MONETARY ECONOMICS AND POLICY

Monetary Economics and Policy

A FOUNDATION FOR MODERN CURRENCY SYSTEMS

PIERPAOLO BENIGNO

PRINCETON UNIVERSITY PRESS

PRINCETON & OXFORD

Requests for permission to reproduce material from this work should be sent to permissions@press.princeton.edu

Published by Princeton University Press
41 William Street, Princeton, New Jersey 08540
99 Banbury Road, Oxford OX2 6JX

press.princeton.edu

All Rights Reserved

ISBN 978-0-691-26264-2
ISBN (e-book) 978-0-691-26532-2

British Library Cataloging-in-Publication Data is available

Editorial: Hannah Paul and Josh Drake
Production Editorial: Jenny Wolkowicki
Jacket and text design: Wanda España
Production: Erin Suydam
Publicity: William Pagdatoon
Copyeditor: Bhisham Bherwani

Jacket image: ugo ambroggio / Alamy Stock Photo

This book has been composed in Arno Pro

Printed in the United States of America

10 9 8 7 6 5 4 3 2 1

Ai miei genitori Ada e Felice
Per i miei figli Andrea, Francesca e Giorgio

CONTENTS

PREFACE

THE FOLLOWING BOOK originated from a collection of lectures delivered during the Spring 2020 course in monetary economics at the University of Bern, where I assumed the position of Professor of Monetary Macroeconomics in January 2020. Some lectures occurred in person, while others were conducted online due to quarantine measures related to the COVID-19 pandemic. The quarantine provided ample time for me to initiate the drafting process and circulate the material in a preliminary form.

Although the initial attempt fell short on various fronts, I have continually revised the material over the years, incorporating additional content and exploring new topics while deepening my understanding of monetary economics.

The ongoing refinement of this project has transformed it into a more ambitious undertaking. It now delves into current theoretical and policy controversies, drawing connections with similar issues that have permeated the history of monetary economics. The overarching goal is to provide a comprehensive and unifying framework to understand monetary economics and policy, shedding light on these controversies or, at the very least, offering a thorough perspective on them. At the core of this framework are micro-founded monetary models, where currency is deemed intrinsically worthless.

A currency devoid of intrinsic value, such as today's government currency or cryptocurrencies, is a relatively new concept in history, quite mysterious, prominently emerging since the abandonment of the Bretton Woods system in 1973. However, it has a precise definition: a claim that makes a promise to pay in units of itself. This definition empowers the currency issuer to print those claims at will, free from ties to a tangible commodity.

Monetary activities during the last fifteen years, marked by extraordinary events such as the 2007–2008 financial crisis, the global COVID-19 lockdown, and the recent inflationary surge, are testaments to the power that central banks wield in the economy. We have witnessed how creatively they have deployed their unseen tools and "weapons."

Part I of this book addresses a compelling issue within monetary economics essential for advancing our understanding of the effectiveness of monetary policy. The central theme revolves around the control of the price level and explores whether the central bank can anchor the currency's value on a desired path. A currency devoid of intrinsic value is in search of real backing, but the definition of currency, giving special properties to the central bank's liabilities, can empower only the central bank as the agent that can fully control its value. This part showcases the diverse array of tools available to the central bank for this purpose. Within a proposed general framework for price determination, controversial theories like "the fiscal theory of the price level" are incorporated, particularly as a special case when the central bank extends the unique properties of its liabilities to the treasury by backing the treasury's debt.

Part I also explores the concept of money, particularly relevant in a paper-currency system. It extends beyond the currency (base money) issued by the central bank to encompass private financial claims, known as safe assets. These assets share similar properties with currency, serving as a store of value and a medium of exchange. This expanded perspective prompts an analysis of past controversies regarding the supply of liquidity, questioning whether it should be provided by the private sector or the government and in what manner. Furthermore, it explores whether private money creation can disrupt the central bank's control over the currency's value. Within this framework, Part I also addresses currency competition involving cryptocurrencies and the implications of a central bank digital currency framework.

Part II is concerned with the role of monetary policy in stabilizing the economy, presenting the New Keynesian monetary model and discussing the optimality of an inflation targeting policy. This part shares similarities with the renowned two books on the topics, by Jordi Galí and Michael Woodford. However, it also proposes a simple graphical analysis that, despite some simplification, can be helpful for understanding some of the main implications. It also includes an interesting departure from the benchmark framework, in which the central bank's only policy tool is the policy rate, adding the quantity of central bank's reserves as relevant for the control of inflation and economic activity.

Part III focuses on "crisis" models, which naturally emerge by enhancing the main framework with relevant variations. It addresses economic conditions observed over the last fifteen years, including liquidity traps, debt deleveraging, credit crunches, and liquidity squeezes resulting from the under-performance of private money. Within this context, this part aims to provide insights into the various policies implemented to counteract these events and stabilize economic activity. Topics covered include forward guidance, general unconventional policies like quantitative and credit easing, and the more unorthodox concept of helicopter money. Addressing the liquidity crunch reopens the debate on how central bank liquidity should substitute for the failure of private liquidity during a crisis and questions whether the supply of money should be left solely to the private sector or to the government, and in what manner.

Part IV focuses on inflation and high inflation episodes, centering on the most controversial theme in macroeconomics—the Phillips curve. The Phillips curve is explored through different theories that have attempted to support or disprove its evidence. The concept of the natural rate of unemployment is presented alongside theories of short-run neutralities. Alternative theories, more aligned with the Keynesian view of unemployment due to the inflexibility of wages and the seldomly reached maximum capacity of output, are also compared to recount the observed inflation experiences in the United States over the last sixty-five years. High inflation episodes or hyperinflations are presented, rooted in the failures of providing a real anchor to the value of currency, aligning with the theoretical findings of Part I. The disanchoring might result as a consequence of subtle connections between monetary and fiscal policies, often made very explicit through monetary financing of deficits, or because of a deteriorated quality of the assets held by the central bank.

Part V draws conclusions, while Part VI contains appendices.

This book's readership ranges from Master's to Ph.D. students. Some sections, such as the graphical analysis in Part II, can also be covered in advanced undergraduate classes. The material of this book is more than what can be taught in a one-semester course. In the Monetary Economics course from the Master in International and Monetary Economics at the University of Bern, I taught Chapters 1 and 2, Chapters 5–7, and some topics in Chapters 9 and 12. Chapters 4, 8, 10, and 11, which connect banking models to monetary economics, can also be taught in more advanced graduate classes.

Becoming a monetary economist was a logical step after my completing a Ph.D. in economics at Princeton University between 1996 and 2000. During that period, the Princeton Department of Economics boasted an impressive faculty engaged in monetary theories and analyses, including notable figures such as Ben Bernanke, Alan Blinder, Paolo Pesenti, Kenneth Rogoff, Argia Sbordone, Chris Sims, Mark Watson, Michael Woodford, and Lars Svensson (who joined the department later). This stimulating environment nurtured a community of students and friends who have made significant contributions to the field over the years, including scholars with whom I interacted, such as Kosuke Aoki, Brian Doyle, Rochelle Edge, Gauti Eggertsson, Marc Giannoni, Gita Gopinath, Refet Gurkaynak, Alejandro Justiniano, Thomas Laubach, Eduardo Loyo, Giovanni Olivei, Bruce Preston, Giorgio Primiceri, Barbara Rossi, Andrea Tambalotti, and Cedric Tille.

Despite its seemingly natural progression, my academic journey began more as an international economist with a focus on open-macro topics, with my maintaining an interest in monetary policy issues. I wrote my thesis, titled "Optimal Monetary Policy for Open Economies," under the joint supervision of Ken Rogoff and Mike Woodford.1 In collaboration with Mike, who served not only as an incredible mentor and friend, but also as a crucial source of inspiration for my understanding of monetary economics through our conversations and his writings, I had the privilege of producing early works in my career while at New York University. These works focused on performing welfare-based analyses of policies in dynamic stochastic general equilibrium models through a linear-quadratic approach, offering clear applications for thinking about optimal monetary policy in various contexts.

Nevertheless, it was only just before my departure from New York University in 2006 to join LUISS in Rome that I began working more intensively on issues in monetary economics. Collaborating with Luca Ricci, we explored the implementation of Tobin's (1972) idea of using inflation to "grease the wheels" of the labor market, resulting in the derivation of a nonlinear Phillips curve based on downward wage inflexibility. The watershed moments, however, occurred during the 2007–2008 financial crisis and the 2011 European sovereign debt crisis. In those periods, we witnessed new approaches to conducting monetary policy that extended beyond merely setting the policy rate. These crises, in my view, unveiled the inherent power of central banks in monetary systems with intrinsically worthless currencies. While contributing columns to Italian newspapers on the observed policies, I began to form

1. Ben Bernanke was also on my thesis committee, while Chris Sims kindly wrote a reference letter for my job market, and Lars Svensson participated in my thesis defense committee.

intuitions about the authority central banks wielded. Nevertheless, I struggled to find a solid theoretical foundation for that power.

I began exploring these uncharted territories by initially considering the importance of substituting central bank liquidity for private liquidity to avert a liquidity crunch. This represented an additional tool for monetary policy, critical alongside the interest rate policy, to mitigate the ensuing contraction in economic activity. This exploration took shape in a joint project with Salvatore Nisticò.

With Roberto Robatto, we delved further into investigating the endogeneity of private liquidity creation and its inefficiencies, aiming to explore the effectiveness and limits of government intervention. Collaborating with Gauti Eggertsson and Federica Romei, we extended the original work of Eggertsson and Krugman (2012) on debt deleveraging. In that context, we explored optimal monetary policy when the zero lower bound becomes a constraint, accounting for the distributional consequences of monetary policy among heterogeneous agents.

I was also interested in dissecting the alternative compositions of the central bank's balance sheet, studying the relevance or irrelevance of various open-market operations based on the interaction between monetary and fiscal policies. This included the study of helicopter money experiments in joint works with Salvatore Nisticò. With these foundations, I began to envision and theorize that the central bank could anchor the value of currency through appropriately specifying an array of tools. I further explored the importance of the size of the central bank's balance sheet in reference to recent operations of quantitative tightening in collaboration with Gianluca Benigno.

Works with Luca Benati on one side, and Linda Schilling and Harald Uhlig on the other, have also enriched my understanding of the functioning of other types of monetary systems, such as commodity money and cryptocurrencies. To close the circle, Gauti Eggertsson has brought me back to rethink the Phillips curve with his idea that its steep part could be helpful in explaining the current inflation we have been experiencing. I am very grateful to all the aforementioned coauthors, without whom it would not be possible for me to understand enough about monetary economics and for this book to come to life.

Over the years, my understanding of monetary economics has been significantly shaped by the writings and conversations with other numerous scholars, including Matthew Canzoneri, Behzad Diba, Jordi Galí, and Chris Sims. Sims's papers, in particular, have been a constant reference, providing continuous insights into fundamental issues in monetary economics. The learning process from their works remains ongoing, and I am uncertain if I have fully completed the endeavor. Additionally, delving into the past works of Carlo Cipolla and Milton Friedman has been invaluable for broadening my understanding, and I believe there is still much to glean from their contributions.

The support and friendship of Lorenzo Infantino and Marcello Messori have also played a crucial role. Lorenzo's encouragement has led to a deeper exploration, albeit still superficial, of the contributions of thinkers like Ludwig von Mises, Friedrich von Hayek, David Hume, and Adam Smith, instilling thoughts of liberalism in my own thinking. Marcello, on the other hand, has been a stimulating collaborator in policy discussions, particularly with Giovanni Di Bartolomeo and Paolo Canofari, as we authored policy papers for the monetary dialogue of the European Parliament with the European Central Bank.

At the University of Bern, I have enjoyed a stimulating environment for studying monetary issues, surrounded by colleagues like Luca Benati, Anastasia Burya, Harris Dellas, Cyrill Monnet, and Dirk Niepelt. Luca Benati, in addition to our early morning conversations on the topic, has generously provided historical data and some references used in this book. I must humbly acknowledge Karl Brunner and Ernst Baltensperger for the rich tradition of monetary economics at the University of Bern, from whom I have inherited the Chair of Monetary Macroeconomics. The academic environment has been fruitful, with engaging interactions at all levels, particularly with Ph.D. students warmly participating in our reading group. I acknowledge financial support from the University of Bern and Swiss National Bank, and the efficient administrative support of Ulrike Dowidat, Fronz Kölliker, Fiona Scheidegger, Manuela Soltermann, and Gabriella Winistörfer.

I have received useful comments on an early draft and single chapters from Gianluca Benigno, Bezhad Diba, Harris Dellas, Gauti Eggertsson, Jordi Galí, Maurice Obstfeld, and Martin Wolf. Stefano Corbellini has provided excellent research assistantship in assembling simulations and figures of the book. Michel De Vroey has been fundamental in driving my interest to publish the initial project. All errors, theoretical flaws, and inconsistencies are my own responsibility.

I am grateful to Hannah Paul, Josh Drake, Jenny Wolkowicki and Princeton University Press for giving me the hope and the honor of publishing this book, and for the careful reviewing process, providing excellent referee comments that have helped to shape the project to a high standard.

Finally, my gratitude to my brother Gianluca, whose guidance has helped me to become an economist, following in his steps, and to my beautiful family for all the continuous support received.

P.B.
December 6, 2023

PART I
Currency and Money

Introduction

THE NATURAL starting point for understanding monetary phenomena lies in the definitions of currency and money. The two concepts are distinct in a "paper" currency system, where currency holds no intrinsic value, which is unlike a commodity currency regime, where currency derives its value from a precious metal, such as gold or silver. However, it is useful to clarify the definitions first in the context of a commodity standard before delving into "paper" currency systems.

In a metallic currency regime, a currency was defined in terms of a specific quantity of grains of a precious metal, and the content in circulating metallic coins was certified by the embossed portrait or coat of arms of the authority minting them. For instance, the Florentine Florin, which circulated from 1252 to 1533, had 54 grains (3.499 grams, 0.1125 troy ounces) of gold.

Defining money can be a nuanced task, as it does not fit neatly into the category of objects or even nouns. Hayek once expressed that ". . . it would be more helpful for the explanation of monetary phenomena if 'money' were an adjective describing a property which different things could possess to varying degrees" (Hayek, 1976, p. 56). Therefore, it is beneficial to delineate money by enumerating its functions and assessing whether a particular security or object qualifies for this property.

The three commonly attributed functions of money are as follows: *unit of account*, *medium of exchange*, and *store of value*. In a metallic currency system, money aligns with circulating coins, essentially making money, coin, and currency interchangeable concepts. Coins, functioning as a *medium of exchange*, facilitate the exchange of goods. Due to their ability to preserve their metallic content over time, they also serve as a *store of value*.

The *unit of account* property refers to the *numéraire* in which the prices of goods are denominated. Interestingly, this *unit of account* was not always

3

served by the currency in circulation. Einaudi (1936) describes an imaginary currency, the lira, used in Europe from the time of Charlemagne to the French Revolution. It functioned solely as a unit of account that never circulated but was defined as "the unit that did not vary in a world of changing coins." According to the definitions provided, it was neither currency nor money.

The transition from a metallic standard to a paper or digital fiduciary currency system marks a significant discontinuity. Paper currency or digital tokens, unlike specie, lack intrinsic value and are not convertible into units of a precious metal. In this context, a currency is a claim that promises to pay in units of itself. In the current dollar monetary system, a dollar is a unit of the central bank's liabilities. This definition allows the central bank to print dollars at will, without significant resource requirements. If currency were defined in terms of a commodity or another currency, the central bank would be unable to increase its amount at will unless the currency were appropriately backed by the commodity or reference currency. In recent examples of a decentralized currency system like Bitcoin, the currency, which is again a claim to itself, is defined by the digital token that can be virtually created through a suitable mechanism or algorithm, making it verifiable and uniquely identifiable.

The existence of an identifiable and verifiable currency is not a sufficient condition for the existence of a fiduciary currency system, since it does not imply that the currency will be used for payments. The road toward the acceptability of an intrinsically worthless currency to one with a value attached to it by agents is not trivial, and certainly controversial according to literature in this field (see Selgin, 1994). Therefore the second essential factor of a currency system is that some transactions should be settled in units of that currency for a prolonged period. With a fiat currency, this is done by its being imposed as legal tender.

Let us consider as the foremost example a monetary system with a central bank. As already mentioned, a currency is defined precisely by the central bank's liabilities. Unlike money, these liabilities are a well-defined accounting object, and are usually called base money or monetary base. They comprise cash (coins and banknotes), as well as reserves, and reserves are the central bank's short-term claims that, unlike cash, potentially carry a nominal interest rate.

In this monetary system, the currency can serve as the *unit of account*, which is the unit of measure in which prices of goods, financial claims, or contracts can be denominated.

Currency, cash and reserves, serves also as a *medium of exchange* (or means of payment). This is an essential element of the fiduciary currency system.

Some transactions should be settled using currency or securities denominated in that currency, meaning that at least on one side of the exchange the settlement takes place through an instrument denominated in the currency. Base money can naturally play this role. The reason depends, again, on a special property of central banks' liabilities: they are free of any risk, by definition. Therefore, under the nontrivial condition that currency is accepted, base money is the most suited type of financial claim for carrying out those transactions, since it provides certain payment in all future contingencies without any risk.

The last property of currency is that of its being a *store of value*. If cash is issued, it can maintain its currency value unchanged across time and contingencies. Reserves paying a positive nominal interest rate can not only store value, but increase it while maintaining the certainty of the payoff. If the central bank supplies cash, the nominal interest rate on reserves (and the risk-free interest rate) cannot go below zero—absent transaction frictions. Otherwise, arbitrage opportunities would be possible, creating unlimited profits for cash holders. In a completely cashless economy, in contrast, the nominal interest rate can go negative. Should this happen, reserves will not store the value of currency unchanged across time, although they will still provide a certain payoff.

It is tempting to define the *store-of-value* property by requiring currency to keep its value unchanged in terms of the purchasing power of goods. This definition, however, would significantly rely on the stability of the value of currency, which is not a property of currency.

Within this framework, money is a claim on base money, i.e., on what defines currency, and shares with currency, to varying degrees, the *store-of-value* and *medium-of-exchange* properties, as underlined above.

Brunner (1989) wrote: "The distinction between monetary base and the nation's money stock is hardly informative or relevant for pure commodity money regimes. The distinction becomes important with the emergence of intermediation. Financial intermediation inserts a wedge between the monetary base and the money stock" (Brunner, 1989, p. 175). He further underscored that privately issued money represents a claim on another type of money, which is an "ultimate money without regress to other types of money."

Private financial institutions or the treasury can also supply liabilities that promise to pay in units of currency at a future date; here, again, the currency is precisely identified by the liabilities of the central bank. However, the promises can only be maintained if the units of currency to fulfill them, or other means of payments in the same units, are available, in one way or another, at the maturing date. The attribute of money is then extended to private and public claims that replicate or approximate the properties of base money in the payment system and, in general, in the financial markets. Indeed, money is defined by its properties. The concept of money is therefore broader than that of base money, encompassing it, with borders between what is money and what is not often vague and prone to creating instabilities in the financial markets, as we will discuss later.

Chapter 1 illustrates a monetary economy with a single currency in which the currency plays the three roles described above, but is cashless in equilibrium. The chapter investigates the intricate issue of how the value of a currency is determined through an appropriate specification of monetary policy that includes setting a target for the nominal interest rate and implementing appropriate balance-sheet policies.

Chapter 2 considers the same framework but gives a privileged role to cash in providing liquidity. It discusses the control of the value of currency by means of the monetary base, exploring whether that makes any difference with respect to interest rate policies. The chapter concludes by examining the conditions under which a currency can prevail as a medium of exchange in a multiple-currency environment.

Chapter 3 discusses the implications of the central bank's issuance of a digital currency in the form of deposits held by households at the central bank. This framework changes the way the central bank controls the value of a currency, giving a significant role to central bank reserves in influencing inflation beside the interest rate policy.

Chapter 4 extends the special liquidity properties that cash has, discussed in Chapter 2, to risk-free debt securities, those issued either by the government or by private intermediaries. These securities characterize a special class of assets called "safe assets." This category plays an important role in the financial system as collateral or as something exchanged for goods or other assets. Moreover, the deterioration of the quality of these assets can make the economy prone to a liquidity crunch, as Chapter 11, later, will show. Chapter 4 further considers who should supply the liquidity, the government or the private sector, through financial intermediaries, and whether this brings any challenges for the control of the value of currency. The chapter concludes by analyzing currency competition for the denomination and payment settlements of "safe assets".

1

The Value of Currency

1.1 Introduction

A fundamental issue in the field of monetary economics revolves around the intricate mechanisms governing the determination of the equilibrium price level within an economy and the extent to which the central bank can effectively exert its influence over this critical process. Nowadays, central banks function under mandates that prioritize either maintaining price stability or managing inflation, which gives rise to inquiries about their capacity to efficiently achieve these goals.

This chapter demonstrates how the central bank possesses a wide array of tools to influence the price level and can effectively determine the equilibrium value as needed. This outcome logically arises when one recognizes that a currency with no intrinsic value is essentially what the central bank can issue at its discretion, and the price level is inversely related to the currency's value. This gives special powers to the central bank in controlling the price level and rationalizes the mandate in terms of inflation for central banks.

The central bank's role in guiding the price level is not that of a regulator that directly steers it onto a predefined path, distinct from the trajectory it would have naturally followed. Without the proper specification of monetary policy tools, there is no predetermined price level that the economy would naturally reach. The central bank's involvement is crucial for determining the value of its currency.

As a result, the challenge of establishing the price level comes down to accurately defining the tools available to the central bank. This comprehensive set of tools goes beyond merely determining current and future nominal interest rates; it also encompasses elements of the central bank's balance sheet, including its asset holdings and policies related to remittances.

A currency with no intrisic value, no longer tied to a physical commodity, seeks a form of real backing. This chapter, as well as the next, suggests that this backing can be internal and can originate from various sources, including central bank equity, asset composition, seigniorage, and a well-defined remittance policy. Two proposals will be discussed in this chapter in the absence of seigniorage resources.[1] In the first, the central bank follows a policy of distributed real earnings, relying on a positive net equity position and investing in default-free assets. Under the second proposal, the value of currency is anchored by appropriately managing the holding of tangible real assets, such as gold, and maintaining an investment in default-free assets.

The real anchor can also come from sources external to the central bank. The framework explored in this chapter includes, as a particular case, what is known as "the fiscal theory of the price level." This arises when the central bank, by effectively guaranteeing the treasury's debt, extends its privilege of issuing completely risk-free liabilities in its monetary system. In this case, the real backing for the price level comes from real taxes. This clarifies that, in the "fiscal theory," the determination of the price level results from the collaborative efforts of both fiscal and monetary authorities, rather than being solely the responsibility of the fiscal authority.

While the theoretical analysis in this chapter is supportive of the monetary authority's control over the price level and inflation, the empirical evidence is less so. Figure 1.1 shows the Consumer Price Index for the United States spanning the period 1774–2022. It highlights distinct periods when the currency was backed by precious metals, such as silver and gold, which held sway for approximately 150 years prior to World War II and continued in a modified form through the Bretton Woods monetary system until 1973. Pure fiat currency regimes, on the other hand, are relatively rare throughout the course of monetary history, with notable exceptions during events like the Civil War, and the last 50 years.[2]

It is noteworthy that in 1774 the price index stood at 7.82 and had only doubled, to 14.09, by 1938, the onset of World War II. During this period, there were alternating periods of inflation, mainly during wartime, and

---

1. The next chapter is going to consider the possibility that the central bank can finance a portion of its liabilities at a lower rate with respect to the market interest rate, giving rise to seigniorage revenues.

2. A fiat currency is an intrinsically worthless currency imposed by the government as a legal tender.

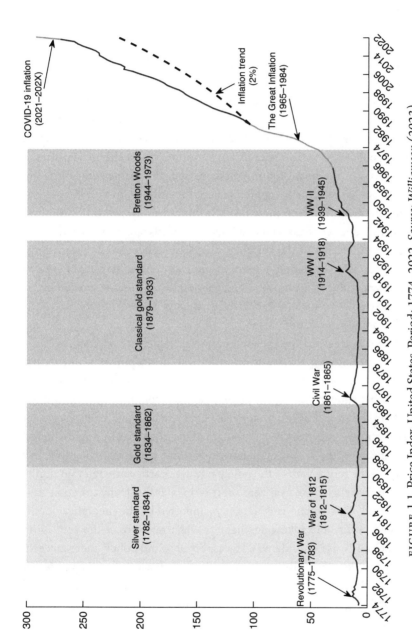

FIGURE 1.1. Price Index, United States. Period: 1774–2022. *Source: Williamson* (2023).

deflation. The overall pattern reveals significant price fluctuations, oscillating around a relatively constant value, which proved highly disruptive to economic activity during periods of declining prices.[3] This contrasts sharply with the rapid surge that followed: the most recent data in 2022 shows a price index of 292.66, more than twenty times higher than the observation in 1938. The shift away from the Gold Standard marked a significant change in the monetary regime, presenting central banks with important challenges in controlling the value of their currencies without being tied to tangible assets like gold. This led to a learning process that culminated in the adoption of inflation targeting policies, which set specific targets for the rate of change in prices.

However, in the post-Bretton-Woods period, the average annual rate of price change has remained at approximately 4%, and it drops to 2.8% when we exclude the Great Inflation period. While this reflects a substantial improvement in the conduct of monetary policy, it still reveals limitations in effectively controlling the value of the currency, especially in light of the recent surge in post-COVID-19 inflation. Figure 1.1 plots a 2% trend starting in 1983 in comparison with the actual data, highlighting the significant erosion in the purchasing power of a dollar, even in relation to the Federal Reserve's recently stated quantitative inflation target.

While it is true that the inflation targeting framework adopted by many central banks around the world preceded the development of theoretical models suitable for its understanding, the evidence presented in Figure 1.1, along with the theoretical results in this chapter, emphasize that there are still aspects in the specification of monetary policy that should be given greater consideration to enhance the stabilization of the price level or its growth rate.

For instance, the recent emphasis on forward guidance, which involves specifying the future path of the policy rate, was particularly relevant during the prolonged episode of near-zero short-term rates that many countries have experienced. This emphasis is not only supported by the theoretical model presented in this and following chapters when rates are at the zero lower bound, but it is also considered a key aspect of sound policy under any economic condition. The suspension of forward guidance, following the recent surge in inflation as the policy rate lifted from zero, may have contributed to destabilizing inflation expectations, as it provided no clear path for future policies.

---

3. Bernanke and James (1991) provide arguments for the importance of the deflationary pressures originating from the Gold Standard at the onset of the Great Depression.

At the same time, the asset purchase programs implemented by many central banks over the past fifteen years have brought attention to the composition of central bank balance sheets. From a theoretical standpoint, this chapter demonstrates that balance sheet policies and asset composition are generally significant factors in controlling the value of a currency. The intricate connections between monetary and fiscal policies, which are also present in asset purchase programs, can be subtle and ambiguous, potentially giving rise to destabilizing movements in prices, as we may have witnessed with the combined monetary and fiscal stimulus in response to the unprecedented COVID-19 crisis.

This chapter explores a model of monetary economy characterized by an inconvertible or irredeemable "paper" currency, such as the U.S. dollar, implying a currency devoid of intrinsic value. A "paper" currency is a claim that represents a promise to be paid by itself, and this concept of currency exactly coincides with the liabilities of the central bank, known as high-powered or base money.

This definition carries two significant implications. First, a dollar claim at a central bank is always repaid independently of the resources available to the central bank. The central bank can indeed "create" that dollar. Second, the central bank can simultaneously determine the quantity of its liabilities and their remuneration. This ability arises from its capacity to "create" its liabilities at will. In contrast, for a dollar claim to be fully paid back at the treasury or any other institution, that institution must possess scarce dollar resources. The treasury cannot "create" dollars; it must obtain them through other means.

In the model that follows, the central bank can issue its liabilities in two different forms: i) cash, i.e., banknotes or coins, and ii) reserves, which are one-period short-term securities paying an interest rate i^X. The central bank sets the interest rate on reserves, i^X. Since the central bank reserves are default-free securities, by definition of currency, the absence of arbitrage opportunities implies that the interest rate at a generic time t, i_t, on any other default-free security issued in the economy should be equal to the interest rate on reserves set by the central bank at the same time, i.e., $i_t = i_t^X$. Hence, by setting the interest rate on reserves, the central bank can influence the short-term risk-free rate in financial markets, establishing the first phase of its policy transmission mechanism.

In the simple economy presented in this chapter, currency serves three key roles: *unit of account, medium of exchange,* and *store of value.*

A *unit of account* represents the standard measure for valuing goods and securities, acting as the *numéraire*. In the model presented in this chapter, there exists a single *unit of account*, the dollar, and all prices for goods and securities are quoted in terms of this unit. Given the definition of currency, the *unit of account* in a paper currency monetary system is defined by the liabilities of the central bank.[4]

This chapter's model presents several securities that serve as a *medium of exchange* alongside base money (i.e., currency), including private and public debt. There is no special role for cash in facilitating transactions, and, indeed, in equilibrium the economy is cashless.

Securities serve as a *store of value* when they preserve currency units over time, like banknotes or coins. In an economy where cash is in circulation, the interest rate on any risk-free security cannot be negative. The reason is simple: negative interest rates would create arbitrage opportunities. Agents could borrow at negative rates and invest in cash, yielding profits without assuming any risk.

1.2   Outline of the Results

The central conclusion of this chapter highlights the complexity of price determination, yet it asserts that monetary policymakers possess the tools necessary for the task. Crafting a policy framework with sufficient richness and appropriateness is crucial. Section 1.4 establishes that relying solely on an interest rate policy falls short in determining a currency's value. Conversely, in Section 1.4.1, we examine the "fiscal theory of the price level," which emphasizes that an appropriate tax policy, when combined with an interest rate policy, can effectively determine the currency value. However, to run its fiscal policy, the treasury's liabilities should be guaranteed by the central bank.

Without this guarantee, there is still hope, however, for the central bank to control the price level. Section 1.4.2 illustrates that currency value can be determined by appropriately defining the central bank's remittance policy, either to the treasury or to the private sector, alongside its interest rate policy. A crucial aspect of this solution is that the central bank must maintain a positive net worth and invest in default-free securities. The requirement of maintaining a positive net worth can be dispensed in an economy with gold

4. See Hall (2005), Sims (1999b), and Woodford (2001c).

by having the central bank invest in gold and sell it at some point in time, as Section 1.5 shows.

1.3 Model

This chapter presents a simple endowment monetary economy under perfect foresight with one currency. There are three agents: the consumer, the treasury, and the central bank. We describe each agent and choice in turn, and then we discuss the overall equilibrium.

1.3.1 Consumers

Consider a representative agent in a closed economy with the following intertemporal utility:

$$\sum_{t=t_0}^{\infty} \beta^{t-t_0} U(C_t),\tag{1.1}$$

where β with $0 < \beta < 1$ is the subjective discount factor in preferences, while $U(\cdot)$ is a concave, twice-differentiable, utility function and (C) is the consumption of the only good available in the economy. The representative agent faces the following budget constraint, expressed in units of currency:

$$\frac{B_t}{1+i_t} + \frac{X_t}{1+i_t^X} + M_t + P_t C_t + T_t = B_{t-1} + X_{t-1} + M_{t-1} + P_t Y. \tag{1.2}$$

There are three types of securities available: bonds (B), reserves (X), and cash (M). All these securities are denominated in the unit of account. The one-period bond (B) has a unitary face value and is issued at a discount with a nominal interest rate (i). Reserves are provided by the central bank, also with a unitary face value, and they yield an interest rate (i^X). Cash (M) consists of banknotes or coins supplied by the central bank, and it does not pay any interest.

The representative agent has the option to take either a long position (where B is positive) or a short position (where B is negative) with respect to bonds. However, when it comes to central bank reserves and cash, the agent can only take a long position, i.e., $X_t \geq 0$ and $M_t \geq 0$ for each $t \geq t_0$.

It is crucial to highlight that both B and X have identical payoffs and are considered default-free. However, they are distinct securities. B is issued by either the private sector or the treasury and must meet specific financial conditions to be considered default-free. In contrast, X is provided by the central bank and is guaranteed since it can be created by the central bank at will.

The central bank establishes the interest rate on reserves and ensures a positive supply of them. Because bonds and reserves offer the same payoff, they should have the same price, eliminating any arbitrage opportunities. This result relies on the requirement that the supply of reserves is strictly positive.[5]

By setting the policy rate, the central bank has direct control over the interest rate on any other default-free security. Therefore, $i_t = i_t^X$, and henceforth, i_t represents the interest rate on reserves. This marks the initial step in the transmission mechanism of monetary policy into the broader economy.

The right-hand side of (1.2) represents the resources available at time t in units of currency. The agent enters time t with assets B_{t-1} and X_{t-1} and a stock of cash M_{t-1}. He receives a constant endowment (Y) of goods. (P) is the price of the only good available, expressed in dollars. The left-hand side of (1.2) says that available currency at time t can be spent to invest in new securities (B_t, X_t, M_t) at their prices, to purchase goods (C_t), and to pay taxes (T_t).[6]

Let us now describe the three properties of currency resulting from the flow budget constraint (1.2): *unit of account*, *means of payment*, and *store of value*.

A currency is a *unit of account* because it is the *numéraire* in which goods, taxes, and securities are denominated, as can be seen from the flow budget constraint (1.2).

Alongside with currency (cash and reserves), the consumer can use every instrument present on the right-hand side of (1.2) as a *means of payment*: bonds and the proceeds obtained by selling the endowment. Therefore, in this model, the property of currency as a *means of payment* applies to a broader set of instruments.

---

5. More formally, consider that the price of a bond offering only a pecuniary payoff cannot be lower than the appropriate discounted value of the payoff; otherwise, investors will bid up its price. It is important to note that X and B have the same payoff. By setting the interest rate, i^X on reserves, and by providing a positive supply of them, the central bank is effectively establishing the discounted value of any default-free securities. As a result, the price of security B cannot be lower than that of X, and therefore the interest rate i is constrained to be no higher than i^X. However, it cannot be lower; otherwise it would be possible to obtain arbitrage gains by borrowing at the market rate and investing in reserves.

6. A negative T indicates transfers from the treasury to the household.

A currency is a *store of value* because it allows for the storage of units of currency intertemporally, through cash, for example. This property has immediate implications for the nominal interest rate. It cannot be negative, i.e, $i_t \geq 0$; otherwise there could be arbitrage opportunities. When $i_t < 0$, the representative agent could borrow $1/(1 + i_t)$ dollars at time t, with $1/(1 + i_t) > 1$, promising to pay one dollar at time $t + 1$. The representative agent can invest the amount borrowed in cash, store its value, pay back debt and obtain profits, with certainty, of the amount $-i_t/(1 + i_t) > 0$.

Note that cash is a perfect substitute for bonds in settling payments, therefore, if the nominal interest rate is positive, cash will be dominated by bonds and its demand will be zero. Only at a zero interest rate will it be held. It is then possible to disregard cash in the following analysis, i.e., set $M_t = 0$ for each $t \geq t_0$, and consider the economy cashless *in equilibrium,* but not without cash. Indeed, the possibility of using cash as a *store of value* implies that interest rates cannot be negative.

In equation (1.2), a negative B_t indicates that the consumer is obtaining a loan through the bond market. When formulating the budget constraint, we have assumed that private debt is free from default, a condition that necessitates sufficient backing with resources.[7]

There exists an upper limit to the amount of debt that the consumer can issue and repay with certainty. This limit can be described as follows. Suppose the representative agent reaches time t with this maximum debt amount. The only way it can repay the loan at that point is by consuming nothing from time t onward and utilizing all its assets, including current and future net income. Therefore, at each time t, with $t \geq t_0$, the consumer's outstanding debt position $(-B_{t-1})$ to be repaid with certainty should respect the following inequality:

$$- B_{t-1} \leq X_{t-1} + \sum_{j=0}^{\infty} \tilde{R}_{t,t+j} \left(P_{t+j} Y - T_{t+j} \right) < \infty, \qquad (1.3)$$

in which $\tilde{R}_{t,t+j}$ is the nominal discount factor to evalute one unit of currency at time $t + j$ with respect to time t, with $\tilde{R}_{t,t} \equiv 1$, and

$$\tilde{R}_{t,t+j} \equiv \prod_{i=1}^{j} \left(\frac{1}{1 + i_{t+i-1}} \right),$$

7. We are assuming commitment to financial obligations or full enforceability of contracts.

for $j \geq 1$. The inequality stated in (1.3) specifies that the outstanding debt at time t must be repaid using the available assets, which are central bank reserves, and current as well as future net income. Only under these circumstances will a lender extend credit at an interest rate devoid of default, thus preventing any Ponzi scheme-like situation involving indefinite borrowing.

The borrowing limit (1.3) can be equivalently written in real terms as

$$
-\frac{B_{t-1}}{P_t} \leq \frac{X_{t-1}}{P_t} + \sum_{j=0}^{\infty} R_{t,t+j} \left(Y - \frac{T_{t+j}}{P_{t+j}} \right) < \infty, \tag{1.4}
$$

where now $R_{t,t+j}$ is the appropriate real discount factor to evaluate one unit of good at time $t+j$ with respect to time t, with $R_{t,t} \equiv 1$, and

$$
R_{t,t+j} \equiv \prod_{i=1}^{j} \left(\frac{1}{1+r_{t+i-1}} \right),
$$

for $j \geq 1$.[8] The real interest rate (r) at time t is defined as $1 + r_t = (1 + i_t) \cdot (P_t/P_{t+1})$. Note that in (1.3) and (1.4) the present discounted value of net income should be finite in order for consumption to also be finite.

The consumer chooses sequences $\{C_t, B_t, X_t\}_{t=t_0}^{\infty}$ with $C_t, X_t \geq 0$ to maximize (1.1) under the flow budget constraint (1.2) and borrowing limit (1.4) at each time $t \geq t_0$, given initial conditions B_{t_0-1} and X_{t_0-1}.[9] Households take as a given the prices, interest rates, endowments, and taxes in their optimization problem. An alternative, and equivalent, formulation of the consumer's optimization problem can be obtained by replacing constraint (1.4) with intertemporal budget constraint

$$
\sum_{t=t_0}^{\infty} R_{t_0,t} C_t \leq \frac{B_{t_0-1} + X_{t_0-1}}{P_{t_0}} + \sum_{t=t_0}^{\infty} R_{t_0,t} \left(Y - \frac{T_t}{P_t} \right), \tag{1.5}
$$

for which the present discounted value of consumption is bounded above by the sum of the initial real value of financial assets and the present discounted value of real net income. A third and equivalent formulation can be obtained

---

8. Transitioning from equation (1.3) to (1.4), we have implicitly assumed the existence of a finite price level in line with a monetary equilibrium. Further discussion on the existence of a monetary equilibrium will be provided later in this chapter.

9. Recall that we have set $M_t = 0$ at all times.

by replacing constraint (1.4) with the following limit:

$$\lim_{t \to \infty} \left\{ R_{t_0,t} \left(\frac{B_{t-1} + X_{t-1}}{P_t} \right) \right\} \geq 0. \qquad (1.6)$$

This condition mandates that the limit of the discounted value of assets owned by the household remain nonnegative.[10]

The optimization problem implies the Euler equation

$$U_c(C_t) = \beta(1 + r_t) U_c(C_{t+1}) \qquad (1.7)$$

in an interior solution and for each $t \geq t_0$ in which $U_c(\cdot)$ is the first derivative of the function $U(\cdot)$ with respect to its argument. The marginal rate of substitution between consumption in subsequent periods, the ratio $U_c(C_t)/(\beta U_c(C_{t+1}))$, is equal to the (gross) real interest rate, $1 + r_t$. Consumption and saving are at their optimum when the marginal utility of one unit of consumption at time t is equivalent to the marginal utility of saving that unit, i.e., postponing consumption to the next period. The last optimality condition requires that all resources for consumption be exhausted. Therefore, intertemporal budget constraint (1.5) holds with equality

$$\sum_{t=t_0}^{\infty} R_{t_0,t} C_t = \frac{B_{t_0-1} + X_{t_0-1}}{P_{t_0}} + \sum_{t=t_0}^{\infty} R_{t_0,t} \left(Y - \frac{T_t}{P_t} \right), \qquad (1.8)$$

or equivalently

$$\lim_{t \to \infty} \left\{ R_{t_0,t} \left(\frac{B_{t-1} + X_{t-1}}{P_t} \right) \right\} = 0, \qquad (1.9)$$

which is the transversality condition.

1.3.2   Government

The government includes the central bank and the treasury. The central bank has a simple composition on the balance sheet. It issues reserves (X^C) and can hold private and/or treasury bonds (B^C). The central bank's flow budget constraint is represented by

$$X_{t-1}^C + \frac{B_t^C}{1 + i_t} + T_t^C = \frac{X_t^C}{1 + i_t} + B_{t-1}^C. \qquad (1.10)$$

10. Appendix A presents equivalence results among (1.4), (1.5), and (1.6).

In this equation (B^C) represents the central bank's holdings of short-term default-free securities, supplied by either the treasury or the private sector, while (X^C) is the supply of the central bank reserves, which, in this cashless economy, are the central bank's only liabilities; (T^C) are the nominal remittances delivered to the treasury, when positive, or transfers received, when negative. On the left-hand side of (1.10), the equation accounts for the central bank's liabilities to pay (X^C_{t-1}), the new purchases of assets (B^C_t), and the transfers made to the treasury (T^C_t), if positive; on the right-hand side these payments are made by issuing new reserves (X^C_t) and through the payoff of previous-period asset holdings (B^C_{t-1}).

A holder presenting a nominal claim like X^C at the central bank is always paid back, regardless of the resources that the central bank has on its balance sheet: X^C are claims of units of the central bank's liabilities that *define* the dollar; they are claims to themselves! The central bank does not even need to hold any asset to pay them, nor rely on any other resource. In (1.10), B^C_t could be set to zero at all times and still the central bank could issue reserves at will and also set the interest rate on them. As a unique agent in the economy, the central bank can indeed decide both the quantity of its liabilities to issue and their price: given X^C_{t-1}, it can set at the same time X^C_t and i_t and let T^C_t or B^C_t appropriately adjust according to (1.10).

The treasury's outstanding debt at time t, instead, given by B^F_{t-1}, represents a nominal claim on B^F_{t-1} dollars that the treasury has to find to be solvent. The debt issued by the treasury is distinct from that of the central bank but shares similarities with private debt, as it must meet specific criteria to be considered free from default. Observe that credit rating agencies do assess the credit risk of treasury debt but not that of central banks. Furthermore, the events surrounding the 2023 debt-ceiling negotiations in the U.S. and the subsequent downgrade by rating agencies of U.S. Treasury debt highlight the significance of fiscal sustainability in safeguarding the security of public debt.

The budget constraint of the treasury is

$$B^F_{t-1} = T_t + T^C_t + \frac{B^F_t}{1 + i_t}. \tag{1.11}$$

At a generic time t, the treasury can pay its obligations B^F_{t-1} by raising lump-sum taxes T_t, or using the remittances transferred by the central bank T^C_t, or issuing new debt B_t^F.[11] However, in the latter case, the treasury cannot decide both quantity and price. As in the case of consumer debt, the treasury debt is subject to a solvency constraint to be deemed safe. In nominal terms, the solvency constraint is

$$B_{t-1}^F \leq \sum_{j=0}^{\infty} \tilde{R}_{t,t+j} \left(T_{t+j} + T_{t+j}^C \right) < \infty,$$

or equivalently in real terms,

$$\frac{B_{t-1}^F}{P_t} \leq \sum_{j=0}^{\infty} R_{t,t+j} \left(\frac{T_{t+j}}{P_{t+j}} + \frac{T_{t+j}^C}{P_{t+j}} \right) < \infty. \tag{1.12}$$

The outstanding treasury debt should be covered through a combination of current and future taxes, as well as the remittances received from the central bank. This is the natural condition a lender would require to extend credit to the treasury at a default-free rate. The inequality referenced in (1.12) should be interpreted as a restriction on how the treasury determines tax levels, taking into account the existing debt, the patterns of prices and interest rates, and the amount of remittances received from the central bank. When taxes are reduced in certain periods, they must subsequently be increased in other periods to ensure compliance with this constraint.

As an alternative, we can substitute (1.12) with the following condition:

$$\lim_{t \to \infty} \left\{ R_{t_0,t} \left(\frac{B_{t-1}^F}{P_t} \right) \right\} \leq 0. \tag{1.13}$$

This constraint ensures that the limit of the discounted value of debt issued by the treasury remains nonpositive, thereby prohibiting Ponzi schemes within the treasury's financial operations.

In the subsequent analysis, we make the assumption that condition (1.12) or, equivalently, (1.13), is satisfied precisely with an equality sign. This assumption can be supported by political-economic considerations, where imposing taxes beyond the debt burden is deemed costly, or by the rationale that the treasury does not intend to accumulate a positive asset position for the long run.

---

11. We are abstracting from government purchases, and T can be interpreted as lump-sum taxes net of transfers.

1.3.3 Equilibrium

Equilibrium in asset markets requires that the debt issued by the government be held by the central bank and the consumer,

$$B_t^F = B_t^C + B_t, \tag{1.14}$$

while the reserves issued by the central bank be held by the consumer only:

$$X_t^C = X_t, \tag{1.15}$$

for each $t \geq t_0$.[12]

Aggregating the budget constraints of the consumer, equation (1.2), and the government, equations (1.10) and (1.11), by using (1.14) and (1.15), the equilibrium in the goods market, $C_t = Y$ for each $t \geq t_0$, follows. Consumption is equal to output, consistently with a closed economy with no investment and government purchases.

To characterize the determination of the value of currency, which is the inverse of the price level, the following equilibrium conditions are relevant. The first is the Euler equation (1.7), which, using $C_t = Y$ for each $t \geq t_0$, implies the Fisher equation,

$$1 + i_t = \frac{1}{\beta} \frac{P_{t+1}}{P_t}, \tag{1.16}$$

saying that the nominal interest rate is equal to the real rate, $1/\beta$, and to the next-period inflation rate. Note that, given the assumption of a constant endowment, the real interest rate is constant and equal to the inverse of β. The second equilibrium condition is the intertemporal budget constraint of the consumers (1.8), which can be written using equilibrium in the goods market as

$$\frac{B_{t_0-1} + X_{t_0-1}}{P_{t_0}} = \sum_{t=t_0}^{\infty} \beta^{t-t_0} \frac{T_t}{P_t}, \tag{1.17}$$

having substituted in equation (1.8) $R_{t_0,t} = \beta^{t-t_0}$ for $R_{t_0,t}$. On the left-hand side of (1.17), we have the overall real net liabilities of the entire government (including the treasury and central bank) in relation to the private sector. On the right-hand side, there is the present-discounted value of real taxes. It is important to note that this equation represents an equilibrium condition and

---

12. We could separate the markets for private and treasury debt, but it will be inconsequential for the analysis.

should not be interpreted as a solvency constraint for the government, requiring taxes to adjust in order to fulfill all government debt obligations to the private sector. Instead, the relevant solvency condition for only the treasury is (1.12), which we restate here with the equality sign following the previous discussion and having substituted in $R_{t_0,t} = \beta^{t-t_0}$ for $R_{t_0,t}$:

$$\frac{B_{t_0-1}^F}{P_{t_0}} = \sum_{t=t_0}^{\infty} \beta^{t-t_0} \left(\frac{T_t}{P_t} + \frac{T_t^C}{P_t} \right). \tag{1.18}$$

This equation should be understood as a constraint on the trajectory of taxes.

To provide a complete characterization of the equilibrium price level, we need to incorporate the budget constraints of both the central bank and the treasury, represented as (1.10) and (1.11). These constraints are here rewritten as:

$$\frac{X_t - B_t^C}{1 + i_t} = X_{t-1} - B_{t-1}^C + T_t^C, \tag{1.19}$$

$$\frac{B_t^F}{1 + i_t} = B_{t-1}^F - T_t - T_t^C. \tag{1.20}$$

Additionally, we need to consider equilibrium in the bond market, (1.14).

An equilibrium is a set of sequences $\{P_t, i_t, X_t, B_t^C, T_t^C, B_t^F, T_t, B_t\}_{t=t_0}^{\infty}$ with $\{P_t, i_t, X_t, B_t^C\}_{t=t_0}^{\infty}$ nonnegative that satisfies conditions (1.14), (1.16), (1.19), and (1.20), holding at each $t \geq t_0$, and conditions (1.17), given initial values $B_{t_0-1}^C, B_{t_0-1}^F, X_{t_0-1}$. Moreover, the sequence of taxes, $\{T_t\}_{t=t_0}^{\infty}$, should satisfy (1.18) for any equilibrium sequences $\{P_t, T_t^C\}_{t=t_0}^{\infty}$, given initial condition $B_{t_0-1}^F$.[13]

There are four degrees of freedom to specify government policy.[14] By inspecting (1.19), we can see that the central bank can specify the sequences of interest rates, reserves, and remittances—i.e., $\{i_t, X_t, T_t^C\}_{t=t_0}^{\infty}$—letting the asset holdings be determined by (1.19). The supply of reserves is assumed to always be positive, a critical assumption for ensuring that the market interest rate, i_t, remains equal to the interest rate on reserves, i_t^X, at all times. With the central bank dictating the sequences $\{i_t, T_t^C\}_{t=t_0}^{\infty}$, the treasury can then determine the trajectory of taxes $\{T_t\}_{t=t_0}^{\infty}$, in accordance with (1.18) and given the

13. It is further required that the infinite sums in equations (1.17) and (1.18) be finite.

14. Equations (1.17) and (1.18) do not reduce the degrees of freedom since they are intertemporal conditions.

equilibrium sequence of prices $\{P_t\}_{t=t_0}^{\infty}$, while the supply of treasury bonds follows from (1.20).

There are significant insights for monetary policy that can be gleaned from this analysis. Firstly, it becomes evident that the economy lacks an inherent tendency to establish an equilibrium price level without the central bank articulating its policy. In fact, without the central bank setting any of the sequences $\{i_t, X_t, T_t^C\}_{t=t_0}^{\infty}$, the economy may be plagued by multiple equilibria.

Secondly, it underscores the importance of the central bank specifying not only the current stance of its monetary policy but also its future trajectories. In line with this, the recent emphasis on forward guidance in monetary policymaking, especially in situations where the zero lower bound is a factor, emerges as a natural element of effective monetary policy under any circumstances.

Lastly, it highlights that it is not only essential for the central bank to define its interest rate policy, but it is also crucial for it to articulate the specifics of its balance-sheet policies. In keeping with this perspective, the next section will demonstrate that an interest rate-only policy cannot uniquely determine the price level.

1.4   Determining the Value of the Currency

The interest rate policy cannot alone determine the value of currency. This can be seen by using the Fisher equation (1.16). If the central bank pegs the interest rate at a constant value, $i_t = i$, then (1.16) will determine only the rate of changes in prices, not the price level. This is Sargent and Wallace's critique (1975) of interest rate pegging. The indeterminacy problem is present even if the central bank sets the interest rate in an active way by reacting to the price level following policy rule

$$1 + i_t = \max \left\{ \frac{1}{\beta} \left(\frac{P_t}{\bar{P}} \right)^{\phi}, 1 \right\},$$

(1.21)

where ϕ is a nonnegative parameter, $\phi \geq 0$, and $\bar{P}$ is positive. The target $\bar{P}$ could represent the target price level specified in the central bank's mandate. When $\phi > 0$, the policy instrument reacts directly to the deviation of the actual price level with respect to the target. When $\phi = 0$, the nominal interest rate is pegged to a constant value, the real rate, but $\bar{P}$ can still be interpreted as the policy's objective. The Fisher equation (1.16) and the interest rate

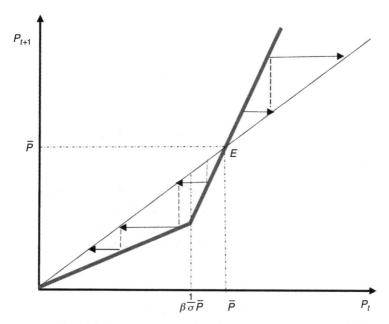

FIGURE 1.2. Plot of difference equation (1.22) in which $\phi > 0$. Point E is the stationary solution $P_t = \bar{P}$ at each date t. If $P_t \leq \beta^{\frac{1}{\phi}}\bar{P}$, the rate of deflation of the price level is β, with $0 < \beta < 1$.

policy (1.21) are two equations in two unknowns, i.e., prices and interest rates. It would seem that there are enough restrictions to determine the path of prices and interest rates. However, this turns out to be incorrect, as the analysis below shows.

Combining (1.16) and (1.21), the price level follows a nonlinear difference equation:

$$\frac{P_{t+1}}{P_t} = \max\left\{\left(\frac{P_t}{\bar{P}}\right)^{\phi}, \beta\right\}. \tag{1.22}$$

Equation (1.22) has infinite solutions irrespective of value $\phi \geq 0$. Consider first the case $\phi > 0$, which is shown in Figure 1.2. There is a stationary solution, with $P_t > 0$, if and only if $P_{t_0} = \bar{P}$. If instead $P_{t_0} > \bar{P}$, the solution will be monotone increasing, which is an inflationary solution. On the other hand, if $P_{t_0} < \bar{P}$, the solution will be monotone decreasing, a deflationary solution, and in particular when $P_t \leq \beta^{1/\phi}\bar{P}$ the rate of deflation is β. Moreover, note that solutions associated with different P_{t_0} never cross in the time dimension.

Therefore, when $\phi > 0$, there are infinite solutions that can be simply indexed by the value assumed by the initial price level, P_{t_0}, in interval $(0, \infty)$.

Consider now the case $\phi = 0$. Infinite solutions are also possible, indexed by the value assumed by initial price level P_{t_0} in range $(0, \infty)$. However, all these solutions are stationary.

It is crucial to emphasize that the limitations of relying solely on an interest-rate-based policy for price determination apply broadly across various interest-rate policy specifications, such as Taylor rules in which the interest rate reacts to the current inflation rate, and more comprehensive frameworks.[15] This issue persists even when considering factors such as uncertainty and nominal rigidities. In the upcoming sections, we investigate the proper specifications of other policy elements necessary to attain a uniquely determined trajectory of prices while maintaining the interest rate policy (1.21).

1.4.1   The Fiscal Theory of the Price Level

This section explores what has been termed the "fiscal theory of the price level," which arises from the coordination between monetary and fiscal policy, as we will discuss in detail. At the core of this coordination lies the central bank's commitment to guarantee the treasury's debt, effectively extending the special default-free status of its own obligations to the treasury. This enables the treasury to formulate a tax policy without being bound by the solvency requirement outlined in (1.12). The literature avoids explicitly addressing this implicit or explicit support because it merges the central bank and treasury within the government, thereby blurring the crucial distinction between the central bank's liabilities and treasury debt.

A theoretical dispute has cast doubt on the validity of the fiscal theory of the price level. Some, like Buiter (1999, 2002), argue that the government's intertemporal budget constraint must always hold as an identity, while others, such as Cochrane (2005), Sims (1999b), and Woodford (2001b), contend that it can be disregarded when considering off-equilibrium prices. The controversy is effectively resolved when we differentiate between the treasury and central bank. By doing so, we recognize that the treasury should adhere to a solvency constraint because it makes commitments to "pay in units of

---

15. Taylor rules are named after the seminal work of Taylor (1993) to identify interest rate rules in which the policy rate reacts to inflation and the output gap.

a commodity (such as dollars) for which it has a limited capacity to produce or obtain in the market" (Sims, 1999b, p. 2). In contrast, the central bank issues securities "that make no promise to pay in units other than the security itself" (Sims, 1999b, p. 4). In the context of the fiscal theory of the price level, the central bank implicitly or explicitly guarantees the treasury's debt, extending the special properties of its liabilities to the treasury. This is why the treasury is not constrained to set taxes to meet the solvency constraint (1.12).

The consolidated budget constraint between the two institutions arises by using (1.19) and (1.20) while netting out the remittances policy:

$$\frac{B_t + X_t}{1 + i_t} = B_{t-1} + X_{t-1} - T_t, \tag{1.23}$$

in which the equilibrium in the bonds market, (1.14), is used.

Given that the tax policy is no longer constrained by (1.18), the three equations (1.16), (1.21), and (1.23) holding at each $t \geq t_0$, together with (1.17), characterize the equilibrium values for the sequences $\{i_t, P_t, X_t, T_t, B_t\}_{t=t_0}^{\infty}$, given initial conditions X_{t_0-1} and B_{t_0-1}.[16] Two other instruments of policy are left to be specified besides the interest rate, as in (1.21), i.e., the sequence of taxes $\{T_t\}_{t=t_0}^{\infty}$ and that of reserves $\{X_t\}_{t=t_0}^{\infty}$. Let the path of reserves be an arbitrary positive sequence.

The key factor influencing the price level is the formulation of the tax policy. It is important to note that not all tax policies are equally effective in achieving this goal. One tax policy that works under the central bank's backing is the constant real tax policy, expressed as $T_t/P_t = (1 - \beta)\tau$, with $\tau > 0$. This policy can be put into practice in two ways: i) the tax authority may set a nominal tax that is fully indexed to the price level, ensuring it consistently generates revenues equivalent to $(1 - \beta)\tau$ worth of goods; ii) it could alternatively collect tax payments directly in the form of goods. Use $T_t/P_t = (1 - \beta)\tau$ in (1.17) to obtain

$$\frac{B_{t_0-1} + X_{t_0-1}}{P_{t_0}} = \tau,$$

which can be solved for P_{t_0} as:

$$P_{t_0} = \frac{B_{t_0-1} + X_{t_0-1}}{\tau}. \tag{1.24}$$

---

16. The infinite sum in (1.17) should be finite.

The full path of the price level is now uniquely determined through-out equation (1.22). An interesting implication of (1.24) is that there exists a proportional relationship between the government's net liabilities with respect to the private sector and the price level. To illustrate, if the government were to double the number of securities that essentially represent claims to themselves, this action could result in a doubling of the price level.

The literature on the "fiscal theory of the price level" has labelled the tax policy $T_t/P_t = (1 - \beta)\tau > 0$ active, capturing the notion that the tax policy should not necessarily adjust to ensure government solvency, or non-Ricardian, meaning that it creates wealth effects on the private sector, as opposed to passive or Ricardian.[17] This line of analysis has given rise to the view that fiscal policy plays a pivotal role in shaping the price level. For instance, in his presidential address to the American Economic Association, Sims (2013) contended that "fiscal policy can be a determinant, or even the sole determinant, of the price level," and that "paper" currency requires fiscal support to control its value. Nevertheless, it's essential to qualify this argument by acknowledging that, to some degree, it is accurate to assert that the tax policy influences the trajectory of prices. Given the interest rate policy (1.21), from among the many possible solutions in (1.22), the tax policy can pick the equilibrium one. If $\tau = \tau^*$, with $\tau^* \equiv (X_{t_0-1} + B_{t_0-1})/\bar{P}$, then the price level is going to be always at $\bar{P}$, as equation (1.24) shows. When taxes are higher, i.e., $\tau > \tau^*$, then $P_{t_0} < \bar{P}$, and a deflationary path will unravel if $\phi > 0$, as shown in (1.22). On the contrary, an inflationary path occurs with a lower tax rate than τ^*.

The qualification to Sims's argument becomes apparent when we observe that the authority of the tax policy to influence the price level stems exclusively from the backing of the central bank. The commitment to the tax policy $T_t/P_t = (1 - \beta)\tau$, regardless of the price level's trajectory, is ensured by the central bank's guarantee of the treasury's debt, rendering the solvency constraint (1.12) no longer a limiting factor.

---

17. The category of active fiscal policies extends beyond constant real tax policies to encompass rules where the real tax rate responds, albeit modestly, to the current level of real debt. A much stronger reaction that ensures the stationarity of the real debt qualifies as a passive fiscal policy. See the analysis of Benhabib, Schmitt-Grohé, and Uribe (2001a,b) and Sims (1994).

To grasp this role, let's insert the tax policy $T_t/P_t = (1 - \beta)\tau$ into (1.12), assuming, for simplicity, that $T_t^C = 0$ at all times. This yields:

$$\frac{B_{t_0-1}^F}{P_{t_0}} \leq \tau.$$

The treasury, acting alone, cannot commit to such a tax policy, regardless of the price level. If, for a given initial debt obligation $B_{t_0-1}^F$, the price level at time t_0 settles at a sufficiently low value, the left-hand side of the equation above could exceed the right-hand side. This implies that at that price level, the treasury may become at least partially insolvent. To ensure the debt remains default-free, it must adjust its tax policy to meet its obligations, and it cannot adhere to $T_t/P_t = (1 - \beta)\tau$, regardless of the price level's trajectory. The central bank's guarantee of the treasury's debt is crucial for completely relaxing constraint (1.12) and allows the treasury to determine the price level through the aforementioned tax policy. This guarantee can be implicit by hypothesizing that the central bank is ready to purchase treasury debt indefinitely, correspondingly issuing reserves, or making appropriate transfers to always back treasury debt, regardless of the price level.[18] The analysis raises some important questions.

Why should the central bank back the treasury and grant it the power to influence the price level? This arrangement carries the risk of extending undue authority to the fiscal branch, potentially endangering price level control, as elaborated in the studies by Bianchi and Melosi (2019) and Bianchi, Faccini, and Melosi (2023), who substantiate their arguments with empirical data. A fiscal authority that has not the ability to deliver a sufficient fiscal capacity can be the source of high inflations or hyperinflations, as we will explore in Chapter 13. Bassetto and Sargent (2020) recount historical instances where the lines of authority between the treasury and the central bank were blurred.

Is it conceivable for the central bank to achieve price determination independently? Given the unique characteristics of the central bank's liabilities, it should come as no surprise that the central bank has the capability to independently influence the price level, without relying on fiscal authority support, as we will demonstrate in the next section.

---

18. On the contrary, trajectories of taxes that guarantee solvency regardless of the equilibrium path of prices do not determine the price level.

1.4.2   Central Bank Theory of the Price Level

The "fiscal theory of the price level" does not account for two practical scenarios of interest. First, in cases where monetary systems evolve toward forms of private currency, it becomes essential to consider how these private entities can maintain control over the value of their currency without depending on fiscal policy. Additionally, even in more traditional monetary systems, such as the European Monetary Union, the conventional perspective of a consolidated government budget constraint appears to be an inadequate representation of reality.[19] Instead, reality is marked by significant boundaries between the central bank and numerous national tax authorities, as evidenced by events such as the Greek default in 2015.

Without the central bank's backing, the treasury should respect solvency condition (1.12) for its debt to be deemed devoid of default. Taxes should be adjusted to pay the initial value of government liabilities for any possible equilibrium path for prices and the remittances policy.[20]

The equilibrium allocation can be analyzed in the following way. Use (1.18), which is (1.12) with equality, to substitute for the path of taxes in (1.17) to obtain

$$\sum_{t=t_0}^{\infty} \beta^{t-t_0} \frac{T_t^C}{P_t} = \frac{B_{t_0-1}^C - X_{t_0-1}}{P_{t_0}}. \tag{1.25}$$

Having set the interest rate policy as in (1.21), the equilibrium can be characterized by nonnegative sequences $\{i_t, P_t, X_t, B_t^C, T_t^C\}_{t=t_0}^{\infty}$ that satisfy (1.16); (1.21); the central bank's budget constraint

$$\frac{X_t - B_t^C}{1 + i_t} = X_{t-1} - B_{t-1}^C + T_t^C \tag{1.26}$$

for each $t \geq t_0$; and (1.25), given initial conditions $B_{t_0-1}^C, X_{t_0-1}$.[21] Condition (1.25) can be also replaced by

$$\lim_{t \longrightarrow \infty} \left\{ R_{t_0,t} \left(\frac{B_{t-1}^C - X_{t-1}}{P_t} \right) \right\} = 0,$$

19. In their works, Canzoneri, Cumby, and Diba (2002) and Sims (1999a) argue that fiscal discipline is essential for maintaining price stability.

20. In the case of not enough resources to pay debt, the default rate would be determined endogenously to align obligations that can be met with available resources.

21. The infinite sum in (1.25) should also be finite.

which is the result of combining (1.9) with (1.13), holding with equality, and (1.14).

There are two additional degrees of freedom to specify policy, but these are solely within the domain of the central bank's tools. In this scenario, the treasury does not exert any influence on the determination of the price level. We assume that the central bank, in addition to its interest rate policy, simultaneously determines an arbitrarily positive sequence of reserves $\{X_t\}_{t=t_0}^{\infty}$ and a nonnegative remittances policy $\{T_t^C\}_{t=t_0}^{\infty}$. While the nonnegativity of the remittances policy is not an absolute necessity, it plays a crucial role in preventing the treasury from providing financial support to the central bank.

The equilibrium condition (1.25) mandates further comments. The present discounted value of remittances in *equilibrium* should be equal to the real value of the net asset position of the central bank. The condition (1.25) is not to be interpreted as a solvency condition for the central bank, since its nominal liabilities are always paid back. Intertemporal constraint (1.25) holds in equilibrium not because the central bank necessarily adjusts its remittances to fulfill (1.25) at equilibrium prices, but because equilibrium prices may adjust given the chosen remittances policy. Indeed, the central bank can determine the initial price level with an appropriate transfer policy.

Let's explore a real transfer policy. Since the central bank lacks endowment of goods, such a policy involves committing to a monetary transfer indexed to the price level, ensuring it maintains a specific purchasing power in terms of goods. Let us consider the policy $T_t^C/P_t = (1 - \beta)\tau^C$ for each $t \geq t_0$, with $\tau^C > 0$; then by using it in (1.25) the initial price level can be determined by

$$P_{t_0} = \frac{(B_{t_0-1}^C - X_{t_0-1})}{\tau^C}. \tag{1.27}$$

This price is positive insofar that $B_{t_0-1}^C > X_{t_0-1}^C$, i.e., the central bank has more assets than liabilities, which can happen if it starts its operations with some positive level of net worth. By setting $\tau^C = (B_{t_0-1}^C - X_{t_0-1})/\bar{P}$, the price level P_{t_0} can be determined at $\bar{P}$ irrespective of whether the parameter ϕ in (1.21) is positive or zero. There is no inherent conflict within the central bank that would hinder its ability to control the price level as desired. This is different from the cooperation required under the "fiscal theory of the price level."

The equilibrium condition (1.25) can be useful to illustrate the intution behind price determination. Let's define central bank's net worth (N^C) as the difference between assets and liabilities,

$$N_t^C \equiv \frac{B_t^C - X_t}{1 + i_t},$$

and write (1.25) as

$$\frac{1}{P_{t_0}}(1 + i_{t_0 - 1})N_{t_0 - 1}^C = \sum_{t=t_0}^{\infty} \beta^{t - t_0} \frac{T_t^C}{P_t}, \qquad (1.28)$$

saying that the real value of equity, compounded, is equal to the current and future discounted real "earnings" that the central bank distributes. The value of currency, the factor $1/P_{t_0}$, is nothing more that the price of central bank's equity in units of goods.[22] Given the nominal value of equity at time $t_0 - 1$, $N_{t_0 - 1}^C$, the central bank can determine the value of its currency, i.e., the price of equity in units of goods, by an appropriate policy of distributed real earnings.

At this point, it would be tempting to draw a parallel with the valuation of equity for private companies, as a function of the stream of dividends, arguing that any of these private intertemporal constraints could determine the price level. This is fallacious, simply because the liabilities of these companies are not claims to themselves. However, for companies whose liabilities are claims to themselves, like today's cryptocurrencies, the above framework could apply to determine the price of goods in units of those claims (currency), but not in units of dollars.[23]

One somehow counterintuitive implication of (1.28) is that an expansion of the reserves of the central bank, given a stream of real remittances, lowers the price level. This is indeed the case because it reduces the nominal value of the central bank's equity. Given no variation in the distributed real earnings, the price of the central bank's equity in units of goods should rise. This, in turn, requires a fall in the price level. This implication will change when considering the possibility that the central bank holds a commodity like gold, as in Section 1.5, or relies on seigniorage revenues, as in Chapter 2.

Equation (1.28) further illustrates that there are some important features of the central bank's ability to control the price level on top of the interest rate,

22. Since equity is a liability of the central bank, the price of one dollar equity is a dollar.

23. In Sims's (1999b) discussion of the fallacy in the notion that any intertemporal dollar constraint would effectively determine the value of dollars, he considers the scenario where companies issuing stocks that essentially represent claims to themselves might have the capacity to set the price level in terms of those stocks.

remittances, and reserve policies. In the framework of this section, the central bank needs i) some transfers, either from the treasury or the private sector, and ii) to have default-free securities in its portfolio, such as B^C.[24]

Consider, first, the need to have a transfer, possibly at the beginning of the central bank's activity. Equation (1.28) shows that this necessarily depends on a positive net worth that the central bank cannot build on its own, at least in the setup of this model.[25] To see this result, rewrite (1.26) using the definition of net worth as

$$N_t^C = N_{t-1}^C + \Psi_t^C - T_t^C,$$

with the central bank's profits (Ψ^C) given by

$$\Psi_t^C = \frac{i_{t-1}}{1+i_{t-1}}(B_{t-1}^C - X_{t-1}) = i_{t-1}N_{t-1}^C.$$

Profits are positive if and only if the interest rate and the net worth are positive. If central bank's net worth is zero at time $t_0 - 1$, profits will always be zero and the net worth can never be positive, since $T_t^C \geq 0$. Thus a transfer, real or nominal, is needed.

Another important feature of the central bank's control of the price level is its holding of default-free nominal securities, issued either by the treasury or the private sector. Although this is not a necessary requirement for controlling interest rates, it is critical in the setup of this chapter for price determination. Equation (1.27) has demonstrated that the central bank should include certain assets in its portfolio, exceeding the value of its liabilities. Furthermore, it is crucial that these assets be default-free because, in the event of a default, the central bank could find itself in a situation of negative net worth, potentially undermining its ability to control the value of its currency, as will be shown in Section 13.5 of Chapter 13.

For a "paper" currency to have value, it needs a real backing. In the previous section, we showed that this backing can be achieved through the power of real taxes imposed by the treasury when monetary and fiscal authorities collaborate. In the absence of such collaboration and any taxation authority,

24. The transfer could take the form of an immediate, tangible transfer of goods, even perishable, at the inception of the central bank's activity or a commitment to a one-time future monetary transfer.

25. This result is going to change in a model in which the central bank has gold holdings, as in Section 1.5, or retrieves seigniorage revenues, as in the models of Chapter 2.

the central bank should seek its own real backing. This section has demonstrated that this can be achieved through a policy of distributing real earnings. However, to have earnings to distribute, there must be profits, which, in the context of this section, can be obtained by having more assets than liabilities. Furthermore, these assets should be of high quality.

We consider now the implications of assuming a different remittances policy, a nominal rather than a real remittances policy. Use

$$T_t^C = T^C = (1-\beta)(B_{t_0-1}^C - X_{t_0-1}^C)$$

together with interest rate policy (1.21), provided again $B_{t_0-1}^C > X_{t_0-1}^C$. By inserting the above transfer policy into (1.25), we obtain restriction

$$(1-\beta)\sum_{t=t_0}^{\infty}\beta^{t-t_0}\frac{1}{P_t}=\frac{1}{P_{t_0}}. \qquad (1.29)$$

To determine the price level, we need to distinguish between two cases: i) a pure interest rate pegging, $\phi = 0$ in (1.21); ii) an "active" interest rate policy, $\phi > 0$. In the first case, $P_t = P_{t_0}$ for each $t \geq t_0$; therefore, (1.29) would imply just the identity $P_{t_0} = P_{t_0}$, and would not be able to determine the initial price level. When, instead, $\phi > 0$, (1.29) can be solved by the desired price target $\bar{P}$, i.e., $P_t = \bar{P}$ at all times. This example shows that it might be desirable to have an "active" interest rate policy, with $\phi > 0$, rather than just interest rate pegging, when the remittances policy is specified in nominal terms. Note, however, that with a nominal, rather than a real, remittances policy, there is always another equilibrium in which the value of currrency is zero (the price level is infinite) and the economy is in a barter system. Indeed, $P_t = \infty$ at all times is a solution of (1.29).[26] In the next section, we are going to show that trading in gold by the central bank can eliminate this equilibrium and imply a unique price level even with a nominal remittances policy and without any need of a transfer from the treasury.

1.5 Holding Gold

We expand upon the framework presented in Section 1.3 to accommodate the inclusion of a durable commodity within the economy, such as gold. Consumers derive utility benefits from holding gold, and it also constitutes a

26. A nominal tax policy in the context of Section 1.4 would similarly fail to rule out the nonmonetary equilibrium.

part of the central bank's assets, which will now play a significant role in price determination. This section demonstrates that through effective management of the gold reserves, the central bank can exercise control over the price level, even in the presence of a nominal remittances policy and a negative net worth.

The intuition behind this result aligns with the observations made in the previous section. A "paper" currency requires a real backing, which can be provided by gold. However, the interesting implication of this section is that there is no need to declare full convertibility of the central bank's liabilities into gold, similarly to a Gold Standard regime, which would constrain policy, as will be shown in Section 2.6 of Chapter 2. In the example provided in this section, the central bank can set its interest rate policy by remunerating reserves and achieve any desired inflation target. It should manage some gold holdings by selling a portion of them at some point in time. Price determination can even occur with zero remittances and with periods of negative net worth. However, asset composition remains crucial for price determination. When gold is sold, the central bank's liabilities should be matched with assets of good quality.

Preferences of the households are given by

$$\sum_{t=t_0}^{\infty} \beta^{t-t_0} [U(C_t) + Z(g_t)],$$

in which $Z(\cdot)$ is a concave, twice-differentiable utility function and g is the stock of gold held by the consumer, which provides utility, like jewelry does. The household's budget constraint expressed in units of currency is:

$$\frac{B_t + X_t}{1 + i_t} + P_{g,t}g_t + P_tC_t + T_t = B_{t-1} + X_{t-1} + P_{g,t}g_{t-1} + P_tY$$
$$+ P_{g,t}(g_t^S - g_{t-1}^S), \quad (1.30)$$

in which (P_g) is the gold price in units of currency and (g^S) is the stock of gold in the economy that is owned by the household. In what follows, we underline the major changes with respect to the analysis of Section 1.3. The set of first-order conditions is enriched by the first-order condition with respect to gold, which can be represented by

$$\frac{P_{g,t}}{P_t} = \frac{Z_g(g_t)}{U_c(C_t)} + \frac{1}{1+r_t}\frac{P_{g,t+1}}{P_{t+1}}, \quad (1.31)$$

in which $Z_g(\cdot)$ is the first derivative of the function $Z(\cdot)$ with respect to its argument. The real value of gold is equal to the nonpecuniary (marginal) benefits of gold, captured by the marginal rate of substitution between gold and consumption, plus the discounted value of the next-period real price. The intertemporal budget constraint of the consumer also changes to

$$\sum_{t=t_0}^{\infty} R_{t_0,t} C_t = \frac{W_{t_0}}{P_{t_0}} + \sum_{t=t_0}^{\infty} R_{t_0,t} \left\{ \left(Y - \frac{T_t}{P_t} \right) + \frac{Z_g(g_t)}{U_c(C_t)} (g_t^S - g_t) \right\}, \quad (1.32)$$

with

$$W_{t_0} \equiv B_{t_0-1} + X_{t_0-1} + P_{g,t_0}(g_{t_0-1} - g_{t_0-1}^S).$$

The last term on the right-hand side of (1.32) represents the gains that the household gets by selling its gold holdings.

We characterize the equilibrium in the case in which the central bank does not back the treasury and therefore is the only one responsible for controlling the value of currency. To keep things simple, let's assume a constant endowment of gold, g^S. Equilibrium in the gold market requires that $g^S = g_t + g_t^C$, in which the g_t^C are the central bank's holdings of gold.

The following set of equations characterizes the equilibrium price level. Equation (1.22) still holds, assuming the interest rate rule (1.21). By considering equilibrium conditions in the goods, asset, and gold markets, and incorporating the relationship (1.18) along with $R_{t_0,t} = \beta^{t-t_0}$, equation (1.32) leads to the following implication:

$$\frac{B_{t_0-1}^C + P_{g,t_0}g_{t_0-1}^C - X_{t_0-1}}{P_{t_0}} = \sum_{t=t_0}^{\infty} \beta^{t-t_0} \left(\frac{Z_g(g_t)}{U_c(Y)} g_t^C \right) + \sum_{t=t_0}^{\infty} \beta^{t-t_0} \left(\frac{T_t^C}{P_t} \right),$$

$$(1.33)$$

which is now key for determining the price level. It's worth noting that the central bank's budget constraint, accounting for its gold holdings, is expressed as:

$$\frac{B_t^C - X_t}{1 + i_t} + P_{g,t}g_t^C = B_{t-1}^C - X_{t-1} + P_{g,t}g_{t-1}^C - T_t^C. \quad (1.34)$$

Equation (1.33) says that in equilibrium the central bank's real net asset position, including gold holdings (the left-hand side of equation (1.33)), is equal to the present-discounted real value of the central bank's costs of maintaining gold holdings together with the present-discounted value of real remittances. Both terms are on the right-hand side of (1.33). Holding gold is costly because the return on gold is lower than that on reserves, since gold provides non-pecuniary benefits (utility benefits) for households. Equation (1.33) boils down to (1.25) when $g_t^C = 0$ at all times.

Define

$$\mathcal{G}_{t_0-1} = \sum_{t=t_0}^{\infty} \beta^{t-t_0} \left(\frac{Z_g(g^S - g_t^C)}{U_c(Y)} (g_{t_0-1}^C - g_t^C) \right)$$

and write (1.33) as

$$\frac{B_{t_0-1}^C - X_{t_0-1}}{P_{t_0}} + \mathcal{G}_{t_0-1} = \sum_{t=t_0}^{\infty} \beta^{t-t_0} \left(\frac{T_t^C}{P_t} \right), \qquad (1.35)$$

using the equilibrium version of (1.31) to substitute for $P_{g,t_0}/P_{t_0}$ as a function of the present-discounted value of the utility services of gold. When compared with (1.25), (1.35) shows the additional term $\mathcal{G}_{t_0-1}$, which is independent of the price at time t_0. A nonzero value of $\mathcal{G}_{t_0-1}$ is enough to exclude the non-monetary equilibrium since in this case an infinite price level is no longer a solution of the equation. To have a nonzero $\mathcal{G}_{t_0-1}$, some time variation in central bank gold holdings is sufficient. Interestingly, a constant g^C, implying $\mathcal{G}_{t_0-1} = 0$, does not work.

As a corollary of these results, it is now possible to determine a unique price level even in the case of a nominal remittances policy and even with interest-rate pegging, unlike in Section 1.4.2. To illustrate the point, consider the policies $T_t^C = (1 - \beta)T^C \geq 0$ and $1 + i_t = 1/\beta$. Equation (1.35) implies

$$P_{t_0} = \frac{T^C + (X_{t_0-1} - B_{t_0-1}^C)}{\mathcal{G}_{t_0-1}}.$$

For the price level P to be positive, numerator and denominator should have the same sign. A convenient assumption is that $T^C > (B_{t_0-1}^C - X_{t_0-1})$, since this implies a downward-sloping consumption demand with respect to the price level.[27] As a consequence, $\mathcal{G}_{t_0-1}$ should be positive.[28] A sufficient condition is for the central bank to hold an initial stock of gold, which is then sold,

---

27. Refer to the discussion in Benigno and Nisticò (2022). The consumer demand function can be derived by combining the Euler equation and the intertemporal budget constraint of the consumer. Furthermore, note that the consumer demand function of Section 1.4.2 is upward sloping.

28. Note also that if $B_{t_0-1}^C < X_{t_0-1}$, given that $T^C \geq 0$, then $\mathcal{G}_{t_0-1}$ should be positive.

even partly, at some future time. Alternatively, the central bank can acquire gold and then sell it in the future. Note that, unlike in Section 1.4.2, doubling the central bank's liabilities results now in a doubling of the price level.

To gain insight into the price determination mechanism, let's simplify the example by assuming that $T_t^C = 0$. This simplification will clearly show two things: i) no monetary transfer is required, and ii) a positive net worth is not necessary. Additionally, let's assume that the central bank initiates its operations at time t_0 with a zero net worth and finances asset purchases and gold holdings through reserves:

$$\frac{B_{t_0}^C}{1 + i_{t_0}} + P_{g,t_0} g_{t_0}^C = \frac{X_{t_0}}{1 + i_{t_0}}. \tag{1.36}$$

Now, consider the following gold holdings management policy. The central bank keeps the stock of gold constant until period $\tilde{t} - 1$ and sells all of it at time $\tilde{t}$, i.e., $g_t^C = g^C$ for $t_0 \leq t \leq \tilde{t} - 1$ and $g_t^C = 0$ for $t \geq \tilde{t}$. Therefore, equation (1.33) at time $\tilde{t}$ implies that:

$$p_{g,\tilde{t}} g^C = \frac{X_{\tilde{t}-1} - B_{\tilde{t}-1}^C}{P_{\tilde{t}}}, \tag{1.37}$$

in which $p_{g,\tilde{t}} = P_{g,\tilde{t}}/P_{\tilde{t}}$ is the real gold price at time $\tilde{t}$, determined by

$$p_{g,\tilde{t}} = \frac{1}{1 - \beta} \frac{Z_g(g^S)}{U_c(Y)},$$

according to (1.31). Note that all gold is in the hands of consumers after, and including, period $\tilde{t}$, and its marginal utility is $Z_g(g^S)$. Equation (1.37) is going to determine the price level at time $\tilde{t}$ as

$$P_{\tilde{t}} = \frac{X_{\tilde{t}-1} - B_{\tilde{t}-1}^C}{p_{g,\tilde{t}} g^C}. \tag{1.38}$$

Equations (1.37) and (1.38) illustrate that the central bank's primary mechanism for anchoring the price level is achieved by exchanging its net liabilities for a tangible asset, gold. Using the interest rate policy $1 + i_t = 1/\beta$, the Fisher equation (1.16) implies that prices remain constant and equal to $P_{\tilde{t}}$ starting from t_0. This is because the nominal interest rate is set to the rate of time preferences, and, as a result, the real and nominal interest rates should equalize.

The mechanism of price determination in this context bears a resemblance to the proposal put forth by Obstfeld and Rogoff (1983), who advocate for the government to partially back the currency by guaranteeing a minimal real redemption value for the currency, within a framework governed by money supply rules. However, there are significant differences between their approach and the one presented in this section. First, in this section, the central bank's policy is based on the interest rate on reserves rather than on the quantity of money, and the economy is cashless. In their context, fractional backing serves as a potential threat, not realized, that requires exchange of all money for real assets at a price ceiling set by the central bank. In contrast, in this framework, the equilibrium involves selling gold, but the central bank does not need to declare any specific convertibility value; the price level is determined endogenously at the time gold holdings are reduced. Furthermore, even after the gold sale, the central bank's liabilities must still be balanced with assets of high quality. This contrasts with the analysis presented by Obstfeld and Rogoff (1983), as elaborated in Section 2.5 of Chapter 2, where a model with positive cash demand is considered.

Now, let's demonstrate that, given (1.36) and the zero remittances policy, the following inequality holds: $X_{\tilde{t}-1} > B^C_{\tilde{t}-1}$. This implies that the price level is positive in (1.38). Unlike in Section 1.4.2, the central bank does not need any monetary transfer, from either the treasury or the private sector. Indeed, (1.36) shows that it starts its operations at time t_0 with a zero net worth. Moreover, the net worth is decreasing and negative until time $\tilde{t} - 1$. Indeed, profits are now represented by

$$\Psi^C_t = \frac{i_{t-1}}{1+i_{t-1}}(B^C_{t-1} - X_{t-1}) + (P_{g,t} - P_{g,t-1})g^C_{t-1} \qquad (1.39)$$

$$= i_{t-1}N^C_{t-1} + (P_{g,t} - (1+i_{t-1})P_{g,t-1})g^C_{t-1},$$

in which in the second line we have used the definition of net worth

$$N^C_t \equiv \frac{B^C_t - X_t}{1+i_t} + P_{g,t}g^C_t.$$

Note from equation (1.31) that

$$P_{g,t} - (1+i_{t-1})P_{g,t-1} = -(1+i_{t-1})P_{t-1}\frac{Z_g(g^S - g^C)}{U_c(Y)} < 0,$$

implying losses on central bank gold holdings for $t_0 \leq t \leq \tilde{t} - 1$, which are accounted for in the second line of equation (1.39).[29] Recall the law of motion for net worth,

$$N_t^C = N_{t-1}^C + \Psi_t^C - T_t^C,$$

considering that we are assuming $T_t^C = 0$. Starting with a zero net worth at time t_0, the central bank makes losses that bring its net worth to negative, and increasing, values. Therefore, the central bank enters period $\tilde{t} - 1$ with a negative net worth and $X_{\tilde{t}-1} > B_{\tilde{t}-1}^C$. Despite this and without any support from the treasury, the central bank can control the price level. At time $\tilde{t}$, the net liabilities are paid by selling gold, and the net worth becomes zero again with a balanced composition of assets and liabilities. This is shown in the flow budget constraint (1.34) at time $t = \tilde{t}$, in which, given that the right-hand side is zero using (1.38) and $T_t^C = 0$, the left-hand side implies $X_{\tilde{t}} = B_{\tilde{t}}^C$ when $g_{\tilde{t}}^C = 0$. The latter result implies that after gold is sold, the central bank matches its liabilities with its default-free assets.

The analyse in this section and chapter have revealed the intricate nature of price determination. However, the key takeaway is a positive one for monetary policymaking: the central bank has the ability to maintain control over the price level at its preferred value. To achieve this goal, the required policy specification goes beyond considering only current and future interest rates; it also entails crucial elements of the balance sheet, including the remittances policy and asset composition.

1.6   References

Woodford (2000, 2001c) and Hall (2005) discuss the unique characteristics of central bank liabilities, highlighting their role in defining the unit of account within the monetary system. Sims (1999b) offers valuable insights into the properties of securities that promise to pay in units of the security itself, like central bank's liabilities, a crucial aspect for comprehending price determination, as explored in the current chapter.

Del Negro and Sims (2015), Hall and Reis (2015), and Reis (2013) underscore the significance of differentiating between the budget constraints

29. As mentioned, the return on gold is lower than that on reserves because gold provides nonpecuniary services to households.

of the treasury and those of the central bank. This distinction serves as a foundational element in constructing the model presented in this chapter.

Benhabib, Schmitt-Grohé, and Uribe (2001a) have established that relying solely on interest rate rules is insufficient for determining the price level in a global analysis of the equilibrium.

The "fiscal theory of the price level" is elaborated upon in the influential works of Sims (1994) and Woodford (1995), as well as in their subsequent publications, including Sims (1999a, 1999b, 2000, 2013) and Woodford (1998, 2001b). Cochrane's recent book (2023) presents his contributions to the literature and provides an extensive analysis of all the implications of the "fiscal theory of the price level," drawing parallels with historical events within the paper-currency regime. Bassetto (2008) offers a concise review of this theory.

Leeper (1991) has explored price determination in a local equilibrium using active/passive fiscal and monetary policies. For insights into a sticky-price model, refer to Benhabib, Schmitt-Grohé, and Uribe (2001b). Additionally, Benhabib, Schmitt-Grohé, and Uribe (2002) have demonstrated how appropriate fiscal policy can prevent deflation when the central bank adopts an active interest rate policy in a global analysis of the equilibrium.

Canzoneri, Cumby, and Diba (2001) explore whether active or passive fiscal policy regimes provide plausible interpretations of postwar U.S. data. Bianchi and Ilut (2017) analyze the inflation surge in the 1970s and subsequent disinflation in the context of different combinations of monetary and fiscal policies. Furthermore, Bianchi, Faccini, and Melosi (2023) discuss how monetary policy accommodation of unfunded fiscal shocks can lead to persistent inflation.

The central bank theory of the price level of Section 1.4.2 is discussed in a more general framework in Benigno (2020). Section 1.5 draws from the setup of Benigno and Nisticò (2022).

2

Cash as a Medium of Exchange

2.1 Introduction

In the previous chapter, coins and banknotes were not in demand, as bonds dominated in a positive interest rate environment. In that context, cash and bonds essentially provided the same payment services. This stands in contrast to the historical role of coins, which primarily facilitated exchanges beyond a barter system. When coins had intrinsic metallic value, they were the sole circulating currency.

Nonetheless, the significance of cash goes beyond historical interest; it retains its importance within the broader definition of money, especially in the framework known as the quantity theory of money, where the quantity of money influences the price level. Historically, however, the origin and relevance of this theory are intertwined with commodity currency systems.

In 1752, David Hume argued that an increase in the quantity of money "has no other effect than to heighten the price of labour and commodities," although he recognized that there could be some effects on economic activity during the adjustment process. He primarily viewed an increase in the quantity of money as equivalent to an increase in the supply of gold and silver in a nation. As a consequence, the price level within that nation would rise above prices in the rest of the world, leading to a reduction in exports and an increase in imports. This, in turn, would result in gold and silver flowing out of the country to other parts of the world, ultimately equalizing prices across nations and restoring balance.

As currency transitioned from metallic coins to paper money, such as banknotes issued by banks that were convertible at predetermined values with specie, a more complex and intriguing financial landscape emerged. The Scottish free-banking system, active from 1716 to 1845, offers an illustrative example. In this system, various banks issued notes and accepted each other's, leading to the development of a note exchange monetary system.

Building upon Hume's analysis, Adam Smith, in *The Wealth of Nations* in 1776, argued that the quantity of notes in circulation would naturally self-regulate when a nation adhered to an international specie standard. He considered the volume of annual production as a given factor that determines the necessary money supply to facilitate that production. Any excess issuance of notes would flow abroad to purchase goods and services.[1]

Adam Smith's insights laid the groundwork for what would later be known as the real-bills doctrine. He envisioned the advantages for a nation in replacing the direct backing of specie with real bills, which represented risk-free private securities. In this system, gold and silver could then be utilized to acquire capital and goods from abroad.[2]

The challenges of implementing a paper-money system, whether fully or partially backed by specie, ignited a lively debate in the early nineteenth century, involving different schools of thought, including the Banking School, the Currency School, and the Free Banking School. The disputes revolved around issues such as the level of backing of notes with gold, the presence of a monopoly issuer or a competitive market, and the necessity or not of a central bank.[3]

In this debate, the origins of monetarism, in general, can be traced back to Henry Thornton's 1802 book, *An Enquiry into the Nature and Effects of the Paper Credit of Great Britain*.[4] Thornton's significant contribution was to emphasize the central bank's role in influencing the price level.[5] According to his theory, the central bank has the ability to control the monetary base, thereby influencing the overall money supply in the economy, and ultimately affecting the price level. This control mechanism is particularly intriguing because Thornton postulated the existence of a natural interest rate that

1. See White (2014).

2. Prior to Adam Smith, in 1705, John Law, a Scottish financier, was among the earliest proponents of the "real bills" doctrine. Smith's presentation in 1776 underscored the crucial feature of the "real bills" system, which allowed for the ultimate convertibility of these bills into gold to prevent excessive money creation.

3. See Schwartz (1989).

4. "Monetarism is the view that the quantity of money has a major influence on economic acitivity and the price level and that the objectives of monetary policy are best achieved by targeting the rate of growth of the money supply" (Cagan, 1989b, p. 195).

5. See Hetzel (1987) for an insightful discussion of the contribution of Thornton.

remains relatively stable in the long run, regardless of fluctuations in the money supply.[6] Money creation, according to Thornton's theory, hinges on the difference between the central bank's policy rate (discount rate) and this natural rate of interest.

Given that an intrinsically worthless paper-currency system emerged almost seamlessly from a system of backed paper money as the backing progressively vanished, it is not surprising that monetarism emerged as one of the most prominent economic theories. Milton Friedman's *A Program for Monetary Stability* in 1960 is often recognized as its modern foundation.[7]

In the early 1970s, following the collapse of the Bretton Woods system, several central banks embraced the goal of controlling money aggregates as part of their monetary policy. However, Canada, the United Kingdom, and the United States soon abandoned this approach due to the perceived unreliability of the relationship between monetary aggregates and inflation. In contrast, Germany successfully implemented a strategy focused on controlling monetary aggregates for more than two decades. In fact, the European Central Bank's monetary policy strategy has inherited a reference to a monetary pillar in its inflation targeting framework.

As previously noted in the introduction to this part, the key observation is that the emergence of an intrinsically worthless paper-money system represents a significant discontinuity, despite its continuous development from a monetary system of backed, and then partially backed, paper currency.

First, in this new system, the value of the currency is no longer tethered to the intrinsic value of tangible assets. Instead, the currency essentially becomes a claim to be paid by itself, aligning with what the central bank can issue at will.[8] Such a system, as we have discussed in Chapter 1, requires the specification of monetary policy for us to have any hope of determining the value of the currency.

The second element of discontinuity is that the distinction between high-powered money and the money stock has less relevance in a commodity-based system but becomes significant in a paper-currency system. In this context, money encompasses not only high-powered money issued by the central bank

6. This concept of a long-run interest rate value anticipated the work of Wicksell in 1898.

7. See also Friedman (1956).

8. Friedman (1989) argued that "such a worldwide fiat (or irredeemable paper) standard has no precedent in history. The 'gold' that central banks still record as an asset on their books is simply the grin of a Cheshire cat that has disappeared." (Friedman, 1989, p. 10).

but also a second type of money. This second type of money, which can be privately issued, represents a potential claim on the first type of money (as discussed by Brunner, 1989, p. 175).

This chapter extends the framework of Chapter 1 to incorporate securities with a distinct transactional role. These securities refer to central bank liabilities bearing zero interest rate, such as coins and banknotes, which offer nonpecuniary (utility) benefits. These benefits can be seen as proxies for the transaction services provided by cash when exchanged for specific goods. Within this context, we explore how the central bank influences the price level and outline the potential differences between controlling the overall monetary base and using interest rates on reserves as policy tools, as discussed in Chapter 1.

Directly controlling high-powered money does not alleviate the necessity of finding a real backing for the currency, as we have previously explored in Chapter 1 through the central bank's balance-sheet policies or treasury-imposed taxes. To provide a glimpse into the subsequent chapters, Chapter 3 delves into a framework in which liquidity is offered through central bank securities, such as reserves, which bear an interest rate. In this context, we examine how the quantity of central bank reserves becomes a pivotal element in the transmission of policy to control money market rates and inflation. The analysis gives a distinct role to central bank reserves in affecting inflation, besides the interest-rate policy.

Chapter 4 further extends this framework to accommodate money creation by the private sector. In a frictionless market with competition among intermediaries, an abundant supply of private liquidity can be obtained to meet all liquidity needs of the economy. Importantly, this does not impede the central bank's ability to control the value of currency, as detailed in the principles outlined in Chapter 1. The same equilibrium can be obtained with the government supplying all liquidity, backing it with either taxes or assets held by the central bank. However, Chapter 4 does not fully do justice to a comprehensive analysis of monetarism since it assumes frictionless private-money creation, which does not destabilize the economy. Chapter 11 will offer a more intricate policy analysis of when private liquidity can become a source of a liquidity crisis, pointing to policies that can stabilize liquidity within the system.

Furthermore, the model presented in this chapter is highly suitable for analyzing price determination in contexts where money is exchangeable for tangible assets such as gold, thus characterizing the historical Gold Standard regime.

Finally, with regard to recent innovations in emerging payment systems, particularly cryptocurrencies, our framework also enables the study of currency competition and the factors that determine the dominance of one currency as a medium of exchange.

2.2   Outline of the Results

The main result of this chapter is aligned with that of Chapter 1, namely that control of high-powered money cannot succeed alone in determining the value of currency. It again requires specification of appropriate tax or remittance policies, as Sections 2.4 and 2.5 in this chapter show. However, in the case where the central bank solely aims to control the price level, there is a novel role played by seigniorage revenues, which are obtained by issuing liabilities (cash) at zero cost. Seigniorage allows us to determine the value of currency even without any initial transfer to the central bank or with negative net worth.

Section 2.6 analyzes a Gold Standard regime, where money is fully convertible to gold, showing that the price level is determined by the backing of gold and appropriately bounded in its variation.

A novelty of this chapter is the analysis of optimal monetary policy, as shown in Section 2.7, that aims to achieve the satiation level in real money balances by setting the interest rate to zero or deflating the economy at the rate of time preference. This is an interesting result since it goes against the interest of a monopolistic supplier of money, whose objective, instead, could be that of keeping seigniorage revenues. When we introduce another currency, such as a cryptocurrency, to compete with government money, Section 2.8 shows that government money might lose its medium-of-exchange property if inflation is too high.

2.3   Model

In the model of this chapter, the liquidity services of "cash" are modelled through "money in the utility function," as in the framework of Sidrausky (1967) and Brock (1974). Besides having this feature, the model is similar to that of Chapter 1.

2.3.1   Consumers

Let us consider a representative agent in a closed economy with the following intertemporal utility:

$$\sum_{t=t_0}^{\infty} \beta^{t-t_0} \left\{ U(C_t) + V\left(\frac{M_t}{P_t}\right) \right\}, \tag{2.1}$$

where β with $0 < \beta < 1$ is the subjective discount factor in preferences, while $U(\cdot)$ is a concave, differentiable utility function in its argument C, the consumption good; $V(\cdot)$ is also a concave, differentiable function of real money balances (M/P) and has a satiation point at $\bar{m} > 0$, i.e., $V_m(M_t/P_t) = 0$ for $M_t/P_t \geq \bar{m}$, in which $V_m(\cdot)$ is the first derivative of $V(\cdot)$ with respect to its argument; and P is the price of the consumption good C.

The consumer is subject to the following budget constraint:

$$\frac{B_t + X_t}{1 + i_t} + M_t + P_t C_t + T_t = B_{t-1} + X_{t-1} + M_{t-1} + P_t Y. \tag{2.2}$$

There are three securities available, as in Chapter 1: bonds (B), reserves (X), and cash (M). All securities are denominated in units of currency. We have already set the interest rate on bonds (i) as equal to that on reserves, following the reasoning given in Chapter 1; (Y) is the constant goods endowment and (T) are lumpsum taxes.

Currency has three properties or roles in this model: *unit of account, store of value*, and *medium of exchange*. The first two roles have features that are similar to those explained in Chapter 1. Regarding the *medium-of-exchange* property, as in Chapter 1, cash and bonds are both means of payment, but, here, cash has an additional liquidity role captured by the utility benefits provided by the real cash balances in (2.1), a proxy of additional transaction (liquidity) services. In what follows, we identify money with just cash (M) and we attribute to it all *medium-of-exchange* properties, remembering that other securities are also means of payment since they are used in purchasing goods C, as shown in (2.2).

Since currency, through cash, still maintains its role as *store of value*, the zero lower bound applies to this model too, i.e., $i_t \geq 0$. The borrowing limit is represented by

$$-\frac{B_{t-1}}{P_t} \leq \frac{M_{t-1} + X_{t-1}}{P_t} + \sum_{j=0}^{\infty} R_{t,t+j}\left(Y - \frac{T_{t+j}}{P_{t+j}}\right) < \infty, \tag{2.3}$$

where the discount factor, $R_{t,t+j}$, has the same definition as in Chapter 1. The consumer chooses sequences $\{C_t, B_t, X_t, M_t\}_{t=t_0}^{\infty}$ with $C_t, X_t, M_t \geq 0$ to maximize (2.1), under constraint (2.2) and borrowing limit (2.3) at each time $t \geq t_0$, given initial conditions $B_{t_0-1}, X_{t_0-1}, M_{t_0-1}$. Moreover, there is an alternative representation of the consumer problem in which the borrowing limit (2.3) is replaced by the intertemporal budget constraint

$$\sum_{t=t_0}^{\infty} R_{t_0,t}\left(C_t + \frac{i_t}{1+i_t}\frac{M_t}{P_t}\right) \leq \frac{B_{t_0-1}+X_{t_0-1}+M_{t_0-1}}{P_{t_0}} + \sum_{t=t_0}^{\infty} R_{t_0,t}\left(Y - \frac{T_t}{P_t}\right).$$
(2.4)

The constraint now shows one additional term with respect to equation (1.8) in Chapter 1: the resources paid to maintain real money balances, the second term on the left-hand side of the constraint. Holding money delivers utility benefits but also carries the cost of the forgone interest from investing in bonds. There is a third, and equivalent, formulation of the consumer problem, in which constraint (2.4) is replaced by

$$\lim_{t\longrightarrow\infty}\left\{R_{t_0,t}\left(\frac{B_{t-1}+X_{t-1}+M_{t-1}}{P_t}\right)\right\} \geq 0, \qquad (2.5)$$

requiring that the limit of the discounted value of assets owned by the household remain nonnegative.[9]

Considering the Lagrange multiplier λ_t attached to constraint (2.2), the first-order condition with respect to C_t implies that $\lambda_t = U_c(C_t)/P_t$, in which $U_c(\cdot)$ is the first derivative of the function $U(\cdot)$, and therefore the first-order condition with respect to X_t, or B_t, is again

$$\frac{U_c(C_t)}{P_t} = \beta(1+i_t)\frac{U_c(C_{t+1})}{P_{t+1}}. \qquad (2.6)$$

The first-order condition with respect to M_t implies that

$$\frac{U_c(C_t)}{P_t} = \frac{1}{P_t}V_m\left(\frac{M_t}{P_t}\right) + \beta\frac{U_c(C_{t+1})}{P_{t+1}}, \qquad (2.7)$$

or, alternatively,

$$1 = \frac{V_m\left(\frac{M_t}{P_t}\right)}{U_c(C_t)} + \frac{1}{1+i_t}, \qquad (2.8)$$

using (2.6).

9. The intertemporal constraint (2.4) and the limit (2.5) can be derived using (2.2) and borrowing limit (2.3) following similar steps as in Appendix A. Refer to Appendix B.

The latter condition provides an intuitive characterization of the optimal choice to invest in money. The consumer equates the cost of investing one dollar in money, represented on the left-hand side of (2.8), to the benefits accounted for on the right-hand side of the equation. These benefits include nonpecuniary benefits, represented by the marginal utility gained from that dollar in money expressed in units of currency (the first term on the right-hand side of (2.8)), as well as pecuniary benefits, which are determined by the discounted value of the unitary payoff of investing one dollar in money. Using (2.8), we can obtain

$$V_m\left(\frac{M_t}{P_t}\right) = \frac{i_t}{1+i_t}U_c(C_t),$$

which implicitly defines the demand of real money balances as a nondecreasing function of consumption, and nonincreasing in the nominal interest rate. Since $i_t \geq 0$, the marginal utility of real money balances, $V_m(\cdot)$, is equal to zero when $i_t = 0$, at which point households may hold any arbitrary amount of real money balances above the satiation level, $\bar{m}$. Therefore, we can write the demand of real money balances as

$$\frac{M_t}{P_t} \geq L(C_t, i_t),$$

which holds with equality whenever $i_t > 0$ and in which $L(C_t, i_t) \equiv V_m^{-1}(U_c(C_t)i_t/(1+i_t))$. Money is now held because, besides being a *store of value*, it also provides nonpecuniary benefits thanks to its utility value (liquidity services). The opportunity cost of holding real money balances is the nominal interest rate; therefore, money demand decreases with the nominal interest rate when $i > 0$, while it increases with consumption.

In the optimal allocation, the intertemporal budget constraint (2.4) holds with equality:

$$\sum_{t=t_0}^{\infty} R_{t,t_0}\left(C_t + \frac{i_t}{1+i_t}\frac{M_t}{P_t}\right) = \frac{B_{t_0-1}+X_{t_0-1}+M_{t_0-1}}{P_{t_0}} + \sum_{t=t_0}^{\infty} R_{t,t_0}\left(Y - \frac{T_t}{P_t}\right).$$

$$(2.9)$$

The present-discounted value of real resources spent for purchasing goods and for holding real money balances is equal to the real value of the initial asset position plus the present-discounted value of real net income. Alternatively, the transversality condition holds:

$$\lim_{t \longrightarrow \infty}\left\{R_{t_0,t}\left(\frac{B_{t-1}+X_{t-1}+M_{t-1}}{P_t}\right)\right\} = 0. \qquad (2.10)$$

2.3.2 *Government*

The central bank's flow budget constraint is represented by

$$\frac{B_t^C - X_t^C}{1 + i_t} - M_t^C = B_{t-1}^C - X_{t-1}^C - M_{t-1}^C - T_t^C, \qquad (2.11)$$

in which money (M^C) and reserves (X^C) are the two types of central bank liabilities. As discussed in Chapter 1, they are claims that promise payment in units of themselves. As before, (B^C) are the central bank's holdings of short-term default-free assets issued by the private sector or the treasury.

The treasury has the same flow budget constraint as in Chapter 1.1

$$\frac{B_t^F}{1 + i_t} = B_{t-1}^F - T_t - T_t^C, \qquad (2.12)$$

where (B^F) is the treasury's debt; (T) are lumpsum taxes; and (T^C) are the nominal remittances received from the central bank. Consistently with the discussion of Section 1.3.2 in Chapter 1, the treasury's debt should satisfy constraint (1.12) to be deemed safe. Furthermore, assuming as before that the treasury does not levy more taxes than needed, the constraint (1.12) holds with equality, imposing restrictions on the trajectory of taxes, given the other variables involved.

2.3.3 *Equilibrium*

Equilibrium in asset markets requires that the debt issued by the government be held by the central bank and by the representative household,

$$B_t^F = B_t^C + B_t, \qquad (2.13)$$

while the reserves and money issued by the central bank be held only by the household:

$$X_t^C = X_t, \qquad (2.14)$$

$$M_t^C = M_t, \qquad (2.15)$$

for each $t \geq t_0$.

Equilibrium in asset markets, together with the flow budget constraints of consumers and the government, implies goods market equilibrium, $C_t = Y$ for each $t \geq t_0$.

Let us now summarize all the equilibrium conditions. The first equation is the Fisher equation,

$$1 + i_t = \frac{1}{\beta} \frac{P_{t+1}}{P_t}, \tag{2.16}$$

derived from (2.6) using equilibrium in the goods market.

Equilibrium in the money market implies that demand is equal to supply, and therefore

$$\frac{M_t}{P_t} \geq L(Y, i_t) \tag{2.17}$$

at each $t \geq t_0$, using equilibrium in the goods market. Equation (2.17) holds with equality whenever $i_t > 0$.

Finally, the intertemporal budget constraint of the consumer (2.9) can be written using the equilibrium condition in goods and asset markets as

$$\sum_{t=t_0}^{\infty} \beta^{t-t_0} \left(\frac{T_t}{P_t} + \frac{i_t}{1+i_t} \frac{M_t}{P_t} \right) = \frac{B_{t_0-1} + X_{t_0-1} + M_{t_0-1}}{P_{t_0}}. \tag{2.18}$$

The government's real revenues match the outstanding real liabilities of the whole government. An intertemporal resource constraint holds in equilibrium. This is again not a solvency constraint but an equilibrium condition. Therefore, it does not require the government to adjust resources to pay its liabilities. Rather, it says that, given outstanding government *nominal* liabilities—the sum $B_{t_0-1} + X_{t_0-1} + M_{t_0-1}$—their real value should be exactly equal to the real resources raised by the government. These real resources are of two sources: taxes and seigniorage—the second term on the left-hand side of the equation. We are going to discuss the meaning of seigniorage in more detail in the next section.

To provide a complete characterization of the equilibrium price level, we need to incorporate the budget constraints of both the central bank and the treasury, represented as (2.11), substituting X_t and M_t for X_t^C and M_t^C, and (2.12). Additionally, we need to consider equilibrium in the bond market (2.13) and the constraint on the trajectory of taxes, (1.12) with equality, which we restate here after substituting $R_{t_0,t} = \beta^{t-t_0}$ for $R_{t_0,t}$:

$$\frac{B_{t_0-1}^F}{P_{t_0}} = \sum_{t=t_0}^{\infty} \beta^{t-t_0} \left(\frac{T_t}{P_t} + \frac{T_t^C}{P_t} \right). \tag{2.19}$$

The model equilibrium conditions are not much different from those of Chapter 1. They share the same Fisher equation, i.e., (2.16), the same budget constraint and solvency condition for the treasury, i.e., equations (2.12) and (2.19), and the same equilibrium in the bonds market (2.13). Equations (2.11) and (2.18) are similar to the previous ones, except for the positive money supply. There is now an additional variable involved in the equilibrium, M_t, and the respective equilibrium condition (2.17).

An equilibrium is a set of sequences $\left\{P_t, i_t, X_t, M_t, B_t^C, T_t^C, B_t^F, T_t, B_t\right\}_{t=t_0}^{\infty}$, with $\left\{P_t, i_t, X_t, M_t, B_t^C\right\}_{t=t_0}^{\infty}$ nonnegative, that satisfies conditions (2.11), (2.12), (2.13), (2.16), and (2.17), holding at each $t \geq t_0$, and condition (2.18), given initial values $B_{t_0-1}^C, B_{t_0-1}^F, X_{t_0-1}, M_{t_0-1}$.[10] Moreover, the sequence of taxes, $\{T_t\}_{t=t_0}^{\infty}$, should satisfy (2.19) for any equilibrium sequences $\left\{P_t, T_t^C\right\}_{t=t_0}^{\infty}$ given initial condition $B_{t_0-1}^F$.

There are four degrees of freedom to specify government policy. As before, we assume that the treasury sets the path of taxes consistently with (2.12) and (2.19), while the central bank simultaneously sets three out of the four sequences $\left\{i_t, M_t, X_t, T_t^C\right\}_{t=t_0}^{\infty}$; but note that, given (2.17), the sequences $\{M_t\}_{t=t_0}^{\infty}$ and $\{i_t\}_{t=t_0}^{\infty}$ cannot be set independently of each other.

2.3.4 Seigniorage

What is seigniorage? In medieval Europe, a period that saw the circulation of metallic coins, the "seigneur," who had the right to issue coins, guaranteed their content by stamping his portrait or coat of arms on the coin. For this service, the "seigneur" retained a share of precious metals when minting the coins. In a fiat-money system, seigniorage should be defined as the central bank's profits. In this chapter's simple model, the central bank makes profits because it can finance at zero cost—with money—the purchase of default-free assets carrying a positive interest rate. When the nominal interest rate is zero, these revenues are also zero. To see this result, note that the central bank's net worth (N^C) at a generic time t is given by

$$N_t^C = \frac{B_t^C - X_t}{1 + i_t} - M_t.$$

10. The infinite sums in (2.18) and (2.19) should be also finite.

According to the flow budget constraint (2.11), its law of motion is

$$N_t^C = N_{t-1}^C + \Psi_t^C - T_t^C,$$

in which profits (Ψ^C) are:

$$\Psi_t^C \equiv \frac{i_{t-1}}{1+i_{t-1}}(B_{t-1}^C - X_{t-1}) = i_{t-1}(N_{t-1}^C + M_{t-1}).$$

In the second equality, we have used the definition of net worth. Profits (seigniorage) depend on the interest income received on asset holdings minus the interest payments on reserves, therefore on the non-interest-bearing liabilities (net worth and money) times the interest rate. With a zero interest rate, seigniorage is zero.

While this is the literal definition of seigniorage, representing the monetary resources that the central bank can extract from its activity, we will also use the term seigniorage to refer to the implicit cost for households when holding certain securities at a lower interest rate compared to the market rate. These costs can be positive even when the central bank's profits are zero, as will be demonstrated. Accordingly, this definition of seigniorage is represented by the infinite sum

$$\sum_{t=t_0}^{\infty} \beta^{t-t_0} \left(\frac{i_t}{1+i_t} \frac{M_t}{P_t} \right)$$

in (2.18), which corresponds to the resources spent by the households in holding real money balances. This interpretation is also consistent with what can be obtained by iterating forward the law of motion of net worth in real terms,

$$\frac{N_t^C}{P_t} = (1+i_{t-1})\frac{N_{t-1}^C}{P_t} + i_{t-1}\frac{M_{t-1}}{P_t} - \frac{T_t^C}{P_t},$$

using the definition of net worth and the equilibrium value for $R_{t,t_0} = \beta^{t-t_0}$ to obtain

$$\frac{X_{t_0-1} + M_{t_0-1}}{P_{t_0}} + \sum_{t=t_0}^{\infty} \beta^{t-t_0} \left(\frac{T_t^C}{P_t} \right) = \frac{B_{t_0-1}^C}{P_{t_0}} + \sum_{t=t_0}^{\infty} \beta^{t-t_0} \left(\frac{i_t}{1+i_t} \frac{M_t}{P_t} \right).$$

$$(2.20)$$

In the derivation of (2.20), we have used the limit

$$\lim_{t \to \infty} \left\{ R_{t_0,t} \left(\frac{B_{t-1}^C - X_{t-1} - M_{t-1}}{P_t} \right) \right\} = 0,$$

which is the result of combining (2.10) with (1.13), holding with equality, and (2.13). Equivalently, (2.20) can be obtained by simply combining (2.18) and (2.19) using (2.13).

An intertemporal resource constraint holds for the central bank's liabilities in the equilibrium. It is important to note that (2.20) should not be mistaken for a solvency condition; rather, it serves as an equilibrium condition. This condition asserts that the real value of the central bank's liabilities, in combination with the present-discounted value of real remittances (found on the left-hand side of the equation), must equal the sum of asset holdings and seigniorage, which are on the right-hand side of the equation. Note that this definition of seigniorage can be positive even if the central bank does not make any profit, meaning that, in its literal definition, seigniorage has a zero value. Consider the simple case in which the central bank merely drops money on the ground, without holding any assets. In this case $M_t = M_{t-1} + T_t^C$ and profits are zero, whereas the last summation on the right-hand of (2.20) can be positive.[11]

One can also represent (2.20) as

$$\frac{X_{t_0-1}}{P_{t_0}} + \sum_{t=t_0}^{\infty} \beta^{t-t_0} \left(\frac{T_t^C}{P_t} \right) = \frac{B_{t_0-1}^C}{P_{t_0}} + \sum_{t=t_0}^{\infty} \beta^{t-t_0} \left(\frac{M_t - M_{t-1}}{P_t} \right)$$
$$- \lim_{t \to \infty} \beta^{t-t_0} \frac{M_{t-1}}{P_t},$$

using (2.16). This could suggest an alternative definition of seigniorage, as indicated by the second addendum on the right-hand side of the equation, a definition often assumed in the literature. However, it is important to note that the above formulation may be less compelling because there is no inherent reason to assume that the limit on the right-hand side, (second line), is necessarily equal to zero in equilibrium. In fact, the consumer's natural borrowing limit should encompass the possibility of his repaying debt with asset holdings, such as money, as shown in (2.3) and (2.5).

2.4 Price Determination through the Interest Rate Policy

Let us first assume that the central bank sets policy in terms of sequences $\{i_t, X_t\}_{t=t_0}^{\infty}$ and therefore controls the nominal interest rate, in which case

---

11. Net worth, in this case, is such that $N_t^C = -M_t$.

the path of money supply becomes endogenous. We start by assuming that the central bank fully backs the treasury's debt. The results do not change much with respect to Section 1.4 of Chapter 1. We maintain the same interest rate policy,

$$1 + i_t = \max \left\{ \frac{1}{\beta} \left(\frac{P_t}{\bar{P}} \right)^{\phi}, 1 \right\},$$

with $\phi \geq 0$ and target price $\bar{P} > 0$, while we modify the tax policy for it to be constant once we take into account a transfer of the seigniorage revenues obtained by issuing money:

$$\frac{T_t}{P_t} = (1 - \beta)\tau - i_{t-1} \frac{M_{t-1}}{P_t}, \tag{2.21}$$

with $\tau > 0.$[12] Inserting this tax policy into (2.18), we obtain

$$\frac{B_{t_0-1} + X_{t_0-1}}{P_{t_0}} + (1 + i_{t_0-1}) \frac{M_{t_0-1}}{P_{t_0}} = \tau,$$

determining then the initial price level P_{t_0}, given initial conditions B_{t_0-1}, X_{t_0-1}, M_{t_0-1}, and i_{t_0-1}. The full sequence of prices follows from (1.22). As in Section 1.4 of Chapter 1, the value taken by τ can determine the type of equilibrium: inflationary, deflationary, or with a constant price level at $\bar{P}$. The sequence of money supply is determined by (2.17).

Whether or not the economy is cashless has no consequence for price determination under an interest rate policy once it is combined with an appropriate tax policy.

The case in which the central bank does not back the treasury follows in a similar way. By inserting in (2.20) an appropriate transfer policy, such as

$$\frac{T_t^C}{P_t} = (1 - \beta)\tau^C + i_{t-1} \frac{M_{t-1}}{P_t}, \tag{2.22}$$

the prices will be determined with the same mechanism as in Chapter 1.4.2. The price level at time t_0 is given by:

$$P_{t_0} = \frac{B_{t_0-1}^C - X_{t_0-1} - (1 + i_{t_0-1})M_{t_0-1}}{\tau^C} = \frac{N_{t_0-1}^C}{\tau^C(1 + i_{t_0-1})}.$$

12. The policy in (2.21) is convenient for simplifying the derivations and, at the same time, it is consistent with a reaction of the tax policy to the past interest rate and money supply. It could be possible to simplify the analysis even further to consider a less appealing reaction to the current interest rate and money supply.

There is one subtle difference, though: parameter τ^C can also be set to negative values because, with a positive supply of money, the central bank earns seigniorage revenues that are transferred to the private sector, according to (2.22). Indeed, remittances policy T_t^C/P_t can be positive, even if τ^C is negative. If τ^C is set to a negative value, an equilibrium with positive prices will exist only if the central bank has a negative net worth, therefore not requiring any monetary transfer from the treasury.[13]

It is worth elaborating more on the role of seigniorage revenues for price determination since the central bank could use them to retrieve resources to back the value of currency. The term $(i_t/(1+i_t))M_t/P_t$ represents a real revenue for the central bank, mirroring the real resources that the consumer forgoes by holding real money balances, as shown in (2.20).

Consider, as an example, a nominal remittances policy $T_t^C = (1-\beta)$ $T^C \geq 0$, and couple it with a pure interest rate pegging policy, i.e., $1 + i_t = 1/\beta$. In Chapter 1.4.2, these policies were unable to determine the price level. Here, by substituting $T_t^C = (1-\beta)T^C$ in (2.20), and together with equilibrium in the money market (2.17) and a constant price level, $P_{t_0} = \ldots = P_t = \ldots = P_T \ldots$, implied by the interest rate policy, we get

$$\frac{T^C + (X_{t_0-1} + M_{t_0-1} - B_{t_0-1}^C)}{P_{t_0}} = L\left(Y, \frac{1}{\beta} - 1\right),$$

which can now determine a positive price at t_0:

$$P_{t_0} = \frac{T^C + (X_{t_0-1} + M_{t_0-1} - B_{t_0-1}^C)}{L(Y, 1/\beta - 1)}, \tag{2.23}$$

provided the numerator is positive.

Two important remarks follow from the price determination in (2.23). First, note the proportionality between the central bank's liabilities and the price level. Second, there is again no need for the treasury's support to determine the price level, since a positive P_{t_0} is set even by a negative net worth. Note from (2.20) that seigniorage resources can provide real backing to the value of currency even with no asset holdings and zero transfers, for a positive inflation rate. However, it's important to note that an infinite price level, a zero value of currency, can still be a possible equilibrium, as demonstrated in Section 1.4.2 of Chapter 1. Indeed, the first-order condition for money

---

13. Note that central bank's profits at time t are positive provided $N_{t-1}^C > -M_{t-1}$, giving a bound to how far net worth can be negative.

demand (2.7) can also be consistent with an infinite price level. Therefore, real money balances can be zero and seigniorage, too, and equation (2.23) can be compatible with two equilibria: one with a finite price level and the other with an infinite price level.

One way to rule out the nonmonetary equilibrium is to assume that

$$\lim_{P_t \to \infty} \frac{1}{P_t} V_m \left(\frac{M_t}{P_t} \right) > 0, \tag{2.24}$$

which is, indeed, a requirement for cash to be essential even at very high interest rates.

Obstfeld and Rogoff (1983) discussed this assumption to rule out hyper-inflationary outcomes when considering money supply rules. However, the assumption is often viewed as implausible because it implies a positive demand for money even at very high interest rates. An alternative, less contro-versial approach to eliminate the nonmonetary equilibrium is by the central bank's holding real assets, such as gold, as demonstrated in Section 1.5 of Chapter 1.

2.5 Price Determination through Money Aggregates

We now switch to a different specification of monetary policy, assuming that the central bank controls the path of money supply (cash) together with that of reserves. The central bank, then, directly determines base money and, there-fore, the size of its balance sheet. The objective of this section is to understand whether this makes any difference with respect to setting an interest rate policy. Can the central bank control the price level through money without relying on fiscal policy or balance-sheet policies? In general, the answer is no.

Let us consider a simple policy of constant money supply, i.e., $M_t = M_{t_0-1} = M$ for a positive M and for each $t \geq t_0$, aimed at achieving a constant, and unique, price level. Using it in (2.7) with $C_t = Y$, we can obtain

$$m_{t+1} = \frac{m_t}{\beta} \left(1 - \frac{V_m(m_t)}{U_c(Y)} \right), \tag{2.25}$$

for each $t \geq t_0$, having defined $m_t = M/P_t$. This difference equation in real money balances has infinite solutions as well, depending on the initial real money balance holdings m_{t_0} or initial price level P_{t_0}. It cannot alone determine the price level. There is a stationary solution in which real money balances and the price level are constant. This solution, denoted with $\tilde{m}$, is implicitly defined by

$$V_m(\tilde{m}) = U_c(Y)(1-\beta).$$

Given M, a certain price level, let's say $\tilde{P}$, is implied. However, given the same M, there could also be other paths for prices consistent with (2.25). If $P_{t_0} > \tilde{P}$, there are inflationary paths; if $P_{t_0} < \tilde{P}$, there are deflationary paths. There can also be solutions in which $m_t = 0$ and the price level is infinite at all times, again the nonmonetary equilibrium. Interestingly, there can be solutions in which $P_{t_0} > \tilde{P}$ and prices rise over time until a finite period $\tilde{t}$, in which $V_m(m_{\tilde{t}}) = U_c(Y)$. Subsequently, prices become infinite, and $m_t = 0$ at all times.

One can assume the positive limit (2.24) to exclude nonmonetary solutions and inflationary paths. It is important to recall, however, that this assumption implies an implausible behavior of money demand. However, deflationary paths would still be equilibria.

In general, similarly to the case of the interest rate policy, controlling monetary aggregates is not sufficient for determining the price level, and other policy tools are needed to uniquely determine it. Consider first the case in which the central bank backs the treasury, and therefore (2.18) is an equilibrium condition. The treasury could set a tax policy like (2.21) and determine the initial price level at

$$P_{t_0} = \frac{X_{t_0-1} + B_{t_0-1} + (1+i_{t_0})M}{\tau}.$$

The tax policy τ should be appropriately set to achieve $P_{t_0} = \tilde{P}$.

When the central bank does not back the treasury's debt, condition (2.19) should hold and therefore intertemporal constraint (2.20), too. In this case, following previous analyses, the central bank remittances would be relevant to determining the price level.

Interestingly, Obstfeld and Rogoff's proposal (1983) to threaten redemption of money with gold can be incorporated into this analysis. Consider their simple case, in which $M_t = M$ at all times; then (2.20) implies

$$\frac{M}{P_{t_0}} = \sum_{t=t_0}^{\infty} \beta^{t-t_0}\left(\frac{i_t}{1+i_t}\frac{M}{P_t}\right) = \sum_{t=t_0}^{\infty} \beta^{t-t_0}\left(\frac{V_m\left(\frac{M}{P_t}\right)}{U_c(Y)}\frac{M}{P_t}\right), \qquad (2.26)$$

since in their analysis $X_t = B_t^C = T_t^C = 0$ for each $t \geq t_0$. To obtain the second equality in (2.26), we have used (2.8) and $C_t = Y$

Note that $\tilde{m}$, and therefore $\tilde{P}$, is a solution of (2.26). Consistently with their analysis, deflationary solutions are ruled out since in that case $i_t = 0$, and the above equilibrium condition is violated. However, inflationary solutions are still possible equilibria. One way to exclude them is through condition (2.24). This condition ensures that the right-hand side of the above equation is always positive, thereby implying a finite price level at all times. Without this condition, it would be possible to rule out inflationary paths by holding a real asset, such as gold, and selling it or threatening to do so at some point in time.

In line with the analysis in Section 1.5 of Chapter 1, when gold circulates, the intertemporal resource constraint of the economy, the mirror image of the intertemporal budget constraint of the consumers, is

$$\frac{M - P_{g,t}g_{t-1}^C}{P_t} = \sum_{T=t}^{\infty} \beta^{T-t} \left(\frac{V_m(m_T)}{U_c(Y)} m_T \right) - \sum_{T=t}^{\infty} \beta^{T-t} \left(\frac{Z_g(g_T)}{U_c(Y)} g_T^C \right),$$

(2.27)

in which P_g is the price of gold; g^C and g are, respectively, the central bank and private sector gold holdings; and $Z_g(\cdot)$ is the marginal utility households derive from their gold holdings, given a concave function $Z(\cdot)$. In (2.27), the central bank's real net debt position (the left-hand side of the equation) is equal in equilibrium to the present-discounted value of seigniorage revenues minus the discounted real value of the central bank's cost of maintaining gold holdings. Note that when g_t^C is constant at all times, then (2.27) is equivalent to (2.26), and $\tilde{m}$ is a solution with the associated price level $\tilde{P}$.

The insight of Obstfeld and Rogoff (1983) is to threaten the redemption of the entire money stock with gold at a generic future time under the contingency that an inflationary path would develop. Recall the first-order condition for money demand (2.7), and write it as

$$\frac{U_c(C_t)}{P_t} = \frac{1}{P_t} V_m(m_t) + \frac{\beta U_c(C_{t+1})}{P_{t+1}}.$$

To hold money, the marginal cost of the forgone consumption of a dollar (on the left-hand side) should be equal to the sum of the marginal benefits of saving that dollar in money, including the nonpecuniary benefits (the first term on the right-hand side), and the pecuniary benefits of purchasing goods in the next period (the second term). If marginal cost is higher than the benefit, demand for money is zero. If the marginal cost is lower than the benefit, agents will hold as much money as possible, reducing consumption. However, this will raise the marginal utility of consumption at time t, to rebalance the equation. In equilibrium, $C_t = Y$ and

$$\frac{1}{P_t} = \frac{1}{P_t} \frac{V_m(m_t)}{U_c(Y)} + \frac{\beta}{P_{t+1}}.$$

On an inflationary path $\bar{P}_{t_0} > \tilde{P}$, in which $\tilde{P}$ is the price level in the stationary equilibrium, $\bar{P}_t$ keeps rising until a generic time $\tilde{t}$ to reach $\bar{P}_{\tilde{t}}$. If the central bank promises to redeem money simultaneously at a price $\bar{\bar{P}}_{\tilde{t}} < \bar{P}_{\tilde{t}}$, then the inflationary path starting from $\bar{P}_{t_0}$ cannot be an equilibrium since the marginal benefits of holding money looking forward would be higher than the costs. The key issue is whether the central bank has the resources for this backing. These are given, within the economy, by (2.27). When central bank gold holdings are sold, (2.27) implies that the value of currency at time $\tilde{t}$ can be backed at

$$\frac{1}{\bar{\bar{P}}_{\tilde{t}}} = \frac{p_{g,\tilde{t}} g^C_{t_0}}{M}$$

by setting $m_T = 0$ and $g^C_T = 0$ for each $T \geq \tilde{t}$, in which $p_{g,\tilde{t}} = P_{g,\tilde{t}}/P_{\tilde{t}}$ is the relative price of gold at time $\tilde{t}$.[14] At time t_0, instead, we assume that the money issued is used to purchase gold at the relative price p_{g,t_0},

$$p_{g,t_0} g^C_{t_0} = \frac{M}{\bar{P}_{t_0}},$$

given the price $\bar{P}_{t_0}$. We can combine the above two equations to obtain that the central bank can redeem money at the price $\bar{\bar{P}}_{\tilde{t}} = (p_{g,t_0}/p_{g,\tilde{t}})\bar{P}_{t_0} > \bar{P}_{t_0}$. The last inequality follows by observing that the relative price of gold falls given that the marginal utility of gold, $Z_g(\cdot)$, decreases. The value obtained for $\bar{\bar{P}}_{\tilde{t}}$ determines the time $\tilde{t}$ at which the central bank would eventually execute the backing of money with gold when $\bar{\bar{P}}_{\tilde{t}}$ satisfies $\bar{P}_{\tilde{t}-1} \leq \bar{\bar{P}}_{\tilde{t}} < \bar{P}_{\tilde{t}}$.

2.6   The Gold Standard

The model presented in this chapter is well suited for examining the implications of the Gold Standard regime, wherein a central bank commits to

---

14. By setting $m_T = 0$ for each $T \geq \tilde{t}$ the worst continuation scenario is considered, where there are no longer seigniorage resources.

fixing the price of gold and allowing the free conversion of national currency into gold at that price. The Gold Standard characterized the international monetary system during a significant period. The United States informally adopted the Gold Standard in 1834, and formally in 1900 with the passage of the Gold Standard Act, as shown in Figure 1.1.[15] Between 1880 and 1914, most countries adhered to the classical Gold Standard, and from 1946 to 1971, they adopted the Bretton Woods system.

We propose an amendment to the model described in Section 2.3 to incorporate the role of gold. Initially, we generalize household preferences as follows:

$$\sum_{t=t_0}^{\infty} \beta^{t-t_0} \left[U(C_t) + L\left(\frac{M_t}{P_t}\right) + Z(g_t) \right].$$

Here, as a novel addition, $Z(\cdot)$ represents the functional form of utility that households derive from gold, as introduced in Section 1.5 of Chapter 1, and g represents the stock of gold held by households in the forms of jewelry. The household's budget constraint, expressed in units of currency, is defined as:

$$\frac{B_t}{1+i_t} + M_t + P_{g,t}g_t + P_t C_t + T_t = B_{t-1} + M_{t-1}$$
$$+ P_{g,t}g_{t-1} + P_t Y + P_{g,t}(g_t^S - g_{t-1}^S),$$

in which (P_g) is the gold price in units of currency and (g^S) is the stock of gold in the economy. All other variables maintain the same interpretations as previously defined. We are abstracting from the issuance of central bank reserves and assuming that the entire monetary base consists of coins and banknotes. The households' problem is subject to an appropriate borrowing limit. In what follows, we underline the major changes with respect to the analysis of this chapter. The set of first-order conditions, (2.6) and (2.7), is enriched with the first-order condition with respect to gold that can be represented by

$$\frac{P_{g,t}}{P_t} = \frac{Z_g(g_t)}{U_c(C_t)} + \frac{1}{1+r_t}\frac{P_{g,t+1}}{P_{t+1}}, \qquad (2.28)$$

where r is the already defined real rate, and is completed by the exhaustion of the intertemporal budget constraint of the consumer.

In a Gold Standard regime, the monetary authority fixes the price of gold, let's say $P_{g,t} = 1$, and supplies any quantity of money backed by gold. Defining

15. See Bordo (1981).

by g_t^C the gold held by the central bank, $M_t = P_{g,t}g_t^C = g_t^C$. Equilibrium in the gold and goods market implies $g_t^S = g_t + g_t^C$ and $C_t = Y$. We can then express (2.7) and (2.28) as

$$\frac{1}{P_t} = \frac{1}{P_t}\frac{L_m\left(\frac{g_t^C}{P_t}\right)}{U_c(Y)} + \frac{\beta}{P_{t+1}}$$

and

$$\frac{1}{P_t} = \frac{Z_g(g_t^S - g_t^C)}{U_c(Y)} + \frac{\beta}{P_{t+1}}. \tag{2.29}$$

From these equations, we can deduce that the nonpecuniary benefits of holding real money balances in units of real income are equal to the marginal utility of gold in units of real income, and thus:

$$P_t = \frac{L_m\left(\frac{g_t^C}{P_t}\right)}{Z_g(g_t^S - g_t^C)}. \tag{2.30}$$

This equation demonstrates that price movements are appropriately constrained as long as the supply of gold is suitably bounded, given that $0 < g_t^C < g_t^S$. We can then iterate forward (2.29) to obtain that the value of currency is given by the present-discounted value of the marginal benefits of gold in units of goods, i.e.,

$$\frac{1}{P_t} = \sum_{j=0}^{\infty} \beta^j \left(\frac{Z_g(g_{t+j}^S - g_{t+j}^C)}{U_c(Y)}\right).$$

Solving the two equations mentioned above allows us to determine the equilibrium values of P_t and g_t^C at each point in time. The value of currency is anchored by the benefits derived from gold for consumers. Furthermore, the constrained supply of gold establishes limits on the price level. Consequently, under the Gold Standard, the price level is firmly determined by the backing of a real asset in limited supply.

The implications of this model align with the observed evidence of complete price stability during the classical Gold Standard period, spanning from 1880 to 1914, during which the United States saw an average annual inflation rate of merely 0.1 percent. However, this stability comes at the expense of heightened sensitivity of the price level to both monetary and real factors. For instance, the model suggests a positive relationship between the price

level and the supply of gold, consistent with historical evidence that gold discoveries, such as the one in California in 1848, were often associated with
inflationary effects.

During the classical Gold Standard period, the variability of the price level
was notably higher compared to the average annual percentage change, and
significantly higher than under an inflation targeting regime.[16] Furthermore,
falling prices could potentially trigger a debt-deflation spiral. Bernanke and
James (1991) have discussed the relevance of deflationary pressures stemming
from the Gold Standard during the onset of the Great Depression.

The model introduced above also aligns with another intriguing phenomenon associated with the Gold Standard known as the Gibson paradox,
which is named after Gibson (1923) by Keynes (1930). This phenomenon
is characterized by a notable positive correlation between long-term interest rates and the level of prices during that era. As Friedman and Schwartz
(1976, p. 288) pointed out, "the Gibson paradox remains an empirical phenomenon without a theoretical explanation."

This is an implication of the model presented in this section, when we apply
(2.8) to (2.30) to derive

$$P_t = \frac{i_t}{1 + i_t} \frac{U_c(Y)}{V_g(g_t^S - g_t^C)}.$$

This equation demonstrates a positive correlation between the price level and
the interest rate, accounting for the restrictions implied by equations (2.29)
and (2.30).[17]

2.7 Optimal Policy

This chapter's model features some implications in terms of optimal monetary
policy for real money balances entering the utility function. Holding money
implies a real cost for households maintaining real money balances instead

---

16. Bordo (1981) documents that the coefficient of variation, i.e., the ratio of the standard deviation of annual percentage changes in the price level to the average annual percentage
change, was 17 for the United States between 1879 and 1913, while only 1.6 between 1946 and
1979.

17. Benati and Benigno (2023) have further deepened the mechanism behind the Gibson
paradox, finding its roots in movements of the natural real rate of interest. They have also shown
that it is hidden in other monetary regimes, such as that of inflation targeting, when eliminating
the drift in prices.

of investing in the bond market. This cost, as we have already argued, is a source of "resources" for the central bank through seigniorage. However, in this model, producing cash is costless. A benevolent policymaker, maximizing the utility of the household, would like to set the marginal benefits of one unit of money, $V_m(\cdot)$, to its zero marginal cost, thus to the point of satiating the economy with real money balances, i.e., $M_t/P_t \geq \bar{m}$, which is also a way to reduce to zero the consumer's cost of holding money. This result represents the famous Friedman rule (see Friedman, 1969), which could be alternatively expressed in terms of the inflation rate or money growth. The policymaker should target the money's negative growth rate to achieve a rate of deflation of prices equal to the rate of time preference, $P_{t+1}/P_t = \beta$.

It should be emphasized that having the monetary policymaker satiate the economy with liquidity is not in its interest. In fact, this model's central bank has monopoly power in the supply of money for which it retrieves seigniorage revenues.[18] Why, then, would a monopolist act against its interest by reducing to zero any seigniorage? Why would it even do that to the point of limiting its power to determine the price level? These questions serve as the motivation for the next section, which explores how currency competition can influence central bank policy and potentially drive the economy toward reducing the monopoly rents associated with currency issuance.

2.8   Cryptocurrency Competition

Let us consider now an economy in which two currencies, for example, a government and a private currency, compete as a *medium of exchange*, extending therefore the model of Section 2.3. Preferences are represented by

$$\sum_{t=t_0}^{\infty} \beta^{t-t_0} \left\{ U(C_t) + V\left(\frac{M_t}{P_t} + \frac{M_t^*}{P_t^*}\right) \right\},$$

in which (M) is the government-issued and (M^*) the privately issued money. (P) is the price of the consumption good in terms of government currency, (P^*) is the price in private currency. Both types of money can now provide utility benefits (liquidity services) and are perfectly substitutable in this

---

18. Note that the central bank's profits can be positive, depending on the appropriate composition of asset holdings.

respect. The function $V(\cdot)$ has again the same properties as before, with $\bar{m}$ being the satiation level.

The consumption good (C) is subject to a budget constraint expressed in units of goods:

$$\frac{B_t}{P_t(1+i_t)} + \frac{M_t}{P_t} + \frac{M_t^*}{P_t^*} + C_t \le \frac{B_{t-1}}{P_t} + \frac{M_{t-1}}{P_t} + \frac{M_{t-1}^*}{P_t^*} + Y - \frac{T_t}{P_t} + \frac{Tr_t^*}{P_t^*},$$

$$(2.31)$$

in which B is an interest-bearing security in units of government currency; Y is the constant endowment of the consumption goods; T are government taxes in units of government currency; and Tr^* are the private issuer's transfers in units of private currency. One important difference between the two currencies, which we are going to explain shortly, is that the private issuer cannot rely on taxation power.[19]

In writing budget constraint (2.31), we made two important assumptions: first, interest-bearing securities provide no liquidity services; second, they are only denominated in the government currency. The significance of the latter assumption is discussed later. B can be positive, in which case it is an asset for the household, or negative, in which case it is debt. We allow the private sector to borrow by issuing debt denominated in the government currency but not in the privately issued currency. And this debt, when issued, is paid back in full, being subject to an appropriate borrowing limit. We abstract for now from the distinction between reserves and bonds, assuming directly that i is the interest rate on reserves set by the central bank. Note again that, given the *store-of-value* properties of money, the nominal interest rate in the government currency is nonnegative, $i_t \ge 0$. The consumer's problem is subject to an appropriate borrowing limit.

Consider the optimization problem. The first-order condition with respect to the consumption good C and with respect to holdings of interest-bearing security B_t implies the standard Euler equation,

$$\frac{U_c(C_t)}{P_t} = \beta(1+i_t)\frac{U_c(C_{t+1})}{P_{t+1}},$$

$$(2.32)$$

19. In a more general framework, one could envision a deeper structure of the balance sheet of the private company issuing money, along the lines of the discussion in Section 1.4.2 of Chapter 1. Here, the modelling is meant to capture more closely the issuance of cryptocurrencies like Bitcoin.

at each time $t \geq t_0$, while the conditions with respect to M_t and M_t^* are:

$$\frac{U_c(C_t)}{P_t} = \frac{1}{P_t} V_m \left(\frac{M_t}{P_t} + \frac{M_t^*}{P_t^*} \right) + \beta \frac{U_c(C_{t+1})}{P_{t+1}} + \psi_t, \qquad (2.33)$$

$$\frac{U_c(C_t)}{P_t^*} = \frac{1}{P_t^*} V_m \left(\frac{M_t}{P_t} + \frac{M_t^*}{P_t^*} \right) + \beta \frac{U_c(C_{t+1})}{P_{t+1}^*} + \psi_t^*, \qquad (2.34)$$

at each time $t \geq t_0$, in which ψ_t and ψ_t^* are the nonnegative Lagrange multipliers associated with nonnegative constraints $M_t \geq 0$ and $M_t^* \geq 0$, respectively, with the Kuhn-Tucker conditions $\psi_t M_t = 0$ and $\psi_t^* M_t^* = 0$. The above two conditions already illustrate which currency is going to dominate as a *medium of exchange*. If we combine them, we get

$$\psi_t P_t - \psi_t^* P_t^* = \beta U_c(C_{t+1}) \left[\frac{P_t^*}{P_{t+1}^*} - \frac{P_t}{P_{t+1}} \right].$$

When the inflation rate is higher for the private currency, $P_{t+1}^*/P_t^* > P_{t+1}/P_t$, then the private currency is not used. In the above equation, the right-hand side is negative; therefore $\psi_t^* P_t^* > \psi_t P_t \geq 0$, implying $\psi_t^* > 0$ and then $M_t^* = 0$, and conversely in the opposite case. When inflation rates are equal, both currencies may compete simultaneously to provide transaction services.

The last first-order condition is the exhaustion of the resources available to the consumer, and therefore its intertemporal budget constraint holds with equality:

$$\sum_{t=t_0}^{\infty} R_{t_0,t} \mathcal{C}_t = \frac{B_{t_0-1} + M_{t_0-1}}{P_{t_0}} + \frac{M_{t_0-1}^*}{P_{t_0}^*} + \sum_{t=t_0}^{\infty} R_{t_0,t} \left(Y - \frac{T_t}{P_t} + \frac{Tr_t^*}{P_t^*} \right),$$

$$(2.35)$$

in which

$$\mathcal{C}_t \equiv C_t + \frac{i_t}{1+i_t} \frac{M_t}{P_t} + \Gamma_t^* \frac{M_t^*}{P_t^*},$$

where

$$\Gamma_t^* \equiv 1 - \frac{P_t^*}{P_{t+1}^*} \frac{P_{t+1}}{P_t} \frac{1}{1+i_t} = \frac{i_t^*}{1+i_t^*}.$$

We have defined the "shadow" nominal interest rate on private currency as[20]

$$1 + i_t^* \equiv \frac{1}{\beta} \frac{P_{t+1}^*}{P_t^*} \frac{U_c(C_t)}{U_c(C_{t+1})}.$$

We will now characterize the conditions for a currency's dominance with respect to another one based on the monetary policy of the two issuers. To this end, we specify their budget constraints. The government's monetary authority is subject to the following budget constraint:

$$M_t^g + \frac{B_t^g}{1 + i_t} = M_{t-1}^g + B_{t-1}^g - T_t, \tag{2.36}$$

where M_t^g is the supply of cash and B_t^g is the debt issued by the government, if positive, or assets held, if negative. We are considering the treasury and the central bank pooled together in the government, with all government debt having the property of being default-free by definition.

The private issuer is instead subject to the constraint

$$M_t^{*p} = M_{t-1}^{*p} + Tr_t^*,$$

which can be interpreted either as the budget constraint of an agent issuing money in a centralized system or simply as an identity regulating how private money is created in a decentralized system. It is important to underline that private money are claims to themselves and not subject to any solvency constraint. We assume that $Tr_t^* = \vartheta^* M_{t-1}^{*p}$, where ϑ^* is the growth rate of private money, with $\vartheta^* \geq 0$. This is a convenient assumption, as well as quite realistic. As an example, Bitcoin issuance is regulated by a time-varying ϑ^* that reaches 0 at some point in time.

Note some important differences between the two issuers arising from the way their budget constraints are modelled. First, the government can rely on taxation power as opposed to the private issuer, and therefore can also reduce the supply of cash while the private issuer cannot lower it.[21] Moreover, the government also issues debt in its unit of account and pays interest on it.

20. This is not a market rate since no interest-bearing security is issued in the private currency.

21. Digital currency provides issuers with the possibility of reducing its supply by invalidating, randomly, some tokens. This is discussed in Benigno (2023).

Equilibrium in the goods market implies that consumption is equal to the constant endowment, $C_t = Y$. Equilibrium in the market for the interest-bearing security in the government currency requires that $B_t = B_t^g$, while equilibrium in the cash market for the two currencies implies that supply and demand equalize for each currency, $M_t = M_t^g$ and $M_t^* = M_t^{*p}$, for each $t \geq t_0$. The consumer's intertemporal budget constraint (2.35) can be written using equilibrium in the goods and asset markets as

$$\frac{M_{t_0-1} + B_{t_0-1}}{P_{t_0}} + \frac{M_{t_0-1}^*}{P_{t_0}^*} = \sum_{t=t_0}^{\infty} \beta^{t-t_0} \left[\frac{i_t}{1+i_t} \frac{M_t}{P_t} + \frac{i_t^*}{1+i_t^*} \frac{M_t^*}{P_t^*} + \frac{T_t}{P_t} - \frac{Tr_t^*}{P_t^*} \right].$$
$$(2.37)$$

In (2.37), the initial value of the real liabilities of both currency issuers should be equal to the seigniorage revenues plus the present discounted value of government taxes minus the private issuer's transfers.[22]

Whereas monetary policy for the private issuer of currency is simply specified in terms of the growth rate of money, the fact that the government also issues interest-bearing securities makes it possible to have an additional degree of freedom to specify policy. We assume that the government sets the interest rate to a target level $i_t = i$ and follows the tax policy

$$\frac{T_t}{P_t} = (1 - \beta)\tau - i\frac{M_{t-1}}{P_t},$$
$$(2.38)$$

for each $t \geq t_0$ and for $\tau > 0$. This is the same tax policy as that in the single-currency framework of Section 2.4.

We can characterize equilibria by first noting that the Euler equation (2.32), under goods market equilibrium, still implies the Fisher equation. Therefore, setting a constant interest rate policy, the inflation rate in government currency, i.e., $\Pi_t = P_t/P_{t-1}$, is constant at $\Pi = \beta(1 + i)$: the price level follows the law of motion $P_{t+1} = \Pi P_t$ for each $t \geq t_0$. Private money growth follows the law of motion $M_t^* = (1 + \vartheta^*)M_{t-1}^*$ for each $t \geq t_0$. To determine the initial price level P_{t_0} and the sequences $\{P_t^*, M_t, B_t\}_{t=t_0}^{\infty}$, the following equilibrium conditions are relevant:

$$\frac{1}{P_t}\frac{i}{1+i} = \frac{1}{P_t}V_m\left(\frac{M_t}{P_t} + \frac{M_t^*}{P_t^*}\right) + \psi_t,$$
$$(2.39)$$

22. The equilibrium condition (2.37) illustrates how, in previous models, it was a coincidence that the intertemporal budget constraint of the consumer was equivalent to the intertemporal resource constraint of the government, using equilibria in goods and asset markets.

$$\frac{1}{P_t^*} = \frac{1}{P_t^*} V_m \left(\frac{M_t}{P_t} + \frac{M_t^*}{P_t^*} \right) + \beta \frac{1}{P_{t+1}^*}, \tag{2.40}$$

$$\beta \frac{(1+i)M_t + B_t}{P_{t+1}} = \frac{(1+i)M_{t-1} + B_{t-1}}{P_t} - (1-\beta)\tau, \tag{2.41}$$

$$\frac{(1+i)M_{t_0-1} + B_{t_0-1}}{P_{t_0}} + \frac{M_{t_0-1}^*}{P_{t_0}^*} = \tau + \sum_{t=t_0}^{\infty} \beta^{t-t_0} \left[\frac{i_t^*}{1+i_t^*} \frac{M_t^*}{P_t^*} - \vartheta^* \frac{M_{t-1}^*}{P_t^*} \right], \tag{2.42}$$

together with the nonnegative constraints $\psi_t, P_t, P_t^*, M_t \geq 0$, and the Kuhn-Tucker condition $\psi_t M_t = 0$. Moreover, the sums on the right-hand side of (2.42) should be finite.

The constraint (2.39) is derived by combining (2.32) and (2.33) with the goods market equilibrium. Constraint (2.40) is (2.34) with $\psi_t^* = 0$, since the supply of private money is positive.[23] Constraints (2.41) and (2.42) are (2.36) and (2.37), respectively, using the tax policy (2.38), the constant interest rate policy, and the law of motion of private money supply.[24] In all the above equations, without losing generality, we have set $U_c(Y) = 1$.

In what follows, it is important to note that constraint (2.42), using $M_t^* = (1+\vartheta^*)M_{t-1}^*$ and (2.41), is equivalent to

$$\lim_{T \to \infty} \beta^{T-t} \left\{ \frac{(1+i)M_{T-1} + B_{T-1}}{P_T} + \frac{M_{T-1}^*}{P_T^*} \right\} = 0. \tag{2.43}$$

Moreover, by appropriately iterating $M_t^* = (1+\vartheta^*)M_{t-1}^*$ forward, equation (2.42) can be written as

$$\frac{(1+i)M_{t_0-1} + B_{t_0-1}}{P_{t_0}} + \lim_{T \to \infty} \beta^{T-t_0} \frac{M_{T-1}^*}{P_T^*} = \tau. \tag{2.44}$$

There are three possible equilibria: i) only government currency is used as a *medium of exchange*; ii) both currencies are used; iii) only private currency is used.

2.8.1 Only Government Money Is Used

There is always an equilibrium in which private currency is worthless and government currency is always valued. By inspection, the first-order condition (2.40) is consistent with an infinite price level for private currency—a zero

---

23. It is still possible that private currency is worthless, i.e., has an infinite price P^*.
24. We have also set $i_{t_0-1} = i$.

value of currency.[25] In contrast, the real taxation policy followed by the government and the interest rate policy are always able to give a positive value to government currency. The inflation rate, $\Pi_t = P_t/P_{t-1}$, is set at $\Pi = \beta(1+i)$ and the price level is determined using (2.42) or (2.44) to obtain

$$\frac{(1+i)M_{t_0-1} + B_{t_0-1}}{P_{t_0}} = \tau. \tag{2.45}$$

This result is a consequence of the asymmetries between how the two types of currency are modelled, with government currency having the privilege of taxation power and of being the unit of denomination of other securities. The limitation for private issuers is not only the absence of taxation power, but, in general, also the absence of resources that can back private currency. We have seen in Section 2.5 that these resources can take the form of a positive net worth or seigniorage revenues, the latter provided by investing in interest-bearing securities.

The converse result—that there is *always* an equilibrium with a zero value for government currency—does not hold. There are two reasons for this: the first is the trade in interest-bearing securities issued in government currency; the second is the government policy of interest rate pegging and real taxes. Setting the nominal interest rate fixes the inflation rate, while the real tax policy pins down the price level. In this way, the value of government currency is never zero. Suppose that P is infinite and P^* is finite; then equation (2.39) is verified. However, equation (2.43) implies that $\lim_{T\to\infty} \beta^{T-t_0} M^*_{T-1}/P^*_T = 0$, which, used in (2.44), leads to a finite price P, and therefore we have a contradiction.

2.8.2 Both Types of Money Are Used

Consider an equilibrium in which both currencies are used as a medium of exchange. In this case, the inflation rates should be the same $\Pi = \Pi^*$, in which $\Pi^*_t = P^*_t/P^*_{t-1}$. But, how should the growth rate of private currency, ϑ^*, be set? Let us first assume $i > 0$, (2.39) implies

$$V_m\left(\frac{M_t}{P_t} + \frac{M^*_t}{P^*_t}\right) = \frac{i}{1+i}.$$

25. Note that $V_m(\cdot)$ is finite for $M > 0$.

Therefore, the sum of real money balances should always be constant, let's say equal to a generic $c > 0$. The above equation implies that

$$\frac{M_t}{P_t} + \left(\frac{1+\vartheta^*}{\Pi}\right)^{t+1-t_0} \Pi \frac{M^*_{t_0-1}}{P^*_{t_0}} = c, \tag{2.46}$$

using the growth rate of private money and its inflation rate equal to Π. For an equilibrium with two currencies as a medium of exchange to exist, it must be that $1 + \vartheta^* \leq \beta(1+i) = \Pi$: otherwise the government money supply will be negative within some finite period of time, which is not feasible. The growth rate of private money should be capped by the inflation rate.

Equation (2.46) shows that, when $1 + \vartheta^* < \Pi$, real money balances in private currency shrink over time and converge to zero in the long run; therefore, real money balances in government currency rise over time to reach in the limit the upper bound, c. This implies that the growth rate of government money is higher than the inflation rate Π and, therefore, higher than that of private money. We have an example of Gresham's law, in which the "bad" money, the one with the higher growth rate, crowds out the "good" money.

In the case $i = 0$ and $\Pi^* = \Pi = \beta$, there is no bound on real money balances. However, an additional requirement for the equilibrium is that the following summation, which is present in condition (2.37) or (2.42), be finite:

$$\sum_{t=t_0}^{\infty} \beta^{t-t_0} \left(\frac{Tr^*_t}{P^*_t}\right) = \vartheta^* \sum_{t=t_0}^{\infty} \beta^{t-t_0} \left(\frac{M^*_{t-1}}{P^*_t}\right) = -\vartheta^* \frac{M^*_{t_0-1}}{P^*_{t_0}} \sum_{t=t_0}^{\infty} (1+\vartheta^*)^{t-t_0},$$
$$\tag{2.47}$$

where the transfer rule of the private issuer is substituted in the first equality and the equilibrium growth rate of prices β is substituted in the second equality. The sum is finite whenever $\vartheta^* = 0$. Therefore, for an equilibrium in which both currencies are used as a medium of exchange, it should be that $\vartheta^* = 0$ when $i = 0$.

Another pervasive result in a world of currency competition is the indeterminacy of the exchange rate, as in Kareken and Wallace (1981). In the above analysis, the exchange rate $\mathcal{E}_t$ (the price of private currency in terms of government currency) is constant at a level that is not determined. This follows from the equalization of the inflation rates, i.e., $\Pi = \Pi^*$, which implies constancy of the nominal exchange rate $\mathcal{E}_t = \mathcal{E}$. However, indeterminacy means that there is no equilibrium condition that pins down the level at which the exchange rate is fixed.

It should be asked whether the indeterminacy of the exchange rate has any consequence for the determination of prices, given the monetary policy assumed. The results depend on the interest rate in government currency being positive or zero. In the case $i > 0$, the government can determine its price level, through the tax policy and the interest rate policy, exactly as in the single-currency framework, and, therefore, (2.45) applies. Note, indeed, that

$$\lim_{T \to \infty} \beta^{T-t_0} \frac{M^*_{T-1}}{P^*_T} = \lim_{T \to \infty} \left(\frac{\beta(1+\vartheta^*)}{\Pi} \right)^{T-t_0} \frac{M^*_{t_0-1}}{P^*_{t_0}} = 0$$

in equation (2.44), given that $(1+\vartheta^*) \leq \Pi$.

Instead, in an equilibrium in which $i = 0$ and $\vartheta^* = 0$, it follows that

$$\lim_{T \to \infty} \beta^{T-t_0} \frac{M^*_{T-1}}{P^*_T} = \lim_{T \to \infty} \left(\frac{\beta}{\Pi} \right)^{T-t_0} \frac{M^*_{t_0-1}}{P^*_{t_0}} = \frac{M^*_{t_0-1}}{P^*_{t_0}},$$

since $\Pi = \beta$. Therefore, (2.44) implies

$$\frac{M_{t_0-1} + B_{t_0-1}}{P_{t_0}} + \frac{\mathcal{E}_{t_0} M^*_{t_0-1}}{P_{t_0}} = \tau,$$

showing that the indeterminacy of the exchange rate translates also into intedeterminacy of the price level in government currency. This price level, at time t_0, is higher than in the single government currency case. The explanation for this result relies on the fact that, when $i = 0$ and $\vartheta^* = 0$, private money is a pure bubble whose real value grows over time at the rate $1/\beta$. Its positive value implies a nominal wealth effect that, to be consistent with equilibrium real resources, requires a higher price level, as the above equation shows.

2.8.3 Only Private Money Is Used

There can be equilibria in which only private money is used as a *medium of exchange*, although there is no equilibrium in which government currency is worthless. Therefore $M_t = 0$, but $P_t > 0$ at all times. Let us discuss the conditions under which this equilibrium arises. For this, the inflation on private money must be lower than that on government currency, i.e., $P^*_{t+1}/P^*_t < P_{t+1}/P_t$. Equation (2.40), when $M_t = 0$, can be written as

$$m^*_{t+1} = \frac{1+\vartheta^*}{\beta} (1 - V_m(m^*_t)) m^*_t, \tag{2.48}$$

for each $t \geq t_0$, having defined $m_t^* \equiv M_t^*/P_t^*$. Moreover, since $M_t = 0$ implies $\psi_t > 0$, equation (2.39) establishes the upper bound

$$V_m(m_t^*) \leq 1 - \frac{\beta}{\Pi}, \tag{2.49}$$

given that $\Pi = \beta(1+i)$. The above inequality represents a lower bound on equilibrium real money balances in private currency. Note that the inflation rate in government currency is still set at Π through the interest rate policy of the government, no matter whether government currency circulates as a medium of exchange or not.

There are many solutions for (2.48). The stationary solution $\tilde{m}^*$, implicitly defined by

$$1 - V_m\left(\tilde{m}^*\right) = \frac{\beta}{1+\vartheta^*},$$

is an equilibrium, provided it satifies (2.49), requiring therefore that $1 + \vartheta^* < \Pi$. In this equilibrium, $\Pi^* = 1 + \vartheta^*$ and $\Pi > \Pi^*$. However, there are no equilibria with real money balances that decrease over time, since they will, at some point, violate constraint (2.49). This interestingly shows that the inflationary path that characterizes the single-currency case, as in (2.25), can be ruled out by the presence of another currency that is always positively valued.[26] On the other hand, there can be equilibria with rising real money balances, provided again that $1 + \vartheta^* < \Pi$. In this case, Π_t^* decreases over time until it reaches the rate β, at which point there is full satiation of real money balances. However, for this to be an equilibrium, the summation (2.47) should be finite, which requires the growth rate of private money to be zero, $\vartheta^* = 0$. As a result, $\Pi > 1$ in this equilibrium.

Issuing private money as a "strong" currency, with a growth rate lower than the inflation rate in government currency $(1 + \vartheta^* < \Pi)$, allows for the possibility of excluding government currency as a *medium of exchange*. Note that $1 + \vartheta^* < \Pi$ is not a sufficient condition to guarantee the exclusive usage of the private currency, since Sections 2.8.1 and 2.8.2 in this chapter have shown that there are also equilibria in which private currency is worthless or in which it coexists with government money, implying a purchasing power that shrinks over time.

---

26. There could be equilibria, however, that start with only private money as a medium of exchange and end up with both private money and public money playing a role, with private money shrinking in real value because $1 + \vartheta^* < \Pi$, as discussed earlier in Section 2.8.2.

Results can also be seen from a different perspective by asking how a government can crowd out private currency as a *medium of exchange*. It has to maintain inflation, Π, low, and bounded by the growth rate of private money, i.e., $\Pi < 1 + \vartheta^*$. Therefore, competition from other currencies can be a useful way to keep inflation low and reduce seigniorage revenues. It could be a way to reach the optimal allocation studied in Section 2.7 when multiple currencies compete to extract rents in the liquidity market.

2.8.4 Launching a Fully Backed Cryptocurrency

In our previous analysis, we examined unbacked private currencies, where there existed an equilibrium in which the currency held no value. If private agents collectively adhere to this equilibrium, it becomes challenging to introduce a new currency successfully. Cryptocurrencies like Bitcoin were created on the premise of trust and utility for transactions, and this has become the prevailing norm. However, it is crucial to acknowledge that there is always a potential equilibrium where they could be deemed worthless if all agents lose faith in them. This inherent possibility might explain their price fluctuations and raises an important question: What are the prerequisites for the successful launch of a new fiduciary currency, ensuring it holds positive purchasing power?

Von Mises (1912), in dealing with this problem, ended up formulating a regression theorem according to which "the value of money today depends upon today's demand for money, today's demand in turn depends, not on the value of money today, but on its value yesterday" (Selgin, 1994, p. 810). The basis of the current purchasing power relies on the previous purchasing power, which condemns any newly created currency to worthlessness unless some exchange value is determined. Another possibility is that of launching a new currency on the basis of a fixed exchange-rate regime with respect to an existing currency or commodity. There is also the possibility of enforcing its use in some transactions through legal requirements. In this chapter, we explore the first avenue, which is akin to the Diem project, first proposed by Meta Platforms.[27]

Diem's main characteristic is its backing through a basket of risk-free securities in other currencies. In our framework, suppose that the consortium

---

27. The theories developed in Section 1.4.2 of Chapter 1 can also be applied to anchor the value of a currency, without the need to establish a fixed exchange rate with another currency. However, they entail other requirements that are not immediately available to a newborn currency, such as the existence of a credit market in the currency. The results of Sections 1.5 and

issuing the private currency backs it with safe bonds denominated in the government currency. Moreover, assume that the consortium is ready to buy and sell any amount of the private currency at the exchange rate $\mathcal{E}_t$. When issuing the amount M_t^* of the private currency at some date t, the consortium invests the proceeds $M_t^* \mathcal{E}_t$ in the safe bonds in units of the government currency. In period $t + 1$, the consortium receives the interest payments on the bonds for a total of $(1 + i_t)M_t^* \mathcal{E}_t$ in the government currency. The consortium keeps a portion of the date $t + 1$ portfolio value as a per-period asset management fee, assumed to be $\phi_t^f M_t^* \mathcal{E}_t$ for some $\phi_t^f \geq 0$ set in t. One may wish to think of these fees as profits paid to the shareholders of the consortium. The consortium then sets the new price $\mathcal{E}_{t+1}$, again trading any amount of private currency at that price.

In order to credibly promise the repurchase of the private currency for $\mathcal{E}_{t+1}$ at $t + 1$, and assuming there are no profits other than the asset management fee, the bond return after the management fee, given by $(1 + i_t - \phi_t^f)M_t^* \mathcal{E}_t$, should be equal to the liabilities, $M_t^* \mathcal{E}_{t+1}$, and therefore

$$\mathcal{E}_{t+1} = (1 + i_t - \phi_t^f)\mathcal{E}_t. \tag{2.50}$$

It is important to remember that the initial exchange rate is arbitrarily determined by the private consortium and that investors should have no reason to doubt that positive value, given the mechanisms of backing underlining the newly issued currency.

Note that for $i_t > \phi_t^f$, the exchange rate of the private currency then appreciates over time, $\mathcal{E}_{t+1} > \mathcal{E}_t$, and therefore $P_{t+1}^*/P_t^* < P_{t+1}/P_t$, while with $i_t = \phi_t^f$, the analysis reproduces stable coins, with a constant exchange rate with respect to the government currency.

Results on the usage of private currency as a *medium of exchange* follow from the analysis made in the previous section, with the qualification that the private currency has now a positive value. In the case $\phi_t^f < i_t$, $P_{t+1}^*/P_t^* < P_{t+1}/P_t$, and the government money is crowded out as a *medium of exchange*. If $\phi_t^f = i_t$, the exchange rate is fixed and both currencies coexist, while if $\phi_t^f > i_t$, only the government currency is used.

The analysis shows that one way to launch a new fiduciary currency is to peg its exchange rate to another currency, in this case a government currency,

---

2.5 can instead provide helpful insights, even to a newborn currency, through the benefits of managing a tangible asset.

by backing its value with investment in risk-free assets denominated in the circulating currency.

2.9 References

The incorporation of money into utility functions can be traced back to the pioneering works of Sidrausky (1967) and Brock (1974). Numerous studies have embraced this framework as a means to model the nonpecuniary benefits offered by specific securities, such as money. This approach is also used in the works of Galí (2008) and Woodford (2003). Alternatively, there are popular methods for modeling the transactional role of money using cash-in-advance constraints, as demonstrated by Lucas (1982) and Svensson (1985). These models highlight how the timing of money choices leads to different forms of money demand.[28] In Lucas (1982), at positive interest rates, the demand for cash aligns with nominal income, while Svensson (1985) introduces variations in this demand, with money decisions made before knowing consumption choices. Walsh (2017) provides a thorough discussion of cash-in-advance models with different timings.

The analysis of price determination under interest rate policies when money provides transaction services, as in Section 2.4, is expounded by Woodford (1995) within the fiscal theory of the price level, discussing also several alternative monetary and fiscal policy regimes.

Studies on price determination, which employ various models for money demand, with monetary policy controlling base money include works by Obstfeld and Rogoff (1983), Sims (1994), and Woodford (1995). These studies reveal the challenges of relying solely on the control of money, and explore alternative policy frameworks along the lines of Section 2.5.

Barro (1979) is a classical study of the price level in a Gold Standard regime, while Bordo (1981) provides an insightful historical perspective. There are numerous studies delving into the Gibson's paradox, including the more recent ones, Barsky and Summers (1988) and Benati and Benigno (2023), that are consistent with the analysis presented in Section 2.6. Jacobson, Leeper, and Preston (2023) discuss the importance for the United States of abandoning the Gold Standard in 1933 to allow for an unbacked fiscal expansion.

---

28. See also Lucas and Stokey (1987).

The literature on currency competition is extensive and spans the fields of monetary and international economics. The work of Kareken and Wallace (1981) serves as a classic benchmark in monetary economics, while Giovannini and Turtelboom (1992) offer a comprehensive review in the international monetary literature. Section 2.8 is based on the analysis by Benigno (2023). Recent contributions in this area, driven by the advent of cryptocurrencies, include studies by Fernandez-Villaverde and Sanches (2019) and Schilling and Uhlig (2019). Benigno, Schilling, and Uhlig (2022) analyze currency competition in a global economy, demonstrating that the introduction of a global currency places bounds on exchange rates and cross-country nominal interest rates. The analysis in Section 2.8.4 draws from their work.

3

Central Bank Digital Currency

3.1 Introduction

Since the creation of the first digital currency, Bitcoin, in 2009, cryptocurrencies have proliferated and attracted the attention of investors, the media, and policymakers. They are revolutionizing the payment system not so much because they allow for payments in a digital form, since other instruments already existed for this purpose (e.g. credit cards), but more because their transactions, through a decentralized verification process based on blockchain, replicate to some extent the anonymity of a traditional exchange using physical money (coins and/or banknotes). The payment system is progressing toward complete digitalization. The revolution is quite remarkable if we look back at the origin of money, when only physical money, of various forms, existed. Cipolla (1967) observes that in the early Middle Ages, "any commodity was considered a potential means of exchange, and coins were considered just like any other commodity, one among hundreds of possible means of exchange, sometimes particularly desired and sometimes not," (Cipolla, 1967, p. 6).

Cryptocurrencies are also threatening monetary sovereignty—the paradigm in which only one currency, the government-issued one, circulates within the borders of a nation. Monetary sovereignty, though, is just a recent phenomenon. Economic history is full of examples in which multiple currencies coexisted within the same borders and multiple types of media of exchange were used for payments.[1]

---

1. Cipolla (1967, 1982, 1990) describes several cases in monetary history of the coexistence of multiple currencies.

Traditional government currencies face several challenges. Chapter 2 has shown that issuing money can be a source of revenue for central banks, which can be critical for backing the value of currency without requiring the treasury's support. Currency competition may erode seigniorage revenues, as the analysis in Section 2.8 of Chapter 2 showed. Central banks can also enter more dangerous territories if several financial instruments start to be denominated in other currencies. In the end, central banks are very powerful, indeed, because their liabilities define the unit of account of their monetary system. But at least some transactions should be settled in that unit of account; otherwise the currency becomes worthless.

Central banks are reacting to the challenges by introducing their own digital currency, which can have two forms. The first one replaces physical money with digital tokens. The second allows the general public to access the central bank's reserves in the form of deposits.

Let us first consider digital tokenization. In this case, the analyses in Chapters 1 and 2 remain unaltered, insofar as government tokens allow for the storage of units of currency in the same way as physical money does. However, due to the digital feature of tokens, the issuer may discretionally change their "face" value. A dollar token today can be declared to be valued less than a dollar at a future date. The absence of securities that can store unaltered the value of currency across time relaxes the zero lower bound on the nominal interest rate, which can go negative. This, however, does not have any consequences on price determination with respect to the findings in Chapters 1 and 2. The only difference, using interest rate rule (1.21), is that the rate of deflation can now go below β. Otherwise, nothing changes in how prices can be determined, either in the case in which the treasury sets an appropriate tax policy to back the price level, or when the central bank uses its remittances policy to determine it.

The situation can differ if the central bank digital currency takes the form of deposits at the central bank accessible to the general public. Deposits, indeed, are money-like securities that, in general, provide liquidity services, such as money in the models in Chapter 2. Therefore, reserves can provide direct nonpecuniary benefits to households, which can be modelled as well through utility benefits. Modeling liquidity using interest-bearing securities, as opposed to the zero interest rate securities discussed in Chapter 2, leads to important differences in the determination of the price level, as this chapter will illustrate. These differences exist regardless of whether digital tokens circulate or not. The latter circumstance only becomes relevant for the zero lower bound on nominal interest rates to apply.

The primary implication of a framework in which central bank reserves directly provide liquidity benefits to households is the decoupling between the policy rate, i.e., the interest rate on reserves, and the credit market interest rate. The latter directly influences the consumption and saving decisions of individuals. The spread between these two interest rates depends on the quantity of reserves supplied by the central bank.

This result has significant policy implications since both the quantity of and the rate on reserves play crucial roles in determining the inflation rate. This is in contrast to the models presented in Chapters 1 and 2, where the inflation rate was solely controlled by the interest rate on reserves. The relevance of these results extends beyond the central bank digital currency environment and can be useful for understanding the effects of both the expansion and the contraction of the central bank's balance sheet that have occurred since the 2007–2008 financial crisis. According to the model, variations in the real value of reserves for the same policy rate influence the credit market rate and then the inflation rate. In the presence of price rigidity, as will be shown in Chapter 8, an increase in central bank reserves stimulates aggregate demand through the lowering of the credit market rate.

These observations raise important questions about what the optimal size of the central bank's balance sheet is and, in general, about the optimal liquidity/debt policy, which can be addressed in the framework of this chapter. The results align with the perspective put forth by Milton Friedman in 1960, who advocated for a system where the central bank could pay interest on its reserves and the banking sector could be subject to a 100% reserve requirement, with deposits fully guaranteed by the central bank. This concept closely resembles a central bank digital currency system. In such a system, the entire liquidity supply in the economy comes from the government, and it could be implemented either by having the central bank as the sole provider of liquidity, backed by potentially safe assets in its portfolio, or by having both the treasury and central bank jointly manage the supply of debt, with overall tax capacity constraining the amount of debt.

The limit to the supply of liquidity is given by the availability of default-free securities in one case and by the fiscal capacity of the treasury in the other. Within these limits, the central bank faces no challenges in maintaining full control over the price level while also optimally supplying liquidity. These outcomes are the result of a well-defined specification of interest rate and overall balance-sheet policies, including the remittances policy.[2]

This chapter's results further show that by paying an interest rate on reserves, the optimal liquidity policy does not interfere with the interest rate policy and the inflation rate, unlike in Section 2.7 of Chapter 2.

3.2 Outline of the Results

In Chapter 1, the central bank controlled the inflation rate primarily through an interest rate targeting policy. Managing the entire trajectory of prices was more intricate, involving other tools such as balance-sheet or tax policies.

In the context of a central bank digital currency framework, the total supply of central bank reserves now also plays a role in influencing the inflation rate, in addition to the interest rate policy. This concept is discussed in Section 3.4, revealing that this new transmission mechanism of policy doesn't fundamentally change the control of the price level, which remains consistent with the principles outlined in Chapter 1.

Section 3.5 further explores how the central bank can optimize its liquidity policy without significant consequences for the interest rate policy, price level, or inflation rate. This optimal liquidity supply can be achieved by maintaining sufficient assets in the central bank's portfolio. Alternatively, coordination with the treasury by backing its liabilities can also ensure an optimal supply of liquidity. In this case, the overall availability of liquidity hinges on the fiscal capacity of the treasury.

3.3 Model

The model in this chapter uses the same framework as the one in Chapter 2, but in it liquidity services are provided by the liabilities of the central bank, including digital tokens and reserves held in the form of deposits.

3.3.1 Consumers

Let us consider a representative agent in a closed economy with the following intertemporal utility:

$$\sum_{t=t_0}^{\infty} \beta^{t-t_0} \left\{ U(C_t) + V\left(\frac{X_t + M_t}{P_t}\right) \right\}, \tag{3.1}$$

2. Control of the price level was a challenging aspect in Friedman's analysis.

where β, with $0 < \beta < 1$, is the rate of time preference, while $U(\cdot)$ is a concave, differentiable utility function in its argument (C), the consumption good; $V(\cdot)$ is also a concave, differentiable function in real liquidity holdings, which now include central bank reserves (X) and digital tokens (M); the function $V(\cdot)$ has a satiation point $\bar{q} > 0$ such that $V_q(q_t) = 0$ for $q_t \geq \bar{q}$, having defined the overall real liquidity as $q_t \equiv (X_t + M_t)/P_t$, and $V_q(q_t)$ is the first derivative of the function $V(\cdot)$ with respect to its argument; and P is the price of the consumption good (C).

The consumer is subject to the following budget constraint:

$$B_t + X_t + M_t + P_t C_t + T_t = (1 + i_{t-1})B_{t-1} + \left(1 + i_{t-1}^X\right) X_{t-1}$$
$$+ M_{t-1} + P_t Y. \tag{3.2}$$

There are three securities available: private and/or treasury bonds (B), the central bank's reserves (X), and digital tokens (M), which are also issued by the central bank. Differently from Chapters 1 and 2, for expositional convenience, the price of bonds at the time of issuance is set to the unitary value, and the interest rate, set at the same time, accrues in the next-period balances.[3] Private and treasury bonds do not provide liquidity services: for this reason the interest rate (i) on the private illiquid securities may be different from the policy rate (i^X), which is the interest rate on reserves set by the central bank. Digital tokens do not pay interest. Y is the constant endowment and T are lumpsum taxes levied by the treasury.

There is a subtle justification for assuming that certain default-free securities, such as reserves and digital tokens, provide liquidity services while others do not. As noted in Section 1.3.2 of Chapter 1, central bank liabilities are always free of default and are repaid. Since reserves are held as deposits by households, we assume that they provide additional liquidity services, as captured by the function $V(\cdot)$. In contrast, private and treasury debt must satisfy a solvency condition to be considered default-free, which sets them apart from central bank reserves. For this reason, we do not attribute a special liquidity role to private securities and treasury debt. Section 3.5 extends the analysis to consider central bank backing of treasury debt, thereby allowing it to provide liquidity services. In Chapter 4, when we explore the creation of default-free securities by intermediaries, we allow intermediaries' debt (deposits) to provide liquidity services.

---

3. This aligns the model with Chapter 2, where liquidity services are provided by the beginning-of-period real value of liquid securities.

In this economy, all securities, including tokens, exist in digital form. Central bank tokens maintain their value over time and do not accrue any interest. Therefore, they are outperformed as an investment by central bank reserves when i^X is positive and are equivalent when $i^X = 0$. Due to the absence of arbitrage opportunities, discussed on page 15 of Chapter 1, the presence of a store of value prevents the interest rate i^X from being negative. Conversely, negative interest rates are feasible when there is no store of value in the form of digital tokens. Additionally, the digital nature of securities enables the central bank to trace them through their digital keys and attribute a negative interest rate to tokens if necessary. One key feature of a central bank digital currency framework is therefore its ability to overcome the zero lower bound on interest rates. Without losing generality, we will assume $M_t = 0$ at all times moving forward and that the policy rate can go negative.

The appropriate borrowing limit on private debt is in this case represented by

$$-\frac{(1+i_{t-1})B_{t-1}}{P_t} \leq \frac{(1+i^X_{t-1})X_{t-1}}{P_t} + \sum_{j=0}^{\infty} R_{t,t+j}\left(Y - \frac{T_{t+j}}{P_{t+j}}\right) < \infty,$$

(3.3)

where discount factor $R_{t,t+j}$ has the same definition as in Chapter 1, with i being the relevant interest rate.[4] The consumer chooses sequences $\{C_t, B_t, X_t\}_{t=t_0}^{\infty}$ with $C_t, X_t \geq 0$ to maximize (3.1), under constraint (3.2) and borrowing limit (3.3) at each time $t \geq t_0$ given initial conditions on $(1+i_{t_0-1})B_{t_0-1}$ and $(1+i^X_{t_0-1})X_{t_0-1}$. Moreover, there is an alternative representation of the consumer problem in which borrowing limit (3.3) is replaced by intertemporal budget constraint

$$\sum_{t=t_0}^{\infty} R_{t_0,t}\left(C_t + \frac{i_t - i^X_t}{1+i_t}\frac{X_t}{P_t}\right) \leq \frac{(1+i_{t_0-1})B_{t_0-1} + (1+i^X_{t_0-1})X_{t_0-1}}{P_{t_0}}$$

$$+ \sum_{t=t_0}^{\infty} R_{t_0,t}\left(Y - \frac{T_t}{P_t}\right).$$

(3.4)

The constraint now shows one additional term with respect to equation (1.8) of Chapter 1: the resources paid to maintain real liquidity balances in the form of deposits at the central bank, the second term on the left-hand side of the

4. Note that in (3.3) the debt being referred to includes both the principal amount and the interest payments that must be repaid.

constraint.[5] Holding liquidity delivers utility benefits, but also carries a possible cost in terms of a lower interest rate with respect to that on investing in bonds.

Considering the Lagrange multiplier λ_t attached to constraint (3.2), the first-order condition with respect to C_t implies that $\lambda_t = U_c(C_t)/P_t$, in which $U_c(\cdot)$ is the first derivative of the function $U(\cdot)$ with respect to its argument. Therefore the first-order condition with respect to B_t is again

$$\frac{U_c(C_t)}{P_t} = \beta(1+i_t)\frac{U_c(C_{t+1})}{P_{t+1}}. \tag{3.5}$$

In what follows, we are going to label i as the "credit market" nominal interest rate, which is the credit market rate that directly affects the saving-consumption choices of the consumer, to distinguish it from the policy rate, i^X. The distinction between the two nominal rates represents a novelty with respect to the analyses of Chapters 1 and 2, and it bears important implications for monetary policy in controlling prices and inflation.

The first-order condition with respect to X_t now implies that

$$\frac{U_c(C_t)}{P_t} = \frac{1}{P_t}V_q\left(\frac{X_t}{P_t}\right) + \beta\frac{U_c(C_{t+1})}{P_{t+1}}(1+i_t^X), \tag{3.6}$$

which can also be written using (3.5) as

$$1 = \frac{V_q\left(\frac{X_t}{P_t}\right)}{U_c(C_t)} + \frac{1+i_t^X}{1+i_t}. \tag{3.7... }$$

The household equates the cost of investing one dollar in deposits at the central bank with the benefits represented on the right-hand side of the equation above. These benefits include nonpecuniary advantages, expressed in terms of the marginal utility provided by one dollar of reserves (the first addendum on the right-hand side), as well as pecuniary benefits derived from the discounted value of the return, $1+i_t^X$. We can also express it as describing the spread between the market nominal interest rate and the policy rate,

$$\frac{1+i_t^X}{1+i_t} = 1 - \varrho_t, \tag{3.7}$$

---

5. The intertemporal constraint (3.4) can be derived using (3.2) and borrowing limit (3.3) following similar steps to those in Appendix A. Refer to Appendix C.

in which

$$\varrho_t \equiv \frac{V_q\left(\frac{X_t}{P_t}\right)}{U_c(C_t)}$$

represents the liquidity premium, with $0 \leq \varrho_t < 1$. Because of the liquidity value that reserves provide, the policy rate is in general lower than the market nominal rate of interest. Equalization of the two rates happens only when liquidity is satiated, i.e., $V_q(\cdot) = 0$.

In the optimal allocation, the intertemporal budget constraint (3.4) holds with equality

$$\sum_{t=t_0}^{\infty} R_{t_0,t} \left(C_t + \frac{i_t - i_t^X}{1+i_t} \frac{X_t}{P_t} \right) = \frac{(1+i_{t_0-1})B_{t_0-1} + (1+i_{t_0-1}^X)X_{t_0-1}}{P_{t_0}}$$

$$+ \sum_{t=t_0}^{\infty} R_{t_0,t} \left(Y - \frac{T_t}{P_t} \right). \tag{3.8}$$

The present-discounted value of real resources spent for purchasing goods and for holding real liquidity balances is equal to the real value of the initial asset position plus the present-discounted value of real net income.

3.3.2 Government

The central bank's flow budget constraint is represented by

$$B_t^C - X_t^C = (1+i_{t-1})B_{t-1}^C - (1+i_{t-1}^X)X_{t-1}^C - T_t^C, \tag{3.9}$$

where (B^C) are the central bank's holdings of short-term assets issued by the treasury or the private sector; (X^C) is the supply of the central bank's reserves; and (T^C) are the nominal remittances.

The treasury has the following flow budget constraint:

$$B_t^F = (1+i_{t-1})B_{t-1}^F - T_t - T_t^C, \tag{3.10}$$

where (B^F) is the treasury's debt and (T) are lumpsum taxes. The treasury is subject to a solvency condition for its liabilities to be deemed safe, which takes the form

$$\frac{(1+i_{t_0-1})B_{t_0-1}^F}{P_{t_0}} = \sum_{t=t_0}^{\infty} R_{t_0,t} \left(\frac{T_t}{P_t} + \frac{T_t^C}{P_t} \right), \tag{3.11}$$

where we have already imposed the equality sign to disregard cases in which the treasury levies more taxes than needed, as discussed in Section 1.3.2 of

Chapter 1. Equation (3.11) represents a constraint on the path of taxes given the other variables involved in it. It is worth noting that treasury debt pays the market nominal interest rate as it doesn't provide liquidity services.

3.3.3 Equilibrium

Equilibrium in asset markets requires that the debt issued by the treasury be held by the central bank and by the representative consumer,

$$B_t^F = B_t^C + B_t,$$ (3.12)

while reserves issued by the central bank are held only by the consumer:

$$X_t^C = X_t,$$ (3.13)

for each $t \geq t_0$.

Equilibrium in asset markets, together with the flow budget constraints of consumers and government, implies the goods market equilibrium, $C_t = Y$ for each $t \geq t_0$.

Let us now summarize all the equilibrium conditions. The first equation is the Fisher equation

$$1 + i_t = \frac{1}{\beta} \frac{P_{t+1}}{P_t},$$ (3.14)

for each $t \geq t_0$, derived from (3.5) using equilibrium in the goods market. The relevant rate that is directly connected to the inflation rate through the Fisher equation is now the market nominal interest rate.

Equilibrium in the liquidity market, using (3.7), implies that

$$\frac{1 + i_t^X}{1 + i_t} = 1 - V_q\left(\frac{X_t}{P_t}\right)$$ (3.15)

for each $t \geq t_0$, relating the market nominal rate to the policy rate, through the liquidity premium. We have used equilibrium in the goods market and set $U_c(Y) = 1$.

Finally, the intertemporal budget constraint of the consumer (3.8) can be written using equilibrium in goods and asset markets as

$$\sum_{t=t_0}^{\infty} \beta^{t-t_0} \left(\frac{T_t}{P_t} + \frac{i_t - i_t^X}{1 + i_t} \frac{X_t}{P_t} \right) = \frac{(1 + i_{t_0-1})B_{t_0-1} + (1 + i_{t_0-1}^X)X_{t_0-1}}{P_{t_0}},$$ (3.16)

or using (3.11) as

$$\sum_{t=t_0}^{\infty} \beta^{t-t_0} \left(\frac{T_t^C}{P_t} \right) = \frac{(1+i_{t_0-1})B_{t_0-1}^C - (1+i_{t_0-1}^X)X_{t_0-1}}{P_{t_0}}$$

$$+ \sum_{t=t_0}^{\infty} \beta^{t-t_0} \left(\frac{i_t - i_t^X}{1+i_t} \frac{X_t}{P_t} \right). \tag{3.17}$$

An equilibrium is a set of sequences $\{P_t, i_t^X, i_t, B_t^C, X_t, T_t^C\}_{t=t_0}^{\infty}$, with $\{P_t, X_t, B_t^C, T_t^C\}_{t=t_0}^{\infty}$ nonnegative, satisfying conditions (3.9), (3.14), and (3.15) for each $t \geq t_0$, and (3.17), with $i_t \geq i_t^X$, given initial conditions $(1+i_{t_0-1})B_{t_0-1}^C$, $(1+i_{t_0-1}^X)X_{t_0-1}$.[6] Therefore, there are three degrees of freedom to specify policy within the tools of the central bank, which can set the interest rate on reserves, its quantity, and the remittances policy $\{i_t^X, X_t, T_t^C\}_{t=t_0}^{\infty}$.

3.4 Price Determination

Price and inflation determination is a bit more complex in this model because the policy rate is no longer sufficient for determining the inflation rate. Indeed, the relevant interest rate in the Fisher equation (3.14) is the market interest rate, which is linked to the policy rate through the liquidity premium. Their spread depends on central bank reserves (see equation 3.15). The framework nests that of Section 1.4.2 of Chapter 1 when liquidity exceeds the full satiation level, in which case market and policy rates coincide.

To illustrate price determination, let us consider an interest rate policy that targets a constant interest rate, $i_t^X = i^X = 1/\beta - 1$, and specify a certain positive path for reserves, $\{X_t\}_{t=t_0}^{\infty}$. To simplify the analysis, consider a central bank's remittances policy of the type

$$\frac{T_t^C}{P_t} = (1-\beta)\tau^C + (i_{t-1} - i_{t-1}^X)\frac{X_{t-1}}{P_t}, \tag{3.18}$$

which substituted in (3.17) implies

$$\tau^C = \frac{(1+i_{t_0-1})(B_{t_0-1}^C - X_{t_0-1})}{P_{t_0}},$$

---

6. The requirement for nonnegative remittances aims to prevent any fiscal support.

and therefore

$$P_{t_0} = \frac{(1+i_{t_0-1})(B^C_{t_0-1} - X_{t_0-1})}{\tau^C}. \tag{3.19}$$

Equation (3.19) determines a positive price level at time t_0 provided that the denominator and numerator have the same sign. When τ^C is positive $(\tau^C > 0)$, the central bank's net worth should be positive $(B^C_{t_0-1} > X_{t_0-1})$. However, if the central bank earns enough seigniorage revenues by issuing its liabilities, then τ^C can be negative in (3.18), in which case the central bank's net worth can also be negative in (3.19).[7] Recall that in Section 1.4.2 of Chapter 1, which is nested when $i_t = i^X_t$, τ^C and net worth were restricted to being positive to determine the price level.

To determine the full sequence of prices, equations (3.14) and (3.15) should be combined to obtain

$$\frac{P_{t+1}}{P_t} = \beta \frac{(1+i^X)}{1 - V_q\left(\frac{X_t}{P_t}\right)}. \tag{3.20}$$

Equation (3.20) determines the inflation rate at a generic time $t+1$, which is on the left-hand side, given prices at time t, and reserves and interest rate policies, X_t and i^X, which are on the right-hand side. The novel result with respect to Section 1.4.2 of Chapter 1 is that now the inflation rate depends on the supply of the central bank reserves. Starting with P_{t_0} determined by (3.19), given the interest rate policy $i^X_{t_0} = i^X = (1/\beta) - 1$ and the reserve policy at time t_0, X_{t_0}, equation (3.20) determines the price level at P_{t_0+1}, and so forth.

It is interesting to examine the impact of an increase in the central bank reserves on interest rates and prices. Assuming a constant policy rate, when reserves (X_{t_0}) increase at time t_0, this reduces the liquidity premium, leading to a lower money market interest rate (i_{t_0}). Importantly, P_{t_0} remains unaffected when the same real remittances policy is maintained, as equation (3.19) shows.

Using equation (3.20), we can determine a lower price level P_{t_0+1}. Note that the expansion in reserves is accompanied by a proportional expansion in bond holdings, $B^C_{t_0}$. This can be seen by inserting the remittances policy (3.18) into the flow budget constraint (3.9), to obtain:

$$B^C_t - X^C_t = (1+i_{t-1})(B^C_{t-1} - X^C_{t-1}) - (1-\beta)P_t\tau^C. \tag{3.21}$$

---

7. In any case, net worth must be appropriately bounded below for profits to be positive.

When evaluated at time t_0, the right-hand side does not change with the expansion of reserves, so $B_{t_0}^C$ (on the left-hand side) should rise by exactly the increase in reserves. There is, however, a dynamic adjustment even if the expansion in reserves is just temporary. At time $t_0 + 1$, the fall in P_{t_0+1} lowers the liquidity premium and the money market rate, which further reduces prices at time P_{t_0+2}. Prices will stabilize at a constant value once the liquidity premium reaches zero. It might appear unusual that an increase in central bank reserves lowers the price level, but this outcome should be understood within the framework of a model where prices are flexible and the Fisher equation (3.14) holds. According to the latter equation, lowering the market interest rate through an increase in reserves reduces the inflation rate. However, in the presence of price rigidity, where the Fisher equation does not hold, the expansion of reserves also leads to a fall in the market interest rate. This reduction, in turn, stimulates aggregate demand, output, and inflation, as will be discussed in Chapter 8.

3.5 Optimal Liquidity Policy

In line with the analysis of Section 2.7 of Chapter 2, we can ask how optimal monetary policy should be set in this environment. Results confirm the optimality of satiating the holdings of liquidity, i.e., setting $V_q(\cdot) = 0$. What is different now is how to achieve this outcome, which coincides with eradicating the difference between the market nominal interest rate and the rate on reserves, $i_t = i_t^X$. Note that the policy that implements satiation of liquidity does not imply anymore a rate of deflation in the economy, which was the case in the discussion in Section 2.7 of Chapter 2. Indeed, by paying an interest rate on the securities providing liquidity and satiating the supply of liquidity, the central bank controls directly the nominal interest rate in (3.14) and therefore can set the inflation rate at a desired value. The remittances policy and other balance sheet policies are still critical for determining the price level. Maintaining the remittances policy as in (3.18), we notice that τ^C should be positive to have determinacy of the price level, since "seigniorage" revenues are missing and there is no treasury support, meaning remittances cannot be negative. Equation (3.19) is still determining the price level at time t_0. We can then use (3.21) to obtain

$$\frac{X_t}{P_t} = \frac{B_t^C}{P_t} - \beta \tau^C,$$

which shows that to maintain a certain real value of liquidity above the satiation level, i.e., $X_t/P_t \geq \bar{q}$, the central bank should have enough assets in its portfolio exceeding the liabilities. This result aligns with Friedman's recommendation in 1960 that the responsibility for supplying liquidity rest with the government, and can be implemented by the central bank through maintaining a sufficiently large asset portfolio on its balance sheet. It is crucial for these assets to be default-free, since any default risk could jeopardize the control of the price level, as already emphasized in Section 1.4.2 of Chapter 1. This risk arises because the value of assets may fall below that of the liabilities, making it impossible to maintain a positive τ^C in the remittances policy. The solution in such a scenario would require challenging the central bank's independence and seeking a monetary transfer from either the treasury or the private sector.

It should be further emphasized that the requirement of having more assets than liabilities is essential both for the supply of liquidity and for the control of the price level. However, this requirement has a quantitative aspect in the first case, necessitating a specific quantity of real liquidity supply. In the second case, this quantitative aspect may not be as necessary.

This parallel with Friedman's proposal illustrates that a central bank digital currency framework aligns with a narrow banking regime, also discussed in Friedman (1960). In such a regime, the central bank exercises full control over the liquidity in the economy by supplying reserves at a positive interest rate and mandating intermediaries that supply liquid securities to maintain a 100% reserve requirement. Relying on the availability of default-free securities, whether issued by the private sector or the treasury, the narrow banking regime envisioned by Friedman is not inconsistent with full control of the price level through appropriate interest rate policies and balance-sheet policies, discussed in Chapter 1 and in this section. The key feature is the availability of default-free securities, above the liabilities issued by the central bank, which should be sufficiently large to sustain the appropriate optimal liquidity policy.

Friedman (1960) also highlights an alternative approach, still within the government's control of liquidity, which involves backing liquidity through taxes. This alternative can be rationalized within the context of the model presented in this chapter by enabling the central bank to back the treasury's liabilities, as discussed in Section 1.4.1 of Chapter 1. This extends the properties of central bank's liabilities to those of the treasury. We can hypothesize that treasury debt held by the household provides the same liquidity services as central bank reserves, entering then into the function $V(\cdot)$ in

(3.1), where now $q_t = (B_t + X_t)/P_t$. In this case, the solvency constraint (3.11) does not apply, and the critical equation to determine the price level is (3.16). Recall that B is the treasury's debt held by the household and $B_t^F = B_t + B_t^C$.

Consider, for simplicity, an interest rate peg $i_t^X = i^X$ for each $t \geq t_0$, and the following specification of the real tax policy:

$$\frac{T_t}{P_t} = (1 - \beta)\tau - (i_{t-1} - i_{t-1}^X)\frac{B_{t-1} + X_{t-1}}{P_t}, \qquad (3.22)$$

in which there is a constant real component, captured by the positive parameter τ, and a second component transferring to the consumers the seigniorage revenues retrieved from issuing liabilities at a lower cost, i^X, with respect to the market rate i. Substituting (3.22) in (3.21) for T, we obtain that

$$\tau = \frac{(1 + i_{t_0-1})(B_{t_0-1} + X_{t_0-1})}{P_{t_0}},$$

and therefore

$$P_{t_0} = \frac{(1 + i_{t_0-1})(B_{t_0-1} + X_{t_0-1})}{\tau},$$

which determines the price level as proportional to the net liabilities of the whole government with respect to the private sector. We can, as well, use the consolidated budget constraint of the government to get that at each point in time the real value of such liabilities is proportional to the parameter τ:

$$\frac{B_t + X_t}{P_t} = \beta\tau. \qquad (3.23)$$

Since τ represents the present discounted value of real taxes, it could be interpreted as indicating the fiscal capacity of the government. Equation (3.15) holds with the argument of the function $V_q(\cdot)$ being now the net liabilities of the government. Combining it with the Fisher equation, inflation is now determined as

$$\frac{P_{t+1}}{P_t} = \beta\frac{(1 + i^X)}{1 - V_q\left(\frac{B_t + X_t}{P_t}\right)} = \beta\frac{(1 + i^X)}{1 - V_q(\beta\tau)}. \qquad (3.24)$$

Both monetary and fiscal policies play pivotal roles in determining the inflation rate. Monetary policy directly influences inflation through the management of interest rates on reserves, while fiscal policy shapes inflation by governing the overall liquidity supply and, consequently, liquidity premiums. To achieve the optimal supply of liquidity, the treasury should raise appropriately τ when unconstrained. The fiscal capacity of the government then becomes crucial in determining both the price level and the overall availability of real liquidity in the economy. Failure to do so, or encountering constraints in this regard, can lead to inefficiencies and threaten price control. It is important to note that the central role of the treasury is based on the support it receives from the central bank. This collaboration makes price and inflation determination a shared concern of both monetary and fiscal policies. Ultimately, in deciding how much real liquidity to supply and at what price level to target, the fiscal capacity plays a critical role.

3.6   References

Canzoneri et al. (2008) and Canzoneri, Cumby, and Diba (2017) were early models that introduced a disconnect between the policy rate and the interest rate relevant for consumption and saving decisions. In monetary analysis, several works have introduced a transaction role for bonds, although an indirect one. In Canzoneri and Diba (2005), current income can also be used for liquidity purposes in a fraction that depends on the quantity of bonds held in the portfolio. In Belongia and Ireland (2006, 2012), money and deposits are bundled together, and can be used for liquidity purposes as in the work of Canzoneri et al. (2011), where bonds are instead imperfect substitutes for money.

Benigno and Nisticò (2017) presented a model in which securities providing liquidity, through a collateral constraint, carried a nominal interest rate. This framework included central bank reserves, making them relevant in the monetary policy transmission mechanism.

Diba and Loisel (2021, 2022) also developed New Keynesian models featuring the central bank employing two policy instruments. Piazzesi, Rogers, and Schneider (2021) emphasized the disconnection between the policy rate and the interest rate relevant for consumption and saving choices. They presented a model of central bank digital currency, primarily through a local analysis of the equilibrium. Niepelt (2023) studies central bank digital currency in a context in which intermediaries have market power in issuing deposits and liquidity transformation creates externalities.

The model presented in this chapter draws inspiration from Benigno and Benigno (2022).

Friedman (1960) proposed paying interest on reserves and discussed cooperation or separation between monetary and fiscal policies in debt-management policies.

4

Private Money

4.1 Introduction

Money cannot be exclusively a creation of the government, as its definition is based on its properties and functions rather than on its being a physical object. In Chapters 2 and 3, government money (cash) and default-free government bonds had a special liquidity role, a *medium-of-exchange* property, along with being a *store of value*. However, even in a monetary system with one *unit of account*, government money is not necessarily the only money with the properties of *store of value* and *medium of exchange*. The private sector, through financial intermediaries, can also create money-like claims that, to a certain degree, share the same properties that government money has. Deposits serve as a clear example of this phenomenon. As Brunner (1989) pointed out, "the distinction [between monetary base and the nation's money stock] becomes important with the emergence of intermediation. Financial intermediation inserts a wedge between the monetary base and the money stock" (Brunner, 1989, p. 175).

Chapter 3 has demonstrated that there is no trade-off between achieving the optimal liquidity supply and controlling prices. Moreover, in a monetary framework where the central bank has an additional policy tool, such as that of paying an interest rate on its reserves and adjusting it, it becomes possible to separate the achievable inflation target from the supply of liquidity.[1]

---

1. In contrast, when money does not pay an interest rate, Section 2.7 of Chapter 2 has demonstrated that the optimal supply of money can be achieved by implementing a deflation rate equivalent to the rate of time preference. In that case, achieving the optimal supply of liquidity affects the inflation rate that can be targeted.

Importantly, the full trajectory of prices and the supply of liquidity within the government are interconnected and rely on the same fundamental principles. The price level necessitates a real anchor, whether in the form of high-quality assets held by the central bank beyond its liquid liabilities or through taxation when the treasury and central bank cooperate in price determination. Exactly the same features are needed for the provision of liquidity, with the only difference being that an abundant supply of liquidity demands an adequately substantial backing.

On a similar note, inefficiencies in liquidity supply and instability in price level control can arise due to inadequate backing. This insufficiency may be attributed to either a lack of high-quality assets within the economy or limited fiscal capacity. Additionally, a government may not have the incentive to satisfy the economy's liquidity needs because it holds a monopoly on money supply and may seek to maintain rent. It is not surprising that some central banks were founded on the "desperate want of money" (Bagehot, 1873, p. 92), such as the Bank of England in 1694.[2]

Leaving rent opportunities in the liquidity market incentivizes the private creation of money-like claims, often referred to as "safe assets," to take advantage of lower financing costs. These money-like claims share properties with government-issued money, serving as a *store of value* since they are risk-free, and maintain their value in terms of currency over time. They also function as a *medium of exchange*, offering liquidity services in the form of transaction services and collateral requirements.

The possibility of private money supply has been the subject of extensive debate, with discussions centered around the potential implications for inefficiencies in liquidity supply and the stability of price level control. Established and influential theories, including the "real bills" doctrine, free banking theory, and narrow banking theory, have attempted to tackle these issues, but they have not produced definitive conclusions.[3]

The results in this chapter demonstrate that the private supply of money does not pose a challenge to the central bank's price level control, provided the latter adheres to the principles outlined in Chapter 1. As a consequence

---

2. See the discussion of White (2014).

3. Sargent (2011), summarizing the debate on the grounds of the monetary analysis of the 1970s and 1980s, concludes that there could be an inherent instability in the control of price when markets of money and credit are not separated, while separating those markets either produces inefficiencies or creates subtle connections between monetary and fiscal authorities.

of this result, it is important to underscore that the entity responsible for determining the price level is the one whose liabilities, which are claims to themselves, define what the currency is. In this context, that entity is the central bank, which may not coincide with the main supplier of liquidity in the economy.[4] In addition, a banking sector characterized by unrestricted competition (free banking) can efficiently provide liquidity. Similarly to government liquidity supply, private liquidity provision requires proper backing, which can be achieved through investments in high-quality assets or by absorbing losses on risky assets with sufficient equity.

The intermediaries supplying liquidity should not necessarily be regulated in their asset holdings, as the "real bills" doctrine might suggest holding private risk-free securities. The competition for safe securities directs private suppliers to also combine risky investments cushioned by an appropriate amount of equity. Backing is needed but not necessarily tied to specific assets.

The conclusions drawn in this chapter combined with those in the previous one suggest that the optimal supply of liquidity can be achieved in multiple equivalent ways. It can be done by the government through the central bank with appropriate asset backing, through collaboration between monetary and fiscal authorities via taxes, or by the private sector in a competitive market, as long as sufficient backing is ensured. A narrow banking regime, advocated by Friedman (1960), or free banking or "real bills" are economically equivalent under certain conditions.

There is a subtle distinction to make. The competitive nature of a private market for liquidity supply naturally eliminates rent-seeking behavior. This happens without relying on the will of a monopolist, who may lack the economic motivation to eliminate such rent.

4.2 Outline of the Results

The existence of liquidity premiums in money markets incentivizes financial intermediaries to create money-like securities, which can be backed by risky assets and equity. Section 4.3.3 shows that, in a frictionless market, intermediaries can create safe securities by raising enough equity to

4. The controversies in past debates largely stem from a failure to distinguish between money, defined by its properties, and currency, defined by the central bank's liabilities. It's essential to recognize that the inverse of the price level reflects the value of the currency, not the value of money.

absorb the possible losses. Moreover, Section 4.3.4 demonstrates two results: i) unfettered competition can reduce to zero any premium in liquidity markets, allowing liquidity satiation with the creation of enough private safe securities to complement government debt, and ii) the efficient private supply of liquidity does not jeopardize the control of the price level by the central bank, which can follow the principles underlined in Chapter 1. The chapter concludes by analyzing competition among different currencies to become the *unit of account* in which intermediaries issue safe securities that are used as a *means of payment*. Section 4.5, in discussing competition between securities denominated in different currencies to provide liquidity services, finds that the security in units of the currency with stable prices is dominant.

4.3 Model

The model is stochastic. Uncertainty is introduced to model the risky characteristics of some securities, a feature that will be important in the following analysis. Let s_t be the state of nature at time t belonging to a set S that is invariant across time; $f(s^t|s_{t_0})$ is the probability distribution of the history s^t conditional on the state of nature s_{t_0} at time t_0. The history s^t is defined as the sequence of states of nature up to time t, i.e., $s^t \equiv (s_t, s_{t-1}, s_{t-2}, \ldots, s_{t_0})$. Moreover, $f(s^t|s_{t_0})$ can be written as $f(s^t|s_{t_0}) \equiv f(s_t|s_{t-1})f(s_{t-1}|s_{t-2})\ldots f(s_{t_0})$, if it is assumed that $f(s^t|s_{t_0})$ has the Markov property. In the following discussion, for a generic random variable X, we will use the notation X_t to represent $X(s^t)$. Accordingly, the conditional expectation at time t_0 of X_t is defined as $E_{t_0}X_t = \sum_{s^t} f(s^t|s_{t_0})X(s^t)$.

There are three agents in the economy: consumers, the government, and financial intermediaries. The key feature of this chapter is that there are certain securities, called "safe assets," which play a special liquidity role in the economy: exchange for goods or collateral services. These securities can be naturally produced by the government, as in Chapter 3. Financial intermediaries can also create safe securities, backing them with risky investment and by appropriately raising equity.

There is a fixed amount of capital, K, used by consumers and financial intermediaries. Output is now a function of capital and its productivity, $Y_t = A_t K$. Capital productivity A_t has a bounded support, $[A_{\min}, A_{\max}]$. Capital has a price Q_t^K in units of currency and therefore its nominal return at time t is $1 + i_t^K \equiv (Q_t^K + P_t A_t)/(Q_{t-1}^K)$.

4.3.1 Consumers

Let us consider a representative agent in a closed economy with the following expected intertemporal utility:

$$E_{t_0} \sum_{t=t_0}^{\infty} \beta^{t-t_0} \left\{ C_t + V\left(\frac{B_t + S_t}{P_t}\right) \right\}, \tag{4.1}$$

where β, with $0 < \beta < 1$, is the subjective discount factor in preferences; (C) is the consumption good, and utility is linear in it;[5] and $V(\cdot)$ is a concave, differentiable function of real "safe assets" holdings, which now include the government's debt (B) and the intermediary's debt (S). The function $V(\cdot)$ has a satiation point $\bar{q} > 0$ such that $V_q(q_t) = 0$ for $q_t \geq \bar{q}$, having defined $q_t \equiv (B_t + S_t)/P_t$, ($P$) is the price of the consumption good (C).

"Safe assets," which are nominal securities free of any risk, provide utility benefits, which can be considered as a proxy of transaction or collateral services. In this chapter, we assume that the central bank fully backs the treasury debt. Therefore, all the government's liabilities are always risk-free. With B in (4.1), therefore, we denote both the treasury's short-term debt and the central bank's reserves. Financial intermediaries can also create risk-free securities, labelled by S. As in the model in Section 3.3 of Chapter 3, liquidity is supplied by securities paying a nominal interest rate, provided they are free of risk. Cash—a non-interest-bearing asset—could also provide liquidity services, but it will be dominated by other, interest-bearing, assets and will therefore not be demanded for liquidity purposes or for other purposes except when the nominal interest rate is zero. We consider the economy cashless in equilibrium, but the possibility of holding cash imposes a zero lower bound constraint on the nominal interest rate.

The consumer is subject to the following budget constraint to purchase good C:

$$B_t + S_t + Q_t^K K_t + N_t + P_t C_t + T_t = (1 + i_{t-1}^X)B_{t-1}$$
$$+ (1 + i_{t-1}^S)S_{t-1} + (1 + i_t^K)Q_{t-1}^K K_{t-1} + \Psi_t^D. \tag{4.2}$$

---

5. The linearity of the utility function in consumption is useful for simplifying the analysis and tying the real interest rate to the inverse of the discount factor, even when output is stochastic. In Chapters 1–3, the same results were obtained under a nonlinear utility function assuming constant endowment.

Consumers can also invest in a risky asset, capital (K), which has price Q_t^K at time t, and a stochastic nominal return, $1 + i_{t+1}^K$, which is contingent on the realization of uncertainty at time $t + 1$. The returns on government and private safe debt are $1 + i_t^X$ and $1 + i_t^S$, respectively, and they are non-stochastic and determined at time t.[6] Consumers can finance financial intermediaries' equity, N_t, and for this reason they receive dividends in the next period, Ψ_{t+1}^D. T_t are lumpsum taxes levied by the government at time t. There can also be other securities traded in the economy, but those are not relevant for the analysis that follows, and therefore we will omit them.

In the optimal plan, the consumer chooses stochastic sequences $\{C_t, B_t, S_t, K_t, N_t\}_{t=t_0}^{\infty}$, with $C_t, B_t, S_t, N_t \geq 0$ to maximize (4.1), under the constraint (4.2) and an appropriate borrowing limit at each time $t \geq t_0$, given initial conditions $(1 + i_{t_0-1}^X)B_{t_0-1}$, $(1 + i_{t_0-1}^S)S_{t_0-1}$, $(1 + i_{t_0-1}^K)K_{t_0-1}$. Consider Lagrange multipliers $\lambda_t \geq 0$ attached to constraint (4.2); the first-order condition with respect to C_t implies that $\lambda_t = 1/P_t$. Let us define $\tilde{R}_{t,t+1} \equiv \beta(P_t/P_{t+1})$. The first-order condition with respect to holding capital, K_t, implies

$$1 = E_t \left\{ \tilde{R}_{t,t+1}(1 + i_{t+1}^K) \right\}, \tag{4.3}$$

while the value of financial intermediaries' equity is equal to the discounted value of dividends,

$$N_t = E_t \left\{ \tilde{R}_{t,t+1} \Psi_{t+1}^D \right\}. \tag{4.4}$$

The optimality conditions with respect to S_t and B_t imply

$$1 \geq \varrho_t + E_t \left\{ \tilde{R}_{t,t+1} \left(1 + i_t^S\right) \right\}, \tag{4.5}$$

$$1 \geq \varrho_t + E_t \left\{ \tilde{R}_{t,t+1} \left(1 + i_t^X\right) \right\}. \tag{4.6}$$

The above inequalities hold with the equality sign when the respective security is used in the liquidity market, in which case the price of the security, which is one dollar, is equal to the present discounted value of its payoff plus the nonpecuniary services represented by term ϱ_t, given by

$$\varrho_t \equiv V_q \left(\frac{B_t + S_t}{P_t} \right),$$

<hr />

6. We are maintaining the notation that i_t^X is the interest rate on reserves, which is set by the central bank.

in which $V_q(\cdot)$ is the first derivative of the function $V(\cdot)$ with respect to its argument. When the inequality holds strictly, the security is not held for liquidity purposes, but it might be held for its pecuniary return. Note that at least one among (4.5) and (4.6) should hold with the equality sign.

The representative agent's optimization problem is completed with the exhaustion of the intertemporal budget constraints, which we omit here.

4.3.2 Government

Let us consider a consolidated government budget constraint

$$B_t = (1 + i^X_{t-1})B_{t-1} - T_t, \tag{4.7}$$

where (T) are taxes. To keep the analysis simple, we do not differentiate between central bank and treasury; (B) denote the overall government liabilities, which are risk-free because they are all backed by the central bank, as discussed in previous chapters, and, therefore, not subject to a solvency condition.

4.3.3 Intermediaries

There is an infinite number of intermediaries that can enter the securities market without any barrier. They invest in risky capital and can raise equity. They are, however, subject to a limited liability constraint, i.e., a nonnegative profit requirement. Depending on the level of equity, they can issue risk-free securities or defaulted securities, the latter in the event the limited liability constraint is binding. We focus on the creation of risk-free securities, since they will be the only type relevant to characterize the equilibrium.

Intermediaries live for two periods, invest in capital, and can finance it by issuing debt securities and equity. A generic intermediary living at times t and $t+1$, issuing risk-free debt S_t, is subject to the following budget constraint at time t:

$$Q^K_t K^I_t = S_t + N_t. \tag{4.8}$$

Intermediaries invest in capital, K^I_t, and finance it by issuing safe debt and equity.

In the following period $t+1$, gross profits are represented by

$$\Psi^I_{t+1} = (1 + i^K_{t+1})Q^K_t K^I_t - (1 + i^S_t)S_t, \tag{4.9}$$

and cannot be negative, given limited liabilities. Therefore $\min \Psi_{t+1}^I \geq 0$ requires

$$(1 + i_{\min}^K) Q_t^K K_t^I \geq (1 + i_t^S) S_t,$$

where $(1 + i_{\min}^K) = \min(1 + i_{t+1}^K)$. Substituting (4.8) for $Q_t^K K_t^I$ in the above inequality, we obtain a lower bound, $\bar{N}_t$, on equity

$$N_t \geq \bar{N}_t = \left(\frac{1 + i_t^S}{1 + i_{\min}^K} - 1 \right) S_t. \qquad (4.10)$$

Since assets are risky, intermediaries should back safe debt with an appropriate level of equity, which would cover losses in the worst-case scenario.

Intermediaries choose how many securities to supply by maximizing their expected rents $(\mathcal{R})$, which are given by the expected discounted value of non-distributed profits $(\Psi^I - \Psi^D)$ as

$$\mathcal{R}_t = E_t \left\{ \tilde{R}_{t,t+1} (\Psi_{t+1}^I - \Psi_{t+1}^D) \right\} = S_t - E_t \left\{ \tilde{R}_{t,t+1} (1 + i_t^S) \right\} S_t,$$

in which we have substituted (4.8) and (4.9) to obtain the second equality, and used (4.3) and (4.4). Maximization of rents implies a positive supply of securities insofar as their prices are such that[7]

$$\frac{1}{1 + i_t^S} \geq E_t \left\{ \tilde{R}_{t,t+1} \right\}.$$

Since there is an infinite number of intermediaries that can potentially enter the market, all rents are zero in equilibrium, and therefore the supply schedule is just

$$\frac{1}{1 + i_t^S} = E_t \left\{ \tilde{R}_{t,t+1} \right\}. \qquad (4.11)$$

Intermediaries creating "safe assets" will then choose an appropriate equity level (4.10) and supply securities at the price (4.11).

4.3.4 Equilibrium

In equilibrium, the bonds issued by the government and the intermediaries' debt are held by the consumer. Aggregate consumption is equal to the output, $C_t = Y_t = A_t K$; capital required by consumers and intermediaries sum to the total available stock, $K_t + K_t^I = K$.

---

7. Note that $1/(1 + i_t^S)$ is the price of the safe security.

The key result is that competition for private safe securities eradicates all rents no matter what the supply of government liquidity is. The economy is always at a level of full satiation of liquidity. This can be seen by combining the demand (4.6) and supply (4.11) schedules of the intermediaries' safe debt, implying $\varrho_t = 0$ at all times. If ϱ_t were positive, it would trigger the intermediaries' entry in the market of safe securities, since they could profit from financing investment at a lower cost. This extra rent would be wiped out by competition in the market, ensuring that there are no liquidity premiums and zero rents.

To complete the characterization of the equilibrium, we analyze the determination of prices and interest rates. This analysis is important for assessing whether a framework in which liquidity is privately supplied could potentially undermine the central bank's control over prices. The bottom line is that it does not.

Note that by combining the intertemporal budget constraint of the consumer with the balance sheets of the intermediaries we get the following intertemporal resource constraint:

$$\frac{(1 + i_{t_0-1}^X)B_{t_0-1}}{P_{t_0}} = E_{t_0} \left\{ \sum_{t=t_0}^{\infty} \beta^{t-t_0} \left(\frac{T_t}{P_t} + \frac{i_t - i_t^X}{1 + i_t} \frac{B_t}{P_t} \right) \right\}, \qquad (4.12)$$

which corresponds to (3.16) of Chapter 3, with the difference that in (4.12) all government debt B provides liquidity services. In the above equation, i_t represents the notional risk-free rate on a bond that does not provide liquidity services; it is priced as

$$\frac{1}{1 + i_t} = E_t \left\{ \tilde{R}_{t,t+1} \right\}. \qquad (4.13)$$

In equilibrium, the real value of debt should be equal to the expected present-discounted value of taxes plus the liquidity rents obtained by government-issued "safe assets."

We make the following assumptions on government policy. The government sets the interest rate on reserves, i_t^X, to a constant value, $1 + i_t^X = \beta^{-1}$. The tax policy is specified in real terms as $T_t/P_t = (1 - \beta)\tau$ for some positive τ. These assumptions fall within the class of policies that have been analyzed in Section 1.4 of Chapter 1.

To solve for the equilibrium prices, note first that when $\varrho_t = 0$, it should necessarily be that $1 + i_t = 1 + i_t^X = 1/\beta$. The money market nominal interest rate should be equalized to the policy rate. Indeed, two cases are possible.

In the first, government debt is not held for liquidity purposes but only for its pecuniary return, i.e., (4.6) holds with equality. However, by absence of arbitrage opportunities, the interest rate i_t on any risk-free but illiquid security should necessarily coincide with i_t^X and, therefore, $1 + i_t = 1 + i_t^X = 1/\beta$. If instead government debt is used for liquidity purposes, $\varrho_t = 0$ in (4.6) implies again that $1 + i_t = 1 + i_t^X = 1/\beta$, using (4.13).

Using the tax policy and the result $1 + i_t = 1 + i_t^X = 1/\beta$ in (4.12), it follows that

$$\frac{(1 + i_{t_0-1})B_{t_0-1}}{P_{t_0}} = \tau,$$

which determines the price level P_{t_0}, given B_{t_0-1}, i_{t_0-1}, and τ. An additional implication is that the price level does not exhibit stochastic behavior.[8] Moreover, it is also not varying over time. Use equation (4.13) to note that

$$\frac{1}{1 + i_t} = E_t\{\tilde{R}_{t,t+1}\} = \beta \frac{P_t}{P_{t+1}}.$$

Since $1 + i_t = 1 + i_t^X = 1/\beta$, the above equation implies that prices are always constant at a level, let's say, P.

There is no challenge coming from private creation of money to the control of the price level. The above follows exactly from the same principles discussed in Chapter 1.

Finally, note that the supply of government liquidity, B_t/P_t, is given at each point in time by $\beta\tau$. Since the overall supply of liquidity is above the satiation level $\bar{q}$, we can determine the supply of private safe security as $S \geq \max\{P(\bar{q} - \beta\tau), 0\}$. If government liquidity is not enough to satiate the economy $(\bar{q} > \beta\tau)$, intermediaries have an incentive to supplement government liquidity by providing a sufficient amount of safe assets to achieve the full satiation of liquidity, which is the efficient allocation for the same reasons discussed in Section 3.5 of Chapter 3.

4.4 The Supply of Public and Private Liquidity

A private securities market under unfettered competition satiates the demand for liquidity in the economy. This result confirms Hayek's view (1976) that the

---

8. This result follows from applying the same reasoning to (4.12) at a generic time t, for which $((1 + i_{t-1}^X)B_{t-1})/P_t = \tau$. The latter equation implies that the price level is deterministic.

process of competition can lead the private sector to supply a sufficiently large quantity of the best available type of asset, namely, "safe assets" in this context.[9] The competitive market structure in the model is in Hayek's spirit (1976, p. 43) and works as follows.[10] If safe securities were not provided, households would attach a premium to them because such securities provide liquidity services. Therefore, intermediaries would find it worthwhile to supply safe debt, because the premium paid by households reduces the intermediaries' financing costs. Free entry and exit would then guarantee that there is enough supply of safe securities so that the households' liquidity constraints are never binding. As a result, the interest of households is perfectly aligned with that of financial intermediaries. Indeed the premium on "safe assets," which reflects the inefficient provision of liquidity from a societal point of view, creates incentives for self-interested intermediaries to supply safe securities. To this end, intermediaries will raise enough equity to absorb any loss they incur on their risky assets.

Unfettered competition achieves efficiency without the need for any type of regulation. This result can be further compared with the "real bills" doctrine and with the view in Friedman (1960) about the separation of money and credit markets. According to the "real bills" doctrine, intermediaries should be required to hold safe (and possibly illiquid) assets to back the supply of private money. This is not necessary. While intermediaries may hold risky assets, competition for the supply of safe securities compels them to raise sufficient equity to absorb any potential losses. Consequently, the supply of private money remains secure.

In light of the findings in this chapter, it may be worthwhile to reexamine and rationalize the "real bills" doctrine by expanding the concept of "real bills" to encompass not only risk-free securities but also risky investments that can be rendered risk-free through the absorption of losses by equity. Free banking, characterized by an unregulated banking sector, enables the efficient supply of liquidity as competition drives down excess profits in the provision of safe securities.

9. It should be noted that Hayek (1976) discusses competition among moneys denominated in different currencies, but that the mechanism of competition in the search for the best money applies here too. Hayek (1937) advocates free banking without national boundary restrictions.

10. See Hayek (1948, ch. V) for a critical analysis of the assumption of perfect competition.

Friedman (1960) argued that the government should have monopoly power in the supply of liquidity. This objective can be obtained if the government passes regulation to achieve a "narrow banking" system; that is, intermediaries are forced to satisfy a 100% reserve requirement. In the context of this chapter's model, intermediaries would buy government debt, B, using deposits. If this were the case, private intermediaries would not create any liquidity, because their deposits would be backed by liquid government debt, instead of illiquid risky investments. As a result, the supply of liquid assets would be determined solely by the amount of government debt in the economy, B. Note that the government has to back the interest payment on such debt, which in the framework of the previous section is achieved by collecting taxes, T. A benevolent government that decides to use this policy can nevertheless achieve the first best by setting $\beta\tau \geq \bar{q}$, so that government debt is of the amount $B/P \geq \bar{q}$.

Milton Friedman's other proposal (1960) is that the supply of public liquidity should be achieved by the central bank through investment in a portfolio of assets. Ideally, the central bank should transform risk-free but illiquid assets issued by the private sector into risk-free but liquid liabilities. This can be done without any need for the government to raise taxes if the illiquid securities are created by the private sector. This separation of monetary and fiscal policies, as discussed in Section 1.4.2 of Chapter 1, can be beneficial for controlling the price level.

If the central bank can invest only in risky securities issued by the private sector, it can fully back its supply of liquidity as long as the risky securities do not default. Otherwise, taxation would be necessary to cover the central bank's losses in cases where private securities defaulted, creating subtle and delicate linkages between monetary and fiscal policies.

Both free banking and centralizing the supply of liquidity within the government can achieve efficiency. In either case, the manner in which liquidity is supplied does not pose challenges for the central bank in controlling the price level, as demonstrated in Section 3.4 of Chapter 3, as well as in this chapter. However, the views are conflicting in terms of decentralized versus centralized supply, i.e., in terms of the forces of private competition versus the benevolence of a government monopoly. But if the monopolist bases its decision on self-interest, it will not achieve the first best. Indeed, in Hayek's words, a monopoly "prevents the discovery of better methods of satisfying a need for which a monopolist has no incentive" (Hayek, 1976, p. 28). The "need" is the efficient supply of liquidity, the "incentive" of a monopolist is to reduce the provision of liquidity to earn rents, and the "discovery" of "better methods" is the creation of private money by financial intermediaries.

As a result of this reasoning, the balance seems to favor free banking. It's preferable to unleash the forces of private competition because acting in private interest also serves society's needs. However, these conclusions hinge on the crucial assumption that, in the absence of risk-free securities backing intermediaries' liquidity, equity can be raised without frictions. At the same time, taxes can be raised without bound to sustain government liquidity. Chapter 11, by relaxing this ideal frictionless framework, will explore the possibility of a liquidity crisis, establishing connections between equilibrium liquidity, interest-rate policy, and government intervention.

4.5   Dominant Currency

In the model of currency competition presented in Section 2.8 of Chapter 2, government currency had a dominant role since it was the *unit of account* in which debt claims were set and paid. This had some implications for excluding the equilibria, in which government currency was worthless under an appropriate policy discussed therein. On the other hand, the previous sections have shown that private debt can also provide liquidity to the economy—not just government debt. Here we present a model of competition between a government currency and a private currency to study the intermediaries' choice of currency for denominating and paying their debt.

The economy has an infinite horizon and is stochastic. There are two agents: households and intermediaries. Households invest in safe securities that provide liquidity services in the next period.

"Safe assets" can be denominated in two different currencies, for example, a government currency and a private currency, and are issued by financial intermediaries. Intermediaries invest in risky real projects and finance them by issuing safe securities in either one of the two currencies, while being subject to a limited liability constraint. The monetary policy of the currency issuers is simplified by assuming that prices of goods in terms of the two currencies follow a specified distribution.[11] Characteristics of this distribution determine the currency in which securities are going to be issued in equilibrium.

---

11. This is an important simplification of and departure from the analysis of price determination undertaken so far.

Households have the same preferences as in (4.1) for consumption and real liquidity balances,

$$E_{t_0} \sum_{t=t_0}^{\infty} \beta^{t-t_0} \left\{ C_t + V \left(\frac{S_t}{P_t} + \frac{S_t^*}{P_t^*} \right) \right\}, \tag{4.14}$$

in which (S) and (S^*) are "safe assets," held from time t, denominated in government and private currency, respectively; (P) and (P^*) are prices in terms of the two currencies. Consumption of good (C) at time t is subject to the following budget constraint, expressed in units of goods:

$$\frac{S_t}{P_t} + \frac{S_t^*}{P_t^*} + C_t = \frac{(1 + i_{t-1}^S)S_{t-1}}{P_t} + \frac{(1 + i_{t-1}^{S^*})S_{t-1}^*}{P_t^*} + Y + \Psi_t^A, \tag{4.15}$$

in which (i^S) and (i^{S^*}) are the returns of the two securities in the respective currencies, (Y) is a constant endowment, and (Ψ^A) are state-contingent intermediaries' aggregate real profits.

Consumption and portfolio choices follow from the maximization of (4.14) under constraint (4.15) and an appropriate borrowing-limit condition. The demand for "safe assets" is influenced by the liquidity value provided by the securities, represented by the variable ϱ_t:

$$1 \geq \varrho_t + E_t \left\{ \tilde{R}_{t,t+1} \left(1 + i_t^S \right) \right\}, \tag{4.16}$$

$$1 \geq \varrho_t + E_t \left\{ \tilde{R}_{t,t+1}^* \left(1 + i_t^{S^*} \right) \right\}, \tag{4.17}$$

in which

$$\varrho_t = V_q \left(\frac{S_t}{P_t} + \frac{S_t^*}{P_t^*} \right),$$

whereas $\tilde{R}_{t,t+1} \equiv \beta P_t / P_{t+1}$ and $\tilde{R}_{t,t+1}^* \equiv \beta P_t^* / P_{t+1}^*$.

Note that both securities carry the same liquidity premium, but prices can be different because of the differences in the realization of inflation rates in the two currencies.[12]

Intermediaries live for two periods and have a sufficient number of risky projects available in which to invest. At time t, each project has a unitary value, expressed in units of goods, and delivers A_{t+1}/β units at time $t+1$, where A_{t+1} is a random variable with $E_t(A_{t+1}) = 1$ distributed on the support

---

12. Prices of the two securities are given by $1/(1 + i_t^S)$ and $1/(1 + i_t^{S^*})$, respectively.

$[A_{min}, A_{max}]$. Intermediaries are restricted to investing in only one project, but, potentially, there can be many (infinite) intermediaries that can enter the market without any barrier to entry. Intermediaries finance this investment by issuing nominal risk-free securities in each of the two currencies and can choose which type of security to issue, and the currency. Differently from the model of the previous section, they cannot raise equity to cover their losses; therefore, they can only rely on liquidity premiums to lower the financing cost of their investment. Intermediaries provide a service of liquidity transformation by issuing safe and liquid securities backed by risky and illiquid investments.

At time t, a generic intermediary is subject to the following budget constraint:

$$1 = \frac{D_t}{P_t} + \frac{D_t^*}{P_t^*}, \tag{4.18}$$

where (D) and (D^*) are the securities issued, denominated in the government and the private currency, respectively, to finance one unit of real investment. At time $t + 1$, profits, expressed in real terms, are state contingent and represented by

$$\Psi_{t+1}^I = \frac{A_{t+1}}{\beta} - \frac{(1 + i_t^S)D_t}{P_{t+1}} - \frac{(1 + i_t^{S*})D_t^*}{P_{t+1}^*}. \tag{4.19}$$

In order to issue safe securities, intermediaries should always be able to pay their debt, irrespective of the contingency in which they find themselves, and therefore of the realization of the project's payoff and price levels. Profits should be nonnegative, $\Psi_{t+1}^I \geq 0$. Without equity issuance, this constraint imposes an upper bound on the interest rate at which intermediaries are willing to supply their safe debt. This interest rate should embed a premium for compensating for the worst realization of price levels and the lowest payoff of the investment project. When the price level at time $t + 1$ falls, intermediaries have to pay a larger amount of real resources. Therefore, they should issue debt at a lower interest rate. Indeed, the premium will compensate for this risk. The constraint that guarantees the safety of the securities can be written as

$$\min \Psi_{t+1}^I = \frac{A_{min}}{\beta} - \frac{(1 + i_t^S)D_t}{P_{min}} - \frac{(1 + i_t^{S*})D_t^*}{P_{min}^*} \geq 0, \tag{4.20}$$

given the support of the distribution of prices, $P_{t+1} \in [P_{min}, P_{max}]$ and $P_{t+1}^* \in [P_{min}^*, P_{max}^*]$, and of the random variable, $A_{t+1} \in [A_{min}, A_{max}]$.

Intermediaries maximize expected discounted real profits,

$$E_t[\beta\Psi^I_{t+1}] = \left[1 - E_t\left(\frac{\beta(1+i^S_t)}{P_{t+1}}\right)D_t - E_t\left(\frac{\beta(1+i^{S*}_t)}{P^*_{t+1}}\right)D^*_t\right],$$

by choosing nonnegative quantities of each security subject to constraints (4.18) and (4.20), and taking market prices as given. Not all intermediaries willing to supply securities will be accommodated by households' demand. Since profits are positive for intermediaries supplying safe securities and zero for those outside the market, intermediaries will bid up their interest rate— provided the safety of the security they issue is maintained—to make sure they are not cut out of the market.[13] As a consequence of this competition, safety constraint (4.20) is going to be binding. Therefore, in equilibrium, the market interest rate of a security in positive supply is equal to the maximum interest rate that guarantees its safety. Let us define with $1+\tilde{i}^S_t$ and $1+\tilde{i}^{S*}_t$ these maximum interest rates. They can be determined as

$$\frac{1}{1+\tilde{i}^S_t} = \frac{\beta}{A_{\min}}\frac{P_t}{P_{\min}}, \tag{4.21}$$

$$\frac{1}{1+\tilde{i}^{S*}_t} = \frac{\beta}{A_{\min}}\frac{P^*_t}{P^*_{\min}}, \tag{4.22}$$

and can be obtained by combining (4.18) and (4.20) with equality and setting $D^*_t = 0$ and $D_t = 0$, respectively. These reservation prices reflect the premium intermediaries need to guarantee the safety of securities. For each security, this premium depends on two factors: a low realization of the payoff of the investment project reduces the resources available to pay debt and so must be compensated for by issuing debt at higher prices (lower interest rate); a low realization of the price level requires more real resources to pay debt, so it must be compensated again by issuing debt at higher prices (lower interest rate). If the interest rate rises above the maximum rate, intermediaries cannot issue a safe security.

We characterize the equilibrium given the exogenous path of prices. We determine which securities are traded; their amount and price; the liquidity

---

13. Households gain resources by purchasing safe securities in each of the two markets at a lower price (higher interest rate), provided their safety is maintained and, therefore, also their liquidity value.

premium; and the mass of intermediaries in the market, and therefore consumption. Note that, in equilibrium, $S_t = n_t D_t$ and $S_t^* = n_t^* D_t^*$, where n_t and n_t^* are the mass of intermediaries in each respective market.

Given the above setup, we run a simple example: prices are stable in the government currency ($P_{t+1} = P$) while the private currency has variable prices on a support $[P_{\min}^*, P_{\max}^*]$. We conjecture that intermediaries will denominate securities only in the stable-price (government) currency. In this equilibrium, competition in the market of government-denominated securities is such that the interest rate is at its maximum value, i.e., $1 + i_t^S = 1 + \tilde{\imath}_t^S$, implying

$$\varrho_t = 1 - A_{\min} > 0,$$

using (4.16) with equality, and (4.21) with a constant price level in government currency imposed. Since

$$\varrho_t = V_q \left(\frac{S_t}{P} \right),$$

it follows that the supply of government securities is constant at

$$S = P V_q^{-1} (1 - A_{\min}).$$

Liquidity is not fully satiated because securities need a premium to be issued in order to absorb the risk of the assets that back them. Using $D_t^* = 0$ in the constraint (4.18), we obtain $D_t = P$, and therefore

$$n_t = \frac{S_t}{D_t} = V_q^{-1} (1 - A_{\min}).$$

To prove that this is the equilibrium, securities denominated in private currency should not be supplied.[14] There can be two reasons for this: i) either their market interest rate is above the reservation interest rate, i.e., $1 + i_t^{S^*} > 1 + \tilde{\imath}_t^{S^*}$, and therefore the liquidity premium is not enough to guarantee the safety of the security; ii) or the market interest rate is below the reservation rate but profits in supplying that security are lower than those in supplying debt in the other currency. It turns out that condition i) applies in this case.

Recall that the liquidity premium is represented by $\varrho = 1 - A_{\min}$. At this liquidity premium, private securities are not supplied because their market (shadow) interest rate is above the maximum rate compatible with their

---

14. Note that in equilibrium, $\Psi_t^A = n_t \Psi_t^I$ and $S_t = n_t D_t = P$, which substituted into the budget constraint (4.15) implies $C_t = Y + n_{t-1} A_t / \beta - n_t$ determining consumption.

safety, i.e., $1 + i_t^{S*} > 1 + \tilde{\imath}_t^{S*}$. Indeed, $1 + i_t^{S*}$ is determined by demand (4.16) evaluated at $\varrho = 1 - A_{\min}$, to obtain

$$\frac{1}{1 + i_t^{S*}} = \frac{\beta}{A_{\min}} E_t \left\{ \frac{P_t^*}{P_{t+1}^*} \right\}.$$

Comparing with (4.22), it follows that $1 + i_t^{S*} > 1 + \tilde{\imath}_t^{S*}$, noting

$$\frac{1}{P_{\min}^*} > E_t \left\{ \frac{1}{P_{t+1}^*} \right\}. \tag{4.23}$$

To understand why price stability can lead to the dominance of a currency as a *unit of account* for "safe assets," let us assume, for simplicity's sake, that the investment payoff is not risky, $A_{\min} = A_{\max} = 1$. Looking at the supply side, price stability in a currency avoids any balance-sheet mismatch between assets and liabilities of intermediaries issuing that currency. Therefore, no premium is required to maintain the safety of the securities. Competition to attract investors of money-like claims drives the liquidity premium to zero, which then lowers the demand price of any safe security. This low price crowds out any supply of safe securities in the other currency, given that safety cannot be guaranteed without earning a liquidity premium.

Stability of prices does not have consequences only for determining which currency dominates in the creation of safe claims, but also for welfare. Note that, in this simple environment, welfare is inversely related to the liquidity premium. Price stability eradicates the liquidity premium to the maximum extent possible. The reason for this result can be intuited by noting that price variability requires an overly high price (low interest rate) for the security to be issued and for it to be safe, which implies a shortage of "safe assets" and also a liquidity premium to hold them.

The results discussed in this chapter complement those shown in Section 2.8 of Chapter 2, in which we analyzed competition for the *medium-of-exchange* role between money supplied by a government and money supplied by a private issuer. There, the prevailing currency was the one with the lower inflation rate. Here, when currencies compete to be a *unit of account* and a means of payment for money-like claims issued by private intermediaries, the prevailing currency has stable prices. Low inflation and stable prices are therefore the characteristics that can make one currency the prevailing currency in money and exchange markets.

4.6   References

The theme of private versus government supply of money has been intensely debated in the economic literature, encompassing various proposals, including the "real bills" doctrine, free banking, and narrow banking theories. The origins of the "real bills" doctrine can be attributed to the works of Law (1705) and Smith (1776), who have also been the inspiration for free banking theories. Von Mises (1912) offered a coherent approach to free banking, while Friedman (1960) is the primary reference for the Chicago plan on narrow banking. Schwartz (1989), Sargent (2011), and White (2014) provide interesting historical accounts of the theoretical and policy controversies.

The analysis in this chapter builds on Benigno and Robatto (2019). The banking literature is rich with models that analyze liquidity creation in the spirit of the seminal contribution of Gorton and Pennacchi (1990). Gorton (2017) is an important reference for understanding the concept of safe assets and the implications that they have for macroeconomic and monetary policy, drawing on the historical experience. Recent works in the banking literature that have modelled safe assets are Greenwood, Hanson, and Stein (2015) and Magill, Quinzii, and Rochet (2020). The latter work focuses on the inefficiency in the private creation of liquidity and the central bank's role in restoring efficiency in the banking equilibrium.

Finally, Doepke and Schneider (2017) develop a theory that rationalizes the use of a dominant unit of account in an economy by reducing exposure to risk and default.

PART II

Stabilization Policies

Introduction

THE MONUMENTAL work of Milton Friedman and Anna Schwartz in 1963, *A Monetary History of the United States, 1867–1960,* is a statement about the importance of stabilization policies by central banks. Thirty years later, in his review of the book, Robert Lucas describes two important tenets underlying the narration of the evolution of the money stock M2 in U.S. history. The first is the concept of a natural rate of output toward which the economy converges and which is not affected by monetary policy. The second hypothesis is the non-neutrality of money in the short run. The efficacy of monetary policy hinges on price rigidities, which are not spelled out in the description but are understood to be "transient" and can be reconciled with long-run neutrality (see Lucas, 1994, p. 6).

The key observation in Friedman and Schwartz's analysis is that economic contractions and depressions are primarily attributed to contractions in the money supply, which plays a significant role in major economic fluctuations. The normative implication is consequential; it suggests that the monetary authority should have had the power to eliminate instabilities in the money supply: "Prevention or moderation of the decline in the stock of money . . . would have reduced the contraction's severity and almost certainly its duration" (Friedman and Schwartz, 1963, p. 301).

Friedman and Schwartz do not provide a theoretical framework to rationalize their policy conclusions beyond the tenets mentioned earlier.[1]

The importance they assign to monetary policy and stabilization policy was largely overshadowed by the theoretical developments of the 1980s,

---

1. Friedman (1970a) provides a theoretical framework to the evidence of Friedman and Schwartz (1963) through the income-expenditure theory, in which prices are fixed.

particularly the real business cycle theories introduced by Finn Kydland and Edward Prescott in 1982. According to this perspective, variations in total factor productivity can account for the observed output fluctuations in the U.S. during the postwar period. Furthermore, the fluctuations generated by the model are seen as efficient responses to these productivity shocks.

The work of Kydland and Prescott (1982), along with many others in the same research area, is characterized by three main features in the modeling framework. First, it models the behavior of consumers and firms by formulating optimization problems for their plans under resource constraints, along the lines of Ramsey (1928). Second, it incorporates the modeling of uncertainty and assumes rational expectations for economic agents, equipping them with the true probability distribution that characterizes the stochastic uncertainty of the model economy. Finally, it addresses the clearing of goods and asset markets, ensuring that excess demand and supply balances are eliminated in the equilibrium.

The New Keynesian literature, which emerged in the 1990s and was synthesized in the works of Woodford (2003) and Galí (2008), builds upon the same general features of the real business cycle model. However, it also maintains consistency with the two tenets of Friedman and Schwartz's analysis, relying on the same fundamental assumption of price rigidities.

The New Keynesian framework is consistent with monetary non-neutrality in the short run. It also incorporates the concept of a natural rate of output to which the economy converges in the long run. This natural rate remains unaffected by monetary policy and is driven by the same fluctuations as those in a real business cycle model.

To model nominal rigidities, a departure from the world of perfect competition is necessary. In a competitive market where all firms' products are perfect substitutes for each other, firms have no control over setting prices; they can only choose quantities. New Keynesian models, on the other hand, introduce price rigidities through the assumption of imperfect (monopolistic) competition. Under imperfect competition, firms have the ability to influence demand by choosing their prices. While imperfect competition alone is insufficient to generate nominal rigidities, when coupled with even small costs of price adjustment, it results in sticky prices as the optimal price-setting behavior, as shown in Mankiw (1985).

The assumption of price rigidity is what attributes to the framework the label "Keynesian," aligning it with the second tenet of Friedman and Schwartz's work, which posits short-run monetary non-neutralities. However, this assumption has been a common feature in the analysis of the effects of monetary policy since the early days of theoretical thought on the subject. As far back as 1752, David Hume stated: "In the progress toward these changes, the augmentation [in the quantity of money] may have some influence by exciting industry, but after the prices are settled . . . it has no manner of influence."

The controversy centers around the duration of the "excitement" period in the industry and the lingering effects of monetary policy on real economic activity. The New Keynesian literature draws its perspective from empirical evidence derived from structural vector autoregression models. These models demonstrate that a monetary policy shock, when identified, produces a peak output effect only in the sixth quarter following the shock, with a significant effect still observed after two years have passed (Woodford, 2003, ch. 3).[2]

The New Keynesian benchmark model is built upon a price-setting mechanism characterized by staggered and forward-looking prices. It aligns with an aggregate supply equation in which inflation depends not only on the current state of the economy but also on expectations of future inflation, following a forward-looking New Keynesian Phillips curve. This framework, known as Calvo's model, corresponds well with an empirically realistic degree of persistence of a monetary shock on real activity, given an empirically realistic average duration of price changes (Woodford, 2003, ch. 2).

The controversy remains unresolved, largely because of the simplified assumptions of the benchmark model. It hypothesizes a homogeneous production sector affected by various sources of aggregate disturbances and a time-dependent price-setting model. Substantial literature, including works by Nakamura and Steinsson (2008, 2013), has investigated price changes at the micro level, revealing significant variations and heterogeneity. It also underscores that estimated probabilities of price adjustments, based on the time since the last price reset, align more closely with a state-dependent model than with the fixed rate of Calvo's model.

However, concerning the effects of monetary shocks on output, there appears to be agreement that Calvo's model serves as a reasonable approximation, even when compared to state-dependent models, while remaining

2. For a review of empirical analysis on the effects of monetary policy shocks, refer to Christiano, Eichenbaum, and Evans (1999), Sims and Zha (2006), Arias, Caldara, and Rubio-Ramirez (2019), and Bauer and Swanson (2023).

empirically relevant.[3] These findings support the foundational elements of the aggregate-supply schedule in the benchmark New Keynesian framework.

On the other hand, the optimizing behavior of consumers within an intertemporal framework yields an aggregate demand function in which one of the key determinants is the real interest rate. Monetary policy influences the economy by adjusting the short-term nominal interest rate or by shaping expectations of future price changes. The real interest rate impacts consumption and saving decisions, with an increase inducing more saving and, consequently, a reduction in aggregate demand. The aggregate demand equation is forward-looking, implying that current demand is also influenced by future real interest rates and, consequently, by the future stance of monetary policy.

Hence, the overall framework supplements the missing theoretical elements of Friedman and Schwartz's analysis by proposing a model for the transmission mechanism of monetary policy. This model is also perturbed by other sources of exogenous shocks similar to the ones that have explained the fluctuations in macroeconomics variables in real business cycle models.

An important innovation is the ability to evaluate alternative policies based on the welfare of optimizing households and establish the optimal monetary stabilization policy. While central banks began endorsing inflation targeting policies in the early 1990s, it's a surprising coincidence that the New Keynesian model suggests that inflation targeting can effectively characterize the optimal approach to conducting stabilization policies for many significant disturbances affecting both demand and supply. This approach appears to outperform rigid interest rate rules, money supply rules, and even the prescriptions of following the natural rate of interest, as suggested by Knut Wicksell in 1898.

However, the events of the 2007–2008 financial crisis challenged the adequacy of the New Keynesian framework in explaining them and providing policy advice. As will be demonstrated in the next part, the framework has not been discarded but rather refined in various directions to account for the missing features. Robert Lucas, in 1994, while mentioning early models in the style of Kydland and Prescott being adapted to include monetary nonneutrality, somewhat prophetically remarked that the "prospects for success depend on our willingness to depart from the familiar world of postwar quarterly time

3. See Alvarez, Le Bihan, and Lippi (2016), Auclert et al. (2024), and Nakamura and Steinsson (2010).

series and test our ideas against the events of the interwar period" (Lucas, 1994, p. 14). These tests have included recent dramatic global events, such as Great Financial Crisis and the COVID-19 pandemic.

This part is divided into four chapters: Chapter 5 presents the New Keynesian benchmark model, Chapter 6 provides a simple graphical analysis through an *AS-AD* representation of how the model economy reacts to various shocks. Chapter 7 analyzes optimal monetary policy by maximizing the welfare of consumers, showing that it can be characterized by an inflation targeting policy. Chapter 8 incorporates in the benchmark New Keynesian model a banking sector. This framework changes the way the policy rate is transmitted into the economy—giving a role to central bank reserves, and, in general, government liquidity—to directly influence aggregate demand, besides policy rate. The significance of liquidity, or general money aggregates, becomes much more relevant when assessing prescriptions such as those proposed by Friedman and Schwartz (1963) for controlling the money supply as a means of stabilizing the economy.

5

The Benchmark New
Keynesian Model

5.1 Introduction

In this chapter, we introduce the benchmark New Keynesian (NK) model, which serves as a foundation for examining the role of monetary policy in stabilizing the economy when it encounters various sources of stochastic disturbances. This model extends the basic framework introduced in Chapter 1 to incorporate a stochastic environment and endogenize production. However, the key departure in this chapter is the presentation of a more refined characterization of aggregate supply, which has significant policy implications for how monetary policy influences economic activity.

The model of Chapter 1 could be represented through a downward-sloping aggregate demand (AD) curve in a diagram depicting the relationship between price (or inflation) and output, alongside a constant vertical aggregate supply (AS) curve. In that context, monetary policy was essentially neutral on the real economy, impacting only prices and nominal interest rates.

However, the NK model, which incorporates the assumption of price rigidity, introduces an upward-sloping AS curve. This alteration results in a non-neutral role for monetary policy in influencing short-run output, justifying a stabilization role for monetary policy within the economy.

The first element of enrichment in the NK model of this chapter is a stochastic structure, introducing several exogenous disturbances that perturb the economy.

The second element is the endogeneity of production. The single-good model from Chapter 1 is extended to encompass a continuum of goods that are not substitutable for consumers. The production of these goods becomes endogenous and is carried out by firms owned by households, which utilize labor as an input.

The distinct feature of the product market in the NK model is its monopolistic-competitive nature. This arises because the goods are not substitutable for consumers and, therefore, firms have the ability to influence demand for their produced goods by setting their prices strategically. Firms optimize their prices to maximize profits while considering demand and technology. Households optimally supply labor, taking into account that it reduces utility but provides labor income, which can be used to support consumption and saving plans, in addition to the firms' profits.

All the above features enrich the model by introducing stochastic variations in output, but they do not alter the vertical position of the *AS* equation. This is because labor and, consequently, output are functions of exogenous real disturbances due to market clearing in the labor market. The demand for labor is a function of the real wages, and so is the quantity supplied. At any point in time, there is an equilibrium level of employment and output corresponding to an equilibrium real wage rate. As a result, the model aligns with the classical dichotomy, wherein monetary policy specification influences inflation and the general price level but remains neutral regarding output and economic activity. The determination of prices can be understood through the framework in Chapter 1, with the necessary adjustments for operating in a stochastic environment.

The primary characteristic of the NK model is the assumption of price rigidity, which results in an upward-sloping *AS* equation. These price frictions are embedded critically in the model of monopolistic competition, restricting firms from adjusting their prices for a stochastic duration of time, following the Calvo-style price-setting mechanism, as described by Calvo (1983).

The resulting *AS* equation not only establishes a positive relationship between inflation and output, but also links the current inflation rate to expectations of future inflation. This linkage arises from the strategic decisions made by price setters when adjusting their prices. They must consider the possibility that prices may remain fixed for some periods in the future and, therefore, need to anticipate the general price index under such circumstances.

With an upward-sloping *AS* equation, monetary policy can influence economic activity in two ways. Firstly, it can act directly on the aggregate demand (*AD*) equation, thereby altering inflation and output along the *AS* curve. Secondly, it can impact inflation expectations, which can, in turn, shift the *AS* equation directly.

5.2   Outline of the Results

Section 5.4 explores the equilibrium of a model that incorporates all the essential elements of the NK framework, with the exception that prices adjust fully flexibly. The resulting equilibrium aligns with the classical dichotomy, where monetary policy exerts neutrality with respect to output. In this setup, output relies solely on real factors, unaffected by monetary policy. As a consequence, the aggregate supply (AS) equation takes on a vertical orientation, while variations in aggregate demand (AD) result solely in price fluctuations.

In Section 5.5, frictions in price adjustment are introduced through Calvo's price-setting model. This addition results in an aggregate supply (AS) equation that slopes upward. In this context, monetary policy takes on the role in mitigating fluctuations in output, signifying its importance in stabilizing the economy.

The AD and AS equations of the benchmark NK model are both forward looking. In the AD equation, output depends negatively on the current and expected values of the real interest rate, which monetary policy can directly influence through the nominal interest rate. In the AS equation, inflation depends on the present-discounted value of current and future output gaps.

5.3   Model

The model is stochastic and the characterization of uncertainty follows the presentation given in Section 4.3 of Chapter 4. Recall that s_t defines the state of nature at time t in a set S that is invariant across time, and $f(s^t|s_{t_0})$ is the probability distribution of the history s^t conditional on the state of nature being s_{t_0} at time t_0. The history s^t is defined as the sequence of states of nature up to time t, i.e., $s^t \equiv (s_t, s_{t-1}, s_{t-2}, \ldots, s_{t_0})$. There are three agents in the economy: households, firms, and the government. We are going to describe them in turn.

5.3.1   Households

Preferences of consumers are now represented by

$$E_{t_0} \left\{ \sum_{t=t_0}^{\infty} \beta^{t-t_0} \xi_t \left[U(C_t) - \int_0^1 H(L_t(j)) dj \right] \right\}, \qquad (5.1)$$

in which $E_{t_0}\{\cdot\}$ is the expectation operator at time t_0; β, with $0 < \beta < 1$, is the utility discount factor; ξ is a preference shock; $U(\cdot)$ is an increasing and concave function of (C), which is the Dixit-Stiglitz aggregator of a continuum of consumption goods produced in the economy,

$$C_t = \left[\int_0^1 C_t(j)^{\frac{\theta-1}{\theta}} dj \right]^{\frac{\theta}{\theta-1}}, \tag{5.2}$$

where $\theta > 1$ is the elasticity of substitution across the goods $(C(j))$, with $j \in [0, 1]$.[1] There is a measure one of consumption goods, which are not perfectly substitutable according to the aggregator (5.2). The parameter θ measures the degree of substitution of the goods in consumption. The higher the θ, the higher the degree of substitution; when $\theta \to \infty$, goods are perfectly substitutable, i.e., $C_t = \int_0^1 C_t(j) dj$.

Given this preference structure and prices $P_t(j)$ for each good, a household's demand for the single good j is represented by

$$C_t(j) = \left(\frac{P_t(j)}{P_t} \right)^{-\theta} C_t, \tag{5.3}$$

which depends on the relative price of good j with respect to the overall price index (P),

$$P_t = \left[\int_0^1 P_t(j)^{1-\theta} dj \right]^{\frac{1}{1-\theta}}. \tag{5.4}$$

P is an appropriate "sum" of the prices of the single good j.[2] Consumption demand (5.3) of good j depends on its price $(P(j))$ because goods are imperfectly substitutable in consumption. This demand function will be the key, later in the firms' problem, to characterizing the model of monopolistic competition.

In the utility function (5.1), $(L(j))$ is hours worked, supplied by the households to the firms producing good j, and $H(\cdot)$ is a convex, differentiable function in its argument. Households supply labor to all firms, in a separable way.

At each point in time, households optimize with respect to their consumption, saving plans, and hours worked. In their saving plans, they have access to an ample spectrum of assets to trade in, for we assume that financial markets are complete. This means that there exists a sufficient number of alternative investments at each date to allow a household to achieve an arbitrary pattern of payoffs across the successor states.

---

1. Refer to Dixit and Stiglitz (1977).
2. The demand function (5.3) and the price index (5.4) are derived in Appendix D.

Let $\mathcal{W}(s_{t+1}|s^t)$ denote the payoff in the state of nature s_{t+1} at time $t+1$ of the household's portfolio chosen at time t conditional on the history s^t. Use $\mathcal{W}_t(s_{t+1})$ to denote $\mathcal{W}(s_{t+1}|s^t)$. Complete markets mean that any desired random pattern $\mathcal{W}_t(s_{t+1})$ with $s_{t+1} \in S$ can be achieved by purchasing the right portfolio of available assets. The number of types of assets traded at date t must be at least as large as the number of states that occur at time $t+1$. Furthermore, the absence of arbitrage opportunities requires that the price at time t of any portfolio that has the same random payoff, $\mathcal{W}_t(s_{t+1})$, be the same regardless of the combination of assets that achieves it.

A way to characterize complete financial markets is to assume the existence of a set of state-contingent securities that at each point in time span all states of nature with the characteristic that each security delivers one unit of currency in one of the states and zero in all others. Let $v_t(s_{t+1})/(1+i_t)$ denote the price at time t, conditional on the history s^t, of the security that delivers one unit of currency at time $t+1$ in state s_{t+1} and zero in all other states. The normalization of the price by the factor $(1+i_t)$ is done for analytical convenience and without losing generality, where i_t is the risk-free nominal interest rate controlled by the central bank.

For a portfolio to achieve a state-contingent payoff $\mathcal{W}_t(s_{t+1})$, households should buy $\mathcal{W}_t(s_{t+1})$ units of the state-contingent security delivering one unit of currency in state s_{t+1} for a total cost of $v_t(s_{t+1})/(1+i_t) \times \mathcal{W}_t(s_{t+1})$ for that security. Therefore, with the absence of arbitrage opportunities, the value of a portfolio held at time t—let's call it B_t—with random payoff $\mathcal{W}_t(s_{t+1})$ is equal to

$$B_t = \sum_{s_{t+1} \in S} \frac{v_t(s_{t+1})}{1+i_t} \mathcal{W}_t(s_{t+1}).$$

Defining the nominal stochastic discount factor $\tilde{R}_t(s_{t+1})$ as

$$\tilde{R}_t(s_{t+1}) \equiv \frac{v_t(s_{t+1})}{f_t(s_{t+1})(1+i_t)},$$

where $f_t(s_{t+1}) \equiv f_t(s_{t+1}|s^t)$, we can write

$$B_t = \sum_{s_{t+1} \in S} f_t(s_{t+1}) \frac{v_t(s_{t+1})}{f_t(s_{t+1})(1+i_t)} \mathcal{W}_t(s_{t+1})$$

$$= \sum_{s_{t+1} \in S} f_t(s_{t+1}) \tilde{R}_t(s_{t+1}) \mathcal{W}_t(s_{t+1})$$

$$= E_t \tilde{R}_{t,t+1} \mathcal{W}_{t+1}.$$

The price of a portfolio with a random return W_{t+1} is equal to the expected discounted value of its payoff, where the discount factor is represented by the random variable $\tilde{R}_{t,t+1} \equiv \tilde{R}_t(s_{t+1})$. Note that for simplicity we have used the notation W_{t+1} in place of $W_{t,t+1}$.

If we consider a portfolio that delivers one unit of currency in each state of nature, i.e., $W_t(s_{t+1}) = 1$ for each $s_{t+1} \in S$, this portfolio replicates the risk-free nominal bond. Note that the price of a risk-free nominal bond is $1/(1+i_t)$. Therefore, applying the above formula, with $W_{t+1} = 1$ and $B_t = 1/(1+i_t)$, it should be that

$$\frac{1}{1+i_t} = E_t \tilde{R}_{t,t+1}$$

and using the definition of $\tilde{R}_{t,t+1}$ it follows that

$$\sum_{s_{t+1} \in S} v_t(s_{t+1}) = 1.$$

Given the structure of financial markets described above, households are subject to a flow budget constraint of the form

$$B_t + P_t C_t = W_t + \int_0^1 W_t(j)L_t(j)dj + \Psi_t - T_t, \qquad (5.5)$$

given that B_t is the value of a portfolio with next-period state-contingent payoff W_{t+1},

$$B_t = E_t(\tilde{R}_{t,t+1}W_{t+1}). \qquad (5.6)$$

The right-hand side of (5.5) represents the resources that a household has at time t: namely, the payoff of the portfolio held from period $t-1$, i.e., W_t; labor income $W_t(j)L_t(j)$ for each variety of labor j supplied, in which $(W(j))$ is the nominal wage specific to the sector producing good j; firms' profits (Ψ), less taxes (T). The resources at time t are spent in purchasing consumption goods C_t, at price P_t, and the portfolio of value B_t.

The central bank can also issue coins and banknotes, but those are dominated by the other securities and will not be held by the households unless the nominal interest rate is zero. We neglect them in the following analysis. However, the potential supply of physical money imposes a zero lower bound constraint on the nominal interest rate.

The household maximizes utility under (5.5), (5.6), and an appropriate borrowing limit condition of the form

$$-W_t \leq E_t \left\{ \sum_{T=t}^{\infty} \tilde{R}_{t,T}(W_T L_T + \Psi_T - T_T) \right\} < \infty,$$

for each time $t \geq t_0$ and contingency at time t; or, alternatively, under intertemporal budget constraint

$$E_t \left\{ \sum_{T=t}^{\infty} \tilde{R}_{t,T}(P_T C_T) \right\} \leq W_t + E_t \left\{ \sum_{T=t}^{\infty} \tilde{R}_{t,T}(W_T L_T + \Psi_T - T_T) \right\}, \quad (5.7)$$

for each time $t \geq t_0$ and contingency at time t, saying that the expected present-discounted value of consumption expenditures should not be greater than the payoff of the portfolio of financial assets held from the previous period plus the present-discounted value of net income of the households. The above intertemporal budget constraint can be equivalently written in real terms for a finite price sequence.

The following set of first-order conditions characterizes the optimal consumption/saving choices at each point in time t

$$\frac{\xi_t U_c(C_t)}{P_t} = \frac{\beta}{\tilde{R}_{t,t+1}} \frac{\xi_{t+1} U_c(C_{t+1})}{P_{t+1}}, \quad (5.8)$$

in which $U_c(\cdot)$ is the first derivative of the function $U(\cdot)$ with respect to its argument. Looking forward from time t, there is a set of first-order conditions (Euler equations) equal to the number of states of nature at time $t + 1$. This is an implication of the complete market assumption, for which households can optimally allocate consumption and savings, looking forward from a generic time t with respect to each of the contingencies at time $t + 1$. The above set of Euler equations can be equivalently written as

$$\frac{v_t(s_{t+1})}{(1 + i_t)} \frac{\xi_t U_c(C_t)}{P_t} = \beta f_t(s_{t+1}) \frac{\xi_{t+1} U_c(C_{t+1})}{P_{t+1}}.$$

The left-hand side represents the marginal costs of saving one unit of consumption at time t invested at the price $v_t(s_{t+1})/(1 + i_t)$ in the state-contingent security that delivers one unit of currency in state s_{t+1} at time $t + 1$; the right-hand side represents the marginal benefits of saving that unit and consuming it at time $t + 1$ in state s_{t+1}. This benefit is positive with probability $f_t(s_{t+1})$.

Multiplying (5.8) by the factor $\tilde{R}_{t,t+1}$ and taking the expectation at time t, we obtain the stochastic Euler equation:

$$\xi_t U_c(C_t) = \beta(1 + i_t) E_t \left\{ \frac{P_t}{P_{t+1}} \xi_{t+1} U_c(C_{t+1}) \right\}, \quad (5.9)$$

using $E_t \tilde{R}_{t,t+1} = 1/(1 + i_t)$. Note that the stochastic Euler equation (5.9) is implied by the set of state-contingent Euler equations (5.8), but it does not imply them.

The marginal rate of substitution between each variety $j \in [0, 1]$ of labor and consumption is equated to the real wage for that variety by the optimal choice on how much labor to supply,

$$\frac{H_l(L_t(j))}{U_c(C_t)} = \frac{W_t(j)}{P_t}, \tag{5.10}$$

in which $H_l(\cdot)$ is the first derivative of the function $H(\cdot)$ with respect to its argument. Given the concavity of utility $U(\cdot)$ and the convexity of $H(\cdot)$ with respect to their arguments, labor supply is a positive function of the real wage and a negative one of consumption. Finally, in the optimal allocation, the intertemporal budget constraint (5.7) holds with equality at each point in time and contingency.

5.3.2 Firms

There is a continuum of firms in which each produces one of the goods supplied in the economy. Consider a generic firm of type j producing good j, with $j \in [0, 1]$. It faces an overall demand

$$Y_t(j) = C_t(j) + G_t(j)$$

at each point in time. Let us assume that government expenditure of good j, $G_t(j)$, is of a form similar to that of demand (5.3), i.e., $G_t(j) = (P_t(j)/P_t)^{-\theta} G_t$, where G_t is aggregate government purchases. The overall demand of the goods produced by firm j at time t, $Y_t(j)$, is

$$Y_t(j) = \left(\frac{P_t(j)}{P_t}\right)^{-\theta} (C_t + G_t). \tag{5.11}$$

Goods are produced according to technology $Y_t(j) = A_t L_t(j)$; A_t is labor productivity, which is the same for all firms producing in the economy and is also a stochastic disturbance.

Firm j's profits are

$$\Psi_t(j) = (1 + \tau_t^s) P_t(j) Y_t(j) - W_t(j) L_t(j)$$

$$= \left[(1 + \tau_t^s) P_t(j) - \frac{W_t(j)}{A_t}\right] Y_t(j), \tag{5.12}$$

in which τ_t^s is a subsidy on firms' revenue. In going from the first to the second line of equation (5.12), we have used $L_t(j) = Y_t(j)/A_t$ through the production function. There is a dual purpose of adding a subsidy to a firm's revenue which is also a stochastic process: first, it can produce stochastic variations in the markup; second, it can be used to make the steady-state equilibrium efficient, which is a convenient simplification for the analysis of optimal policy, as we will see in Chapter 7. Firms operate in a market characterized by monopolistic competition. The key feature is that the goods consumed are not perfectly substitutable for the consumers in the aggregator (5.2). Therefore, firms have some power to influence their demand by varying the price $P_t(j)$ they set through (5.11). However, they are small with respect to the overall market and also take aggregate price P and quantities C and G as a given.

5.3.3   Government

Let us consider a consolidated budget constraint between the treasury and the central bank, represented by

$$
\begin{aligned}
B_t^g &= (1 + i_{t-1})B_{t-1}^g + \int_0^1 P_t(j)G_t(j)dj + \tau_t^s \int_0^1 P_t(j)Y_t(j) - T_t \\
&= (1 + i_{t-1})B_{t-1}^g + P_t G_t + \tau_t^s P_t Y_t - T_t,
\end{aligned}
\tag{5.13}
$$

which now includes government nominal spending, $P_t G_t$, and government subsidy to all firms, $\tau_t^s P_t Y_t$; B_t^g is government debt and T_t are lumpsum taxes. In going from the first to the second line of equation (5.13), we have used the demand functions $G_t(j) = (P_t(j)/P_t)^{-\theta}G_t$ and $Y_t(j) = (P_t(j)/P_t)^{-\theta}Y_t$, and the price index P_t defined by (5.4). It is assumed that the central bank backs the treasury along the lines discussed in Section 1.4 of Chapter 1 and, therefore, all government debt is not subject to a solvency condition.

5.4   Equilibrium with Flexible Prices

With flexible prices, a generic firm j sets its price, $P_t(j)$, to maximize its profits (5.12) given the demand (5.11). The optimal choice implies that the price $P_t(j)$ is set as a markup over marginal cost,

$$
P_t(j) = \mu_t \frac{W_t(j)}{A_t},
$$

in which

$$\mu_t \equiv \frac{1}{1+\tau_t^s}\frac{\theta}{\theta-1}$$

is the markup, which also includes variations in the tax subsidy, and $W_t(j)/A_t$ are nominal marginal costs specific to firm j. The firm j's labor demand is flat at the real wage,

$$\frac{W_t(j)}{P_t(j)} = \frac{A_t}{\mu_t},$$

which is constant across all firms j. Equating the demand for labor and its supply (5.10), we obtain

$$\frac{H_l(L_t(j))}{U_c(C_t)} = \frac{A_t}{\mu_t},$$

for each j. It follows that equilibrium labor to produce each good j is equal across firms, $L_t(j) = L_t$. Therefore, output $Y(j)$ is also equal across firms producing different goods. Given the demand function (5.11), prices are also equalized, $P_t(j) = P_t$ for each j.

We can substitute L_t in the above expression with Y_t/A_t, using the aggregate production function $Y_t = A_t L_t$, and C_t with $Y_t - G_t$, using equilibrium in the goods market $Y_t = C_t + G_t$, to determine the output level, which we label as the natural rate of output (Y^n).[3] It is implicitly defined by

$$\frac{H_l\left(\frac{Y_t^n}{A_t}\right)}{U_c(Y_t^n - G_t)} = \frac{A_t}{\mu_t}. \tag{5.14}$$

Given the properties of utility, this natural level of output is a positive function of productivity and government purchases, while it is negatively related to the markup. When productivity rises, firms are willing to hire labor at a higher real wage. Since labor supply is upward sloping in real wage, equilibrium labor increases. Output rises also for the increase in productivity. A rise in markup pushes down labor demand, as well as equilibrium labor. In contrast, an increase in government purchase leads to a positive wealth effect that raises labor supply and equilibrium labor. Output rises but consumption falls.

An important implication of equation (5.14) for output, in this flexible-price equilibrium, is that the model features the classical dichotomy in which the real allocation is independent of monetary policy. Monetary policy does

---

3. In the asset markets, the state-contingent securities are in zero-net supply within households and government debt is held by households.

not influence output. On the contrary, it can affect the determination of nominal variables, such as interest rates and prices, as in the model of Chapter 1. Indeed, the analysis in Chapter 1 applies here with the caveats that the model economy is now stochastic and the output is endogenous.

It is interesting to compare the natural rate of output implied by (5.14) with the efficient level. The latter solves a central planner problem in which the utility of consumers (5.1) is maximized under the resource constraint $Y_t = C_t + G_t$ and technology $Y_t = A_t L_t$. The problem becomes static and boils down to maximizing $U(Y_t - G_t) - H(Y_t/A_t)$ with respect to Y_t. The first-order condition defines the efficient level of output (Y_t^e) through

$$\frac{H_l\left(\frac{Y_t^e}{A_t}\right)}{U_c(Y_t^e - G_t)} = A_t. \tag{5.15}$$

Comparing (5.14) and (5.15) shows that markup shocks perturb the natural rate of output but not the efficient level, and therefore they are inefficient shocks. In contrast, productivity and public spending shocks move natural and efficient levels of output in the same proportion.

5.5   Price Rigidities

The neutrality result of monetary policy's effect on output can be broken by assuming some form of price rigidity. In this chapter, we will consider a price-setting mechanism as in the Calvo-Yun model,[4] which has become the benchmark paradigm for modelling price rigidities in the New-Keynesian literature. Given a continuum of firms on the segment [0, 1], there is a lottery each period for which a measure, $1 - \alpha$, with $0 < \alpha < 1$, is selected to change their prices at each point in time, t, independently of the last time they reset their price. A firm understands that the price chosen at time t is going to be in place also at the next time, $t + 1$, with probability α, in the event the firm is not chosen again to reset its price. Therefore, the price chosen, $P_t(j)$, is going to apply at a generic future time $T > t$ with a probability α^{T-t}. During the periods in which firms are not chosen to reset their price, prices are going to be automatically indexed to the inflation target (Π). Therefore, if the price $P_t(j)$ chosen at time t still applies at time T, it becomes $P_t(j)\Pi^{T-t}$. Adjusting

4. Refer to Calvo (1983) and Yun (1996).

firms choose prices to maximize the presented discounted value of the profits under the circumstances that the price chosen, appropriately indexed to the inflation target, still remains in place. Consider profits at time $T > t$ in the contingency in which the price chosen at time t still applies. They are represented by

$$\Psi_T(j) = (1 + \tau_T^s) P_t(j) \Pi^{T-t} Y_T(j) - W_T(j) L_T(j)$$

$$= (1 + \tau_T^s) P_t(j) \Pi^{T-t} Y_T(j) - \frac{W_T(j)}{A_T} Y_T(j),$$

in which the price that applies in that contingency is indeed $P_t(j) \Pi^{T-t}$ and in which from the first to the second line we have substituted $L_T(j) = Y_T(j)/A_T$ and demand at time T is represented by

$$Y_T(j) = \left(\frac{P_t(j) \Pi^{T-t}}{P_T} \right)^{-\theta} Y_T. \qquad (5.16)$$

Therefore, the expected present-discounted value of profits under the contingencies in which the price chosen at time t still applies is represented by:

$$E_t \sum_{T=t}^{\infty} (\alpha)^{T-t} \tilde{R}_{t,T} \left[(1 + \tau_T^s) \Pi^{T-t} P_t(j) Y_T(j) - \frac{W_T(j)}{A_T} Y_T(j) \right]. \qquad (5.17)$$

A generic firm j chooses price $P_t(j)$ to maximize (5.17) given demand (5.16).[5] The first-order condition can be written as

$$\frac{P_t(j)}{P_t} = \frac{E_t \left\{ \sum_{T=t}^{\infty} (\alpha\beta)^{T-t} \xi_T U_c(C_T) \left(\frac{P_T}{P_t} \frac{1}{\Pi^{T-t}} \right)^{\theta} \frac{W_T(j)}{A_T P_T} Y_T \right\}}{E_t \left\{ \sum_{T=t}^{\infty} (\alpha\beta)^{T-t} \xi_T U_c(C_T) \left(\frac{P_T}{P_t} \frac{1}{\Pi^{T-t}} \right)^{\theta-1} \frac{Y_T}{\mu_T} \right\}}, \qquad (5.18)$$

where the discount factor $\tilde{R}_{t,T}$ has been replaced by

$$\tilde{R}_{t,T} \equiv \beta^{T-t} \frac{\xi_T U_c(C_T)}{\xi_t U_c(C_t)} \frac{P_t}{P_T}.$$

5. Firms take wages $W(j)$ as given, which could be rationalized more formally by considering that each good j is produced in a sector j with a measure one of identical firms. A generic firm in the sector can then be considered small and a wage-taker.

using the Euler equation (5.8) and we have used the definition $\mu_t \equiv \theta/[(1 + \tau_t^s)(\theta - 1)]$. Note that in equilibrium all firms that adjust their prices set them at the same level, i.e., $P_t(j) = \mathcal{P}_t^*$.[6]

To simplify the analysis, we make a special isoleastic assumption on the disutility of labor:

$$H(L(j)) = \frac{L(j)^{1+\eta}}{1+\eta},$$

in which η is the Frisch elasticity of labor supply, with $\eta \geq 0$.

We now use (5.10), $L_T(j) = Y_T(j)/A_T$ and (5.16) to substitute $W_T(j)/P_T$ in (5.18), obtaining

$$\left(\frac{\mathcal{P}_t^*}{P_t}\right)^{1+\theta\eta} = \frac{E_t\left\{\sum_{T=t}^{\infty}(\alpha\beta)^{T-t}\xi_T \left(\frac{P_T}{P_t}\frac{1}{\Pi^{T-t}}\right)^{\theta(1+\eta)} \left(\frac{Y_T}{A_T}\right)^{1+\eta}\right\}}{E_t\left\{\sum_{T=t}^{\infty}(\alpha\beta)^{T-t}\xi_T U_c(C_T) \left(\frac{P_T}{P_t}\frac{1}{\Pi^{T-t}}\right)^{\theta-1} \frac{Y_T}{\mu_T}\right\}}.$$

$$(5.19)$$

The remaining fraction α of firms—not chosen to adjust their prices—index their previously adjusted prices to the inflation target Π. Calvo's model further implies the following law of motion for the general price index P_t:

$$P_t^{1-\theta} = (1-\alpha)(\mathcal{P}_t^*)^{1-\theta} + \alpha\Pi^{1-\theta}P_{t-1}^{1-\theta}, \qquad (5.20)$$

using (5.4). The above expression can be derived formally by noting that

$$P_t^{1-\theta} = (1-\alpha)\sum_{j=0}^{\infty}\alpha^j(\Pi^j\mathcal{P}_{t-j}^*)^{1-\theta}$$

$$= (1-\alpha)(\mathcal{P}_t^*)^{1-\theta} + \alpha\Pi^{1-\theta}\left\{(1-\alpha)\sum_{j=0}^{\infty}\alpha^j(\Pi^j\mathcal{P}_{t-1-j}^*)^{1-\theta}\right\}$$

$$= (1-\alpha)(\mathcal{P}_t^*)^{1-\theta} + \alpha\Pi^{1-\theta}P_{t-1}^{1-\theta},$$

using the law of large numbers. The first line says that at time t a mass $(1-\alpha)$ sets the price $\mathcal{P}_t^*$, a mass $(1-\alpha)\alpha$ sets $\mathcal{P}_{t-1}^*\Pi$, a mass $(1-\alpha)\alpha^2$ sets $\mathcal{P}_{t-2}^*\Pi^2$, and so forth. From the second line to the third line, the term in the curly brackets is $P_{t-1}^{1-\theta}$.

---

6. It should be noted that the left-hand side of (5.18) increases in $P_t(j)$, while the right-hand side decreases, because of the dependence of $W_T(j)$ on $P_t(j)$, using (5.10), $L_T(j) = Y_T(j)/A_T$, and (5.16), therefore ensuring uniqueness of the optimal price $\mathcal{P}_t^*$.

By substituting equilibrium in the goods market, $Y_t = C_t + G_t$, for consumption, and the labor supply (5.10) for the real wage, and by using (5.20) to substitute $\mathcal{P}_t^*/P_t$, we can further write (5.19) as

$$\left(\frac{1 - \alpha \left(\frac{\Pi_t}{\Pi}\right)^{\theta-1}}{1 - \alpha}\right)^{\frac{1+\theta\eta}{\theta-1}} = \frac{F_t}{J_t}, \qquad (5.21)$$

where $\Pi_t = P_t/P_{t-1}$, and F_t and J_t satisfy:

$$F_t = \xi_t U_c(Y_t - G_t)\frac{Y_t}{\mu_t} + \alpha\beta E_t\left\{\left(\frac{\Pi_{t+1}}{\Pi}\right)^{\theta-1} F_{t+1}\right\}, \qquad (5.22)$$

$$J_t = \xi_t \left(\frac{Y_t}{A_t}\right)^{1+\eta} + \alpha\beta E_t\left\{\left(\frac{\Pi_{t+1}}{\Pi}\right)^{\theta(1+\eta)} J_{t+1}\right\}. \qquad (5.23)$$

5.5.1 Equilibrium with Price Rigidities

We will succinctly describe the equilibrium allocation. This is a set of stochastic processes $\{P_t, i_t, Y_t, F_t, J_t, T_t, B_t^g\}_{t=t_0}^{\infty}$ that satisfy the aggregate demand equation,

$$\xi_t U_c(Y_t - G_t) = \beta(1 + i_t)E_t\left\{\frac{P_t}{P_{t+1}}\xi_{t+1}U_c(Y_{t+1} - G_{t+1})\right\}, \qquad (5.24)$$

the aggregate supply block represented by (5.21), (5.22), (5.23), and the government's flow budget constraint (5.13), together with the intertemporal resource constraint of the economy (which is the mirror image of the intertemporal budget constraint of the households through goods and asset market equilibrium),

$$\frac{B_{t-1}^g}{P_t} = E_t\left\{\sum_{T=t}^{\infty}\beta^{T-t}\frac{\xi_T U_c(Y_T - G_T)}{\xi_t U_c(Y_t - G_t)}\left(\frac{T_T}{P_T} - \tau_T^s Y_T - G_T\right)\right\}, \qquad (5.25)$$

given the zero lower bound on the nominal interest rate, $i_t \geq 0$, exogenous stochastic processes $\{\xi_t, A_t, G_t, \tau_t^s\}_{t=t_0}^{\infty}$, and the appropriate initial conditions.[7] There are two degrees of freedom left to specify the monetary/fiscal

---

7. Recall that the markup shock, μ_t, is a function of τ_t^s.

policy regime. In what follows we assume that the government sets the stochastic path of lumpsum taxes and interest rates, $\{T_t, i_t\}_{t=t_0}^{\infty}$.

5.5.2 Log-linear Approximation

Solving for the equilibrium in closed form is not feasible. An alternative approach involves two key steps: 1) characterizing the steady-state equilibrium of the economy; 2) approximating the equilibrium conditions around the steady state using log-linear approximation techniques.

This method allows for the examination of how the equilibrium responds to small perturbations in the shocks relative to their steady-state values.

The first step is to characterize the steady-state equilibrium. We assume that the shocks are all constant, $\xi_t = \xi$, $A_t = A$, $G_t = G$, and $\mu_t = 1$. In particular, $\mu_t = 1$ is obtained by setting the tax subsidy in the steady state to $\tau^s = 1/(\theta - 1)$. In this steady state, monetary policy sets the inflation rate at the target Π. Using $\Pi_t = \Pi$ in the non-stochastic version of (5.24), it follows that the nominal interest rate is $1 + i = \beta^{-1}\Pi$ in the steady state. Again, setting $\Pi_t = \Pi$ in the non-stochastic version of (5.21), (5.22), and (5.23), it follows that $F = J$ and that $F = \xi U_c(Y - G)Y/(1 - \alpha\beta)$ and $J = \xi(Y/A)^{1+\eta}/(1 - \alpha\beta)$. Therefore, the steady state of output is implicitly given by $(Y/A)^{\eta} = AU_c(Y - G)$, which coincides with the efficient steady-state level of output (5.15).[8]

The second step involves taking a log-linear approximation of the equilibrium conditions around the above-determined steady state. The aggregate demand equation (5.24) can be written as

$$\hat{Y}_t = \hat{G}_t + E_t(\hat{Y}_{t+1} - \hat{G}_{t+1}) - \sigma\left(\hat{i}_t - E_t(\pi_{t+1} - \pi) + E_t(\hat{\xi}_{t+1} - \hat{\xi}_t)\right),$$
(5.26)

while the aggregate supply block, which consists of equations (5.21)–(5.23), collapses to the AS equation

$$\pi_t - \pi = \kappa(\hat{Y}_t - \hat{Y}_t^n) + \beta E_t(\pi_{t+1} - \pi),$$
(5.27)

with

$$\kappa \equiv \frac{1 - \alpha}{\alpha}\frac{(1 - \alpha\beta)(\sigma^{-1} + \eta)}{(1 + \theta\eta)},$$
(5.28)

8. Indeed, the steady-state tax subsidy is set to completely offset the monopolistic distortions.

where variables with hats denote log deviations of the related variables with respect to the steady state, while $\hat{\imath}_t = \ln[(1 + i_t)/(1 + i)]$, $\hat{G}_t = (G_t - G)/Y$, $\pi_t \equiv \ln \Pi_t$, $\pi \equiv \ln \Pi$, and $\sigma \equiv -U_c/(U_{cc}Y)$, with U_c, and U_{cc} representing the first and second derivatives of the function $U(\cdot)$ evaluated at the steady state.[9] In a log-linear approximation, the natural and efficient levels of output, implicitly defined by equations (5.14) and (5.15), are respectively represented by

$$\hat{Y}_t^n = \frac{1 + \eta}{\sigma^{-1} + \eta}\hat{A}_t + \frac{\sigma^{-1}}{\sigma^{-1} + \eta}\hat{G}_t - \frac{1}{\sigma^{-1} + \eta}\hat{\mu}_t \qquad (5.29)$$

and

$$\hat{Y}_t^e = \frac{1 + \eta}{\sigma^{-1} + \eta}\hat{A}_t + \frac{\sigma^{-1}}{\sigma^{-1} + \eta}\hat{G}_t. \qquad (5.30)$$

Some comments are worth making to describe the main features of the NK model in its log-linear approximation. First, the AD and AS schedules represent a set of two equilibrium conditions in two unknowns, inflation and output, given that monetary policy sets the nominal interest rate.[10] In the models of Chapters 1–4 monetary policy was neutral on output; but it is sufficient to add some friction on price adjustment, as in this framework, to have monetary policy influencing output.

Secondly, the consequence of price rigidity is reflected in the upward-sloping AS equation, which demonstrates a positive comovement between inflation and output. An increase in output exerts pressure on firms' marginal costs and, as a result, on inflation. To determine output, one must consider how inflation and output move together within the AS equation, in conjunction with the AD schedule and the interaction with monetary policy. The case of neutrality can be obtained when all firms, in Calvo's model, are free to set their prices at each point in time, i.e., $\alpha = 0$. In this case, $\kappa \longrightarrow \infty$, and the AS equation becomes vertical with $\hat{Y}_t = \hat{Y}_t^n$ at all times. With price rigidities,

9. Appendix E presents the log-linear approximation of equations (5.26) and (5.27).

10. In what follows, we consider tax policies such that constraints (5.13) and (5.25) do not impose restrictions on the equilibrium in a local analysis. Using the terminology of Section 1.4.1 of Chapter 1, these policies are identified as (locally) passive fiscal policies.

what matters, however, is not much the variations in output, but those with respect to the natural rate of output, i.e., the output gap. The *AS* equation has also another important characteristic, that of being forward looking, since current inflation depends not only on the output gap but also on the discounted expectations of the future inflation rate. Iterating equation (5.27) forward, we can write

$$\pi_t - \pi = \kappa E_t \sum_{T=t}^{\infty} \beta^{T-t} \left(\hat{Y}_T - \hat{Y}_T^n \right),$$

showing that variations of the future output gap, appropriately discounted, also matter for the deviations of inflation with respect to the target. A positive output gap in the future leads to pressure on current inflation above target.

Third, the *AD* equation also has two main characteristics: i) it displays a relationship between output and the real interest rate; ii) it is forward looking. With respect to the first characteristic, equation (5.26) shows that output at time t is negatively related to the real interest rate, captured in a log-linear approximation by the term $\hat{\imath}_t - E_t(\pi_{t+1} - \pi)$, through the parameter σ, the intertemporal elasticity of substitution. An increase in the real interest rate lowers output because households would like to save more and, therefore, current consumption falls, driving demand, and then output, down. The higher the elasticity of substitution in consumption, the greater are the sensitivities of consumption and output to variations in the real interest rate. The real rate is the key transmission channel through which monetary policy acts in the model, and it does so in two ways: i) by maneuvering the policy rate $\hat{\imath}$; ii) by influencing inflation expectations with respect to the target, the term $E_t(\pi_{t+1} - \pi)$. The second characteristic of the *AD* equation can be seen through the dependence of current output on its next period value. Iterating the equation forward, we obtain

$$\hat{Y}_t = \hat{G}_t + \sigma \hat{\xi}_t - \sigma E_t \sum_{T=t}^{\infty} \left(\hat{\imath}_T - (\pi_{T+1} - \pi) \right) + \lim_{T \to \infty} (\hat{Y}_T - \hat{G}_T - \sigma \hat{\xi}_T).$$

Output depends not only on the current real rate but also—on an equal ground—on its expected future path. Same variations in current or future rates have the same effects on current output.

Finally, equations (5.29) and (5.30) show, respectively, the determinants of the natural and the efficient levels of output in a log-linear approximation.

As already noted, markup shocks produce variations only in the natural level of output and, therefore, they are inefficient shocks. The natural rate of output falls as markup shocks increase. In contrast, productivity and public spending shocks have a positive relationship with the two measures of output. An interesting result is that a public spending shock has a multiplier on output that is less than the unitary value, therefore crowding out consumption, unless the disutility of labor is linear, i.e., $\eta = 0$. The multiplier of a productivity shock is higher or lower than the unitary value, depending on the elasticity of substitution σ being higher or lower than the unitary value.

5.6 References

The New Keynesian model is extensively discussed in the works of Woodford (2003) and Galí (2008). The original Calvo-Yun price-setting model, which further developed Calvo's (1983) model, can be found in Yun (1996). Some of the early precursors to microfounded models with monopolistic competition and sticky prices include Blanchard and Kiyotaki (1987), Ball and Romer (1990), and Mankiw (1985). In a log-linear approximation, the AS equation derived from Calvo's model can also be equivalently obtained through a model with quadratic costs of price adjustments, as discussed in Rotemberg (1982). Ascari and Sbordone (2014) analyze the implications of the AS equation when there are stochastic shifts in trend inflation to which prices are not indexed.

The Calvo-Yun model belongs to the class of time-dependent price adjustment models such as the one in Taylor (1979). Alternative models have been proposed, allowing prices to adjust depending on contingencies, as seen in Mankiw (1985), which considers the cost of changing prices. Dotsey, King, and Wolman (1999) and Golosov and Lucas (2007) are early examples of quantitative analyses comparing state-contingent models with time-dependent models. Subsequent literature has further explored these comparisons. An important insight derived from this literature for the New Keynesian model in this chapter comes from Auclert et al. (2024), showing that a canonical state-dependent model is equivalent to a mixture of two time-dependent models, and numerically this mixture is closely approximated by the Calvo-Yun model.

Mankiw and Reis (2002) discuss an alternative price-setting mechanism based on the assumption of delays in the information set of price setters.

Finally, the benchmark model in this chapter has been extended in various directions to include features such as investment, wage rigidity, and more, to align with empirical data. Christiano, Eichenbaum, and Evans (2005) and Smets and Wouters (2007) provide early examples of estimated medium-scale models that have served as the foundation for the large-scale models developed by various central banks.

6

An AS-AD Graphical Analysis

6.1 Introduction

This chapter analyzes the implications of the model set up in Chapter 5 through a graphical analysis and using some simplifying assumptions. We focus on a perfect foresight economy that adjusts in two periods, t, the short run, and $t+1$, the long run. In the long run, we assume that prices are completely flexible and therefore output is at the natural rate, $\hat{Y}_{t+1} = \hat{Y}_{t+1}^n$. Long-run prices are anchored at $p_{t+1} = p^*$ by an appropriate fiscal and monetary policy.[1] To further simplify the analysis, we set the inflation target to zero, $\pi = 0$, and the initial price level at time $t-1$ to $p_{t-1} = p^*$. Under these assumptions and in a perfect-foresight equilibrium, the AD equation (5.26) can be written as

$$\hat{Y}_t = \hat{G}_t + \hat{Y}_{t+1}^n - \hat{G}_{t+1} - \sigma\left(\hat{i}_t + p_t - p^* + \hat{\xi}_{t+1} - \hat{\xi}_t\right), \qquad (6.1)$$

which is a negative relationship, in the short run, between output, $\hat{Y}_t$, and price level, p_t, since σ is a positive parameter. Figure 6.1 plots this negatively sloped function. The relationship is negative because, following an increase in the current price level, given other variables, the real interest rate rises, creating incentives for consumers to postpone consumption. This leads to a cut in current consumption and then to a fall in output.

Several factors can shift the AD equation. Starting from those of an exogenous nature, short-run and long-run shocks such as $\hat{G}_t$, $\hat{G}_{t+1}$, $\hat{\xi}_t$, and $\hat{\xi}_{t+1}$ and those influencing the long-run natural level of output, $\hat{Y}_{t+1}^n$, move the AD

---

1. This is an important assumption in the context of this analysis, which is supported by the results of Chapter 7, showing that under optimal policy prices revert back to their initial value in the long run.

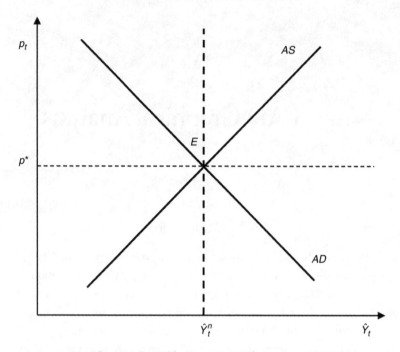

FIGURE 6.1. The initial equilibrium is in E, where AS and AD intersect.

equation. Recall that G is public spending and ξ is a shock that affects the preferences of the consumer. Monetary policy also has an important role in shifting the AD equation, acting on the policy rate $\hat{\imath}_t$ and on the future price level p^*.

The same assumptions applied to the AS equation (5.27) imply the following simplification:

$$p_t - p^* = \frac{\kappa}{1+\beta}(\hat{Y}_t - \hat{Y}_t^n), \tag{6.2}$$

displaying a positive relationship between the current price level and output since κ and β are positive parameters. As output rises, marginal costs of firms increase, putting upward pressure on the price level. Only short-run shocks influencing the natural level output, $\hat{Y}_t^n$, matter as shifters of the equation.[2] The AS equation is plotted in Figure 6.1, showing that it goes through point $\hat{Y}_t = \hat{Y}_t^n$, $p_t = p^*$. Figure 6.1 shows the initial equilibrium E at which AS and AD intersect.

2. Note from equation (5.27) that monetary policy can also influence the AS equation by moving the target price p^* in the long run, while the price at time $t - 1$ remains unchanged.

As a useful reminder for the analysis that follows, note the relationships between short-run (long-run) natural, efficient levels of output and the primitive shocks:

$$\hat{Y}_t^n = \frac{1+\eta}{\sigma^{-1}+\eta}\hat{A}_t + \frac{\sigma^{-1}}{\sigma^{-1}+\eta}\hat{G}_t - \frac{1}{\sigma^{-1}+\eta}\hat{\mu}_t, \qquad (6.3)$$

$$\hat{Y}_{t+1}^n = \frac{1+\eta}{\sigma^{-1}+\eta}\hat{A}_{t+1} + \frac{\sigma^{-1}}{\sigma^{-1}+\eta}\hat{G}_{t+1} - \frac{1}{\sigma^{-1}+\eta}\hat{\mu}_{t+1}, \qquad (6.4)$$

$$\hat{Y}_t^e = \frac{1+\eta}{\sigma^{-1}+\eta}\hat{A}_t + \frac{\sigma^{-1}}{\sigma^{-1}+\eta}\hat{G}_t, \qquad (6.5)$$

$$\hat{Y}_{t+1}^e = \frac{1+\eta}{\sigma^{-1}+\eta}\hat{A}_{t+1} + \frac{\sigma^{-1}}{\sigma^{-1}+\eta}\hat{G}_{t+1}, \qquad (6.6)$$

in which A is a productivity shock, μ is a markup shock, Y^e is the efficient level of output, and η is a positive parameter, which is the inverse of the elasticity of labor supply. In what follows, we are going to assume that natural and efficient levels of output coincide in the long run, i.e., $\hat{Y}_{t+1}^n = \hat{Y}_{t+1}^e$ by setting $\hat{\mu}_{t+1} = 0$, so that inefficient shocks, like markup disturbances, have only transitory effects.

It is useful to define also the concept of frictionless real rate of interest, which would capture in this analysis the original idea of Wicksell (1898) of the natural rate of interest. This is given by

$$r_t^e = \frac{1}{\sigma}(\hat{Y}_{t+1}^e - \hat{Y}_t^e - (\hat{G}_{t+1} - \hat{G}_t)) + \hat{\xi}_t - \hat{\xi}_{t+1} \qquad (6.7)$$

or, equivalently,

$$r_t^e = \frac{1+\eta}{1+\sigma\eta}(\hat{A}_{t+1} - \hat{A}_t) - \frac{\eta}{1+\sigma\eta}(\hat{G}_{t+1} - \hat{G}_t) - (\hat{\xi}_{t+1} - \hat{\xi}_t). \qquad (6.8)$$

The frictionless real rate of interest is driven by the variations over time of productivity, public spending, and preference shocks. Using it in (6.1), we can write the AD equation as

$$\hat{Y}_t - \hat{Y}_t^e = -\sigma\left(\hat{\imath}_t - (p^* - p_t) - r_t^e\right). \qquad (6.9)$$

This shows that r_t^e is the real rate in the economy that, if achieved by the policy rate, is compatible with price stability, $p_t = p^*$, while at the same time reaching the efficient level of output in the short run. According to Knut Wicksell, the concept of frictionless rate of interest should guide the policy rate $\hat{\imath}_t$ in response to the shocks.[3] Central banks also consider a closely related concept, R-star, as seen in works such as Williams (2016), when setting their policy rate. However, as this chapter and the next one will demonstrate, the Wicksellian rate serves as a suitable guide for policy only when the shocks affecting the economy originate from efficient sources.

6.2 Outline of the Results

This chapter shows that, when the economy is hit by efficient shocks related to productivity and public spending, there is no trade-off between achieving price stability and stabilizing the output gap in terms of the efficient level of output. The direction of interest rate adjustments to attain these targets depends on whether the shock is a temporary, a permanent, or a news shock. The guidance for these adjustments is provided by the movements in the frictionless rate of interest. However, a trade-off arises when inefficient shocks, such as markup shocks, perturb the economy. In such cases, the frictionless rate of interest may no longer be the primary guide for determining the policy rate.

The chapter is divided into the following sections. Section 6.3 analyzes pertubations originating from productivity shocks. Section 6.4 discusses markup disturbances, while Sections 6.5 and 6.6 discuss variations in public spending and in the preference shock, respectively. Finally, Section 6.7 considers the possibility that shifts in expectations on future prices perturb the economy.

6.3 Productivity Shock

We will study how inflation and output react to a productivity shock and their interaction with monetary policy.

6.3.1 A Temporary Productivity Shock

First, we analyze the case in which the economy undergoes a temporary productivity gain, meaning that productivity rises in the short run but does not

---

3. Note that what is literally the natural rate of interest in our model, i.e., r_t^n, in which the natural level of output replaces the efficient level in the definition (6.7), would vary in response to inefficient shocks. Thus, it does not represent the appropriate definition for capturing the Wicksellian concept within the NK framework.

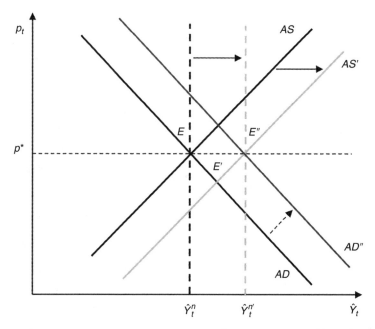

FIGURE 6.2. A temporary productivity shock: $\hat{A}_t \uparrow$. AS shifts to AS' and the equilibrium moves from E to E'. If monetary policy lowers the nominal interest rate, AD moves to AD'' and equilibrium E'' is reached with stable prices and zero output gap.

vary in the long run. A rise in $\hat{A}_t$ increases the short-run natural level of output $\hat{Y}_t^n$, as shown in (6.3), which in turn influences the AS equation. Starting from the equilibrium E, shown in Figure 6.2, the short-run natural level of output rises to $\hat{Y}_t^{n'}$ and AS shifts downward, crossing E'' where output equals the natural level at the initial price level. The AD equation is not affected by movements in current productivity, and the new equilibrium is found at the intersection, E', of the new AS equation, AS', with the old AD equation.

The adjustment from equilibrium E to E' occurs as follows. A temporary increase in productivity lowers the real marginal costs. The firms that can adjust their prices lower them. The real interest rate falls, stimulating consumption. Output increases, but not enough to match the rise in the natural level, because of sticky prices. The economy reaches the equilibrium point E' with lower prices and higher output, but with a negative output gap. The efficient level of output rises in the same proportion as the natural level.

This is the equilibrium that can be reached without any policy intervention. An interesting question is how monetary policy should respond to the shocks

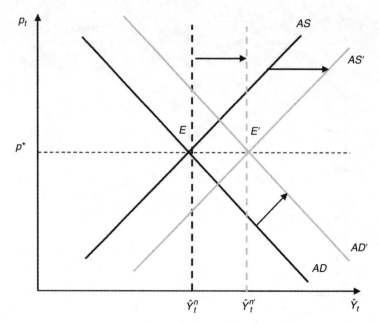

FIGURE 6.3. A permanent productivity shock: $\hat{A}_t \uparrow$ and $\hat{A}_{t+1} \uparrow$. AS shifts to AS' and AD to AD'. The equilibrium moves from E to E' without any monetary policy intervention.

in order to close the output gap and/or stabilize prices if both objectives can be reached simultaneously. In this case, monetary policy can attain both by bringing the economy to equilibrium E''. By lowering the nominal interest rate, monetary policy shifts AD upward to the point at which it crosses E''. The curve thus shifts to AD''. The rise in output also increases firms' marginal costs, driving prices up. Production expands. At E'', prices are stable at the initial level. An accommodating monetary policy can thus achieve both the natural and the efficient levels of output and stable prices. As will be discussed later, this is also the optimal policy, maximizing consumers' utility. It is worth noting that the result of this experiment can be also read in terms of the movements in the frictionless rate of interest, r_t^e, which, according to (6.8), falls. To achieve efficient output and price stability, the policy rate should follow the frictionless rate of interest.

6.3.2 A Permanent Productivity Shock

Figure 6.3 analyzes the case of a permanent productivity shock, which increases $\hat{A}_t$ and $\hat{A}_{t+1}$, and therefore $\hat{Y}_t^n$ and $\hat{Y}_{t+1}^n$, in the same proportion.

As in the previous case, the short-run natural and efficient levels of output increase and the *AS* curve shifts downward through E'. However, now the *AD* equation shifts upward because the future natural level of consumption rises along with long-run productivity. Households would like to increase current consumption because of the desire to smooth the future increase. The *AD* equation shifts exactly to intersect E'. And this is the new equilibrium.

A permanent gain in productivity does not change the frictionless real interest rate, because both $\hat{Y}_t^n$ and $\hat{Y}_{t+1}^n$ increase in the same proportion: this is why the new equilibrium requires no change in monetary policy to achieve price stability while simultaneously closing the output gap. In the next chapter, we will show that this equilibrium outcome corresponds to the optimal monetary policy.

6.3.3 Optimism or Pessimism on Future Productivity

Let us consider now the case of an expected increase in long-run productivity, raising only $\hat{A}_{t+1}$ and, therefore, $\hat{Y}_{t+1}^n$. This can be taken either as an increase that will really occur, or just an optimistic belief about future output growth, or a combination of the two. Conversely, a decrease in long-run productivity can also be interpreted as a pessimistic belief concerning future growth. The case of optimism is analyzed in Figure 6.4.

AS does not move, since there is no change in current productivity. *AD* does shift upward, however, because households expect higher consumption in the future and to smooth the upward shift they want to increase their consumption immediately. Output expands, driving up real wages and real marginal costs, so that firms adjust prices upward. The economy reaches the equilibrium point E' with higher prices and production higher than the natural and efficient level. What should monetary policy do to stabilize prices and close the output gap? It should counter future developments in productivity or such optimistic beliefs by raising the nominal interest rate so as to bring *AD* back to the initial point E. Note that, according to (6.8), the frictionless rate of interest increases and, therefore, the policy rate should rise.

Some lessons can be drawn from these analyses. Regardless of the properties of the shock (temporary, permanent, or expected), monetary policy can always move interest rates to stabilize prices and the output gap simultaneously. But the direction of the movement depends on the property of the shock. When shocks are positive and transitory, monetary policy should be expansionary; when permanent, it should be neutral; and with merely

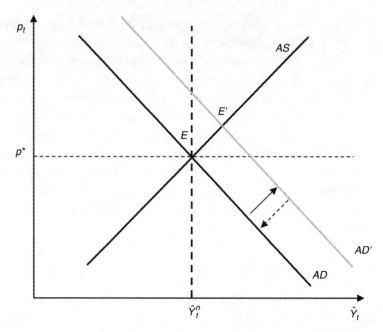

FIGURE 6.4. An increase in long-run productivity: $\hat{A}_{t+1} \uparrow$. AD shifts up to AD'. The equilibrium moves from E to E'. An increase in the nominal interest rate can bring the equilibrium back to the starting point.

expected positive productivity shocks, it should be restrictive. The key point is that changes in the Wicksellian interest rate should guide the policy rate in response to productivity fluctuations, as equation (6.8) shows.

6.4   Markup Shock

When there are productivity shocks, monetary policy does not face a trade-off between stabilizing prices and offsetting the output gap, in terms of either the natural or the efficient level of output.[4] With markup shocks, things are different. First, the efficient level of output does not move, while the natural level does, as shown in equations (6.3)–(6.6). Second, there is a trade-off between stabilizing prices and reaching the efficient level of output.

Let us consider then a temporary increase in the markup (see Figure 6.5), moving up $\hat{\mu}_t$ and leading to a fall in the short-run natural level of output, $\hat{Y}_t^n$,

---

4. An important assumption here is that of wage flexibility. Trade-offs will occur with sticky wages, as discussed in Erceg, Henderson, and Levin (2000).

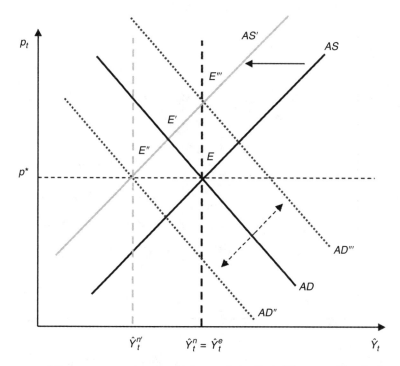

FIGURE 6.5. A temporary increase in the markup: $\hat{\mu}_t \uparrow$. The natural level of output $\hat{Y}^n$ falls while the efficient level of output $\hat{Y}^e$ does not move. AS shifts to AS'. The equilibrium moves from E to E'. By raising the nominal interest rate, monetary policy can stabilize prices and reach equilibrium E''. By lowering it, the efficient level of output can be achieved at equilibrium point E'''. There is a trade-off between the two objectives, stabilizing prices and reaching the efficient level of output.

as shown in (6.3). The AS curve shifts upward following the fall in the natural level of output, but the efficient level of output is unchanged, as shown in (6.5). Firms raise prices because of the higher markup. The real interest rate goes up and households increase savings and postpone consumption. Demand falls along with output. The economy reaches equilibrium E' with a contraction in output and higher prices: a situation dubbed "stagflation." Now, monetary policy does face a dilemma: a choice between maintaining stable prices and keeping the economy at the efficient level of production. To attain the price objective, the nominal interest rate should be raised so as to further increase the real rate and damp down economic activity. In this case, AD shifts downward to AD'' and the economy reaches equilibrium E''. To obtain

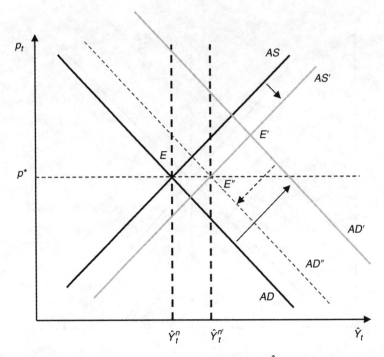

FIGURE 6.6. A temporary increase in public spending: $\hat{G}_t \uparrow$. The natural and efficient level of output $\hat{Y}_t^n$ increases. AS shifts to AS'. AD moves to AD' because public spending increases output for the given consumption. The equilibrium moves from E to E' with a positive output gap. By raising the nominal interest rate, monetary policy can stabilize prices and the output gap, reaching equilibrium E'', with AD' moving to AD''.

the output objective, policymakers should cut the nominal interest rate to stimulate economic activity and consumption. In this case, AD shifts to AD''' and the economy reaches equilibrium E'''.

It is interesting to discuss the implications in the terms of the frictionless rate of interest, which is unchanged when markup shocks hit, as shown in (6.8). This no longer serves as guidance to the nominal interest rate, as will be also shown in the next chapter.

6.5   Public Spending Shock

We consider a temporary increase in public spending, raising $\hat{G}_t$, which affects directly the AD equation and, through $\hat{Y}_t^n$, the AS equation, too. As shown in Figure 6.6, an increase in current public spending expands aggregate demand,

and thus current output, shifting the aggregate demand equation upward from AD to AD'. At the same time, the natural rate of output increases, together with the efficient level, shifting AS downward. Moreover, note that short-run movements in public spending enlarge the output gap. Starting from no gap, public spending creates a positive output gap. This means that AD' and AS' cross to the right of the new natural level of output, $\hat{Y}_t^{n'}$. Prices rise from the initial equilibrium; the real interest rate rises, reducing consumption as equilibrium E becomes E'. The economy is overheated by a positive output gap. To close it and stabilize prices, policymakers should raise nominal interest rates to increase the real rate, which dampens private consumption. In this case, AD moves from AD' to AD'', reaching equilibrium E''. The analysis of a public spending shock is fully consistent with the policy rate following the increase in the frictionless rate of interest, as equation (6.8) shows.[5]

6.6 Preference Shock

Preference shocks have a distinct impact on the economy since they affect only the AD, as was the case for changes in future productivity shock. The analysis here then parallels that case, with the appropriate qualifications. Seen from a different perspective, equation (6.8) shows that preference shocks affect the frictionless rate of interest and therefore, accordingly, the policy rate should move proportionally.

A fall in ξ_t in the short run relative to the long run causes households to be more patient, according to their utility (5.1), and raises their incentives to save. In a frictionless economy, this excess saving is balanced by a reduction in the frictionless rate of interest, which ensures that household consumption and saving decisions remain consistent with the fact that the efficient level of output has not changed.

The adjustment in the AS-AD model with price rigidities unfolds as follows. After a fall in $\hat{\xi}_t$, the AD equation shifts downward, leading to a decline in output and prices along the AS curve. To restore price stability and ensure that output remains at the efficient, natural level, the monetary policymaker should proportionally reduce the policy rate, matching the decrease in the

---

5. When $\eta = 0$, AS and AD shift proportionally to cross the new natural level of output, closing the output gap, with stable prices $(p = p^*)$ and without any monetary policy intervention. This is consistent with the fact that the frictionless rate of interest in (6.8) does not move.

frictionless real interest rate. This adjustment would shift the *AD* equation upward, returning it to the initial equilibrium.

In Chapter 9, we will utilize this type of shock to model a liquidity trap. When such a shock is sufficiently large in magnitude, it can drive the frictionless rate of interest into negative territory. This situation would require an unattainable negative nominal interest rate to restore price stability and return output to the efficient (natural) level.

6.7   Disanchoring of Price Expectations

The framework of this chapter can allow us also to study how shifts in private sector expectations can affect the equilibrium. To this end, we have to relax the assumption that expectations on the long-run price level, which are present in both the *AD* and the *AS* equations, are exactly anchored at the long-run price p^*. We can then write the *AD* and *AS* equations as:

$$\hat{Y}_t - \hat{Y}_t^e = -\sigma \left(\hat{i}_t - (E_t^d p_{t+1} - p_t) - r_t^e \right)$$

and

$$p_t = \frac{1}{1+\beta} p^* + \frac{\kappa}{1+\beta}(\hat{Y}_t - \hat{Y}_t^n) + \frac{\beta}{1+\beta} E_t^s p_{t+1}.$$

In these equations, we distinguish between consumers' expectations on the long-run price $(E_t^d p_{t+1})$, which affect demand, and those of the firms $(E_t^s p_{t+1})$, which influence supply.

Starting from the equilibrium point E in Figure 6.1, if consumers adjust their long-run price expectations downward, it leads to an increase in the real interest rate, which, in turn, dampens current consumption. Consequently, the *AD* curve shifts downward, resulting in reduced output and a decrease in the price level. These shifts in expectations can potentially trigger a deflationary spiral.

To counteract this situation and restore the economy to its initial equilibrium, monetary policy becomes crucial. The central bank should consider lowering the policy rate to stimulate demand and shift the *AD* curve back to its original position, thereby stabilizing the economy.

When it comes to the supply side, shifts in expectations matter for the strategic pricing decisions made by firms. These decisions take into account future demand when setting present prices. Let us consider a scenario where price setters anticipate a future increase in the price level, starting from the equilibrium point E in Figure 6.1.

In this situation, the AS curve shifts upward, leading to a rise in current prices. This, in turn, reduces aggregate demand and contracts the economy. It's important to note that such shifts in expectations can potentially trigger an inflationary spiral.

Given that the natural and efficient levels of output remain constant, the central bank encounters a trade-off between stabilizing prices and maintaining output at its original level. Stabilizing prices may result in reduced output, while focusing on output stabilization can contribute to fueling higher inflation.

This simple analysis shows the potentially destabilizing consequences of shifts in private expectations on the long-run price level, and therefore it underlines the importance for monetary policy to anchor those expectations with an appropriate monetary policy strategy.

6.8   References

This chapter is based on Benigno (2015). There are other works which have analyzed simplified versions of New Keynesian models. Romer (2000) presents a modern view of a Keynesian non-microfounded model without the LM equation, which typically describes money market equilibrium, and instead represents the demand side through an aggregate demand-inflation curve derived from the Euler equation and a monetary policy rule. Eggertsson (2011) maintains stochastic uncertainty, plotting the dynamics of aggregate supply and aggregate demand in an output-inflation diagram using an interest rate rule, under specific assumptions about stochastic disturbances. In contrast, the model we present here interprets the Euler equation as an AD equation without imposing an interest rate rule.

Walsh (2002) introduces a two-equation system where the aggregate demand equation stems from the optimal transformation between prices and output, as desired by an optimizing central bank. This concept closely aligns with the IT equation, which we will analyze further in the next chapter while studying optimal monetary policy.

Finally, Carlin and Soskice (2005) present a simple three-equation non-microfounded model that employs a modern approach to central bank operational targets and requires the display of two graphs.

7

Inflation Targeting as an
Optimal Policy

7.1 Introduction

In 1990, New Zealand became the first country to introduce inflation targeting as a monetary policy strategy for its central bank. The key features of an
inflation targeting regime include the announcement of a numerical inflation
target set for a well-defined price index, for which the central bank is held
accountable. Canada announced its inflation target in 1991, followed by the
United Kingdom in 1992. Subsequently, Sweden and Finland declared their
inflation targets in 1993. It wasn't until 2012 that the United States officially
announced its 2 percent inflation rate target. In general, quantitative targets
for developed countries are between 1 to 3 percent.[1]

The adoption of inflation targeting in practical policymaking preceded the
availability of academic research suitable for its analysis. What is particularly
surprising is that the NK benchmark model, developed in the late 1990s and
presented in Chapter 5, is based on microfoundations that rationalize inflation
targeting as the optimal monetary policy. This approach is found to be superior to interest rate rules or the guidance of the Wicksellian frictionless real
rate.

The microfoundations of the NK model of Chapter 5 provide a natural
criterion for evaluating optimal policy based on the maximization of consumers' utility. Since the equilibrium conditions have been approximated
up to a first-order approximation, a second-order approximation of the

---

1. See Bernanke and Mishkin (1997) and Svensson (2010) for a thorough analysis of
inflation targeting.

utility is needed for a correct ranking of policies. This is consistent with the linear-quadratic approach to optimal policy.[2] Appendix F shows that the second-order approximation of (5.1) implies that at time t_0 the welfare-based loss function $L_{t_0}^{CB}$ is given by

$$L_{t_0}^{CB} = E_{t_0} \sum_{t=t_0}^{\infty} \beta^{t-t_0} \left[\frac{1}{2} (\hat{Y}_t - \hat{Y}_t^e)^2 + \frac{1}{2} \frac{\theta}{\kappa} (\pi_t - \pi)^2 \right], \qquad (7.1)$$

in which the efficient level of output $\hat{Y}_t^e$ has the same definition as in (6.5), while θ and κ are positive parameters defined in the previous chapter. The approximation is simplified by the fact that the steady state is efficient; otherwise, one needs to take a second-order approximation of the equilibrium conditions for a correct linear-quadratic approximation of the optimal policy problem.[3]

The objective of the policymaker involves minimization of a loss function (7.1) that involves two target variables, output ($\hat{Y}_t$) and inflation (π_t). The target of output is the efficient level of output, $\hat{Y}_t^e$, which is self-explanatory, while that of inflation is the inflation target, π. The microfoundations of the model provide the reason for why deviations of inflation from the target are costly. This is because they create price dispersion with the consequence of a misallocation of demand across goods, which is inefficient, considering that the goods are produced using the same technology and should ideally have the same price.

The loss function also provides the weight that the policymaker should attach to the inflation objective versus the output objective. The objectives are fully minimized when output is at the efficient level and inflation is at the target. However, these two targets might not be reached simultaneously since inflation and output are constrained in their movements by the AS equation (5.27) of Chapter 5. The optimal policy should minimize (7.1) under the AS equation (5.27), which we now rewrite as

$$\pi_t - \pi = \kappa (\hat{Y}_t - \hat{Y}_t^n) + \beta E_t (\pi_{t+1} - \pi), \qquad (7.2)$$

for positive parameters κ and β, in which $\hat{Y}_t^n$ is the natural rate of output defined in (6.3).

2. See Woodford (2002).

3. Benigno and Woodford (2005, 2012) discuss the generalization when the steady state is not efficient.

Following a productivity or public spending shock, the optimal policy is to stabilize inflation at the target and at the same time close the output gap, consistently with the graphical analysis made in Chapter 6. Note that when inflation is at the target, output is at the natural rate in the *AS* equation (7.2), which coincides with the efficient level, except when markup shocks hit the economy. A trade-off arises only with markup shocks.

Optimal monetary policy can in general be characterized by a flexibile inflation targeting policy or a price level targeting policy, accounting for deviations from the price stability objective with corresponding variations in output gap growth. Furthermore, optimal monetary policy under commitment is history-dependent and implies long-run price stability, meaning that upward deviations of prices with respect to the trend implied by the central bank's target should be undone gradually so that prices revert to the implied initial trend.

7.2 Outline of the Results

In Section 7.3, we analyze optimal monetary policy when policymakers commit from a "timeless perspective." This analysis demonstrates that it can be represented by targeting rules that rationalize a flexible inflation targeting strategy. In this strategy, policymakers permit deviations of inflation from the target, along with corresponding deviations of output growth from the efficient trend. Notably, this strategy is equivalent to price level targeting and is consistent with the goal of achieving long-term price stability.

Sections 7.4 and 7.5 discuss sub-optimal policies, such as those implied by optimizing behavior without commitment and interest rate rules, respectively. These policies are compared with the optimal policy under commitment, revealing two distinct features of the latter: the inertia in accommodating inefficient shocks, which showcases the policymaker's commitment to fulfilling past promises, and the reversion of prices to the pre-shock trend.

Finally, Section 7.6 delves into the existing literature regarding the numerical value of the inflation target π in the loss function (7.1).

7.3 Optimal Policy under Commitment

We first characterize optimal policy when the policymaker can commit, once and for all, to a state-contingent path of inflation and output. Commitment means that the policymaker will not change its state-contingent optimal plan at future dates. However, commitment does not mean that the policymaker abides by a strict rule. Instead, the policymaker specifies a state-contingent plan for all future periods and commits to it.

Optimal monetary policy under commitment minimizes loss function (7.1) under the sequence of *AS* constraints (7.2) for each $t \geq t_0$. Consider the following Lagrangian:

$$\mathcal{L}_{t_0} = E_{t_0} \left\{ \sum_{t=t_0}^{\infty} \beta^{t-t_0} \left[\frac{1}{2} (\hat{Y}_t - \hat{Y}_t^e)^2 + \frac{1}{2} \frac{\theta}{\kappa} (\pi_t - \pi)^2 + \right. \right.$$

$$+ \lambda_t \left((\pi_t - \pi) - \kappa (\hat{Y}_t - \hat{Y}_t^n) - \beta (\pi_{t+1} - \pi) \right) \right] +$$

$$\left. - \lambda_{t_0 - 1} (\pi_{t_0} - \pi) \right\},$$

in which λ_t is the Lagrange multiplier associated with constraint (7.2) at time t.[4] Note that *AD* equation (5.26) is not a constraint on the optimal policy since the equation will residually determine the path of the interest rate consistent with the optimal path of inflation and output gap. This is true if the optimal path of the interest rate does not violate the zero lower bound. Section 9.5 of Chapter 9 characterizes optimal policy when the zero lower bound constraint is binding. Note that in the above Lagrangian we are analyzing a stronger form of commitment, called commitment from a "timeless perspective," in which even at time t_0 the policymaker takes into consideration constraints on variables at time t_0 that entered into expectations of the same variables formed in period $t_0 - 1$.[5] This stronger form of commitment adds the last set of state-contingent constraints on the third line of the above Lagrangian.

The first-order conditions with respect to inflation and output are

$$\theta (\pi_t - \pi) + \kappa \lambda_t - \kappa \lambda_{t-1} = 0$$

and

$$(\hat{Y}_t - \hat{Y}_t^e) - \kappa \lambda_t = 0,$$

respectively, for each $t \geq t_0$. Note that the first-order conditions have the same form in each period, including at time t_0, because of the additional constraint represented by the last line of the Lagrangian. Otherwise, the

---

4. Note that in writing the Lagrangian we have used the law of iterated expectations, to write $E_{t_0} E_t (\pi_{t+1} - \pi) = E_{t_0} (\pi_{t+1} - \pi)$.

5. See Woodford (2003) for a detailed discussion of commitment from a timeless perspective.

first-order condition at time t_0 with respect to π_{t_0} will not display the Lagrange multiplier at time $t_0 - 1$, i.e., λ_{t_0-1}.

Commitment from a "timeless perspective" renders the optimization problem stationary and its solution time-consistent, as opposed to the time-inconsistent solution when the additional constraint $\lambda_{t_0-1}(\pi_{t_0} - \pi)$ in the above Lagrangian is not considered.

The nature of time inconsistency in the "standard" commitment optimization problem depends on a crucial factor: the constraint in the optimization problem, the AS equation, includes expectations of future variables. When we calculate the optimal policy with a commitment at time t_0, we take into account constraints that involve expectations of variables like $E_t(\pi_{t+1} - \pi)$ for each $t \geq t_0$, and we consider them in our optimal state-contingent plan.

However, we are not bound by constraints related to expectations formed in the past that affect our current choices. For example, we do not consider $E_{t_0-1}(\pi_{t_0} - \pi)$ as a constraint to our policy since it does not appear in the set of constraints, and in particular in the AS equation at time t_0. Time inconsistency arises when we reoptimize at any future time T, assuming the same type of commitment, and considering AS equations for each $t \geq T$ as constraints. In this optimization problem at time T, the policymaker is not bound by past promises, as constraints on $E_{T-1}(\pi_T - \pi)$ do not apply. Therefore, it may deviate from the plan chosen at time t_0.

Looking at commitment from a "timeless perspective," the optimization problem accounts for a constraint related to fulfilling previous expectations on the current inflation rate, represented by the state-contingent term $\lambda_{t_0-1}(\pi_{t_0} - \pi)$ in the Lagrangian. This setup ensures that the policymaker does not deviate from the plan chosen at time t_0 when optimizing at a future date T. In this case, a policymaker acting with commitment from a "timeless perspective" faces the AS equation constraints for each $t \geq T$ and state-contingent constraints in the form of $\lambda_{T-1}(\pi_T - \pi)$ in the Lagrangian.

One significant advantage of "standard" commitment, in general, is its ability to effectively specify a state-contingent plan, which can influence private sector expectations about future variables such as inflation in a way that maximizes the objective function. In addition to this, commitment from a "timeless perspective" is particularly attractive for practical policymaking. It necessitates the fulfillment of past expectations, for which current choices are relevant, as the policymaker commits to doing the same in the future. This approach enhances the credibility of the plan, as it demonstrates how the policymaker will behave today and in the future in a consistent way.

To get further insights into the solution, the above first-order conditions can be combined to obtain

$$(\pi_t - \pi) + \theta^{-1}(\Delta\hat{Y}_t - \Delta\hat{Y}_t^e) = 0 \tag{7.3}$$

by eliminating the Lagrange multipliers.

Equation (7.3) has important implications. Under the optimal monetary policy with commitment from a "timeless perspective," the policymaker should follow a targeting rule, equation (7.3), which aims at stabilizing a particular combination of deviations of inflation from its target, and of output growth from the efficient growth path. Positive deviations of inflation from the target are allowed as long as output growth is below the efficient growth rate.

This type of targeting rule can justify the adoption of a monetary-policy framework that can be dubbed "flexible inflation targeting." This is broader than a strict inflation-targeting regime because the policymaker also considers economic activity, specifically the growth of output with respect to its efficient trend. Three essential elements of the "flexible inflation targeting" framework are described in (7.3).

First, it involves specifying the target variables, which, in this case, include both inflation and output growth. Second, the objectives for these target variables should be defined. In this framework, these objectives are represented by the inflation target (π) and the efficient trend of output ($\Delta\hat{Y}_t^e$). Finally, it requires specifying the relative weight in the linear combination of the deviations of the actual realization of the target variable from its target. This weight is given by the structural parameter θ in (7.3).

The NK framework provides a rationale for adopting "flexible inflation targeting" as a guiding principle for effective monetary policymaking, in contrast to following a determined interest rate rule or relying solely on the Wicksellian frictionless rate of interest as a reference for setting the policy rate. Under an inflation-targeting regime, the policy rate is adjusted to ensure that the objective defined in (7.3) is met at each point in time or within a chosen time horizon, regardless of the economic disturbances at play. Deviations from the targeting rule dictate how the policy rate should respond to various contingencies, considering the transmission mechanism of the policy rate into the target variables. The targeting rule itself remains constant across these contingencies, except that the target for output growth is time-varying.

The targeting rule in (7.3) can also rationalize the optimality of a price level targeting regime. In this case, the policymaker should target a reference price $\tilde{p}_t$, at a level $\tilde{p}_t^*$, where $\tilde{p}_t$ is a combination of the price level and the output gap, as

$$\tilde{p}_t = p_t + \theta^{-1}(\hat{Y}_t - \hat{Y}_t^e),$$

and $\tilde{p}_t^*$ is represented by

$$\tilde{p}_t^* = \tilde{p}_{t-1}^* + \pi.$$

The price level targeting rule $\tilde{p}_t = \tilde{p}_t^*$ is equivalent to the flexible inflation-targeting rule (7.3). The target $\tilde{p}^*$ is trending with the inflation target; the reference price $\tilde{p}$ is not just the price level, but a combination of it and the output gap with respect to the efficient level. Optimal policy requires the reference price $\tilde{p}_t$ to be at the trending target. As an interesting departure from this equivalence result, Section 9.5 of Chapter 9 shows that, when the zero lower bound is binding, optimal policy can only be characterized by a price level targeting rule, and no longer by a flexible inflation targeting policy.

Another interesting implication of the price level targeting rule can be drawn by assuming that the parameter θ is equal to the unitary value. In this case, it can be represented by a nominal GDP targeting rule: nominal GDP (in logs), $p_t + y_t$, should target a reference value $\tilde{y}_t$, i.e.,

$$p_t + y_t = \tilde{y}_t,$$

with

$$\tilde{y}_t = \tilde{y}_{t-1} + \pi + \Delta \hat{Y}_t^e.$$

The nominal-GDP target $\tilde{y}_t$ follows a combination of the inflation target and growth rate of the efficient level of output.

Even in this simplified version, the NK model can support policy discussions on the adoption of inflation targeting policies versus price level targeting and nominal GDP targeting. Flexibile inflation targeting and price level targeting are equivalent policies once target variables and targets are appropriately defined. Nominal GDP targeting is nested under some special parametrization.

Since AS equation (7.2) does not show any trade-off between stabilizing inflation at the target and closing output in terms of the natural level of output, complete stabilization of inflation to the target coincides with the optimal monetary policy following efficient shocks, such as productivity and public spending, as we have already noted in Chapter 6. Instead, for inefficient shocks like markup shocks, the above targeting rule shows how to optimally deal with the trade-off. The monetary policymaker is willing to tolerate some inflation above the target insofar as it is accompanied by a contraction of output growth with respect to the efficient rate, and vice versa.

Before characterizing the optimal path of output and inflation, we analyze the optimal stabilization problem by using the graphical analysis of Chapter 6. Under the assumption $\pi = 0$ and $(p_{t-1} - p^*) + \theta^{-1}(\hat{Y}_{t-1} - \hat{Y}^e_{t-1}) = 0$, the above targeting rule involves a negative relationship between the price level and the output, implicit in

$$(p_t - p^*) + \theta^{-1}(\hat{Y}_t - \hat{Y}^e_t) = 0, \tag{7.4}$$

that can be plotted in the same graph as AS and AD. Recall that p^* represents in the analysis of Chapter 6 the log of the price level both at time $t - 1$ and at time $t + 1$.

Let us call (7.4) the IT equation. The slope is represented by $-1/\theta$, and IT crosses the point $(p^*, \hat{Y}^e_t)$. In particular, IT is flatter than AD whenever $\theta > \sigma$, which is the empirically relevant case.[6]

Returning to markup shocks (see Section 6.4 of Chapter 6), let us focus on a central bank maximizing the welfare of the consumer, with a relatively flat IT. Following a temporary increase in the markup, without monetary policy intervention the economy reaches equilibrium E' in Figure 7.1.

Optimal monetary policy should place the economy on the IT curve, which in this case does not move since $\hat{Y}^e_t$ did not move, at the intersection with AS. It should reach E'' by raising the nominal interest rate. A central bank less concerned about price stability, with IT steeper than AD, should lower the nominal interest rate to achieve its own optimal allocation.

The optimal policy analysis can be repeated for productivity shocks, and similarly for public spending shocks, in which case IT shifts to cross the optimal equilibrium point of stable prices and the contemporaneous closure of the output gap, as discussed in Section 6.3 of Chapter 6.

The graphical representation of the optimal policy problem shown in Figure 7.1 offers a straightforward way to illustrate the guidance provided to policymakers when they follow the targeting rule IT in response to economic shocks. The targeting rule, particularly its intersection with the AS equation, represents the point at which the policymaker should aim to stabilize the

6. Indeed, θ is related to the markup: a value of 10 gives an 11% markup; σ is the elasticity of substitution in consumption, which is usually assumed to be close to 1.

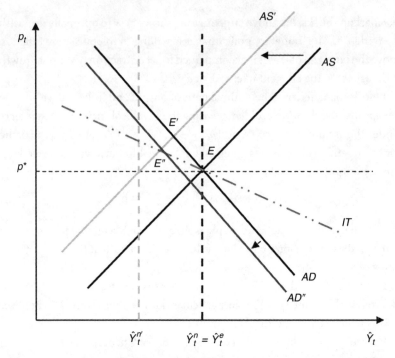

FIGURE 7.1. A temporary markup shock: $\hat{\mu}_t \uparrow$. AS shifts to AS'. The equilibrium moves from E to E'. IT equation describes the optimal combination of prices and output according to the preferences of a welfare-maximizing monetary policymaker. The optimal equilibrium is E'' where IT intersects AS'. Monetary policy should raise the nominal interest rate to move the equilibrium from E' to E''.

economy. By adjusting the policy rate and thereby affecting the AD equation, the monetary policymaker can work toward achieving the desired goal by shifting the AD equation along the AS curve at the intersection with the IT. The transmission mechanism of the policy rate encompasses the effects of the policy rate on AD and the relationship between prices and output as defined by the AS curve, which have to be understood by the policymaker.[7] This framework is superior to the Wicksellian prescription of following the frictionless rate of interest, which would imply that the policy rate should remain invariant to markup shocks, assuming complete knowledge of that rate.

7. The simplifying assumptions needed to provide a graphical analysis do not allow us to consider the channel through which monetary policy, by influencing inflation expectations, can also directly shift the AS equation.

Let us consider again the dynamic model to compute the optimal response to markup shocks. Recall the *AD* equation (5.26) and write it as

$$x_t = E_t x_{t+1} - \sigma \left(\hat{\imath}_t - E_t(\pi_{t+1} - \pi) - r_t^e \right), \qquad (7.5)$$

while the aggregate supply equation (7.2) can be written as

$$\pi_t - \pi = \kappa x_t + \upsilon_t + \beta E_t(\pi_{t+1} - \pi), \qquad (7.6)$$

where we have defined the gap between output and its frictionless level as x_t, i.e.,

$$x_t \equiv \hat{Y}_t - \hat{Y}_t^e.$$

The frictionless real interest rate is represented by

$$r_t^e \equiv E_t \left\{ \frac{1+\eta}{1+\sigma\eta} \left(\hat{A}_{t+1} - \hat{A}_t \right) - \frac{\eta}{1+\sigma\eta} (\hat{G}_{t+1} - \hat{G}_t) - (\hat{\xi}_{t+1} - \hat{\xi}_t) \right\},$$

while the shock (υ) is a reparametrization of the markup shock

$$\upsilon_t = \kappa(\hat{Y}_t^e - \hat{Y}_t^n) = \frac{\kappa}{\sigma^{-1} + \eta} \hat{\mu}_t.$$

Consistent with the definition provided in Chapter 6, the frictionless real interest rate represents the level that would arise in an economy with flexible prices without the inefficiency brought about by markup shocks. The frictionless real rate depends on productivity, government spending, and preference shocks. For each of these three shocks, what matters is their variation over time. Expected growth of productivity raises the real rate, while expected growth of public spending lowers it. Both these shocks move the natural and efficient levels of output and therefore create shifts in the *AS* equation. This is not true for preference shocks, ξ, which do not perturb the natural rate of output but move only the frictionless real rate. An expected increase in future ξ relative to the current level lowers the real rate.

We combine the *AS* equation (7.6) with the targeting rule (7.3) to obtain a second-order stochastic difference equation in x_t,

$$E_t x_{t+1} - \left(1 + \frac{1}{\beta} + \frac{\kappa\theta}{\beta} \right) x_t + \frac{1}{\beta} x_{t-1} = \frac{\theta}{\beta} \upsilon_t, \qquad (7.7)$$

whose characteristic equation is represented by

$$P(\gamma) = \gamma^2 - \left(1 + \frac{1}{\beta} + \frac{\kappa\theta}{\beta} \right) \gamma + \frac{1}{\beta}. \qquad (7.8)$$

The first step is to ask under what conditions there is a unique and locally bounded solution of the stochastic difference equation (7.7). This requirement is important for two purposes: first, uniqueness is a desiderata for the policymaker, or otherwise it cannot be really claimed that there is control of inflation or output since, with multiplicity, there are multiple paths associated with the same policy; second, stability is required since we are working with an approximation of the equilibrium conditions that is only valid for solutions that stay close to the steady state around which the approximation is made. The Blanchard-Kahn conditions discussed in Appendix G say that there is a unique and bounded solution when the number of eigenvalues within the unit circle, of the characteristic polynomial associated with the stochastic linear difference equation, is equal to the number of predetermined variables. The second-order equation (7.7) has one predetermined variable. To obtain a unique and stable solution, we need one eigenvalue within the unit circle and one outside. Note that $P(0) = 1/\beta > 0, P(1) = -\kappa\theta/\beta < 0$ and $P(\infty) = \infty$. The polynomial is positive when evaluated at zero and negative when evaluated at 1; therefore, it should cross in between. One root is surely within the unit circle and the two roots satisfy the following inequalities: $0 < \gamma_1 < 1 < \beta^{-1} < \gamma_2$. Their product is represented by $\gamma_1\gamma_2 = \beta^{-1}$ and their sum is equal to the term in parenthesis on the right-hand side of equation (7.8). The conditions for determinacy are satisfied.

We move now to solve equation (7.7) for the unique and bounded solution. Let us define the lag operator (L) with properties $L \cdot x_t = x_{t-1}$ and $L^{-1} \cdot x_t = E_t x_{t+1}$, or, more generally, $L^k \cdot x_t = x_{t-k}$ and $L^{-k} \cdot x_t = E_t x_{t+k}$; we can then write (7.7)

$$\left[L^{-1} - \left(1 + \frac{1}{\beta} + \frac{\kappa\theta}{\beta} \right) + \frac{1}{\beta}L \right] x_t = \frac{\theta}{\beta} v_t,$$

and therefore

$$\left[L^{-1} - (\gamma_1 + \gamma_2) + \gamma_1\gamma_2 L \right] x_t = \theta\gamma_1\gamma_2 v_t$$

and

$$(1 - \gamma_1 L)(L^{-1} - \gamma_2)x_t = \theta\gamma_1\gamma_2 v_t.$$

We can further simplify the above expression to

$$(1 - \gamma_1 L)(1 - \gamma_2^{-1}L^{-1})x_t = -\theta\gamma_1 v_t,$$

from which it follows that

$$(1 - \gamma_1 L)x_t = -\frac{\theta \gamma_1}{(1 - \gamma_2^{-1}L^{-1})} v_t$$

$$= -\theta \gamma_1 E_t \sum_{j=0}^{\infty} \gamma_2^{-j} v_{t+j}. \qquad (7.9)$$

In going from the first to the second line, we notice that

$$\frac{v_t}{1 - \gamma_2^{-1}L^{-1}} = (1 + \gamma_2^{-1}L^{-1} + \gamma_2^{-2}L^{-2} + \gamma_2^{-3}L^{-3} + \cdots)v_t$$

$$= E_t \sum_{j=0}^{\infty} \gamma_2^{-j} v_{t+j},$$

in which we have used the properties of the operator L^{-k} for $k \geq 1$. To remember the above expansion, recall that for a generic real number c with $|c| < 1$,

$$\frac{1}{1 - c} = \sum_{j=0}^{\infty} c^j.$$

Set $c = \gamma_2^{-1}L^{-1}$ and note that $\gamma_2 > 1$; therefore the result follows.

Using $Lx_t = x_{t-1}$, we can write (7.9) as:

$$x_t = \gamma_1 x_{t-1} - \theta \gamma_1 E_t \sum_{j=0}^{\infty} \gamma_2^{-j} v_{t+j}.$$

For the sake of simplicity, let us assume that v_t is a white noise shock; therefore $E_t v_{t+j} = 0$ for each $j > 0$, and then

$$x_t = \gamma_1 x_{t-1} - \theta \gamma_1 v_t.$$

The above equation represents the dynamic solution for the output gap, showing that it falls on impact when markup increases.

The path of inflation follows from (7.3) and is represented by

$$(\pi_t - \pi) = -\theta^{-1}(\gamma_1 - 1)x_{t-1} + \gamma_1 v_t,$$

having substituted the solution for the output gap. Inflation rises above target at the time at which the markup shock hits.

We can also use the *AD* equation (5.26) to derive the path of the interest rate consistent with optimal policy,

$$\hat{\imath}_t = r_t^e + E_t(\pi_{t+1} - \pi) + \sigma^{-1}E_t(x_{t+1} - x_t),$$
$$\hat{\imath}_t = r_t^e - (\sigma^{-1} - \theta^{-1})(1 - \gamma_1)x_t, \tag{7.10}$$

showing that the nominal interest rate, under optimal policy, should follow in a proportional way the frictionless real rate and react inversely to the output gap. Note the importance of the coefficient $(\sigma^{-1} - \theta^{-1})$ in determining the response of the interest rate to the markup shock consistently with the graphical analysis of Figure 7.1. The figure was plotted under the assumption that $\theta > \sigma$ and, consistently, equation (7.10) says that, in this case, the nominal interest rate increases following a positive markup shock to curb the rise in inflation, while the output gap falls.

It is important to note that (7.10) should not be interpreted as the interest rate rule that the monetary policymaker should follow to implement the optimal policy. Instead, it represents the resulting path of the policy rate once the central bank sets it to achieve the targeting rule (7.3). Furthermore, if (7.10) were considered as an interest rate rule, it would lead to equilibrium indeterminacy. Equation (7.10) also demonstrates that matching the Wicksellian real rate of interest with the equilibrium policy rate serves as a useful check when policy is optimally conducted in response to efficient shocks, but not when dealing with inefficient disturbances. This observation carries important policy implications for current monetary policy strategies in which the central bank pays attention to a concept labelled R-star that captures the frictionless rate of interest.

Under optimal policy with commitment, inflation and output gap show inertial behavior, which is the way commitment to future promises is taken into account in the formulation of the optimal policy problem. The aggregate supply equation (7.6) has a term in expectations, which is related to the next-period inflation rate, and managing those expectations is indeed critical for achieving maximum welfare. The way commitment works is by fulfilling past promises in a way that makes it credible that future promises will be fulfilled as well. This is why the optimal policy shows inertial behavior. Note the reaction of inflation. It rises on impact above target when a positive markup shock hits, but then falls below target to meet it in the long run. From this response, we can back up on the path of prices. Prices rise on impact by more than what would be required by the inflation target, but then their growth rate falls below the target rate and meets it in the long run. The policy rate also follows, inversely, the path of the output gap, inheriting its persistent behavior. Although the shock lasts for only one period, the interest rate remains above the steady state for a long time and declines only gradually.

7.4   Optimal Policy under Discretion

Optimal policy without commitment, the so-called optimal policy under discretion, implies a different path for inflation and output because of the implications of the forward-looking AS equation, which embeds expectations of future endogenous variables. Without commitment, in each period the policymaker reconsiders his optimization problem, having looked at the state of the economy. Therefore, he does not fulfill past promises and the private sector understands that he does not commit to future policies, too. To construct this equilibrium, we have to guess the solution and optimize it. As said before, in each period the policymakers will make the best choice, given the state of the economy. Inflation and output will be a linear function of the state variables. Since the only state variable is the markup shock, which is a white noise process in our example, the guessed solution is of the form

$$(\pi_t - \pi) = \pi_d v_t,$$

$$x_t = x_d v_t.$$

Parameters x_d and π_d are obtained by minimizing the loss function, taking into account the constraints of the economy. Since in the guessed solution inflation and output are a function of only the markup shocks, what is relevant in the optimization problem is just the one-period loss function. Therefore, π_d and x_d are going to be determined by minimizing the loss function

$$\frac{1}{2}(x_t)^2 + \frac{1}{2}\frac{\theta}{\kappa}(\pi_t - \pi)^2 = \frac{1}{2}(x_d v_t)^2 + \frac{1}{2}\frac{\theta}{\kappa}(\pi_d v_t)^2$$

under constraint

$$(\pi_t - \pi) = \kappa x_t + v_t + \beta E_t(\pi_{t+1} - \pi),$$

which can be written as

$$\pi_d v_t = \kappa x_d v_t + v_t,$$

given that under the guessed solution $E_t(\pi_{t+1} - \pi) = 0$. Optimal choices of π_d and x_d are therefore represented by

$$x_d = -\frac{\theta}{1+\theta\kappa},$$

$$\pi_d = \frac{1}{1+\theta\kappa},$$

which can be combined to imply the following targeting rule:

$$(\pi_t - \pi) + \theta^{-1}(\hat{Y}_t - \hat{Y}_t^e) = 0. \tag{7.11}$$

Differently from commitment, the optimal policy under discretion does not feature any inertia and also implies a different short-run response to the shock. By comparing the inflation targeting rule under discretion, (7.11), with that under commitment, (7.3), it can be noticed that (7.11) includes a trade-off only between inflation and the output gap, and not with respect to output-gap growth. The fact that the policymaker cares about the growth rate of output, and therefore internalizes the past level of output, reflects again the importance of fulfilling past promises under optimal policy with commitment, which appears in a more inertial plan.

7.5   Interest Rate Rules

This section studies the implications for inflation and output when the policymaker does not necessarily follow an optimal policy, but instead follows an interest rate rule of the form

$$\hat{\imath}_t = r_t^e + \phi_\pi (\pi_t - \pi) + \phi_x x_t. \tag{7.12}$$

The monetary policymaker reacts one-to-one to the frictionless real rate, meaning that the policymaker can make a perfect forecast of the rate's drivers, which is not as obvious as it may seem.[8]

The policymaker also reacts to the deviations of inflation from the target and to the output gap with nonnegative parameters $\phi_\pi, \phi_x \geq 0$. Each parameter measures the sensitivity of the interest rate with respect to the target variables. The value to assign to ϕ_π and ϕ_x is an important choice for the

---

8. The reaction to the frictionless real rate is undertaken for the sake of simplicity in order to concentrate solely on the inefficient shocks that create a trade-off between inflation and output.

policymaker and can distinguish one central bank from another with respect to its preferences concerning inflation or its output objectives when it follows an interest rate rule of the type (7.12).

Adding (7.12) to the two equations (7.5) and (7.6) gives us three equations to determine the path of the three endogenous variables $(\hat{\imath}_t, \pi_t, x_t)$, given the stochastic processes driving r_t^e and υ_t. Using (7.6) and (7.12) in (7.5) to substitute for $\hat{\imath}_t$ and $E_t(\pi_{t+1} - \pi)$, respectively, we can compress the model into a system of two stochastic linear difference equations:

$$E_t \begin{pmatrix} \pi_{t+1} - \pi \\ x_{t+1} \end{pmatrix} = \begin{bmatrix} \frac{1}{\beta} & -\frac{\kappa}{\beta} \\ \sigma(\phi_\pi - \frac{1}{\beta}) & 1 + \sigma\phi_x + \sigma\frac{\kappa}{\beta} \end{bmatrix} \begin{pmatrix} \pi_t - \pi \\ x_t \end{pmatrix}$$
$$+ \begin{bmatrix} -\frac{1}{\beta} \\ \frac{\sigma}{\beta} \end{bmatrix} \upsilon_t. \tag{7.13}$$

Note again that, given the reaction of interest rates to the frictionless real rate, inflation and the output gap are completely insulated from movements in r^e and will be perturbed only by the markup shock υ_t.

The first step is to study the conditions for the existence of a unique and bounded solution. The number of eigenvalues within the unit circle should be equal to the number of predetermined variables. In (7.13) there is no predetermined variable; therefore all eigenvalues should be outside the unit circle.[9]

To compute the characteristic polynomial, consider matrix $\mathcal{V}$ associated with system (7.13):

$$\mathcal{V} = \begin{bmatrix} \frac{1}{\beta} & -\frac{\kappa}{\beta} \\ \sigma(\phi_\pi - \frac{1}{\beta}) & 1 + \sigma\phi_x + \sigma\frac{\kappa}{\beta} \end{bmatrix}.$$

The characteristic polynomial is represented by

$$P(\gamma) = \gamma^2 - tr[\mathcal{V}]\gamma + \frac{1}{\beta}\det[\mathcal{V}],$$

where the trace and the determinant of matrix $\mathcal{V}$, are respectively,

$$tr[\mathcal{V}] = \left(1 + \frac{1}{\beta} + \sigma\phi_x + \sigma\frac{\kappa}{\beta}\right) > 0,$$

9. An easy rule of thumb to determine the number of predetermined variables is to see whether in the system written in a canonical form at time t, such as (7.13), there are variables with time index $t - 1$.

and

$$\det[V] = \frac{1}{\beta}(1 + \sigma\phi_x + \sigma\kappa\phi_\pi) > 0.$$

Given that the trace and the determinant are positive, the two roots are positive, too. Note that $P(0) = \beta^{-1}(1 + \sigma\phi_x + \sigma\kappa\phi_\pi) > 0$, $P(\infty) = \infty$, and $P(1) = \sigma\phi_x(\beta^{-1} - 1) + \sigma\kappa\beta^{-1}(\phi_\pi - 1)$. A necessary and sufficient condition for the two roots to be out of the unit circle is $P(1) > 0$, requiring

$$\sigma\phi_x(\beta^{-1} - 1) + \sigma\kappa\beta^{-1}(\phi_\pi - 1) > 0. \tag{7.14}$$

In the simple case in which $\phi_x = 0$, the above restriction implies that $\phi_\pi > 1$, which is called Taylor principle. To obtain a unique and stable solution, the interest rate rule should react more than proportionally to the deviations of inflation with respect to the target.

Under condition (7.14), we can now characterize the unique and stable solution. For simplicity, let us assume again that υ_t follows a white-noise process. One way to characterize the solution is to use the method of undetermined coefficients and guess that it is linear in shock υ_t:

$$\pi_t - \pi = \pi_r \upsilon_t,$$

$$x_t = x_r \upsilon_t,$$

for some values of the parameters π_r and x_r to be determined.

Inserting the hypothesized solution into (7.13), we see in the first line that

$$\pi_r E_t \upsilon_{t+1} = \frac{1}{\beta}\pi_r \upsilon_t - \frac{\kappa}{\beta}x_r \upsilon_t - \frac{1}{\beta}\upsilon_t,$$

and therefore we obtain the following restriction between the unknown parameters:

$$\pi_r = \kappa x_r + 1, \tag{7.15}$$

since $E_t \upsilon_{t+1} = 0$. From the second line of (7.13), we instead see that

$$x_r E_t \upsilon_{t+1} = \sigma\left(\phi_\pi - \frac{1}{\beta}\right)\pi_r \upsilon_t + \left(1 + \sigma\phi_x + \sigma\frac{\kappa}{\beta}\right)x_r \upsilon_t + \frac{\sigma}{\beta}\upsilon_t,$$

from which we obtain the following restriction:

$$\left(\frac{1}{\beta} - \phi_\pi\right)\pi_r = \left(\sigma^{-1} + \phi_x + \frac{\kappa}{\beta}\right)x_r + \frac{1}{\beta}. \tag{7.16}$$

Combining (7.15) and (7.16), we obtain

$$x_r = -\frac{\phi_\pi}{\sigma^{-1} + \phi_x + \kappa \phi_\pi},$$

$$\pi_r = \frac{\sigma^{-1} + \phi_x}{\sigma^{-1} + \phi_x + \kappa \phi_\pi}.$$

Parameters π_r and x_r satisfy the following inequalities: $\pi_r \geq 0$ and $x_r \leq 0$. Similarly to the analysis in Section 6.4 of Chapter 6, a markup shock puts pressure on inflation and reduces the output gap computed as deviation from the efficient level of output. There is then a trade-off between stabilizing inflation at the target and offsetting the fall in the output gap. By varying policy parameters ϕ_x and ϕ_π appropriately, we can describe this trade-off. The larger the reaction with respect to inflation, the more muted is the reaction of inflation to the shock, and the larger that of the output gap. At the limit in which $\phi_\pi \to \infty$, $\pi_r = 0$, and $x_r = -1/\kappa$, the entire shock is absorbed by the fall in output. On the contrary, when $\phi_x \to \infty$, $x_r = 0$, and $\pi_r = 1$, there is full pass-through of the markup shock on inflation.

Figure 7.2 compares the impulse responses following a positive temporary markup shock under the three policies considered in this chapter: optimal policy with commitment, optimal policy under discretion, and the interest rate rule.[10] The figure shows the inertial response of the macroeconomic variables under commitment even if the shock lasts only for one period. Instead, under the two other policies, the response of the variables dies out as the shock reverts to zero.

Figure 7.3 shows the path of prices under the three different policies, emphasizing the important difference between the optimal policy under commitment and the other two sub-optimal policies. Under commitment, the leap of the price level above what would have been implied by the growth rate of the inflation target is undone in the subsequent periods, as the price level goes back to the trend it would have followed without the shock, which is represented by the line $\tilde{p}^*$. Instead, under the interest rate policy or the optimal policy under discretion, the price level jumps above the trend and then grows at that point at the 2% annual rate without reconnecting to the initial trend. Bygones are bygones. The picture is consistent with the idea

---

10. Figure 7.2 uses the following parametrization: $\beta = 0.995$, $\kappa = 0.02$, $\sigma = 0.5$, $\theta = 10$, $\eta = 0.47$, $\phi_y = 0.5$, $\phi_\pi = 1.5$. The one-period markup shock υ is set at 0.25%. The model is calibrated quarterly. Inflation target π is set at a 2% annual rate.

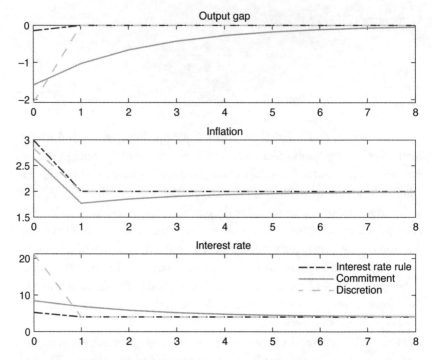

FIGURE 7.2. New Keynesian model: paths of output gap, inflation, and interest rate following a positive temporary markup shock, υ, under optimal policy with commitment, optimal policy under discretion, and the interest rate rule. Output gap is in %, inflation and interest rate are in % and at annual rates.

that optimal policy can be described as following a price level targeting rule, where the price level eventually returns to its pre-shock trend in the long run. The commitment-based optimal policy carries significant implications for maintaining price stability in the long term.

7.6   Optimal Inflation Target

This chapter has demonstrated that a flexible inflation targeting policy provides guidance for policymakers to effectively stabilize the economy under various sources of disturbances. However, one crucial aspect of the framework remains unexplained—the inflation target π in (7.3). In the model presented in Chapter 5, nothing precisely determines this inflation target, except that it represents the rate at which the economy would naturally converge in the absence of stochastic disturbances, on which firms base their price indexing.

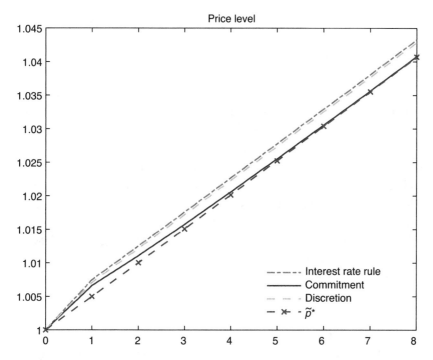

FIGURE 7.3. New Keynesian model: price paths following a positive temporary markup shock, υ, under optimal policy with commitment, optimal policy under discretion, and the interest rate rule. The price level target $\tilde{p}^*$ grows at a 2% annual rate.

Furthermore, this inflation rate is the threshold above and below which any deviations lead to price dispersion and misallocation of resources among goods produced using the same technology. So, what should this target be? Should it be positive, zero, or negative?

Three observations suggest that the inflation target should be a positive value. The first observation, firmly grounded in the model presented thus far, pertains to the presence of the zero lower bound on the nominal interest rate. As Chapter 9 will elucidate, in the face of significant shocks to the frictionless real interest rate that do not result in variations in the efficient level of output, the zero lower bound can impede the achievement of output and inflation stabilization at their targets. If the inflation target is set at zero, a negative frictionless real interest rate alone would necessitate pushing the nominal interest rate below zero to stabilize output at its efficient level. However, if the inflation target is set higher, the zero lower bound constraint binds at a more negative frictionless real rate. Essentially, the higher the target, the larger the shock required to make the constraint binding. For these reasons, a positive inflation target can minimize the occurrence of the zero lower bound and the losses associated with it.

The second observation relies on the existence of downward nominal wage rigidity, which is a well-documented fact in the literature.[11] Downward wage rigidity prevents wages from adjusting when shocks require a decrease in real wages. If real wages remain too high, it can squeeze firms' profits and necessitate a reduction in employment, with adverse consequences for both supply and aggregate demand. As Tobin (1972) suggested, inflation can "grease the wheels" of the labor market in this case, allowing for a decrease in real wages without the need for nominal wages to fall. With a positive inflation target, it is less likely that the downward rigidity constraint will bind, resulting in fewer employment and output costs.

The third observation pertains to the economic costs of deflation for debtors, as they are required to pay more real resources when prices fall due to their fixed nominal debt. When the inflation target is zero, it is likely that shocks will push prices downward. This could trigger a deflation-debt spiral, as first described by Fisher (1933). Debtors have to save more to pay their debt, leading to reduced consumption and aggregate demand. This, in turn, further contracts economic activity, reducing prices and making it more difficult for debtors to repay their debts. The costs of deflation became evident during the Gold Standard era when inflation was, on average, close to zero. Bernanke (1983) and Bernanke and James (1991) have warned about the disinflationary pressures associated with the Gold Standard at the onset of the Great Depression.

All of the above arguments provide a rationale to support a positive inflation target, but how large positive is still left unexplained.[12] Quantitative studies using a more general class of models than the one presented in this Chapter have shown that the optimal inflation rate could fall within the range targeted by many central banks. Coibion, Gorodnichenko, and Wieland (2012) quantified the optimal inflation rate to be just below 2 percent when accounting for the costs associated with reaching the zero lower bound. In their

---

11. See, among others, Holden (2004) and Dickens et al. (2007).

12. Furthermore, there is also to consider that a positive inflation target acknowledges imperfections in adjustments to the prices of existing goods for quality improvements and to the prices of new goods not previously included in the price index.

model, a positive inflation rate is considered costly because firms do not index their prices to a target rate. This approach might underestimate the optimal inflation rate.

Bilbiie, Fujiwara, and Ghironi (2014) showed that deviations from long-run price stability are optimal in the presence of endogenous entry and product variety, and that plausible preference specifications and parameter values justify positive long-run inflation rates. Furthermore, Adam and Weber (2019) have shown that in a framework with heterogeneous firms, each having its own productivity trend, the optimal inflation rate is generally positive and can be estimated to fall within the range of 1 percent to 3 percent.

There are, however, further arguments to consider in order to establish bounds on how high the inflation target could be. In an economy where inflation is high and contracts are fully indexed to it, there are no costs. However, this is rarely the case in practice. A high inflation rate can create costs when interacting with tax systems in which tax brackets are not indexed, as discussed by Feldstein (1997, 1999). Moreover, inflation might obscure changes in relative prices rather than in the overall price level, as well as temporary versus permanent changes in prices, making it more difficult for economic agents to plan their spending. This can also apply to long-term investments, debt, and credit contracts that are not indexed. An International Monetary Fund (2005) study has shown that a high rate of inflation can be associated with high volatility in inflation itself, leading to more misallocation of real resources. Finally, when inflation is high and volatile, and less predictable, economic agents begin to pay more attention to price changes. This increased attention affects their inflation expectations, which, in turn, become more volatile, making it harder for monetary policy to control them.

All of these observations suggest that the quantitative targets currently employed by inflation targeting central banks, typically in the range of 1 percent to 3 percent, are reasonable.

7.7   References

The optimal monetary policy in the NK model, whether from commitment or discretion, has been extensively discussed in works by Woodford (2003) and Galí (2008). In earlier works, Woodford (2002) characterized a welfare-based linear-quadratic approach to the optimal monetary policy problem in the benchmark NK model, assuming an efficient steady state. Clarida, Galí, and Gertler (1999) was the first work to compare optimal policy outcomes under commitment and discretion. Afrouzi et al. (2023) analyze the equilibrium under absence of commitment in the nonlinear version of the New Keynesian model.

Benigno and Woodford (2005, 2012) generalized the characterization of the optimal policy problem under commitment using a linear-quadratic approach, even when the steady state is inefficient. They showed that the solution to this problem corresponds to the first-order approximation of a Ramsey formulation of the optimal policy problem, analyzed under commitment from a "timeless perspective." An example of optimal monetary policy analysis using a Ramsey approach to the optimal monetary policy problem in the NK framework is found in Khan, King, and Wolman (2003).

Additionally, Giannoni and Woodford (2017) demonstrated that the solution of a general linear-quadratic problem yields targeting rules that, if followed, uniquely implement the optimal plan.

Nisticò (2007) showed that the welfare implications of using a Calvo-style price-setting model are equivalent, with an appropriate mapping of the parameters, to using Rotemberg's model. However, this result does not generalize to a distorted steady state, as shown by Lombardo and Vestin (2008).

Aoki (2001) analyzed a two-sector economy, demonstrating that the inflation rate to which higher weight is given in the inflation targeting policy is that with stickier prices. Aoki (2015) extends this analysis to state-contingent pricing models.

Svensson (2010) offers a comprehensive review of the inflation targeting regime adopted by many central banks. He frames it as a linear-quadratic optimal policy problem, underscoring the significance of targeting rules over interest rate rules. For practical insights into the implementation of inflation targeting, Bernanke and Mishkin (1997) provide valuable perspectives.

The interest rate policies discussed in Section 7.5, where the policy rate responds to inflation and the output gap, are commonly known as Taylor rules, named after Taylor's seminal work in 1993. Clarida, Galí, and Gertler (2000) estimated forward-looking Taylor rules for the U.S. economy with the aim of characterizing changes in the response to inflation during two distinct periods: the inflation episode of the 1970s and the disinflation era under Volcker's chairmanship. Williams (2016) discusses the implications of R-star, the frictionless real rate, for the conduct and efficacy of monetary policy.

Coibion, Gorodnichenko, and Wieland (2012) evaluate quantitatively the optimal inflation target when the zero lower bound constraint can occasionally bind as well as when wages are prevented from falling because of a downward rigidity constraint. Kim and Ruge-Murcia (2009) and Benigno and Ricci (2011) show that a positive inflation rate can alleviate the output costs of downward rigid wages.

8

NK Model with a Banking Sector

8.1 Introduction

The standard NK model has several limitations, some of which became evident after the 2007–2008 financial crisis. Specifically, this model assumes a single interest rate that applies to both money and credit markets, all equalized to the policy rate. However, the crisis revealed significant disparities in interest rates based on different credit standards and liquidity markets. Additionally, the standard NK model does not account for the banking sector, traditionally considered a crucial element of the policy transmission mechanism. Banks play a pivotal role by creating liquidity, which households use for transactions (the liquidity channel), and providing credit (the credit channel) to both households and firms operating in the economy, whose activities are vital for production.

In this chapter, we incorporate a banking model into the standard NK model, similarly to the approach taken in Chapter 4, with a primary focus on the liquidity channel. Chapter 10 will further explore the credit channel.

The model in this Chapter introduces two financial frictions, each emphasizing the unique role of specific securities. In terms of households, deposits issued by financial intermediaries serve a transactional purpose, modeled as utility that households gain from holding them. As a result, the deposit rate includes a liquidity premium compared to the rate in the credit market, which directly influences the consumption and saving choices of households. At the intermediary level, central bank reserves provide collateral benefits for issuing deposits. As a result, the interest rate on reserves also carries a liquidity premium relative to the deposit rate.

This framework yields three key results. Firstly, it establishes a hierarchy among risk-free interest rates, distinguished by their liquidity properties: the policy rate is the lowest, followed by the deposit rate, and then the credit market rate. Secondly, the policy rate transmits first through the banking sector before influencing the broader economy, in contrast to directly affecting consumer behavior. Consequently, the credit market rate that directly influences household saving decisions may not necessarily align with the policy rate, as seen in the standard NK model.

The third key result is that government liquidity indirectly impacts the credit market rate and, therefore, consumption and saving choices. This is unlike in the standard NK model, where only the policy rate influences these factors. This divergence occurs because liquidity premiums explain the difference between the credit market rate and the policy rate. Since the demand for deposits is inversely related to the liquidity premium between the deposit rate and the credit market rate, this premium becomes dependent on deposit levels and, through the collateral constraint in the banking sector, is related to overall government liquidity.

One important consequence of these findings is that the model assigns a distinct role to central bank reserves in influencing economic activity alongside adjustments to the policy rate. This feature has gained significance recently, as central banks have expanded their balance sheets and have begun reducing them. Section 9.6 of Chapter 9 uses this model to discuss the management of government liquidity during and after a liquidity trap.

8.2   Outline of the Results

Section 8.3.1 introduces the banking model and its equilibrium, demonstrating that the deposit rate is a weighted average of the credit market rate and the policy rate, with the policy rate being the lowest among them. In Section 8.3.2, the households' optimization problem is studied, particularly exploring their demand for deposits. This demand exhibits an inverse relationship with the premium between the deposit rate and the credit market rate.

One novel finding of the equilibrium, discussed in Section 8.4, is that the policy rate may not necessarily coincide with the rate relevant for consumption and saving decisions. This wedge depends on the overall liquid assets in the economy and therefore can be driven by the overall fiscal stance or/and supply of central bank reserves. Notably, this channel allows government liquidity, and central bank reserves, to exert a direct impact on the inflation rate, in addition to the traditional policy rate. There are specific scenarios in which this framework collapses into the single money market rate paradigm observed in the benchmark NK model of Chapter 5. This convergence occurs under three conditions: i) complete satiation of liquidity; ii) absence of securities that provide liquidity services; or iii) exclusion of reserves, and government debt, from the category of securities offering liquidity services.

In Section 8.5, we present the novel aggregate demand (AD) equation that arises from the model's log-linear approximation. This AD equation differs from the one in the benchmark NK model due to the direct influence of deposits and a reduced impact of future short-term rates on current demand. The optimal supply of liquidity and the optimal stabilization policy are explored in Section 8.6. With lumpsum taxes available, the optimal liquidity supply aims to fully satisfy the economy's liquidity needs. This outcome does not affect the choice of the inflation target. Consequently, the optimal approach to stabilizing shocks can be described in a manner similar to that for the standard NK framework.

8.3 Model

In this chapter, we present the model in blocks, starting from the banking sector, then moving to households, firms, and, finally, the government, which includes the treasury and the central bank. In the presentation we underline the main changes with respect to the benchmark New Keynesian model of Chapter 5.

8.3.1 Banking Model

At a generic time t, there is potentially an infinite number of intermediaries that can start the intermediation activity without any entry cost. Each intermediary lives for two periods. Intermediaries entering at time t face the following balance sheet constraint:

$$X_t + B_t^F + B_t = D_t + N_t, \tag{8.1}$$

in which (X) are the holdings of central bank reserves that are remunerated at the policy rate (i^X), (B^F) are treasury bills, and (B) are the holdings of short-term private debt that carries an interest rate (i). Intermediaries can finance their assets by issuing deposits (D) at the interest rate (i^D), and by raising equity (N). The key feature of this framework, with respect to the benchmark NK model, is that in equilibrium only banks hold central bank reserves. Therefore, the transmission mechanism of the policy rate, i^X, occurs through the banking sector.

In line with Chapter 5, when presenting the NK model, we assume that the treasury's debt is fully backed by the central bank, so it inherits the properties of being repaid with certainty, just like the central bank reserves. Therefore, it is perfectly substitutable for the central bank reserves and carries the same interest rate, denoted as i^X. From now on, we denote B^g as the overall government debt, including central bank reserves and treasury debt, i.e., $B^g = X + B^F$.

Intermediaries are subject to a collateral requirement of the form $B_t^g \geq \rho D_t \geq 0$, with $0 \leq \rho \leq 1$, saying that government debt should cover at least a fraction, when ρ is positive, of deposits. The two extremes of the interval characterize two interesting cases. When $\rho = 1$, intermediaries need to back all deposits with government debt, as in a narrow banking system. When $\rho = 0$, there is no collateral requirement.

Intermediaries can also invest in cash, which is going to be dominated by reserves. The economy is therefore cashless in equilibrium, but not without cash as a store of value. The possibility that reserves can be transformed into cash implies the existence of a zero lower bound on the interest rate on reserves, $i_t^X \geq 0$, at each point in time.

In general, note that B can be also negative, meaning—in this case—borrowing. As will be shown later in the household problem, the following inequality holds: $i_t \geq i_t^D$. Therefore, deposits are a better way of financing intermediaries' assets. The reason for such inequality is that B represents a form of private indebtedness that is risk-free but not liquid, whereas deposit provides also liquidity services and therefore receives a liquidity premium. However, given the demand for deposits and the supply of equity, intermediaries might rely on a more costly way of financing, if needed. Note also that i represents, as in Chapter 3, the credit market nominal interest rate, since it is the one that directly influences the consumption and saving choice of households, as the following analysis is going to show.

Intermediary profits, Ψ_{t+1}^I, at time $t + 1$ are represented by

$$\Psi_{t+1}^I = (1 + i_t)B_t + (1 + i_t^X)B_t^g - (1 + i_t^D)D_t. \qquad (8.2)$$

In this chapter, intermediaries' profits are certain and, therefore, noncontingent on the state, since all securities are free of risk. As in Section 4.3.3 of

Chapter 4, we introduce a limited-liability constraint on intermediaries, for their profits should be nonnegative in all contingencies. It can be represented by

$$\Psi_{\min}^I = (1+i_t)B_t + (1+i_t^X)B_t^g - (1+i_t^D)D_t \geq 0, \qquad (8.3)$$

which is independent of the state.

Intermediaries maximize expected rents, which are equal to the expected discounted value of profits minus the value of equity,

$$\mathcal{R}_t = E_t \left\{ \tilde{R}_{t,t+1} \Psi_{t+1}^I \right\} - N_t \qquad (8.4)$$
$$= E_t \left\{ \tilde{R}_{t,t+1} \left[(1+i_t)B_t + (1+i_t^X)B_t^g - (1+i_t^D)D_t \right] \right\} - N_t.$$

In the first line of (8.4), we have discounted profits with the stochastic nominal discount factor $\tilde{R}_{t,t+1}$, which is the same as that for the consumers, since they own intermediaries. In the second line we have substituted, in the equation, profits Ψ_{t+1}^I using equation (8.2).

Intermediaries choose B_t, B_t^g, D_t, and N_t, with B_t^g, D_t, $N_t \geq 0$ to maximize (8.4) under the budget constraint (8.1), the limited liability constraint (8.3), and the collateral constraint, $B_t^g \geq \rho D_t$.

To solve the above-defined linear programming problem, first substitute the balance-sheet constraint (8.1) for B_t in (8.4) to obtain

$$\mathcal{R}_t = \left[\frac{(1+i_t^X)}{(1+i_t)} - 1 \right] B_t^g - \left[\frac{(1+i_t^D)}{(1+i_t)} - 1 \right] D_t. \qquad (8.5)$$

In deriving equation (8.5), we have used $E_t \left\{ \tilde{R}_{t,t+1}(1+i_t) \right\} = 1$, anticipating a result of the household problem.

The rent function (8.5) should be maximized under the limited liability constraint (8.3) and the collateral constraint. The first result is that raising equity is not costly, which implies that the limited liability constraint is not binding, for equity can be raised to satisfy it.

We now use (8.5) together with $B_t^g \geq \rho D_t$ to draw implications for the supply of deposits. Consider first the case in which there are excess reserves, i.e., $B_t^g > \rho D_t$, meaning that banks are holding reserves in excess with respect to the required collateral constraint. It should follow in (8.5) that the market and the policy rates are equalized, i.e., $i_t = i_t^X$; otherwise rents will be positive. Using, again, the zero-rent condition applied to (8.5) implies that also the deposit rate will be fixed at the rate on reserves; therefore $i_t^D = i_t^X = i_t$. The first interesting result is that when $B_t^g > \rho D_t$, all risk-free rates are equalized.

Consider now the case of a binding collateral constraint, $B_t^g = \rho D_t$. We can substitute it in (8.5) in place of B_t^g to obtain that

$$(1 + i_t^D) = \rho(1 + i_t^X) + (1 - \rho)(1 + i_t) \tag{8.6}$$

when rents are zero. The interest rate on deposits is a weighted average of the interest rate on reserves and that on illiquid bonds. Consider two special cases: i) $\rho = 1$; ii) $\rho = 0$.

The first case $\rho = 1$ characterizes a narrow-banking regime in which all deposits are backed by reserves. Using (8.6), it follows that the deposit rate coincides with the policy rate, $i_t^D = i_t^X$, but in general $i_t > i_t^D = i_t^X$. At the other extreme, when $\rho = 0$ and government debt no longer provide nonpecuniary benefits, it follows that $i_t^D = i_t$ whereas it should necessarily be the case that $i_t = i_t^X$ when reserves are positively supplied by the central bank. Therefore, when $\rho = 0$, all risk-free interest rates are equalized, $i_t = i_t^X = i_t^D$.

To summarize the findings thus far, the standard NK model discussed in Chapter 5, where there exists only one interest rate (as the policy rate coincides with the credit market rate), is a subset of the model when reserves/government debt are in excess, meaning $B_t^g > \rho D_t$, or when they do not offer nonpecuniary benefits, that is, when $\rho = 0$.

To conclude the characterization of the banking problem, the demand for equity, as discussed, is such as to make the limited liability constraint not binding. Therefore, using (8.1) in (8.3), we obtain the following inequality:

$$N_t \geq \frac{i_t^D - i_t}{1 + i_t} D_t + \frac{i_t - i_t^X}{1 + i_t} B_t^g,$$
$$N_t \geq 0,$$

in which we have used (8.6) in moving from the first to the second line. Equity can also be zero in this simple model, since there is no risk in the assets held by intermediaries, unlike in Chapter 4.

8.3.2 Households

Consider a representative consumer maximizing the following intertemporal utility:

$$E_{t_0} \left\{ \sum_{t=t_0}^{\infty} \beta^{t-t_0} \xi_t \left[U(C_t) + V\left(\frac{D_t}{P_t}\right) - \int_0^1 \frac{(L_t(j))^{1+\eta}}{1+\eta} dj \right] \right\}. \tag{8.7}$$

E_{t_0} is the conditional-expectation operator at time t_0; β with $0 < \beta < 1$ is the utility discount factor; ξ is a preference shock; $U(\cdot)$ is a concave, differentiable function of C, the aggregate consumption good. As in the NK model, C is a Dixit-Stiglitz aggregator of a continuum of measure one of goods produced in the economy. $V(\cdot)$ is a concave, differentiable function of D, deposits from which the households get nonpecuniary benefits (liquidity services); it displays a satiation point $\bar{d} > 0$, such that its first derivative satisfies $V_d(\cdot) = 0$ for all $D_t/P_t \geq \bar{d}$, (P) is the consumption-based price index; $(L(j))$ is the supply of labor of variety j; and $\eta \geq 0$ is the inverse of the Frisch elasticity of labor supply. The only difference with respect to the utility function of the benchmark NK model in Chapter 5 is that households also receive utility from deposits. This is similar to what was seen in Chapter 3, where, in a central bank digital currency framework, households hold deposits directly at the central bank, which provides liquidity services. In this chapter, liquidity services are offered by securities issued by intermediaries, potentially backed by central bank reserves.

The household is subject to the following flow budget constraint:

$$P_t C_t + D_t + (1 + i_{t-1})B_{t-1} + N_t + T_t \leq (1 + i^D_{t-1})D_{t-1} + B_t +$$

$$+ \int_0^1 W_t(j)L_t(j)dj + \Psi^I_t + \Psi_t.$$

Households can save in deposits (D) that pay an interest rate i^D and can borrow or lend through private risk-free bonds (B), which pay an interest rate i.[1] We might allow households to also hold treasury debt and central bank reserves. However, given that the only securities used for transaction purposes are deposits, these alternative assets would be dominated in return and thus not held.

Households can also finance intermediaries with equity (N); (T) are lump-sum taxes levied by the government. On the right-hand side of the budget constraint, it receives payment for work at the nominal wage $(W(j))$ for variety j, and nominal profits from firms (Ψ) and intermediaries (Ψ^I). The consumption/saving choices are subject to an appropriate borrowing limit.

---

1. The debt B of households is specular to the assets B held by intermediaries in (8.1). A positive value of B denotes debt. Note that, differently from Chapter 1, bonds are issued not at discount but at the unitary value.

The following asset-pricing condition characterizes the choice with respect to the illiquid bonds:

$$E_t \left\{ \tilde{R}_{t,t+1} \right\} = \frac{1}{1+i_t}. \tag{8.8}$$

The expected nominal value of the stochastic discount factor is equal to the price of the illiquid bonds—the inverse of the gross nominal interest rate. As noted, we label this interest rate, i, as the nominal interest rate in the credit market, since it is the one that directly affects the consumption and saving choices. The nominal stochastic discount factor is represented by

$$\tilde{R}_{t,t+1} = \beta \frac{\xi_{t+1} U_c(C_{t+1})}{\xi_t U_c(C_t)} \frac{P_t}{P_{t+1}},$$

in which $U_c(\cdot)$ is the first derivative of the function $U(\cdot)$ with respect to its argument. The optimal choice with respect to deposits D_t implies that

$$1 = \varrho_t + (1+i_t^D) E_t \left\{ \tilde{R}_{t,t+1} \right\}, \tag{8.9}$$

in which ϱ_t, with $\varrho_t \geq 0$, is the liquidity premium represented by

$$\varrho_t = \frac{V_d \left(\frac{D_t}{P_t} \right)}{U_c(C_t)}.$$

Combine (8.8) and (8.9) to obtain

$$(1+i_t^D) = (1 - \varrho_t)(1+i_t),$$

saying that the interest rate on deposits is lower than, or almost equal to, the rate on illiquid bonds.[2] Only when the economy is satiated with liquidity, $\varrho_t = 0$, do the two rates coincide. The optimal supply of equity, N, implies that its value is equal to the discounted value of intermediary profits:

$$N_t = E_t \left\{ \tilde{R}_{t,t+1} \Psi_{t+1}^I \right\}.$$

Finally, the intertemporal budget constraint of the consumer holds with equality at all times.

8.3.3 Firms

The firm problem is unchanged with respect to Section 5.5 of Chapter 5. Firms, of a unitary mass on the segment $[0, 1]$, use labor to produce goods

---

2. It is required that $0 \leq \varrho_t < 1$.

$(Y(j))$ according to the technology $Y_t(j) = A_t L_t(j)$, in which A_t is labor productivity, facing a demand function of the form $Y_t(j) = (P_t(j)/P_t)^{-\theta} Y_t$, in which $P_t(j)$ is the price of good j and θ is the elasticity of substitution among the variety of goods produced, with $\theta > 1$. In this chapter, we abstract from government purchases. Prices are sticky following the Calvo model, in which a fraction, $1 - \alpha$, is allowed to change its prices, maximizing the expected present discounted value of its profits. Firms that do not adjust prices index them to the target Π. As shown in Section 5.5 of Chapter 5, the described framework delivers an AS equation characterized by equations (5.21), (5.22), and (5.23), in which the only difference is that $G_t = 0$.

8.3.4 Government

The government is composed of the treasury and the central bank, which are consolidated together. Their flow budget constraint is

$$B_t^g = (1 + i_{t-1}^X) B_{t-1}^g + \tau_t^s P_t Y_t - T_t, \qquad (8.10)$$

showing that the government can pay the overall debt and the subsidy to firms' revenues, $\tau^s PY$, via taxes, T, and new borrowing. As mentioned, we are assuming that the central bank backs the treasury. Therefore the overall government debt is not subject to a solvency condition. See the discussion in Section 1.3.2 of Chapter 1.

8.4 Equilibrium

We will now characterize the equilibrium of the model. Asset-market equilibrium requires that all government bonds B^g be held by the intermediaries; their deposits D are held by the households, while B issued by the households is an asset for the intermediaries. Equilibrium in the goods markets implies $Y_t = C_t$ for each $t \geq t_0$.

Recall the relationship between the deposit rate, the policy rate, and the credit market nominal interest rate:

$$(1 + i_t^D) = \rho(1 + i_t^X) + (1 - \rho)(1 + i_t), \qquad (8.11)$$

for each $t \geq t_0$, with $i_t \geq i_t^X \geq 0$.

On the other hand, the household's demand for securities implies that the spread between the deposit rate and the market nominal rate satisfies

$$\frac{(1 + i_t^D)}{(1 + i_t)} = \left(1 - \frac{V_d\left(\frac{D_t}{P_t}\right)}{U_c(Y_t)}\right), \qquad (8.12)$$

with

$$\frac{1}{1+i_t} = E_t \left\{ \beta \frac{\xi_{t+1}U_c(Y_{t+1})}{\xi_t U_c(Y_t)} \frac{P_t}{P_{t+1}} \right\}. \tag{8.13}$$

The three equations above represent the *AD* block of the model, holding for each $t \geq t_0$. Note the difference with respect to the benchmark NK model of Chapter 5. The two models share the Euler equation (8.13), but here the relevant rate is the credit market nominal interest rate, i, which does not necessarily coincide with the policy rate. The transmission mechanism of monetary policy is now enriched by multiple money market rates and the role of liquidity in these markets.

The *AS* block of the model remains as in Chapter 5, which is here restated in the following three equilibrium conditions holding for each $t \geq t_0$:

$$\left(\frac{1-\alpha\left(\frac{\Pi_t}{\Pi}\right)^{\theta-1}}{1-\alpha} \right)^{\frac{1+\theta\eta}{\theta-1}} = \frac{F_t}{J_t}, \tag{8.14}$$

in which F_t and J_t are represented by

$$F_t = \xi_t U_c(Y_t)\frac{Y_t}{\mu_t} + \alpha\beta E_t \left\{ \left(\frac{\Pi_{t+1}}{\Pi}\right)^{\theta-1} F_{t+1} \right\}, \tag{8.15}$$

$$J_t = \xi_t \left(\frac{Y_t}{A_t}\right)^{1+\eta} + \alpha\beta E_t \left\{ \left(\frac{\Pi_{t+1}}{\Pi}\right)^{\theta(1+\eta)} J_{t+1} \right\}, \tag{8.16}$$

where μ_t is the markup disturbance.[3]

The government flow budget constraint is:

$$B_t^g = (1+i_{t-1}^X)B_{t-1}^g + \tau_t^s P_t Y_t - T_t. \tag{8.17}$$

The last equation relevant for the determination of equilibrium is the following intertemporal resource constraint:

$$\frac{(1+i_{t-1}^X)B_{t-1}^g}{P_t} = E_t \left\{ \sum_{T=t}^{\infty} \beta^{T-t} \frac{\xi_T U_c(Y_T)}{\xi_t U_c(Y_t)} \left[\frac{T_T}{P_T} - \tau_T^s Y_T + \frac{i_T - i_T^X}{1+i_T} \frac{B_T^g}{P_T} \right] \right\}, \tag{8.18}$$

---

3. Recall that the markup is represented by $\mu_t = \theta/[(\theta-1)(1+\tau_t^s)]$, and its variations depend on variations of the tax/subsidy τ_t^s, which we maintain as exogenously given.

holding for each $t \geq t_0$. Equilibrium condition (8.18) holds as the mirror image of the intertemporal budget constraint of the private sector, taking into account equilibrium in the goods and asset markets. Note the difference with respect to the intertemporal constraint (5.25) for the "seigniorage" revenues that the government extracts from the households by issuing liabilities at a lower cost with respect to the market nominal interest rate. Finally, recall the collateral constraint

$$B_t^g \geq \rho D_t. \tag{8.19}$$

The equilibrium is a set of stochastic processes $\{P_t, i_t, i_t^D, i_t^X, Y_t, F_t, J_t, D_t, T_t, B_t^g\}_{t=t_0}^{\infty}$ that satisfy equations (8.11)–(8.17), (8.19) for each $t \geq t_0$, and (8.18), considering the inequality constraint, $i_t \geq i_t^X \geq 0$ and the definition $\Pi_t \equiv P_t/P_{t-1}$ and given exogenous stochastic processes, $\{\xi_t, A_t, \tau_t^s\}_{t=t_0}^{\infty}$, and the appropriate initial conditions. There are two degrees of freedom left to specify the monetary/fiscal policy regime. In what follows we assume that the central bank sets the interest rate on reserves $\{i_t^X\}_{t=t_0}^{\infty}$, and jointly the central bank and the treasury set the path of the overall government liabilities, $\{B_t^g\}_{t=t_0}^{\infty}$, which include the central bank reserves.

The key difference with respect to the equilibrium of the benchmark NK model discussed in Section 5.5.1 of Chapter 5 is that now the overall level of government debt matters directly in affecting aggregate demand through equations (8.12) and (8.19). The NK model is nested when liquidity is fully satiated, i.e., $V_d(\cdot) = 0$.

The model is also equivalent in a perfect foresight setting to that developed in Section 3.5 of Chapter 3, when $\rho = 1$, since a narrow-banking regime corresponds to a model in which government debt provides liquidity services directly to households. The case in which $\rho < 1$, in its perfect foresight, would not change the conclusion of that chapter. Furthermore, it is worth noting that we could have also modeled an environment in which the central bank does not back the treasury's liabilities. This approach would have allowed us to mimic the analysis presented in Section 3.3 of Chapter 3. In this case, central bank reserves would be the only securities to directly influence aggregate demand through (8.12).

8.5   Log-linear Approximation

In this section, we discuss the log-linear approximation of the model previously presented, comparing it with the benchmark NK model. We consider a steady state in which shocks are all constant, $\xi_t = \xi$, $A_t = A$, and $\mu_t = 1$. In particular, $\mu_t = 1$ is obtained by setting the tax subsidy in the steady state at $\tau^s = 1/(\theta - 1)$. In this steady state, (gross) inflation is at the target Π. Setting $\Pi_t = \Pi$ in the non-stochastic version of (8.14), (8.15), and (8.16), it follows that $F = J$ and that $F = \xi U_c(Y)Y/(1 - \alpha\beta)$ and $J = \xi(Y/A)^{1+\eta}/(1 - \alpha\beta)$. Therefore, the steady state of output is implicitly given by $(Y/A)^\eta = AY \cdot U_c$, which coincides with the efficient level of output, in line with the discussion in Chapter 5.

Using $\Pi_t = \Pi$ in the non-stochastic version of (8.13), it follows that the market nominal interest rate is $1 + i = \beta^{-1}\Pi$ in the steady state. We assume that monetary and fiscal policies are such that, in this steady state, the real value of government debt implies that the overall real deposits are below the satiation level, i.e., $D/P < \bar{d}$, and therefore $B^g = \rho D$. Given a constant interest rate on reserves, i^X, and defining ν as the ratio of the marginal utility of liquidity versus that of consumption evaluated at the steady state, i.e., $\nu = V_d/U_c$, we can obtain using equations (8.11)–(8.13) that the spreads between the money-market rates and the policy rate are given by

$$\frac{1+i}{1+i^X} = \frac{\rho}{\rho - \nu}$$

and

$$\frac{1+i^D}{1+i^X} = \frac{\rho(1-\nu)}{\rho - \nu},$$

showing that $i \geq i^D \geq i^X$.[4] The benchmark NK model is nested when $\nu = 0$, implying equalization between both money market rates and the policy rate. Note, instead, that under narrow banking ($\rho = 1$), the deposit rate coincides with the policy rate, $i^D = i^X$, while i can be higher.

We take a log-linear approximation of the equilibrium conditions around the above defined steady state.[5] We start from the AS equation, which is exactly the same as the New Keynesian AS equation,

$$\pi_t - \pi = \kappa(\hat{Y}_t - \hat{Y}_t^n) + \beta E_t(\pi_{t+1} - \pi), \qquad (8.20)$$

for a positive parameter κ defined in (5.28); $\pi_t \equiv \ln P_t/P_{t-1}$ and $\pi \equiv \ln \Pi$. Inflation deviations from the target depend positively on the output gap

---

4. Note that it should necessarily be the case that $\nu < \rho$.

5. Details of the derivations are in Appendix I.

$\hat{Y}_t - \hat{Y}_t^n$ and on the one-period ahead inflation expectations.[6] We maintain the same notation and parameters' definition as in Chapter 5, with the natural level of output now represented by

$$\hat{Y}_t^n = \frac{1+\eta}{\sigma^{-1}+\eta}\hat{A}_t - \frac{1}{\sigma^{-1}+\eta}\hat{\mu}_t,$$

in which $\sigma = -U_{cc}Y/U_c$ and the derivatives of the function $U(\cdot)$ are evaluated at the steady state.

The aggregate demand equation, instead, differs from that of the standard New Keynesian model. Although in both models the consumption Euler equation links output to the real rate, here, as noted, the relevant nominal rate is the credit market nominal rate, i, and not the policy rate (see equation 8.13). In a log-linear approximation, we obtain

$$\hat{Y}_t = E_t\hat{Y}_{t+1} - \sigma(\hat{i}_t - E_t(\pi_{t+1} - \pi) + E_t\Delta\hat{\xi}_{t+1}), \qquad (8.21)$$

in which $\Delta\hat{\xi}_{t+1} = \hat{\xi}_{t+1} - \hat{\xi}_t$ and $\hat{i}_t = \ln(1+i_t)/(1+i)$.

The banking model determines the relationship between money-market rates and the policy rate,

$$\hat{i}_t = \hat{i}_t^X + \frac{1-v}{\rho-v}(\hat{i}_t - \hat{i}_t^D), \qquad (8.22)$$

as a first-order approximation to equation (8.11), in which $\hat{i}_t^X = \ln(1+i_t^X)/(1+i^X)$ and $\hat{i}_t^D = \ln(1+i_t^D)/(1+i^D)$.

Equilibrium in the deposit market—see equation (8.12)—implies that the real value of deposit, d with $d = D/P$, is positively related with output and negatively with respect to the liquidity premium through the relationship

$$\hat{d}_t = d_y\hat{Y}_t - d_i(\hat{i}_t - \hat{i}_t^D), \qquad (8.23)$$

in which the elasticity of the demand of liquidity with respect to output is given by $d_y = \sigma_d/\sigma$, and that with respect to the money market spread is $d_i = \sigma_d(1-v)/v$; σ_d is the intertemporal elasticity of substitution in the real value of liquidity, defined as $\sigma_d = -V_d/(V_{dd}d)$, in which V_d and V_{dd} are the first and second derivatives of the function $V(\cdot)$ evaluated at the steady state.

Some interesting cases are nested in the above framework. Consider first the one in which there is full satiation of liquidity, which is captured by

---

6. A variable with a hat, unless otherwise noted, defines the log deviation of the variable with respect to the steady state.

the parameter ν going to zero. The interest rate on deposits and that on reserves and the market nominal rate are all equalized in and out of the steady state. The AD equation collapses to that of the benchmark New Keynesian model,

$$\hat{Y}_t = E_t\hat{Y}_{t+1} - \sigma(\hat{i}_t^X - E_t(\pi_{t+1} - \pi) + E_t\Delta\hat{\xi}_{t+1}), \qquad (8.24)$$

in which the policy rate directly affects the real rate relevant for the consumption/saving choices. In the more general case, we can combine (8.22) and (8.23) into (8.21) to obtain

$$\hat{Y}_t = \nu_\rho E_t\hat{Y}_{t+1} - \sigma\nu_\rho(\hat{i}_t^X - E_t(\pi_{t+1} - \pi) + E_t\Delta\hat{\xi}_{t+1}) + d_y^{-1}(1 - \nu_\rho)\hat{d}_t.$$
$$(8.25)$$

There are two important novel features shown by the AD equation in this framework with respect to the NK model (see equation 5.26): first, there is a role for liquidity in affecting the aggregate demand equation; second, the coefficient $\nu_\rho \equiv (1 - \rho^{-1}\nu)$ in front of the expected level of output is positive and less than the unitary value, which has implications for the effectiveness of future rates in influencing current output. To gauge the difference with respect to the standard AD equation, solve equation (8.25) forward:

$$\hat{Y}_t = -\nu_\rho\sigma E_t \sum_{T=t}^{\infty} \nu_\rho^{T-t}(\hat{i}_T^X - (\pi_{T+1} - \pi) + \Delta\hat{\xi}_{T+1})$$

$$+ d_y^{-1}(1 - \nu_\rho)E_t \sum_{T=t}^{\infty} \nu_\rho^{T-t}\hat{d}_T. \qquad (8.26)$$

Not only does the current real rate have less impact on output for given intertemporal elasticity of substitution in consumption σ; movements in the expected future rates also influence current output less and with a decaying weight. A similar argument applies to the effectiveness of the supply of deposits in moving current demand. Note that a rise in the supply of liquidity has an expansionary effect on output.

Figure 8.1 shows the impulse responses of the output gap, inflation, interest rate on reserves, and real deposit to a shock to the policy rate, which is modelled to follow the policy rule

$$\hat{i}_t^X = \phi_\pi(\pi_t - \pi) + \phi_y\hat{Y}_t + e_t,$$

with

$$e_t = \rho_e e_{t-1} + \varepsilon_{1,t},$$

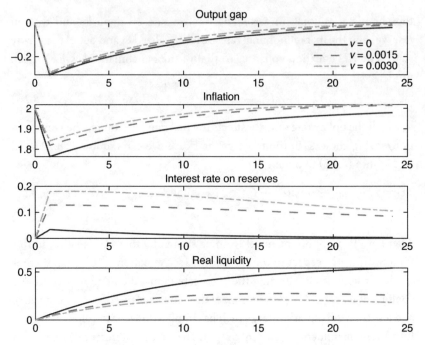

FIGURE 8.1. New Keynesian model with a banking sector: paths of output gap, inflation, interest rate on reserves, and real liquidity (deposit) following a shock to the interest rate on reserves using an interest rate rule for different steady-state spread between the credit market nominal interest rate and the deposit rate (parameter ν). Output gap is in %, inflation and interest rate on reserves are in % and at annual rates, interest rate is in deviation from the steady-state value, and real liquidity is in percentage deviations with respect to the steady state.

in which $\varepsilon_{1,t}$ is the white noise shock perturbing the model economy and $0 \leq \rho_e \leq 1$; ϕ_π and ϕ_y are nonnegative parameters. In Figure 8.1, impulse responses are plotted for three values of the parameter ν, namely $\{0, 0.0015, 0.0030\}$, corresponding to spreads between i and i^D of zero, sixty, one hundred and twenty basis points at annual rates.[7] When ν is equal to zero, the benchmark NK model is nested. Starting from this case, a positive interest rate

7. The model is calibrated quarterly. The following parametrization, as in Benigno and Benigno (2022), is used: $\beta = 0.995$, $\kappa = 0.02$, $\sigma = 0.5$, $\sigma_d = 0.1367$, $\rho = 0.21$, $\theta = 10$, $\eta = 0.47$, $\phi_y = 0.5$, $\phi_\pi = 1.5$, $\rho_e = \rho_b = 0.9$. The one-period shock on the nominal interest rate ε_1 is set at 1% at annual rates; the one-period shock to nominal liquidity ε_2 is set at 10%, in deviation with respect to the steady state. Inflation target π is set at a 2% annual rate.

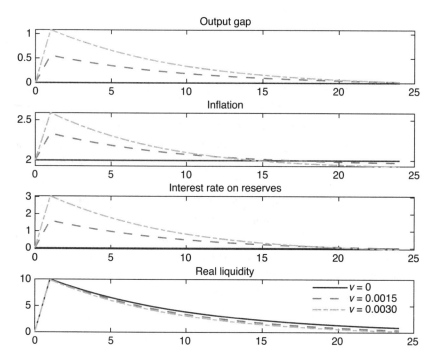

FIGURE 8.2. New Keynesian model with a banking sector: paths of output gap, inflation, interest rate on reserves, and real liquidity (deposit) following a shock to nominal liquidity, for different steady-state spreads between the credit market nominal interest rate and the deposit rate (parameter ν). Output gap is in %, inflation and interest rate on reserves are in % and at annual rates, interest rate is in deviation from the steady-state value, and real liquidity is in percentage deviations with respect to the steady state.

shock has a contractionary effect, lowering the output gap and inflation with respect to the target. Liquidity does not matter in this case. However, since nominal liquidity stays constant and inflation falls below the target, real liquidity rises in deviations from the steady state. When $\nu > 0$, liquidity influences aggregate demand, as shown in equation (8.26). The increase in real liquidity mitigates the output-gap fall, which is not quantitatively significant in the figure, and that of inflation with respect to the target. Since inflation is higher when $\nu > 0$, real liquidity evaluated in deviations with respect to the steady state increases less than in the case in which $\nu = 0$.

   Figure 8.2, using the same calibration of Figure 8.1, shows, instead, the impulse responses following a shock to the overall liquidity supplied by the government, assuming the following process for nominal government debt,

B^g, in deviations from the steady state:

$$\hat{B}^g_t = \rho_b \hat{B}^g_{t-1} + \varepsilon_{2,t},$$

in which $\varepsilon_{2,t}$ is a white noise shock and $0 \leq \rho_b \leq 1$. When $\nu = 0$, liquidity has no effect on output gap and inflation. With a positive ν, liquidity pushes up output gap through the aggregate demand equation and, therefore, inflation.

The analysis above highlights a crucial way in which monetary and fiscal policies can affect the economy, distinct from the usual practice of adjusting interest rates. In this context, government debt and central bank reserves influence economic activity, complementing conventional policies.

Expanding government liquidity can boost overall demand and economic activity. This effect occurs because government liquidity impacts the AD equation. As government liquidity rises, deposits increase, which, in turn, encourages greater consumption rather than saving. People tend to spend more, leading to higher aggregate demand. This increase in economic activity, in turn, affects inflation through the AS equation (8.20).

8.6   Optimal Policy

We discuss in this section the optimal policy along the lines of the discussion in Section 7.6 of Chapter 7 and the optimal stabilization policy.

The noteworthy finding is that the analysis presented in Section 7.6 remains largely consistent with some important qualifications. When considering optimal policy, it should now include the optimization of the liquidity policy alongside the selection of the optimal inflation target. This should be done with the overarching goal of maximizing household utility, as outlined in equation (8.7). The key departure from the standard NK model lies in the fact that, in this context, households derive utility from the real value of their deposit holdings.

When it comes to liquidity management, the optimal liquidity policy is to satiate the economy with liquidity, therefore achieving $V_d(\cdot) = 0$, provided there are no bounds on real lumpsum taxes. In fact, the total real amount of government liquidity in the economy is constrained by the intertemporal resource constraint, as indicated in equation (8.18), and thus by the real value of taxes.

This recommendation aligns with the concept known as the Friedman (1960) rule. According to this rule, it is desirable to eliminate the gap between money-market interest rates and the policy rate, effectively setting it to zero; see equation (8.12). Importantly, reducing this interest rate wedge does not impose any restrictions on the inflation target that the central bank can choose. This is because the central bank sets policy in terms of the interest rate on reserves.

As a result, the same issue of indeterminacy regarding the optimal inflation target discussed in Section 7.6 of Chapter 7 arises in this context. The arguments presented there in favor of having a positive inflation target remain relevant here as well.

It is important to discuss the case in which taxes are distortionary. In this scenario, the policymaker, by a second-best argument, does not aim to achieve full satiation of liquidity because doing so would require imposing excessive distortions in taxation.[8] However, this does not alter the fact that the optimal inflation target remains indeterminate under optimal policy (from a "timeless perspective"). The arguments presented earlier continue to hold, with the caveat that when arguing against an excessively high inflation rate, it should be taken into consideration that the costs of such a high rate should be, at least in part, endogenously connected to the distortionary nature of taxation.

In the context of optimal stabilization policy, we examine the problem when lumpsum taxes are available, employing a similar linear-quadratic approach as the one discussed in Chapter 7.[9] For the sake of simplifying the derivation of the loss function, we assume that τ_t^s is adjusted, in the steady state, to completely offset the monopolistic distortions.

Concerning liquidity, we assume that in the steady state the economy is close to the first-best satiation level, i.e., V_d is nonzero but of a small order. This corresponds to an economy in which the parameter ν is of a small order. We also assume that as d_t approaches from below the satiation level $\bar{d}$, the limiting value of $V_{dd}(\cdot)$ from below is negative. The latter assumption corresponds to the existence of a well-defined interest rate semi-elasticity of liquidity demand for values of d_t below the satiation level.[10] In the limit in which V_d becomes small, the demand for liquidity will still be of the same form as (8.23), with parameters $d_y = 0$ and $d_i = -U_c/(V_{dd}d)$.

---

8. This result is in line with Calvo (1978) and Woodford (1990).

9. In Section 9.6 of Chapter 9 the management of liquidity is analyzed during periods of zero nominal interest rates when taxes are distortionary.

10. See Woodford (2003, Ch. 6, p. 422) for an analysis in which cash provides utility.

Appendix I shows that under these assumptions the second-order approximation of the utility of the consumers implies the following loss function:

$$E_{t_0}\left\{\sum_{t=t_0}^{+\infty}\beta^{t-t_0}\left[\frac{1}{2}(\hat{Y}_t-\hat{Y}_t^e)+\frac{1}{2}\Lambda_d\left(\hat{d}_t-d^*\right)^2+\frac{1}{2}\frac{\theta}{\kappa}(\pi_t-\pi)^2\right]\right\},$$

$$(8.27)$$

for some positive parameter Λ_d defined in the appendix. The policymaker should weigh deviations of output, real liquidity, and inflation from their respective targets.[11] Given the separability of utility, nothing changes with respect to Chapter 5 for what concerns the output and inflation targets. There is an additional term, though, represented by the deviation of real liquidity, $\hat{d}_t$, with respect to the target d^*. The target d^* captures the liquidity distortions in the steady state, since liquidity is not fully satiated; d^* is such that $d^* = vd_i$ showing that it is of the same order as v. In the first best, liquidity should satiate the economy and therefore $\hat{d}_t = d^*$.

The minimization of the loss function is subject to the AS equation

$$\pi_t-\pi=\kappa(\hat{Y}_t-\hat{Y}_t^e)+v_t+\beta E_t(\pi_{t+1}-\pi),\qquad(8.28)$$

in which $v_t=(\kappa/(\sigma^{-1}+\eta))\hat{\mu}_t$ and

$$\hat{Y}_t^e=\frac{1+\eta}{\sigma^{-1}+\eta}\hat{A}_t.$$

The minimization problem is subject also to the AD equation. When v is of a small order, the equilibrium in the market of liquidity is still of the same form as in (8.23), with $d_y=0$ and $d_i=-U_c/(V_{dd}d)$. The functional form of (8.21) is also unchanged while (8.22) holds, imposing that v is equal to zero in a first-order approximation. In the limit $v\to0$, the AD equation (8.25) becomes[12]

$$\hat{Y}_t=E_t\hat{Y}_{t+1}-\sigma(\hat{i}_t^X-E_t(\pi_{t+1}-\pi)+E_t\Delta\hat{\xi}_{t+1})+\rho^{-1}d_i^{-1}\sigma\hat{d}_t.\quad(8.29)$$

When evaluating the optimal stabilization policy in this context, results do not change with respect to Chapter 7. Optimal monetary policy under

11. The loss function considers deviations of d_t, which are bounded above by $\bar{d}$.
12. Note that $d_y^{-1}\rho^{-1}v=-\rho^{-1}\sigma vV_{dd}d/V_d$. Since $v=V_d/U_c$ as $v\to0$, it follows that $d_y^{-1}\rho^{-1}v$ converges to $-\rho^{-1}\sigma V_{dd}d/U_c$, which is equivalent to $\rho^{-1}d_i^{-1}\sigma$, given the definition of d_i in the limit as v goes to zero.

commitment can still be represented by the same inflation targeting policy,

$$(\pi_t - \pi) + \theta^{-1}(\Delta \hat{Y}_t - \Delta \hat{Y}_t^e) = 0.$$

Combining the above targeting rule with (8.28) implies the same optimal response to shocks as in Section 7.3 of Chapter 7. The reason for this result is that, in this optimal stabilization problem, liquidity is another instrument of policy and would be optimally set to achieve full satiation; therefore $\hat{d}_t = d^*$ at all times. The steady-state spread between the money market rates and the policy rate is closed at any point in time, and the two rates coincide following the movements implied by the AD equation (8.29), given the optimal response of output and inflation. Absent markup shocks, the first best can be achieved, and therefore the central bank can reach all three objectives in (8.27). With markup shocks, a trade-off arises between stabilizing inflation and output at their targets, but it still remains optimal to satiate liquidity and close all money-market rates. In general, liquidity would play a role when sub-optimal policies are in place, as shown in Figure 8.2.

The findings in this section somehow minimize the "relevance" of the frictions we have introduced in this chapter, which set the model apart from the standard NK model. These frictions give certain securities special advantages, such as facilitating transactions or serving as collateral. As a result, this chapter has shown that an additional policy tool emerges—the management of government liquidity.

A benevolent policymaker may seek to employ this tool to alleviate the frictions introduced in a manner that ensures an ample supply of these special securities, in line with the discussion in this section, which suggests that the policymaker strives to operate within the confines of the benchmark NK model, where such frictions do not exist.

Chapter 9 introduces an additional friction, stemming from the distortive nature of taxation. This friction places constraints on the optimal provision of liquidity and alters the nature of the optimal policy for economic stabilization, deviating from the results of this section.

8.7 References

Canzoneri et al. (2008), Goodfriend (2005), and Goodfriend and McCallum (2007) are early models that incorporated a banking sector into the New Keynesian framework to study the role of liquidity policy. More recently, studies incorporating a banking sector have investigated the transmission mechanism of the policy rate, specifically the interest rate on reserves, through the banking sector. These studies have also emphasized the liquidity channel of monetary policy.

In particular, Diba and Loisel (2021, 2022) and Piazzesi, Rogers, and Schneider (2021), in line with the early work of Canzoneri et al. (2008), have developed models that highlight the distinction between the policy rate and the market interest rate, which directly affects consumption and saving choices.[13] The spread between these two rates uncovers the liquidity channel of monetary policy, through which central banks directly operate by setting the quantity of reserves.

In Diba and Loisel (2021, 2022), intermediaries demand reserves to reduce the costs associated with supplying loans, which are sought by firms due to working capital constraints. Reserves directly factor into the aggregate supply equation. This chapter builds upon the modeling framework proposed by Piazzesi, Rogers, and Schneider (2021) and Benigno and Benigno (2022), in which the liquidity channel operates directly through aggregate demand. Piazzesi, Rogers, and Schneider (2021) also extend their banking model to analyze monetary policy operations through a corridor versus a floor system. They demonstrate that equilibrium can be determined even if the policy rate does not follow a Taylor rule. Arce et al. (2020) focus on the relationship between the size of the balance sheet and the interbank rate.

Bigio and Sannikov (2021) integrate monetary policy analysis through a corridor system via a banking model that incorporates both a liquidity channel and a credit channel.

When it comes to determining the optimal supply of liquidity, early studies by Calvo (1978) and Woodford (1990) explored monetary economies in which government liabilities that offer liquidity services, such as money, do not bear interest rates, and taxes are distortionary. Calvo and Woodford showed that, in this context, it is optimal to supply money below the satiation level, in contrast to the Friedman rule, which would typically arise with lumpsum taxes.

Benigno and Benigno (2022) expanded upon these findings, generalizing them to a monetary economy with sticky prices where liquidity is provided by interest-bearing government liabilities, and where the policymaker commits from a "timeless perspective." Sims (2022) presented similar results in a

13. See also Benigno and Nisticò (2017).

non-stationary solution to a Ramsey problem, albeit with flexible prices. Sims (2022) also discussed that the satiation of liquidity might be optimal when the government possesses sufficient asset holdings, even if they are of an illiquid nature, to offset the debt supplied. Angeletos, Collard, and Dellas (2023) characterized similar results in a context where debt is real, and provided a foundation for the liquidity services offered by government debt, rather than apply the ad hoc assumptions made in this chapter.

PART III

Crisis Models

Introduction

ECONOMIC CRISES ARE recurrent phenomena. Their history dates back to 33 A.D., when one of the first economic and financial crises took place in the Roman Empire. The crisis originated from the sudden decision to enforce an old law requiring cash to back real estate loans exactly at a time when cash was scarce. This led to an attempt to liquidate investments, mostly in land, which was followed by a fall in land prices, ruining people in debt. Emperor Tiberius resolved the crisis by providing 100 million sesterces as three-year, interest-free loans to everyone in trouble (see Thornton and Thornton, 1990).

Although financial crises occasionally repeat, they always present novel characteristics, due to the source of the shock, the actors involved, the mechanism, or the policy intervention. They are unique events simply because history does not exactly repeat itself and the economic system is in a continuous metamorphosis.

Economists, policymakers, and economic agents in general have the tendency to forget about how prone the economic system can be to crises, especially deep ones. The recent experience of the Great Moderation—the period between 1987 and 2007 in which volatility in business-cycle fluctuations for advanced economies was reduced—misled us to believe that not only were economic depressions far away but that the duration and severity of cyclical recessions could also be contained. Robert E. Lucas, in the introduction to his presidential address to the American Economic Association (2002), said: "Macroeconomics was born as a distinct field in the 1940s, as a part of the intellectual response to the Great Depression. The term then referred to the body of knowledge and expertise that we hoped would prevent the recurrence of that economic disaster. My thesis in this lecture is that macroeconomics in this original sense has succeeded: Its central problem of depression prevention has been solved, for all practical purposes, and has in

199

fact been solved for many decades." Even in the wake of the 2007–2008 financial crisis, policymakers in the U.S. overestimated the resilience of the financial system to the growing crisis in a tiny fraction of the mortgage market, that of subprime borrowers.

The 2007–2008 financial crisis, and the ensuing Great Contraction, as well as the COVID-19 pandemic with the consequent collapse of the world economy, have surely shown that macroeconomics has not solved the occurrence of depression-like events, nor prevented them. What brings relief is that policy, monetary and fiscal, to some extent has been able to dampen the depth and duration of the economic contractions, turning depression-prone events into great contractions. At least, macroeconomics has learned from the mistakes of the Great Depression—the main one being the belief that monetary policy was ineffective, as indicated by various aphorisms circulating at the time: "You can lead a horse to water but you can't make him drink" and "Monetary policy is like a string: you can pull on it but you can't push on it."

To resurrect monetary policy, Milton Friedman in 1970 said: "It turns out, as I shall point out more fully below, that on re-examination, the depression is a tragic testament to the effectiveness of monetary policy, not a demonstration of its impotence. But what mattered for the world of ideas was not what was true but what was believed to be true. And it was believed at the time that monetary policy had been tried and had been found wanting" (Friedman, 1970b, p. 4). Friedman's view was a defense of the quantity theory of money, which assigns money the primary role of controlling nominal spending. The caveat, and the warning, is that, as we explained, money is not an object or a noun, but rather a property that some securities have. The range of securities that qualifies for the money attribute changes over time due to the evolution of financial markets and payment systems; therefore, the policymaker, to be able to control nominal spending through "money," should not only be aware of such changes but also be able to control the relevant "money" aggregates. The other aspect of this awareness is the understanding that money-like private securities can be the cause of a drop in nominal spending when their moneyness deteriorates. From time to time, when financial crises occur, this observation revives the debate on who should be the supplier of broadly defined money aggregates and how their safety should be guaranteed.

One thing is sure and not subject to change in a fiduciary currency system: the special role of the central bank in supplying securities with the highest degree of moneyness in the system. As Bernanke (2002) noted in one of his speeches on deflation: "the U.S. government has a technology, called a printing press (or, today, its electronic equivalent), that allows it to produce as many U.S. dollars as it wishes at essentially no cost. By increasing the number of U.S. dollars in circulation, or even by credibly threatening to do so, the U.S. government can also reduce the value of a dollar in terms of goods and services, which is equivalent to raising the prices in dollars of those goods and services. We conclude that, under a paper-currency system, a determined government can always generate higher spending and hence positive inflation."

In more practical terms, since the 2007–2008 financial crisis central banks around the world have increased their ammunition beyond all expectations, while losing their standard policy tool—the short-term rate. Instruments have ranged from purchases of the treasury debt at various maturities to purchases of risky private assets to emergency lending programs, and so forth. Central banks have enlarged in a substantial way the supply of high-powered money, providing the best substitute in some cases or the best backing in others for money-like private claims. All these policies have been able to prevent the shocks from translating into a substantial fall in the nominal spending of the economy. The reason is that they are policies that can reflate the economy and that, if appropriately tailored, can maintain a trajectory of an appropriately defined price target, on a path compatible with the most adequate stabilization of the economy around output and inflation targets.

This part is divided into three chapters. Chapter 9 discusses the conditions under which an economy can fall into a liquidity trap through the lens of the New Keynesian model of Part II. It then discusses policy interventions of the types undertaken or discussed in the last fifteen years: from forward guidance to unconventional policies to the more unorthodox helicopter money. Chapter 10 explores more deeply the sources of shocks that can plunge the economy into a liquidity trap, examining debt-deleveraging dynamics and turbulences in the banking sector, which limit lending to the economy. Chapter 11 extends money properties to a broader range of private assets that have money-like properties during booms but that create liquidity crises during downturns since they are not appropriately backed by good investments. It studies unconventional monetary policy, deposit insurance, and financial regulation. It also revisits the debate on public versus private provision of liquidity, which was described in Chapter 4.

9

Liquidity Trap

9.1 Introduction

Hicks (1937) describes *General Theory* as the "economics of depression," the reason being that Keynes said something about an increase in investment not raising the nominal interest rate. In the traditional Keynesian world, the *LM* equation, which describes the equilibrium in the money market, is a positive relationship between nominal interest rates and sales, given money supply. However, the curve is nearly flat on the left and nearly vertical on the right. In particular, it is horizontal on the left because there is a minimum below which the nominal interest is unlikely to go. For low income, movements in the *IS* curve, which represents the equilibrium in the goods market, increase employment without affecting the interest rate. On the other hand, a monetary expansion cannot further reduce the nominal interest rate. The economy is in a trap: whatever liquidity the authorities inject is absorbed by agents without affecting the nominal interest rate and hence the income.[1]

In modern central banking, the monetary policy instrument is the nominal interest rate, and money is endogenous given the policy rate. There is still a limit to lowering the interest rate when money can circulate in physical form. A liquidity trap describes a condition in which the economy is in a slump due to a shortage of aggregate demand even if the nominal interest rate is zero, at which point the monetary policymaker loses its standard policy instrument.

Figure 9.1 shows the stay at the zero lower bound for the Euro area, Japan, the United Kingdom, and the United States during the last three decades. Japan first experienced low interest rates as a response to the economic

---

1. Eggertsson and Petracchi (2021) revisit these arguments through microfounded models, asserting that the effectiveness of money expansion depends on whether it signals a change in regime.

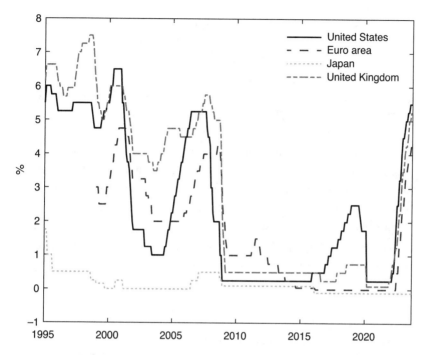

FIGURE 9.1. Policy rate: Euro Area, Japan, U.K., U.S. Period: January 1995 to October 2023. Euro Area since January 1999. *Source: Refinitiv Eikon.*

stagnation caused by the asset price bubble's collapse in late 1991. Since 1995, the policy rate has been set below 1% and during the last six years at minus ten basis points. Following the 2007–2008 financial crisis, the United States entered a period of quasi zero policy rate in December 2008 for seven years, while the Euro area entered one in 2014. The figure also shows the liftoff of rates, except for Japan, started in 2022 to counter the surge in inflation, a topic that will be discussed in Chapter 12.

To see how the zero lower bound coupled with a demand shock can create a shortage of aggregate demand, let us consider the *AD* equation of the NK model in its nonlinear Euler-equation version, equation (5.9), under perfect foresight,

$$U_c(C_t) = \beta(1 + i_t)\frac{P_t}{P_{t+1}}\frac{\xi_{t+1}}{\xi_t}U_c(C_{t+1}), \qquad (9.1)$$

in which C is consumption, i the nominal interest rate, P the price level, ξ is a preference shock, β is the discount factor of the household, and $U_c(\cdot)$ is the first derivative of the utility $U(\cdot)$ with respect to consumption.

Let time t_0 denote the short run and $t_0 + 1$ the long run. Short and long runs are different for two reasons: i) prices are rigid in the short run and flexible in the long run; ii) the preference shock is high in the long run, let's say at $\xi_{t_0+1} = \bar{\xi}$, and low in the short run, at ξ_{t_0}, with $\xi_{t_0} < \bar{\xi}$. Recall from the utility function (5.1) that the preference shock ξ_{t_0+1} is a multiplicative shock to the utility flow, and that a higher ξ_{t_0+1} implies a higher discount factor between t_0 and $t_0 + 1$. Agents become more patient since they care more about future utility. This creates a reason in the short run to save more and postpone consumption to the long run. Prices are rigid in the short run at $P_{t_0} = \bar{P}$ and flexible in the long run at a level determined by monetary and fiscal policies, let's say, $P_{t_0+1} = P^*$. In this long run, the goods market clears because of flexible prices and therefore consumption is equal to the natural rate of output. Let us set it to a constant $Y^n_{t+1} = Y$; therefore $C_{t_0+1} = Y$. Using this information in the above Euler equation at time t_0, we obtain

$$U_c(C_{t_0}) = \beta(1 + i_{t_0})\frac{\bar{P}}{P^*}\frac{\bar{\xi}}{\xi_{t_0}}U_c(Y). \tag{9.2}$$

Short-run consumption depends negatively on the nominal interest rate, because $U_c(\cdot)$ decreases in its argument. Lower nominal rates can boost consumption.

We assume isoelastic utility of the form $U(C) = C^{1-\sigma^{-1}}/(1 - \sigma^{-1})$, with $\sigma > 0$, to obtain in logs an equation similar to (6.9) of Chapter 6:

$$c_{t_0} = y - \sigma(i_{t_0} - (p^* - \bar{p}) - r^e_{t_0}), \tag{9.3}$$

where a lowercase letter represents the logarithm of the corresponding uppercase letter, while $i_{t_0} \approx \ln(1 + i_{t_0})$ and the frictionless real rate is defined by

$$r^e_{t_0} = -\ln \beta + \ln \xi_{t_0} - \ln \bar{\xi}.$$

Note that the frictionless rate, as in (6.7), should also depend on the growth rate of output, but we are assuming, for simplicity, that output is constant. A low realization of ξ_{t_0} with respect to $\bar{\xi}$ implies a fall in the frictionless real rate.

Let us assume that the shock to preference is large enough to bring the frictionless real rate to a negative large value so that:

$$r^e_{t_0} + (p^* - \bar{p}) < 0. \tag{9.4}$$

Under these conditions, the economy is in a slump with a shortage of aggregate demand, $c_{t_0} < y$, as can be seen from (9.3). Demand can be stimulated by

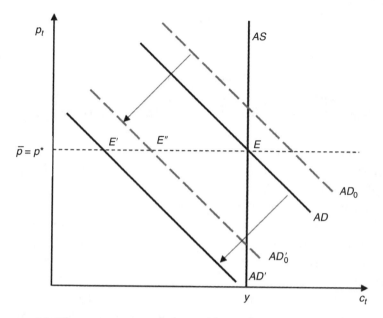

FIGURE 9.2. The economy starts from equilibrium E and is hit by a demand shock, which shifts AD down to AD', and moves the equilibrium to E'. If the central bank lowers the nominal interest rate, it can push at most AD' up to AD'_0, reaching equilibrium E''.

lowering the nominal interest rate down to the zero floor. Even at this point, short-run consumption remains below potential and therefore the economy finds itself in a liquidity trap.

We can illustrate this situation by referring again to our AS-AD graphical representation, but in a diagram with consumption on the x-axis. In Figure 9.2 the starting equilibrium is E, in which AS and AD cross at price $\bar{p}$ and at consumption equal to the constant output, y in logs. The AS equation is vertical. The interest rate is assumed to be positive, and inflation, zero; therefore $\bar{p} = p^*$. The figure displays also the schedule AD_0 which corresponds to AD when the nominal interest rate is set to zero.

When a demand shock of the type described above hits the economy, lowering the frictionless rate by a substantial fall of ξ_{t_0} below $\bar{\xi}$, consumers are willing to save more and this depresses short-run consumption. The AD equation shifts into AD', together with AD_0 shifting into AD'_0. The economy moves to equilibrium E', where consumption falls below output, since prices are fully rigid. Monetary policy can react to the shock by lowering the nominal interest rate, pushing the AD' equation up to AD'_0. However, even at a zero nominal interest rate the economy is still in a slump stuck at E'' on AD'_0.

Three factors are key to creating the conditions for a liquidity trap: a negative demand shock, price rigidities, and the zero lower bound. Without one of these elements, there is no liquidity trap. Indeed, with flexible prices, the goods market clears even in the short run, and $c_{t_0} = y$. Using interest rates that can go below the zero lower bound, the central bank could in principle expand consumption to fill the shortage of demand.

To illustrate a way out of the liquidity trap, we should note that it implies a condition in which the frictionless real rate $r^e_{t_0}$ is too low because of the path of the preference shock, as in the previous discussion, while the actual real rate r_{t_0} is too high because the nominal rate cannot fall below the zero floor. Note that the real rate in (9.3) is given by $r_{t_0} = i_{t_0} - (p^* - p)$. A real rate that is too high, with $r_{t_0} > r^e_{t_0}$, creates excess saving in the economy, which depresses consumption, aggregate demand, and output.

Figure 9.2 shows that the central bank can run out of ammunition with respect to conventional policy. As in the Keynesian model, the liquidity trap is a state of depression. In equilibrium E'' of Figure 9.2, the real interest rate is too high and a lower real rate cannot be achieved only by lowering the nominal interest rate. Given that $r_{t_0} = i_{t_0} - (p^* - p)$, a lower real rate can also be achieved by raising expectations of future inflation, thereby increasing p^*. The objective of this chapter is to discuss the types of policy that the central bank can deploy to reflate the economy and exit the liquidity trap.

9.2   Outline of the Results

The upcoming sections explore the "unconventional" tools designed to raise inflation expectations, lower the real interest rate, and stimulate short-term aggregate demand.

In Sections 9.3 and 9.4, we explore helicopter money and unconventional balance-sheet policies, respectively. A prominent mechanism through which both approaches operate involves transferring resources to the private sector, bolstering its wealth, increasing consumption, and reigniting economic activity. Helicopter money can be executed through collaboration between the central bank and the treasury or solely by the central bank. In the former case, the treasury provides a transfer to the private sector, funded by debt purchased by the central bank through the issuance of reserves. In the latter scenario, the central bank reduces its net worth by augmenting remittances or writing off specific (private) assets from its balance sheet. Unconventional monetary policy, via asset purchase programs, is effective when the central bank absorbs some losses that would otherwise be shouldered by the private sector, thereby creating an implicit transfer.[2]

Section 9.5 examines forward guidance, which involves explicit guidance on future policy rate trajectories. The primary finding is that keeping interest rates at the zero lower bound for an extended period beyond the duration of a shock can boost inflation expectations and reduce both current and future real interest rates.

In Section 9.6, we investigate the management of central bank reserves during a liquidity trap, either in conjunction with or as a substitute for forward guidance. This analysis is particularly relevant when distortionary taxes suggest that satiating liquidity in the economy is not optimal. Our key insight is that reserves should be gradually accumulated during the zero lower bound period, reaching their peak just before the policy rate liftoff. Withdrawal and normalization of reserves should align with the normalization of the policy rate.

Section 9.7 outlines additional channels through which asset purchase programs can be effective, such as by serving as lenders of last resort. In this capacity, the central bank can offer liquidity against illiquid assets or collateral under specific conditions, which can help alleviate credit market conditions.

9.3   Helicopter Money

The term "helicopter money" refers to the concept introduced by Milton Friedman (1969) to illustrate the effects of monetary policy on inflation using the following analogy: "Let us suppose that one day, a helicopter flies over a community and drops an additional $1,000 in bills from the sky, which, of course, is hastily collected by the community members. Further, let us assume that everyone is convinced that this is a unique event that will never be repeated."

Friedman's helicopter experiment is useful for understanding the role of central banks in defeating deflations. They are just monetary phenomena. In Chapter 1, we underlined the power of central banks given their ability to print

---

2. Section 10.5 of Chapter 10 and Section 11.7 of Chapter 11 discuss other cases of the relevance of asset purchase programs, namely via credit easing or via the backing that they provide to support the supply of government liquidity.

default-free securities without facing any solvency constraint. Since a deflation is a condition in which the price of currency is too high—the price level
too low—it is sufficient to print those special central bank liabilities and leave
them on the ground, so that people will hastily collect and spend them to
reflate the economy. This helicopter drop, however, should be understood to
be a gift, never to be taken away in the future in some form or another.

Helicopter money is the natural follow-up of Section 9.1's analysis, since
the way out of the liquidity trap described there is that of raising long-
run prices to boost current consumption. A popular implementation of
Friedman's proposal is having the government carry out a transfer to citizens financed by issuing debt, which is in turn purchased by the central bank
through additional supply of money or reserves. The transfer raises agents'
wealth, stimulating consumption and aggregate demand.

Although central banks are reluctant to acknowledge the deployment of
helicoper money, episodes of coordination between monetary and fiscal policies have been frequent following the 2007–2008 financial crisis and the
COVID-19 pandemic.

In February 2009, the U.S. government launched the American Recovery
and Reinvestment Act, a $787 billion plan including tax cuts and unemploy-
ment benefits. At the March 2009 meeting, the Federal Open Market Committee (FOMC) started a plan of purchasing $300 billion long-term Treasury
debt together with government-guaranteed mortgage-backed securities, a policy dubbed Quantitative Easing 1 (QE1). On November 2010, it expanded
the purchases of Treasury debt by an amount of $600 billion under QE2.

During the pandemic crisis, the Federal Reserve had accumulated around
$3 trillion of Treasury securities, while the government implemented five
stimulus and relief packages in the period March 2020–March 2021 of the
amounts, respectively, of $8.3 billion, $3.5 billion, $2.3 trillion, $900 billion,
and $1.9 trillion. Measures included, among others, direct cash transfers to cit-
izens, tax credits, and increased unemployment benefits. In the meantime, the
Federal Reserve had deployed many programs to lend directly or indirectly to
small and medium-sized business.

In Europe, the European Central Bank activated a Pandemic Emergency Purchase Programme (PEPP) of €1.8 trillion by purchasing sovereign
debt of the euro-area national treasuries.[3] For the first time, the European
Commission relaxed the 3.0% deficit rule, allowing member countries to

---

3. The ECB had already started its QE program in 2015, but without a coordinated fiscal
policy expansion.

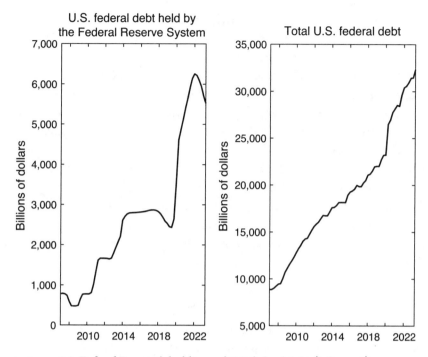

FIGURE 9.3. Federal Reserve's holdings of U.S. federal debt (left panel); U.S. federal debt (right panel), $ billions. Period: March 2007–June 2023. *Source: Board of Governors of the Federal Reserve System (U.S.).*

run substantial deficits. A pan-European fiscal stimulus of €800 billion was implemented.

Figure 9.3 presents two plots: the left panel illustrates the government debt held by the Federal Reserve starting from 2007, while the right panel displays the overall federal debt. The figure shows the increase in the debt held by the Federal Reserve under its asset purchase programs. There is a notable large jump in federal debt following the pandemic crisis and the corresponding increase in the Fed's holdings.

We investigate the effectiveness of a money-financed fiscal transfer, and of equivalent policies, using the simple model of Chapter 2, which is also useful for nesting the analysis of Section 9.1. We refer the reader to Chapter 2 for a full presentation of the model. Here, we underline the changes and address the analysis directly using the equilibrium conditions. The only change with respect to Chapter 2 is in the preferences

$$\sum_{t=t_0}^{\infty} \beta^{t-t_0} \xi_t \left[U(C_t) + V\left(\frac{M_t}{P_t}\right) \right],$$

which now include preference shock (ξ), and where β, with $0 < \beta < 1$, is the subjective discount factor in preferences, while $U(\cdot)$ is a concave, differentiable utility function in its argument C, the consumption good; $V(\cdot)$ is also a concave, differentiable function, of real money balances (M/P), and has a satiation point at $\bar{m} > 0$, i.e., $V_m(M_t/P_t) = 0$ for $M_t/P_t \geq \bar{m}$, in which $V_m(\cdot)$ is the first derivative of $V(\cdot)$ with respect to its argument; (P) is the price of the consumption good (C); and (M) is central bank money, cash and banknotes.

The departure from the model of Chapter 2 is minor, assuming furthermore that $\xi_t = \bar{\xi}$ for each $t \geq t_0 + 1$ while $\xi_{t_0} \leq \bar{\xi}$. As in Section 9.1, prices at time t_0, the short run, are fixed at $\bar{P}$, while they are fully flexible at any point in time after t_0, defined as the long run. This implies that $C_t = Y$ for each $t \geq t_0 + 1$ since we continue to assume that endowment is constant.

The Euler equation (9.1) applies here, and can be written under the above assumptions as

$$U_c(C_{t_0}) = \beta(1 + i_{t_0})\frac{\bar{P}}{P_{t_0+1}}\frac{\bar{\xi}}{\xi_{t_0}}U_c(Y), \tag{9.5}$$

in which $U_c(\cdot)$ is the first derivative of the function $U(\cdot)$ with respect to its argument. The equilibrium in money market at time t_0 implies that real money balances satisfy

$$\frac{M_{t_0}}{\bar{P}} \geq L(C_{t_0}, i_{t_0})$$

for a functional form $L(\cdot, \cdot)$, discussed in Section 2.3 of Chapter 2. In the case of the interest rate at the zero lower bound, the above equation can hold with strict inequality.

The key insight, which is the unknown element in equation (9.5), is that the price level at time $t_0 + 1$, P_{t_0+1}, is exactly determined by the same equilibrium conditions described in Section 2.3.3 of Chapter 2. We restate them here since they will be critical for understanding price determination. The Fisher equation relates the nominal interest rate to the real rate, given by $1/\beta$, and the inflation rate,

$$1 + i_t = \frac{1}{\beta}\frac{P_{t+1}}{P_t}. \tag{9.6}$$

The equilibrium in the money market requires real money balances to satisfy the following relationship:

$$\frac{M_t}{P_t} \geq L(Y, i_t). \tag{9.7}$$

Equation (9.7) holds with equality whenever $i_t > 0$.

Finally, the intertemporal budget constraint of the consumer implies the following equilibrium conditions:

$$\sum_{t=t_0+1}^{\infty} \beta^{t-t_0-1} \left(\frac{T_t}{P_t} + \frac{i_t}{1+i_t} \frac{M_t}{P_t} \right) = \frac{B_{t_0} + X_{t_0} + M_{t_0}}{P_{t_0+1}}, \tag{9.8}$$

in which (T) are the treasury's lumpsum taxes and (B), (X), and (M) are government liabilities with respect to the private sector given by treasury's bonds, central bank reserves, and cash, respectively. The characterization of the equilibrium is completed by the budget constraints of both the central bank and the treasury. The budget constraint of the central bank is represented by

$$\frac{B_t^C - X_t}{1+i_t} - M_t = B_{t-1}^C - X_{t-1} - M_{t-1} - T_t^C, \tag{9.9}$$

in which (B^C) are the central bank's holdings of short-term default-free assets issued by the private sector or the treasury and (T^C) are the remittances to the treasury, if positive. The budget constraint of the treasury is given by

$$\frac{B_t^F}{1+i_t} = B_{t-1}^F - T_t - T_t^C, \tag{9.10}$$

where (B^F) is treasury debt, and, in equilibrium,

$$B_t^F = B_t + B_t^C. \tag{9.11}$$

Moreover, the trajectory of taxes is constrained by the following solvency condition:

$$\frac{B_{t_0}^F}{P_{t_0+1}} = \sum_{t=t_0+1}^{\infty} \beta^{t-t_0-1} \left(\frac{T_t}{P_t} + \frac{T_t^C}{P_t} \right). \tag{9.12}$$

The long-run equilibrium, which begins at time $t_0 + 1$, is a set of sequences $\{P_t, i_t, X_t, M_t, B_t^C, T_t^C, B_t^F, T_t, B_t\}_{t=t_0+1}^{\infty}$ with $\{P_t, i_t, X_t, M_t, B_t^C\}_{t=t_0+1}^{\infty}$ non-negative that satisfies conditions (9.6), (9.7), (9.9), (9.10), and (9.11), holding at each $t \geq t_0 + 1$, and condition (9.8) given the values inherited from period t_0: $B_{t_0}^C, B_{t_0}^F, X_{t_0}, M_{t_0}$. Moreover, the sequence of taxes $\{T_t\}_{t=t_0+1}^{\infty}$ is restricted to satisfying (9.12), given the equilibrium sequences $\{P_t, T_t^C\}_{t=t_0+1}^{\infty}$ and the inherited value $B_{t_0}^F$.[4] There are four degrees of freedom to specify government policy, which we will discuss in the next sections.

---

4. The infinite sums in (9.8) and (9.12) should be also finite.

9.3.1   Helicopter Money Coordinated by Monetary and Fiscal Policy

This section studies an experiment of helicopter money through the collaboration between monetary and fiscal policies. The key element of this collaboration is the implicit or explicit backing of treasury debt by the central bank, which relaxes the constraint (9.12). To make the analysis simple, we assume a constant interest rate policy for each $t \geq t_0 + 1$ that targets a constant rate of inflation $\Pi > \beta$, such that

$$1 + i_t = \frac{\Pi}{\beta}.$$

Substituting it in (9.6), we obtain that

$$\frac{P_{t+1}}{P_t} = \Pi$$

for each $t \geq t_0 + 1$: inflation is constant after $t_0 + 1$ and at the level Π targeted by the central bank. Given P_{t_0+1}, the above equation determines the full sequence of prices for $t \geq t_0 + 2$.

Using the interest rate policy in the money market equilibrium (9.7), we obtain that

$$\frac{M_t}{P_t} = L\left(Y, \frac{\Pi}{\beta} - 1\right)$$

for any $t \geq t_0 + 1$. Given P_{t_0+1}, it determines the full sequence of money M_t for $t \geq t_0 + 1$.

What is left to determine is the price at time P_{t_0+1}. To this end, we rewrite (9.8), assuming a constant real tax policy $T_t/P_t = (1 - \beta)\tau$ given a positive parameter τ, to obtain

$$\frac{B_{t_0} + X_{t_0} + M_{t_0}}{P_{t_0+1}} = \tau + \mathcal{S}(\Pi, Y),$$

in which we have defined the present discounted value of real seigniorage as

$$\mathcal{S}(\Pi, Y) \equiv \frac{\Pi - \beta}{\Pi(1 - \beta)} L\left(Y, \frac{\Pi}{\beta} - 1\right).$$

The price level at time $t_0 + 1$ is then determined by

$$P_{t_0+1} = \frac{B_{t_0} + X_{t_0} + M_{t_0}}{\tau + \mathcal{S}(\Pi, Y)}, \tag{9.13}$$

showing that it is proportional to the outstanding government liabilities.

We discuss the options that the government has for reflating the economy by raising P_{t_0+1} and, through (9.5), short-run consumption C_{t_0}.

In the traditional account of the so-called "helicopter money," the government (treasury or central bank) permanently increases the long-run nominal liabilities—namely, B_{t_0}, X_{t_0}, or M_{t_0}—in order to finance a tax cut in the short run. Since the short-run nominal interest rate is zero, which liability to raise is irrelevant, as can be seen from the government budget at time t_0,

$$B_{t_0} + X_{t_0} + M_{t_0} = B_{t_0-1} + X_{t_0-1} + M_{t_0-1} - T_{t_0}, \qquad (9.14)$$

which is obtained by consolidating (9.9) and (9.10) and setting $i_{t_0} = 0$. The key feature is that all the government's liabilities have the special properties of the central bank: B_{t_0}, X_{t_0}, and M_{t_0} are always paid in full since they are guaranteed by the "printing press" of the central bank without any need to raise taxes or seigniorage revenues. And, indeed, taxes and seigniorage should not move (at least not proportionally) with an increase in government debt to produce an effect on long-run prices, as equation (9.13) clearly shows.

Moreover, equation (9.14) clarifies that the increase in government liabilities outstanding at $t_0 + 1$ can be generated by a tax cut at t_0, and therefore by a larger current deficit. This larger deficit can equivalently be financed issuing treasury debt, which can be held by either the private sector or the central bank. In the former case, B_{t_0} increase for given X_{t_0}, while in the latter case, the opposite occurs, as the central bank raises its liabilities to absorb the new issuance of treasury debt, leaving unchanged the stock of debt held by the private sector, B_{t_0}. In the latter case, it does not really matter whether the central bank permanently holds the treasury's debt or writes it off.

In general, a policy where the central bank conducts large-scale asset purchases of government debt, increasing its reserves at time t_0, produces equivalent effects, regardless of whether the purchase program includes long- or short-term debt.[5] What matters is the transfer made to the private sector.

For all these policy options to succeed, equation (9.13) underscores that it is important that the denominator not change (at least not proportionally): the treasury should therefore commit to never undoing the short-run tax relief. Friedman's helicopter-money experiment requires that the drop of special central bank liabilities, or backed ones, be permanent, or recognized as such.

---

5. The model can be generalized to include long-term debt and prove the result.

The mechanism by which the increase in government liabilities raises the long-term price level can be understood as stimulating consumption due to positive wealth effects on households. However, since output remains unchanged, the increase in aggregate demand in the long run will lead to the desired increase in the long-term price level, P_{t_0+1}.

9.3.2 Helicopter Money by Central Bank Only

This section considers the case in which the central bank does not back the treasury's liabilities, as in Section 1.4.2 of Chapter 1, showing that there are still ways of implement helicopter money through actions of the central bank only.

When taxes are restricted to satisfying condition (9.12) to maintain solvency of treasury debt, the equilibrium condition (9.8), using (9.12), can be equivalently written as

$$\frac{X_{t_0} + M_{t_0} - B_{t_0}^C}{P_{t_0+1}} = \sum_{t=t_0+1}^{\infty} \beta^{t-t_0-1} \left(\frac{i_t}{1+i_t} \frac{M_t}{P_t} - \frac{T_t^C}{P_t} \right). \tag{9.15}$$

We maintain our assumption of a fixed interest rate policy, targeting the inflation rate at Π. Additionally, we specify a constant central bank remittance policy in nominal terms: $\{T_t^C = T^C\}_{t=t_0+1}^{+\infty}$, with $T^C \geq 0$.[6] Inserting it into (9.15) and using previous results, we can write

$$\frac{X_{t_0} + M_{t_0} + \mathcal{T}^C - B_{t_0}^C}{P_{t_0+1}} = \mathcal{S}(\Pi, Y),$$

where

$$\mathcal{T}^C \equiv \frac{\Pi}{\Pi - \beta} T^C. \tag{9.16}$$

The long-run price level P_{t_0+1} is then determined by

$$P_{t_0+1} = \frac{X_{t_0} + M_{t_0} + \mathcal{T}^C - B_{t_0}^C}{\mathcal{S}(\Pi, Y)} = \frac{\mathcal{T}^C - N_{t_0}^C}{\mathcal{S}(\Pi, Y)}, \tag{9.17}$$

where the central bank's net worth (N^C) is equal to

$$N_{t_0}^C = B_{t_0}^C - X_{t_0} - M_{t_0},$$

---

6. See Benigno and Nisticò (2022) for a discussion of the case of a real remittances policy.

having imposed that at time t_0 the nominal interest rate is at the zero lower bound. Since $\mathcal{S}(\Pi, Y) > 0$, the numerator in equation (9.17) should be positive, to support a positive price level P_{t_0+1} at equilibrium.[7] The remittances policy, therefore, should be set so as to ensure $\mathcal{T}^C > N_{t_0}^C$ regardless of the net financial position of the central bank.[8]

Having determined the price level, similarly to the way in Section 2.4 of Chapter 2, we can now study how the central bank can raise its level at time $t_0 + 1$ to stimulate the economy. Note that the law of motion of net worth is given by

$$N_{t_0}^C = N_{t_0-1}^C - T_{t_0}^C, \tag{9.18}$$

since the central bank's profits are zero at time t_0 because $i_{t_0} = 0$.

To raise the price level at time $t_0 + 1$, the central bank could act on the numerator of (9.17), by cutting its net worth, *ceteris paribus*. This can be accomplished by increasing short-run transfers to the treasury, as shown by (9.18), which implies on the one hand an increase in the monetary base and, on the other hand, lower current taxes for the private sector, and is therefore equivalent to the traditional narrative of helicopter money. An alternative, but equivalent, way of cutting nominal net worth would be for the central bank to write off some of the assets in its portfolio held from period $t_0 - 1$. In particular, by writing off private securities from its balance sheet, the central bank can trigger a positive and reflationary wealth effect directly on the private sector, without any involvement from the treasury.

9.4 Unconventional Monetary Policy

The 2007–2008 financial crisis and the COVID-19 pandemic saw unprecedented interventions by central banks around the world that in various waves purchased private and government securities with long-term maturities and non-negligible credit risk. This category of interventions is considered unconventional monetary policy because it involves an atypical composition of the central bank's asset holdings. It differs from the conventional approach, which typically involves central banks holding only treasury bills. Indeed, before

---

7. Equation (9.17) can still be consistent with the nonmonetary equilibrium unless condition (2.24) is imposed. Alternatively, to have a unique equilibrium, an appropriate managing of a real asset like gold should be assumed, as in Section 1.5 of Chapter 1.

8. If net worth $N_{t_0}^C$ is negative, $\mathcal{T}^C$ can also be equal to zero.

the 2007–2008 financial crisis, central banks held, besides foreign reserves and gold, only short-term treasury bills. Additionally, these interventions are unconventional because they are used to compensate for the absence of the conventional policy instrument, the policy rate, when it is constrained to the zero lower bound.

These asset purchase programs, dubbed QE, had two effects on central bank balance sheets. First, as already mentioned, they changed the composition of the asset holdings. Second, the expansion in the asset position was financed by increasing the central bank's reserves to unprecedented amounts.

Figure 9.4 shows, in the left-hand side panel, the increase in the assets held by the Federal Reserve in the aftermath of the 2007–2008 financial crisis and their subsequent doubling following the coronavirus pandemic. The largest component of assets is represented by purchases of long-term securities, while liquidity-assistance programs were very sizeable during the financial crisis.[9] The central panel of the figure displays the corresponding increase in the Federal Reserve's liabilities, primarily stemming from the growth in deposits held by depositary institutions at the Federal Reserve. What is particularly noteworthy, as shown in the chart on the right-hand side of the figure, is the significant surge in money aggregates, M1 and M2, in response to the pandemic crisis.

The mechanisms through which QE works remain, however, controversial. Bernanke (2022, pp. 141–143) considers the contrast within the FOMC between two prominent views.[10] At the time of starting the programs, some participants saw the main benefits from the expansion of the central bank's reserves, which would induce banks to lend them out, putting extra liquidity in circulation and therefore stimulating aggregate demand. On the other hand, most FOMC members viewed the main mechanism as working via a portfolio rebalancing channel. The greater demand for the purchased securities would lower their yields. Investors would then reallocate their portfolio to other asset markets, lowering their yields, too.

9. All liquidity facilities include: Term Auction Facility; primary credit; secondary credit; seasonal credit; Primary Dealer Credit Facility; Asset-Backed Commercial Paper Money Market Mutual Fund Liquidity Facility; Term Asset-Backed Securities Loan Facility; Commercial Paper Funding Facility; Money Market Mutual Fund Liquidity Facility; and central bank liquidity swaps. Support to specific institutions includes: Maiden Lane LLC; Maiden Lane II LLC; Maiden Lane III LLC; and AIG.

10. Bernanke (2022, p. 144) labelled this policy "credit easing," but the "name never caught on. QE it would be."

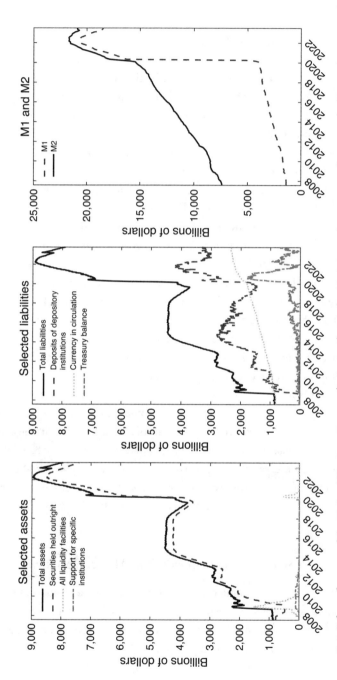

FIGURE 9.4. Selected assets of the Federal Reserve System (left panel), selected liabilities (center panel), and M1 and M2 (right panel). Billions of dollars. Period: July 2007–October 2023. *Source: Board of Governors of the Federal Reserve System (U.S.).*

This section examines the portfolio-rebalancing channel via a frictionless financial-market model in which securities have only pecuniary values. In this environment, unconventional asset-purchase programs are effective only insofar as they produce wealth effects on the private sector, similarly to helicopter money. The key feature of their effectiveness is the central bank's bearing some losses that were before in the hands of the private sector, relying therefore on appropriate transfers and the central bank's remittance policies. Asset purchase programs are irrelevant if losses or gains on the asset purchased by the central bank are transferred back to the private sector, therefore providing no foundations for the portfolio-rebalancing mechanism.

Section 9.6 studies the theoretical grounds of the other view within the FOMC, namely, the reserve channel activated by the expansion of the central bank's reserves. In the context of the model analyzed in that section, reserves provide some nonpecuniary benefits because they can relax a collateral/regulatory constraint. Under these conditions, an increase in reserves lowers money market rates and can influence aggregate demand, stimulating the economy. The increase of M1 and M2 shown in Figure 9.4 could be exemplificative of this channel.

Finally, Section 9.7 draws further conclusions on the effectiveness of asset purchase programs, anticipating results discussed in Sections 10.5 and 11.7 of Chapters 10 and 11, respectively. In credit markets, the central bank, in its role as lender of last resort, can step in by purchasing securities under stress, therefore reducing spreads in credit markets and providing backstop liquidity to avoid fire-sale cascades. Moreover, in the event of a liquidity crunch, the central bank and the treasury can overcome the shortage of private "safe assets" in the economy by increasing the government supply through central bank reserves and treasury debt. Moreover, the central bank's purchases of risky private securities, under certain conditions, can be a less costly way to provide liquidity to the economy.

9.4.1   Irrelevance of Unconventional Open Market Operations

This section provides one simple example of the irrelevance of open-market operations and then discusses the generality of the results. What is key in the exercise that follows is determining whether unconventional policy represents an additional tool with respect to conventional policy.

The framework is the same as in Section 9.3, except that it considers a stochastic economy because of random variations in the preference shock, ξ, and output, Y. There is also long-term debt in the economy, which can be issued by the private sector and/or by the treasury. We now denote with B_S and B_L the short-term and long-term assets in the hands of the private sector, where B_S replaces B in the notation of Section 9.3. The equilibrium conditions for the two bond markets are:

$$B_{S,t}^F = B_{S,t} + B_{S,t}^C,$$
$$B_{L,t}^F = B_{L,t} + B_{L,t}^C,$$

in which B_S^F and B_L^F represent the short-term and long-term debt issued by the treasury, while B_S^C and B_L^C denote the respective central bank holdings of these debts. We denote with Q_t^L the price of the long-term debt at time t. The security available has decaying coupons: by lending Q_t^L units of currency at time t, geometrically decaying coupons are delivered equal to $1, \delta, \delta^2, \delta^3, \ldots$ in the following periods.[11] An implication of the stochastic environment is that the return, i_t^L, on long-term bonds between period $t-1$ and t, given by $i_t^L = (1 + \delta Q_t^L)/Q_{t-1}^L - 1$, is not necessarily equal to that on short-term bonds on the same horizon, i.e., $i_t^L \neq i_{t-1}$.

The equilibrium is characterized by the same conditions as in Section 9.3, with the appropriate qualifications, including an asset-pricing condition for the return on long-term bonds.

In this section we study the case in which the central bank does not back the treasury. Similar arguments can be made to the case of backing.

The following is our experiment. We start with a specification of policy where the central bank holds a certain portfolio of bonds, given by the stochastic sequences $\left\{ \tilde{B}_{L,t}^C, \tilde{B}_{S,t}^C \right\}_{t=t_0}^{\infty}$, and analyze the equilibrium. We then have the central bank change its portfolio by purchasing more long-term bonds but leave all other specifications of policy unchanged. Is the resulting equilibrium the same or different? In the first case, we obtain a result of irrelevance of open market operations; in the second case, we obtain a relevance result.

Let us assume that the central bank sets the interest rate to a constant $i_t = i = 1/\beta - 1$ at all times and specify the exogenous purchase of long- and short-term bonds, $\tilde{B}_{L,t}^C$ and $\tilde{B}_{S,t}^C$. Given the specification of the asset holdings $\left\{ \tilde{B}_{L,t}^C, \tilde{B}_{S,t}^C \right\}_{t=t_0}^{\infty}$, there is still one additional degree of freedom to specify policy, which can be the remittances policy, which turns out to be the relevant

11. See the analysis of Woodford (1998).

feature for characterizing an irrelevance or relevance result. The following remittances policy is first assumed:

$$\frac{T_t^C}{P_t} = (1 - \beta)\tau^C + \frac{i_{t-1}M_{t-1} + (i_t^L - i_{t-1})Q_{t-1}^L \tilde{B}_{L,t-1}^C}{P_t}, \qquad (9.19)$$

in which the central bank follows a real remittances policy captured by the parameter τ^C, and rebates the seigniorage revenues obtained by issuing money and by holding long-term assets.

The relevant equilibrium condition to determine prices is the stochastic version of equation (9.15), which can be appropriately written as

$$\frac{X_{t-1} + M_{t-1} - \tilde{B}_{S,t-1}^C - (1 + i_t^L)Q_{t-1}^L \tilde{B}_{L,t-1}^C}{P_t}$$

$$= E_t \sum_{T=t}^{\infty} R_{t,T} \left(\frac{i_T}{1 + i_T} \frac{M_T}{P_T} - \frac{T_T^C}{P_T} \right), \qquad (9.20)$$

accounting for the central bank holdings of long-term debt and in which the real stochastic discount factor is represented by $R_{t,T} = \beta^{T-t} \xi_T U_c(Y_T) / \xi_t U_c(Y_t)$.

To simplify the analysis we assume that $\xi_t U_c(Y_t)$ is a martingale, i.e., $E_t \xi_T U_c(Y_T) = \xi_t U_c(Y_T)$ for each $T > t$. We can then use this assumption together with (9.19) and (9.20) to obtain

$$\frac{N_{t-1}^C(1 + i_{t-1})}{P_t} = \tau^C,$$

and, therefore, using $1 + i_t = 1/\beta$,

$$\frac{N_{t-1}^C}{P_t} = \beta \tau^C. \qquad (9.21)$$

To obtain this result, we have used the definition of central bank net worth,

$$N_t^C = Q_t^L \tilde{B}_{L,t}^C + \frac{\tilde{B}_{S,t}^C - X_t}{1 + i_t} - M_t. \qquad (9.22)$$

Equilibrium condition (9.21) determines the price level at any time t, showing that it is not contingent on the state. Using the stochastic version of the Euler equation (9.5),

$$\xi_t U_c(Y_t) = \beta(1 + i_t)E_t \left\{ \frac{P_t}{P_{t+1}} \xi_{t+1} U_c(Y_{t+1}) \right\},$$

the martingale property of $\xi_t U_c(Y_t)$, and the interest rate policy, it follows that the price level is always constant, let's say, fixed at a generic level P^*. For this to be an equilibrium, the level of the net worth should be constant, too, which can be verified by the following steps, starting from its law of motion:

$$N_t^C = N_{t-1}^C + \Psi_t^C - T_t^C$$
$$= (1 + i_{t-1})N_{t-1}^C + i_{t-1}M_{t-1} + (i_t^L - i_{t-1})Q_{t-1}^L \tilde{B}_{L,t-1}^C - T_t^C, \quad (9.23)$$

having substituted into the expression of the first line the central bank's profits, given by the formula

$$\Psi_t^C = \frac{i_{t-1}}{1 + i_{t-1}}(\tilde{B}_{S,t-1}^C - X_{t-1}) + i_t^L Q_{t-1}^L \tilde{B}_{L,t-1}^C$$
$$= i_{t-1}(N_{t-1}^C + M_{t-1}) + (i_t^L - i_{t-1})Q_{t-1}^L \tilde{B}_{L,t-1}^C, \quad (9.24)$$

in which, in the second line, we have used the definition of net worth given by (9.22). Using (9.19) to substitute for T_t^C in the second line of (9.23), we obtain

$$N_t^C = (1 + i_{t-1})N_{t-1}^C - (1 - \beta)P_t \tau^C$$

or

$$N_t^C = N_{t-1}^C + P_t \left[i_{t-1}\frac{N_{t-1}^C}{P_t} - (1 - \beta)\tau^C \right].$$

By examining the above equation, it follows that $N_t^C = N_{t-1}^C$, since the term in square brackets is zero considering (9.21) and, therefore, net worth is always constant at the initial level $N_{t_0-1}^C$. After our having determined prices at all times, $P_t = P^*$, (9.7) determines the path of money for each $t \geq t_0$. We have therefore characterized the whole equilibrium, starting from a specification of policy with a certain balance-sheet policy $\left\{\tilde{B}_{S,t}^C, \tilde{B}_{L,t}^C\right\}$, which can allow for zero holding of long-term bonds, $\tilde{B}_{L,t}^C = 0$. Note, however, that equilibrium prices, interest rates, and money will not change under an alternative specification of balance-sheet policies, let's say $\left\{\bar{B}_{S,t}^C, \bar{B}_{L,t}^C\right\}$, with $\bar{B}_{L,t}^C > 0$. Prices are always fixed at P^* since in (9.21) $N_t^C = N_{t_0-1}^C$ at each date $t \geq t_0$ and at each contingency at time t. Most importantly the equilibrium allocation does not depend on whether or not the central bank holds long-term securities. The only variable that is affected, eventually, is the central bank reserves.

This result does not depend on the simplified policies assumed, but on one important feature of the transfer policy (9.19) that provides for the transfer of gains or losses out of the central bank's balance sheet.[12] Whether the central bank holds a riskless portfolio of securities or instead purchases risky assets does not really affect the equilibrium level of prices. How is it possible?

For the central bank's long-term asset purchases to have an effect, there should be some change in total (financial and human) wealth of households to induce them to vary their consumption choices. The consequent change in aggregate demand, given an exogenous stream of output, would then result in a variation of equilibrium prices. This is indeed the same mechanism for which helicopter money was effective, as shown in Section 9.3. However, rule (9.19) makes sure that there is no such change in the households' total wealth. There are only offsetting adjustments of human and financial wealth. Indeed, if the central bank purchases some risky securities that were previously held by the private sector, that risk does not stay with the central bank because the rule (9.19) ensures that the central bank transfers fewer resources to the treasury, or receives a transfer in the event the risk materializes as negative profits. Meanwhile, under the solvency constraint (9.12), the treasury obtains these resources from the private sector through higher lumpsum taxes. In the end, the materialization of risk goes back to the private sector, whose total wealth does not change when evaluated at the initial equilibrium prices. Therefore, equilibrium prices do not need to change.

The role of reserves is indeed critical for the validity of this result. To see this, let us consider that a constant nominal net worth, as implied by remittance rule (9.19), requires that, in equilibrium,

$$Q_t^L B_{L,t}^C + \frac{B_{S,t}^C}{1+i_t} - \frac{X_t}{1+i_t} - M_t = N_{t_0-1}^C.$$

This equation shows that alternative compositions of the central bank's assets, $B_{S,t}^C$ and $B_{L,t}^C$, can be accommodated by variations in central bank reserves, X_t, without any change in equilibrium prices, Q_t^L, interest rate, i_t, and money supply, M_t.

The result of this section is quite striking, as it suggests that the massive purchases carried out by central banks in recent decades could be ineffective if not accompanied by an appropriate transfer policy. In the next section, building on this framework, we will discuss cases of relevance. Before doing that, let

---

12. Benigno and Nisticò (2020) have shown this result in a more general environment and for a more general remittances policy. See also Wallace (1981) and Eggertsson and Woodford (2003).

us draw another important conclusion to better understand the effectiveness of unconventional policies on an empirical basis. In the examples provided in this section, we varied the combination of assets held by the central bank, while keeping all other elements of the policy specification constant. However, if the specification of future interest rates varies contextually with the purchase of long-term securities, a different equilibrium allocation could be achieved. This change occurs not because of the asset purchase program, but, rather, because of the change in conventional policy through the specification of interest rates. This observation suggests that open market operations could, in practice, work if they are interpreted as a way to signal changes in future rates, enhancing the forward guidance, which will be discussed in Section 9.5.[13]

9.4.2   Relevance of Unconventional Open Market Operations

This section discusses cases of the relevance of asset purchase programs. The first result builds on the previous section. In that context, to break irrelevance, one needs to specify a different remittances policy for which some gains or losses of the asset purchase programs remain in the central bank's balance sheet. One simple case is the constant real remittances policy $T_t^C/P_t = (1 - \beta)\tau^C$, with $\tau^C > 0$. In this case, equilibrium condition (9.20) implies

$$L(Y, \beta^{-1} - 1) + \frac{N_{t-1}^C + \Psi_t^C}{P_t} = \tau^C, \tag{9.25}$$

in which we have also substituted in the interest rate policy and the equilibrium in the money market. To further simplify the expression, without losing generality, we have assumed that Y_t is constant at Y and $E_t\xi_{t+1} = \xi_t$. Given the constant real remittances policy, alternative combinations of short-term versus long-term securities in the central bank's balance sheet affect the price level differently. If we start with an equilibrium in which the central bank holds only risk-free short-term bonds, then profits, represented by (9.24), do not vary with the excess return on long-term bonds, since $B_{L,t}^C = 0$. Consider now either an expansion of the central bank's balance sheet with purchases of long-term bonds financed by issuing reserves or a substitution between short- and long-term securities, leaving unchanged the size of the central bank's balance

---

13. Bernanke (2022, p. 144) mentions that in the early Japanese experience, QE worked as a *forward guidance* tool. Bhattarai, Eggertsson, and Gafarov (2023) provide a theoretical analysis of the signaling channel.

sheet. Profits will now depend on the excess return on long-term bonds. If the return falls, then the central bank will make losses. With lower profits—a fall of Ψ_t^C in (9.25)—the price level should also fall in equilibrium. Therefore, unconventional monetary policy can have effects on prices for a "constant" conventional policy and a remittances policy.

The above analysis suggests some more interesting results in the event losses on the central bank balance sheet are large. If we suppose they are, bringing the left-hand side of (9.25) to negative numbers, there cannot be an equilibrium with the interest rate pegged at $1/\beta$. What is possible, instead, is that the central bank changes its future interest rate policy to be consistent with a different inflation rate (in the example, inflation was at zero) and higher seigniorage revenues. If we consider a policy in which the central bank targets the nominal interest rate at $i = \Pi/\beta - 1$, then we can write (9.20) or (9.25) as

$$\frac{\Pi - \beta}{\Pi(1 - \beta)} L\left(Y, \frac{\Pi}{\beta} - 1\right) + \frac{N_{t-1}^C + \Psi_t^C}{P_t} = \tau^C,$$

showing that a large loss, a quite negative Ψ_t^C, can be absorbed by an increase in Π for an equilibrium with a positive P_t to arise. Therefore, the central bank can cover its losses by permanently increasing inflation and seigniorage.[14] If all these forces are strong, then prices can be pushed up even at time t. In this way, unconventional policy can help to reflate the economy, as required in a liquidity trap.

In general, a central bank's remittances policy is more complex than the constant remittances policy analyzed here. The U.S. Federal Reserve, for example, rebates profits to the Treasury during normal times, while it stops making remittances in the event of losses until the point in which they are completely recovered. If we assume a target level for nominal net worth represented by $\bar{N}^C$, the remittance's rule can be written as $T_t^C = \max(\Psi_t^C, 0)$ if $N_{t-1}^C \geq \bar{N}^C > 0$; otherwise, $T_t^C = 0$. Benigno and Nisticò (2020) show that results of relevance of open market operations can arise also in this case if losses are large enough.

To summarize the results in Sections 9.3 and 9.4, it is important to remark that the effectiveness of helicopter money and unconventional monetary policy depends on whether they are able to generate wealth effects on households. In the helicopter money experiment, the government implements a certain

---

14. It is assumed that we are on the increasing side of the seigniorage-revenue function with respect to inflation, so that an increase in inflation raises seigniorage.

transfer to households, which is not undone in the future. With unconventional monetary policy, given certain transfer rules, the asset purchases by the central bank also imply a transfer of wealth to the private sector.

9.5 Forward Guidance

One limitation of our analysis so far is the perfect alignment between the timing of an exogenous shock hitting the economy and the duration of the zero lower bound policy, as in the example of Section 9.1. This alignment has somewhat reduced the significance of properly setting the interest rate policy, even when the central bank's short-term nominal interest rate adjustments are restricted.

In policy formulation, it is not just the current interest rate that matters; the central bank should also specify future interest rates, offering *guidance* on its *future* policy direction. This is known as *forward guidance*. As previously discussed in Section 1.4 of Chapter 1, this type of policy is not unconventional. To determine the equilibrium allocation of output and inflation, the monetary policymaker must define not only the interest rate at the current time but also those at all future times and under different scenarios. This comprehensive specification of interest rates is crucial for uniquely determining current output and inflation. Both the *AD* and the *AS* equations are influenced by expectations of future output and inflation, so the central bank's influence on these expectations plays a pivotal role in shaping current output and inflation.

While guidance on future interest rates should naturally be a part of conventional monetary policy, it has gained increased attention in recent years due to the experience of zero interest rate policies in many advanced economies, as shown in Figure 9.1. The inability to further lower short-term interest rates has placed greater importance on the appropriate setting of future rates, emphasizing the concept of *forward guidance*. In a liquidity trap, *forward guidance* possesses unique features that distinguish it from practices during normal conditions. One interesting aspect is the specification of the potential duration for which interest rates remain at zero, which can be conditional on achieving specific inflation targets over certain time horizons. In this way, *forward guidance* becomes a valuable tool for stimulating economic growth.

The dynamic New Keynesian model is suitable for studying some of the peculiar features of *forward guidance* in a liquidity trap because the duration of the zero interest rate does not necessarily coincide with the duration of the negative demand shock and, therefore, can be an important variable for the policymaker. One direction to explore is that of understanding how optimal policy in Section 7.3 of Chapter 7 changes in the liquidity trap and studying whether this policy can be rephrased in terms of an appropriate *forward guidance* on the paths of interest rates and inflation.

In Section 7.3, the *AD* equation (7.5) was not a constraint on the problem since it was implicitly assumed that the interest rate could freely adjust given the optimal paths of the other variables involved in the equation, such as inflation and output. The interest rate path under optimal policy followed

$$\hat{\imath}_t = r_t^e - (\sigma^{-1} - \theta^{-1})(1 - \gamma_1)x_t;$$

therefore, it was mirroring movements of the frictionless real interest rate (r^e) and, inversely, the output gap (x); σ, θ are parameters and γ_1 is a function of parameters, with the same interpretations as in Section 7.3 of Chapter 7. Shocks were implicitly assumed not to be large enough to push the nominal interest rate below the zero floor. For large negative shocks to r^e, however, the constraint can become binding. In this case, the *AD* equation (7.5) and the zero lower bound itself have to be considered restrictions to the optimal policy problem. To account for this, consider the following Lagrangian to replace that of Section 7.3 of Chapter 7:

$$\mathcal{L}_{t_0} = E_{t_0} \left\{ \sum_{t=t_0}^{\infty} \beta^{t-t_0} \left[\frac{1}{2} \left(\hat{Y}_t - \hat{Y}_t^e \right)^2 + \frac{1}{2} \frac{\theta}{\kappa} (\pi_t - \pi)^2 + \right. \right.$$
$$+ \varphi_t \left((\hat{Y}_t - \hat{Y}_t^e) - (\hat{Y}_{t+1} - \hat{Y}_{t+1}^e) + \sigma \left(\hat{\imath}_t - (\pi_{t+1} - \pi) - r_t^e \right) \right) +$$
$$+ \lambda_t \left((\pi_t - \pi) - \kappa(\hat{Y}_t - \hat{Y}_t^e) - \upsilon_t - \beta(\pi_{t+1} - \pi) \right) \right] +$$
$$\left. - \varphi_{t_0-1}\beta^{-1}(\hat{Y}_{t_0} - \hat{Y}_t^e) - \varphi_{t_0-1}\beta^{-1}\sigma(\pi_{t_0} - \pi) - \lambda_{t_0}(\pi_{t_0} - \pi) \right\},$$

in which notations and variables follow those of Section 7.3.

The first-order conditions with respect to inflation and output are, respectively:

$$\theta(\pi_t - \pi) - \beta^{-1}\sigma\kappa\varphi_{t-1} + \kappa\lambda_t - \kappa\lambda_{t-1} = 0, \qquad (9.26)$$

$$(\hat{Y}_t - \hat{Y}_t^e) + \varphi_t - \beta^{-1}\varphi_{t-1} - \kappa\lambda_t = 0, \qquad (9.27)$$

where φ_t is the Lagrange multiplier attached to the *AD* constraint (7.5), with $\varphi_t \geq 0$, and λ_t the Lagrange multiplier attached to the *AS* constraint (7.6).[15] The Kuhn-Tucker condition associated with the nonnegative constraint on the nominal interest rate is $i_t \cdot \varphi_t \geq 0$.[16] When $\varphi_t = 0$, we can retrieve the same first-order conditions as those of Section 7.3 of Chapter 7.

First-order conditions (9.26) and (9.27) can be used to eliminate all the Lagrange multipliers and synthesize optimal policy through the use of a price level targeting rule. The central bank should set the interest rate in a way that an appropriate "price" $\tilde{p}_t$, defined as $\tilde{p}_t = p_t + \theta^{-1}(\hat{Y}_t - \hat{Y}_t^e)$ as in Section 7.3 of Chapter 7, is set equal to a target $\bar{p}_t^*$ when it is feasible; otherwise the interest rate is set to zero. The target $\bar{p}_t^*$ is updated following the law of motion,

$$\bar{p}_{t+1}^* = \pi + \bar{p}_t^* + \beta^{-1}(1 + \kappa\sigma)(\bar{p}_t^* - \tilde{p}_t) - \beta^{-1}(\bar{p}_{t-1}^* - \tilde{p}_{t-1}).$$

It is adjusted upward during the periods in which it is not achieved $(\bar{p}_t^* > \tilde{p}_t)$ and the zero lower bound is tight.[17] Indeed, the increase in the target during the liquidity trap works to push up inflation expectations. In contrast, when the zero lower bound is no longer binding, the price target decreases at that moment. This is captured by the last term on the right-hand side of the above equation. Meanwhile, under normal conditions of a positive nominal interest rate, $\tilde{p}_t = \bar{p}_t^*$ and $\bar{p}_t^*$ grow at the rate π, as in Section 7.3 of Chapter 7.

It is interesting to compare the outcome of the above policy with one in which the central bank never adjusts the target price level. In this case, the target price level follows $\tilde{p}_{t+1}^* = \pi + \tilde{p}_t^*$, as in Section 7.3 of Chapter 7, and $\tilde{p}_t = \tilde{p}_t^*$ whenever it is feasible; otherwise the interest rate is set to zero. This policy would be optimal without the zero lower bound, but it turns out to be suboptimal when the zero lower bound is binding since it does not allow the central bank to catch up to the lost trajectory in the price level.

Figure 9.5 compares the optimal policy to the, now, suboptimal policy. The economy is hit by a negative shock to the natural rate of interest, which brings it to -4%, at an annual rate, for twelve quarters. Given that the steady-state policy rate is set at 4%, accounting for a 2% inflation target, the shock to the

---

15. The Lagrangian has been augmented with appropriate constraints at time t_0 that allow us to characterize the optimal policy with commitment from a "timeless perspective," as in Section 7.3 of Chapter 7.

16. Note that $i_t \approx \hat{i}_t + \ln(1 + i) \geq 0$, where i is the steady-state interest rate.

17. The price target $\bar{p}_t^*$ is obtained by eliminating Lagrange multiplier λ_t from equations (9.26) and (9.27) and defining $\bar{p}_t^* \equiv \varphi_t + \tilde{p}_t$.

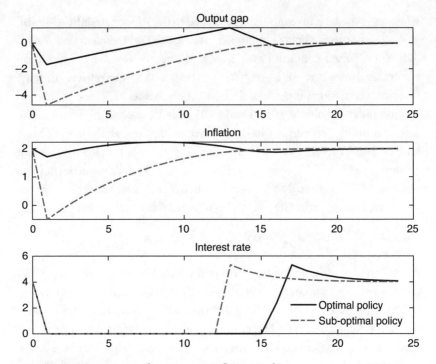

FIGURE 9.5. Responses of output gap, inflation and interest rate to a negative shock to the natural rate of interest with a duration of twelve quarters. Comparison between optimal policy and the suboptimal policy $\tilde{p}_t = \tilde{p}_t^*$ (whenever feasible) or $i_t = 0$ otherwise. Variables are in %. Interest rates and inflation at annual rates.

natural rate of interest could be fully accommodated only if the policy rate could fall to -2%. The zero lower bound prevents this fall and creates an interesting trade-off between stabilizing output and inflation. Under the suboptimal policy, the nominal interest rate stays at the zero lower bound for the same duration as that of the negative shock, and the economy experiences a significant contraction, a fall in the output gap, and deflation.[18] Optimal policy, instead, mitigates the contraction and the fall in inflation. The interest rate is kept at the zero lower bound for longer than twelve quarters, up to fifteen quarters. This observation suggests a way to communicate *forward guidance* as a commitment to keeping short-term rates at zero for longer than the duration of the shock. This type of communication has been used by several central banks during the last few decades. In August 2003, facing a deflation scare,

18. Parameters are calibrated as in Figure 7.2.

the Federal Reserve stated that "policy accommodation can be maintained for a considerable period." In the aftermath of the 2007–2008 financial crisis, when the policy rate reached the zero floor, the wording was changed from "for some time" to an "extended period of time." In August 2011, the FOMC introduced a specific date making *forward guidance* time-contingent, stating that conditions would likely warrant keeping the federal funds rate target near zero at least through mid-2013. The date in the guidance was pushed out twice in 2012, first to late 2014 and then to mid-2015. At the end of 2012, *forward guidance* became state-contingent on economic objectives related to unemployment and inflation.[19]

Another important element of the optimal policy of Figure 9.5 is that inflation is kept above target starting after five quarters and beyond the duration of the negative shock. This is consistent with the need to reduce the real interest rate, as discussed in Section 9.1. Therefore, another way to communicate *forward guidance* is to promise higher inflation than the target, even after the negative shock is over.

Figure 9.6 shows another dimension of *forward guidance* through price-level targeting rule $\tilde{p}_t = p_t + \theta^{-1}(\hat{Y}_t - \hat{Y}_t^e)$ under the optimal policy and the suboptimal one. In the latter case, $\tilde{p}_t$ decreases significantly during the initial stay at the zero lower bound and then increases at the rate of 2% annually, as required by target $\tilde{p}_t^*$. Note, however, that the path implied by the target is completely missed: bygones are bygones. Under optimal policy $\tilde{p}_t$ does not fall but grows at a slower pace at the beginning of the trap and then catches up to its target, $\bar{p}_t^*$, after the liftoff from zero interest rate policies. Note that under optimal policy, $\tilde{p}_t$ increases, at some point, even at a faster rate than 2%, as it is shown in the graph.

It is crucial to recognize that the implications of this straightforward NK model have also lent support to recent reviews of monetary policy strategies carried out by both the Federal Reserve, in 2020, and the European Central Bank, in 2021. These reviews introduce a novel element: the possibility of inflation surpassing the target after periods of zero interest rate policies. The Federal Reserve has adopted an average inflation targeting approach of 2%, which means that periods of inflation persistently below 2% should be followed by periods of inflation above the target. Meanwhile, the European

19. The FOMC announced that no increase in the federal funds rate target should be anticipated so long as unemployment remained above 6-1/2 percent and inflation and inflation expectations remained stable and near target.

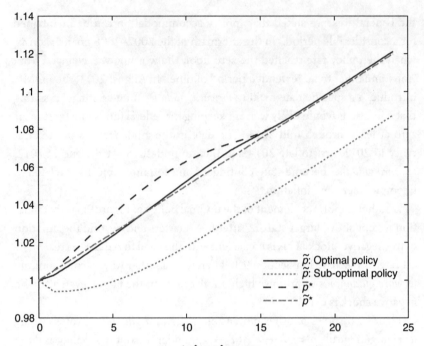

FIGURE 9.6. Plot of $\tilde{p}_t = p_t + \theta^{-1}(\hat{Y}_t - \hat{Y}_t^e)$ under optimal policy and under the sub-optimal policy $\tilde{p}_t = \tilde{p}_t^*$ (whenever feasible) or $i_t = 0$ otherwise. The price level targets $\tilde{p}_t^*$ (sub-optimal) and $\bar{p}_t^*$ (optimal) are also plotted.

Central Bank has emphasized the symmetry of its quantitative inflation target of 2%, replacing the previous notion of staying "below (even if close to) 2%." Despite the symmetric reference to 2%, the ECB's new strategy recognizes the significant asymmetry that comes into play when an economy is "operating near the lower bound on nominal interest rates." In such a scenario, it becomes plausible to design a monetary policy stance that allows for "a temporary period during which inflation moderately exceeds the target," implying a period in which the inflation rate exceeds 2% even in the medium term.

9.6 Managing the Central Bank's Reserves

Whereas much has been written on the guidance of interest rates during a liquidity trap (see Section 9.5), not much has been said about the path and timing of asset purchases. The episode of the "taper tantrum" in June 2013 well describes the uncertainty in the market perception of the timing of reduction in asset purchases, dubbed "tapering," and in general of the withdrawal of the stimulus in combination with the liftoff of the policy rate.[20]

Concerning the working of QE, this section investigates the theoretical relevance of the alternative hypothesis to the portfolio-rebalancing theory, namely the central bank reserves channel. According to the monetarist view, an increase in reserves would trigger the creation of liquidity via financial intermediaries and stimulate aggregate demand. Although the term "quantitative easing" has been applied to almost all types of asset purchase programs deployed by central banks around the world during the last two decades, it was meant at the time of its first implementation, in Japan in 2001, to capture the easing of central bank reserves.

The NK model of Chapter 8 is suitable for studying the relevance of the easing or tightening of reserves, for it characterizes a banking channel through which reserves provide nonpecuniary benefits to intermediaries with regard to some collateral/regulatory constraints. This section investigates the implications of that model.

Following the analysis in Section 9.5, we can first consider the zero lower bound constraint applied to the optimal policy problem presented in Section 8.6 of Chapter 8. The striking result is that the optimal liquidity policy is unchanged with respect to the result in Section 8.6, i.e., it is set to the point of satiating the liquidity needs of the economy. Therefore, all the other implications of optimal policy are also unchanged with respect to the analysis of Section 9.5.[21] Once the economy is at the satiation level, further increases of central bank reserves are irrelevant. Clearly, reserves and tax policy, the drivers of d, become relevant when satiation is not reached.

The role and dynamics of liquidity become more significant when it is costly to vary it, such as in a context in which lumpsum taxes are not available. We reconsider the model of Chapter 8 under this assumption, where the only available tax is the distortionary tax on firms' revenues. The overall supply of government liquidity, B_{t-1}^{g}, is now directly related to the distortionary

---

20. "Taper tantrum" refers to the 2013 collective reactionary panic that triggered a spike in U.S. Treasury yields, in response to the Federal Reserve's announcement that it would begin to scale back or "taper" its quantitative easing (QE) program.

21. When liquidity and goods complement each other in utility, there is some departure at the exit of the liquidity trap, since variations in liquidity have direct effect on the marginal utility of consumption.

tax through the intertemporal resource constraint of the economy:

$$\frac{(1+i^X_{t-1})B^g_{t-1}}{P_t} = E_t \left\{ \sum_{T=t}^{\infty} R_{t,T} \left[\tau_T Y_T - Tr_T + \frac{i_T - i^X_T}{1+i_T} \frac{B^g_T}{P_T} \right] \right\}, \quad (9.28)$$

in which $R_{t,T}$ is the stochastic discount factor for real income, i^X is the policy rate, P is the price level, i is the market nominal interest rate, Y is output, and Tr is a nonnegative transfer. This equation replaces (8.18) of Chapter 8, where τ is a distortionary tax on firms' revenues, which is the opposite of the subsidy τ^s previously used.

Supplying liquidity, in this case, can lead to taxation-related distortions that have the potential to impact overall welfare. As previously discussed in Section 8.6 of Chapter 8, the optimal supply of liquidity is deemed to be below the satiation level. This is because increasing it beyond this point would necessitate significant distortions in taxation. In the following discussion, we analyze the optimal government stabilization problem, employing a linear-quadratic approach with approximations centered around the optimal steady state. In this state, inflation is at the target level, and liquidity remains below the satiation threshold.

The quadratic welfare-based loss function takes the form

$$L^{CB}_{t_0} = E_{t_0} \sum_{t=t_0}^{\infty} \beta^{t-t_0} \left\{ \frac{1}{2} \Lambda_x x^2_t + \frac{1}{2} \Lambda_\pi (\pi_t - \pi)^2 + \frac{1}{2} \Lambda_d \hat{d}^2_t \right\} \quad (9.29)$$

for positive parameters Λ_x, Λ_π, and Λ_d.[22] The policymaker should care about the deviation of the output gap, x, inflation, π, and real liquidity (deposit), d, from their steady state values. The only stochastic disturbances considered in the following analysis are the preference shock ξ and the exogenous transfer Tr.[23]

The optimal policy problem is subject to a modified AS equation with respect to (8.20) in Section 8.5 of Chapter 8:

$$(\pi_t - \pi) = \kappa[x + \psi_\tau(\tilde{\tau}_t - \tilde{\tau}^*_t)] + \beta E_t(\pi_{t+1} - \pi),$$

---

22. See Benigno and Benigno (2022).

23. Variations in the exogenously given transfer Tr are necessary for characterizing an equilibrium in which all targets in the loss function are achieved absent the zero lower bound constraint.

which accounts for the time-varying effects of the distortionary tax on firms' revenue, for a positive parameter ψ_τ. The variable $\tilde{\tau}_t$ is defined as $\tilde{\tau}_t = \tau_t - \tau$, in which τ is the steady state value of the tax rate, whereas $\tilde{\tau}_t^*$ represents a combination of the shocks such that when $\tilde{\tau}_t$ achieves that value, output and inflation can be stabilized at their respective targets.

The AD equation (8.25) simplifies to

$$x_t = v_\rho E_t x_{t+1} - \sigma v_\rho (\hat{i}_t^X - E_t(\pi_{t+1} - \pi) - r_t^e) + d_y^{-1}(1 - v_\rho)\hat{d}_t, \quad (9.30)$$

for an appropriately defined (constrained) efficient real rate of interest, r_t^e, which is a function of the shocks; v_ρ, σ, and d_y are positive parameters.

An additional constraint of the optimal policy problem is the first-order approximation of (9.28), which can be written as

$$\hat{d}_{t-1} - (\pi_t - \pi) - \sigma^{-1} x_t + (\hat{i}_{t-1}^X - r_{t-1}^e)$$

$$= -f_t + E_t \sum_{T=t}^{\infty} \beta^{T-t}[b_x x_T + b_\tau(\tilde{\tau}_T - \tilde{\tau}_T^*) + b_d \hat{d}_T], \quad (9.31)$$

in which b_x, b_τ and b_d are combinations of the primitive parameters of the model; the variable f, as in Eggertsson and Woodford (2004), captures the "fiscal stress," which measures the extent to which full stabilization of output, inflation, and liquidity at their targets implied by the loss function (9.29) is not compatible with the intertemporal budget constraint of the government. When $f_t = 0$ at all times, it is feasible to reach all three targets provided the movements in the efficient real rate of interest, r^e, do not imply violation of the zero lower bound for the nominal interest rate.[24] Indeed, when all targets in (9.29) are achieved, $\hat{i}_t^X = r_t^e$ at all times. In contrast, when the efficient real rate of interest, r^e, falls substantially, there could be violation of the zero lower bound for the policy rate, i^X; therefore a trade-off emerges between the stabilizing of the relevant variables.

The analysis considers, therefore, how policy should be set when the only constraint on the full stabilization of the relevant variables in (9.29) is given by the existence of the zero lower bound on the policy rate.[25]

24. In this reasoning, we are considering zero values for the initial conditions $\hat{d}_{t_0-1}$, $\hat{i}_{t_0-1}^X, r_{t_0-1}^e$. We could also allow for different initial conditions requiring, in this case, f_{t_0} to adjust appropriately.

25. Note that when the optimal supply of liquidity is close to eliminating the distortions in the money market, i.e., $v \to 0$, the problem collapses to exactly that analyzed by Eggertsson and Woodford (2004) in the standard New Keynesian model with distortionary taxes. Indeed, the

We assume a shock that brings the efficient real rate of interest, r^e, from the steady-state level of 2% to -4% at annual rates for twelve quarters.[26]

Figure 9.7 compares the optimal policy with sub-optimal policies in which (i) the central bank sets inflation at the target, i.e., $\pi_t = \pi$, whenever it is feasible, and otherwise sets the policy rate to zero and (ii) the fiscal authority keeps the tax gap $\tilde{\tau}_t - \tilde{\tau}_t^*$ at a level that it expects to maintain indefinitely without violating the intertemporal government budget constraint; that is, an expected path of the tax gap such that $E_t(\tilde{\tau}_T - \tilde{\tau}_T^*) = \tilde{\tau}_t - \tilde{\tau}_t^*$ for all $T \geq t$ is consistent with (9.31).

The second comparison is with the "constant liquidity policy." In the latter, fiscal policy moves the tax gap to fully stabilize liquidity at the steady state while the monetary authority minimizes loss function (9.29) under the same constraints as in the general optimal policy problem, but considering as given the path of the fiscal variables $\tilde{\tau} - \tilde{\tau}^*$ and the fact that the intertemporal solvency of the government is ensured by the tax policy. This better characterizes how optimal policy would cope with the shock when liquidity is not used.

The figure shows the costs of the sub-optimal policy with respect to the optimal one in terms of contraction in the output gap and inflation below the target. The liftoff of the policy rate from the zero lower bound occurs exactly at the time at which the shock vanishes. Optimal policy, instead, succeeds in stabilizing inflation while keeping moderate variations in the output gap.

We discuss three important features of the optimal policy and the managing of liquidity during zero lower bound episodes.

First, in line with the analysis in Section 9.5, optimal policy requires a stay at the zero lower bound longer with respect to the duration of the shock. In the figure, the interest rate remains at the zero lower bound for one additional quarter. Note that the liquidity channel in the AD equation implies a shorter stay at the zero lower bound than under a "constant liquidity policy," in which, to compensate for the lack of this instrument, the interest rate

---

AD equation boils down to the standard one, in which liquidity does not affect, directly, aggregate demand. The AS equation is already the same as in their framework, as are the parameters Λ_x and Λ_π in loss function (9.29). With $\nu \to 0$, Λ_d goes instead to zero as does b_d in constraint (9.31); b_x and b_τ also approach the same values as in Eggertsson and Woodford (2004).

26. The model is calibrated quarterly. The following parametrization is used: $\beta = 0.995$, $\kappa = 0.02$, $\sigma = 0.5$, $\sigma_d = 0.1367$, $\nu = 0,01$, $\theta = 10$, $\eta = 0.47$, $\psi_\tau = 0.5068$, $\Lambda_x = 114.9313$, $\Lambda_\pi = 1117.64$, $\Lambda_d = 0.8750$, $b_x = 0.1367$, $b_\tau = 0.0050$, $b_d = -0.313$. Inflation target π is set at a 2% annual rate; ν is set at 0.01 to imply a 4% spread at annual rates in money markets, similar to the values observed at the onset of the 2007–2008 financial crisis.

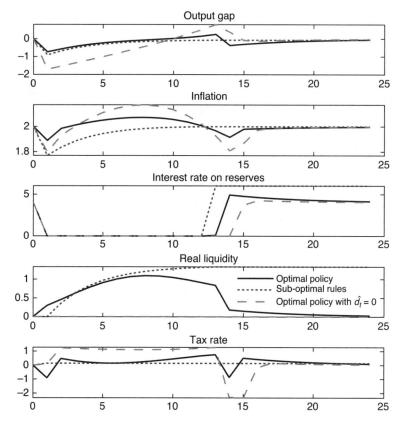

FIGURE 9.7. Responses of output gap, inflation, interest rate on reserves, real liquidity (deposit), and tax rate to a negative shock to the natural rate of interest with a duration of twelve quarters. Comparison between optimal policy and sub-optimal rules. Variables are in %. Interest rates and inflation at annual rates. Real liquidity is in % deviations from the steady state. Tax rate is in percentage points and in deviations from the steady-state value.

stays one quarter longer at the zero lower bound. With respect to the *forward guidance* studied in the previous section, a model in which government liquidity influences directly aggregate demand implies an early liftoff of the policy rate.

The second feature of optimal policy is the path followed by liquidity, which increases at the beginning of the trap. Then, liquidity gradually peaks and remains elevated at the time at which the shock vanishes. The majority of the withdrawal occurs precisely at the liftoff of rates, followed by a gradual reduction. As shown in the figure, optimal policy requires a reversal of liquidity to the steady-state values, unlike what happens under the sub-optimal policy in which liquidity persistently remains high.[27] Moreover, the increase of liquidity during the trap is not much more than under sub-optimal policies, because of the success of the optimal policy in stabilizing inflation and output. Indeed, the fall in the output gap under the sub-optimal rules produces lower revenues from taxes, which lead to a large accumulation of public liabilities. With respect to QE, the framework implies that it should be used during a liquidity trap, but then withdrawn as conditions normalize, and the central bank's balance sheet returns to initial conditions.

The third result is the use of the tax policy that should be lowered at the beginning and at the end of the trap: at the beginning to raise the supply of government liquidity, at the end to mute the overshooting of inflation with respect to the target through the AS equation.[28]

9.7   Other Channels for Unconventional Monetary Policies

The responses of central banks to the 2007–2008 financial crisis and the COVID-19 pandemic extended beyond their traditional macroeconomic stabilization role, which primarily involved using rate cuts and innovative policies to reduce long-term interest rates. These two significant crises revived the more traditional role of central banks as lenders of last resort. Interestingly, the Federal Reserve was originally established for precisely this role. In December 1913, after years of bank crises and runs, President Woodrow Wilson signed the Federal Reserve Act into law, granting the Federal Reserve the authority to conduct monetary policy for the nation and maintain the stability of the financial system, including containing systemic risk in financial markets.

Bagehot (1873) effectively outlines how central banks should address financial panics. The central bank should provide unlimited lending at a penalty rate relative to the risk-free rate to any entity in the economy. Loans

---

27. In contrast to Eggertsson and Woodford (2004), public liabilities do return to the initial steady state in this framework, because there is an optimal steady-state value of liquidity.

28. The initial tax rate reduction during the zero lower bound episode contrasts with the finding of Eggertsson and Woodford (2004), in which the tax rate rises, but where liquidity does not have a stabilizing role in the economy. It would re-emerge in this context also for low values of v.

should be granted in exchange for collateral, which should be evaluated as "good" under normal conditions. A crucial aspect of this proposal is the valuation of collateral under normal conditions rather than under stress, as this can be used to differentiate between solvency and insolvency when providing assistance.[29]

Through these interventions, the central bank can prevent the illiquidity issues of financial intermediaries from resulting in their bankruptcy. The central bank, as the issuer of currency and risk-free liabilities, plays a crucial role in averting systemic financial crises.

Central banks have long had the discount window as a lender-of-last-resort tool. However, the complexity of financial crises has necessitated the use of additional instruments. Over time, central banks have become the "buyers of last resort" (Bernanke, 2022, p. 136).

During severe financial stress, intermediaries may witness a deterioration in the quality and value of their assets, leading to stricter margin requirements on their funding. This raises funding costs and could result in asset liquidation. In cases of systemic risk, this could trigger fire sales across multiple intermediaries, further deteriorating asset quality and exacerbating funding problems. Central banks can step in by purchasing the assets of intermediaries or supplying them with low-rate liquidity, reducing collateral requirements, and accepting assets under stress as collateral. Section 10.5 of Chapter 10 theoretically explains how these policies can mitigate the adverse effects of a financial crisis on aggregate demand.

One complexity of the 2007–2008 financial crisis was its connection to the shadow banking system, which was not eligible for direct lending from the Federal Reserve. One of the initial measures taken was to lend outside the traditional banking system by invoking Section 13(3) of the Federal Reserve Act, which allows such lending under extraordinary circumstances. Eventually, this provision was extended to lend to nonfinancial borrowers as well. The Commercial Paper Funding Facility aimed to provide loans to corporations, while the Term Asset-Backed Securities Loan Facility (TALF) lent to investors purchasing credit securities. The Fed also launched the Money Market Mutual Fund Liquidity Facility (MMLF), which lent to banks against collateral they purchased from prime money market funds that invest in Treasury securities and short-term corporate commercial paper.

---

29. A collateral evaluated under stress conditions would reflect an unnecessarily low quality due to panic.

All of the aforementioned programs, once again invoking Section 13(3), were reactivated during the coronavirus pandemic. In addition to these, numerous other programs were initiated to provide direct assistance to small businesses, households, and local and state governments. Among these, the Main Street Lending Program, introduced in April 2020, aimed to support small and medium-sized businesses. The Paycheck Protection Program (PPP) played a vital role in helping businesses maintain their workforce during the lockdowns. The central bank's interventions were instrumental in preventing foreclosures and bankruptcies. This time, the impact began with the real economy (Main Street) and extended to the financial economy (Wall Street). Indeed, the economic repercussions of the pandemic shock initially affected Main Street, as many businesses struggled to cover their fixed costs and payroll expenses due to the lockdowns.

Figure 9.4, in the left-hand side panel, shows the size of these programs in relationship with the overall asset purchase programs, pointing out their importance during the financial crisis and the pandemic.

Figure 9.8 provides evidence of the surge in credit spreads during the financial crisis and the pandemic, at both short and long maturities, and the effectiveness of the government programs in reducing them.

Chapter 11 will explore another scenario where unconventional open market operations can be effective—when the economy faces a liquidity crunch and a shortage of "safe assets." These are private or government debts that offer liquidity services, serving as collateral or easily exchangeable assets. The 2007–2008 financial crisis revealed the existence of a class of money-like securities within the shadow banking system. These securities, initially perceived as safe, lost not only their value but also their ability to provide liquidity services during the crisis, impacting the real economy.

Chapter 11 suggests how a liquidity crunch can have real economic consequences, leading to a contraction of economic activity. The central bank can address this issue by providing high-quality assets, as its reserves are inherently risk-free. An expansion of reserves can naturally counter the shortage of "safe assets" during a liquidity crisis.

In response to the financial crisis, as previously discussed, the U.S. government increased both the direct supply of public liquidity and its support for the liquidity provided by private intermediaries. These measures included the Federal Reserve's asset purchase programs, raising the deposit insurance limit, and the Temporary Liquidity Guarantee Program offered by the Federal Deposit Insurance Corporation (FDIC).

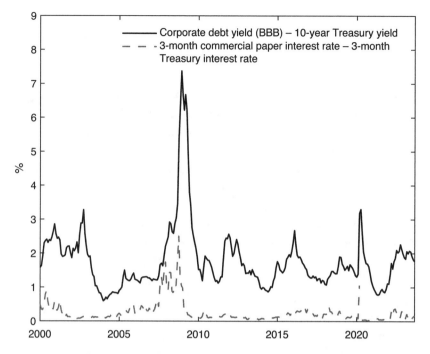

FIGURE 9.8. Credit Spreads. Short-term spread: differential between 3-month commercial paper interest rate and 3-month Treasury interest rate. Long-term spread: differential between corporate debt yield (BBB) and 10-year Treasury yield. Period: January 2000–October 2023. *Sources: Board of Governors of the Federal Reserve System (U.S.) and Ice Data Indices, LLC; ICE BofA BBB US Corporate Index Effective Yield retrieved from FRED, Federal Reserve Bank of St. Louis.*

9.8   References

Krugman (1998) is the main reference for the discussion of the liquidity trap in Section 9.1. See also Eggertsson (2010) for a review. Bernanke (2002) discusses several tools that monetary policymakers can deploy to avert deflation and a liquidity trap. Benigno and Fornaro (2018) and Eggertsson, Mehrotra, and Robbins (2019) study the possibility that a secular stagnation can arise in a liquidity trap.

The original parable of helicopter money is in Friedman (1969). The analysis in Section 9.3 draws from Benigno and Nisticò (2022). Buiter (2014) presents also a discussion of helicopter money via a coordination of monetary and fiscal policy. Galí (2020) studies the effects of a money-financed fiscal stimulus. An interesting discussion on the theme, involving Adair Turner and Michael Woodford, is presented in Reichlin, Turner, and Woodford (2013). This discussion highlights the equivalence between different methods of implementing helicopter money. Moreover, Reis and Tenreyro (2022) provide a thorough analysis on the topic. An historical example of helicopter money is discussed in Masciandaro, Goodhart, and Ugolini (2021), analyzing the money-financed fiscal stimulus implemented in Venice during the famine and plague of 1629–31.

The classical work on the irrelevance of open-market operations is Wallace (1981), which has been restated in more general frameworks by Eggertsson and Woodford (2003) and Benigno and Nisticò (2020).

The results regarding the relevance of open-market operations can be found in Benigno and Nisticò (2020), Berriel and Bhattarai (2009), Park (2012), Bhattarai, Eggertsson, and Gafarov (2023), as well as Del Negro and Sims (2015). Benigno and Nisticò (2020) underscore the importance of alternative tax and remittances policies. Berriel and Bhattarai (2009) examine a scenario with a fiscally independent central bank, demonstrating the effectiveness of specific balance-sheet policies on inflation and output. Del Negro and Sims (2015) discuss conditions under which, in the absence of fiscal support, central bank open-market operations involving risky debt can lead to inflation. Bhattarai, Eggertsson, and Gafarov (2023) illustrate how quantitative easing can be effective in signaling future short-term interest rates when the central bank cannot commit.

Empirical evidence of the effectiveness of asset purchase programs can be found in Krishnamurthy and Vissing-Jorgensen (2011), Ueda (2012), D'Amico et al. (2012), and D'Amico and King (2013). A quantitative model of the effectiveness of asset-purchase programs is presented in Del Negro et al. (2017).

The analysis of forward guidance of Section 9.5 is based on Eggertsson and Woodford (2003); see also Werning (2011) for a continuous-time version and richer interaction between commitment and discretion in fiscal and monetary policy. Eggertsson and Woodford (2004) analyze the exit from the liquidity trap when taxation is distortionary. Correia et al. (2013) discuss alternative fiscal instruments that can alleviate the zero lower bound constraint. Wolf (2023), in a heteregenous-agent model, has shown the equivalence between interest rate policies and transfer policies, which, however, does not affect the importance of forward guidance at the zero lower bound from a normative perspective, as shown by Corbellini (2024). Fujiwara et al. (2013)

study the emergence of global liquidity traps in an international context and exit policies.

Section 9.6 is based on Benigno and Benigno (2022). Diba and Loisel (2022) also analyze the normalization of monetary policy, placing emphasis on the pivotal role of central bank reserves in the adjustment process. Del Negro et al. (2017) present a comprehensive model that quantifies the effects of liquidity policies in the New Keynesian framework. Vissing-Jorgensen (2023) studies the size of a central bank balance sheet to reduce spreads in certain money market rates.

For an insightful exploration of all the monetary policy interventions conducted by the Federal Reserve in the past two decades and their interactions with fiscal policy, refer to Bernanke (2022) and Blinder (2022).

10

Deleveraging and Credit Crunch

10.1 Introduction

The analysis in Chapter 9 left unanswered the question of what triggers the shock that can push the economy into a liquidity trap. The driver was indeed of a pure exogenous source related to a shift in the intertemporal preferences of households, implying more patience and incentive to save. After the financial crisis, economic literature began to model in greater detail how the economy finds itself at the zero bound. This literature primarily focuses on two narratives. One powerful narrative suggests that the source of the shock is a deleveraging cycle on the household side (for theoretical contributions inspired by the crisis, see, for example, Eggertsson and Krugman, 2012, while Mian and Sufi, 2011, provide extensive empirical evidence for this mechanism).

Another powerful narrative traces the origin of the crisis to turbulence in the banking sector (see, for instance, Curdia and Woodford, 2010, 2011; Gertler and Karadi, 2011; and Gertler and Kiyotaki, 2010).

Let us start by exploring the narrative of household debt deleveraging. It begins with a phase of excessive optimism about debt, during which debtors borrow and spend aggressively by accumulating debt, a process referred to as leveraging. Since one person's debt represents another's asset, creditors must be encouraged to spend less, often through adjustments in real interest rates. Then comes the "Minsky moment," as described by Eggertsson and Krugman in 2012. This is the point where people realize that things have gone too far. They come to understand that the newly issued debt may not be sustainable, and the economy transitions from a period of leveraging to deleveraging. In other words, overextended agents must now repay their debt.

The challenge lies in the asymmetry of this process. The central bank may not be able to significantly reduce interest rates to induce enough spending among those who are not heavily indebted due to the zero bound. Hence, one way to explain a decline in the natural rate of interest is to suggest that debtors are trying to deleverage rapidly, requiring the real interest rate to fall to negative levels to encourage savers to spend enough to sustain full employment. A negative natural rate of interest can make the zero lower bound on the nominal interest rate binding.

Now, let us shift our focus to the banking turbulence narrative. In this scenario, a crisis unfolds in the interbank market, leading to increased funding costs for banks. Such a crisis may result from a shock to the banks' capital or the need to reduce leverage ratios. During stressful periods, banks' capital constraints tighten, making them less willing to lend, which, in turn, triggers an economic downturn. Interestingly, the mechanism through which this impacts the macroeconomy shares significant similarities with the household debt-deleveraging story.

This chapter demonstrates that both narratives are consistent with the same movements in spreads in the credit market, particularly between lending and borrowing rates. Whether it is debt deleveraging or a credit crunch, both scenarios lead to an increase in the spread and a fall in the natural, frictionless real rate of interest. By incorporating these insights into a multi-agent New Keynesian model, interesting implications emerge—spreads in the credit market serve as sources of movements in the natural real rate of interest, the one that is compatible with stabilization of output at potential and inflation at the target. An increase in the spread lowers this real rate of interest and requires the policy rate to fall for stabilization purposes, facing the zero lower bound limit.

The main implication is that decisions about the policy rate should consider changes in credit market conditions as reflected in credit spreads. A second important aspect highlighted here is that the spread itself is endogenous, influenced by macroeconomic and financial conditions, as well as policy variables. Financial conditions encompass considerations related to the balance sheets of intermediaries and borrowers. For the former, this involves factors like frictions in raising equity to absorb potential losses, while for the latter it relates to their ability to repay debt, which depends on their current and future income as well as the prevailing credit conditions.

The central bank, through adjustments to the policy rate, can impact the macroeconomic and financial conditions that drive the spread, ultimately affecting the spread itself. However, it can go even further by implementing unconventional credit easing policies, similar to those employed during the 2007–2008 financial crisis. These policies act on the balance sheets of intermediaries and borrowers, improving the determinants of the spread and leading to its reduction. Such policies become particularly necessary when the central bank reaches the zero lower bound on the policy rate. In general, both conventional and unconventional policies can help mitigate the increase in the spread, thus reducing the magnitude of the initial disturbance that pushed the economy into a liquidity trap. Consequently, the natural rate of interest falls to a lesser extent. Improving conditions in credit markets not only have financial consequences but also enhance the stabilization of inflation and output following severe financial conditions.

Considering all these factors suggests the importance of financial conditions within the standard monetary policy framework of an inflation targeting central bank.

This chapter complements Chapter 8 by emphasizing the transmission of monetary policy through a credit channel, in addition to the liquidity channel emphasized there. It also highlights the complexity of the various interest rates toward which monetary policy aims to operate in its macroeconomic stabilization efforts, both in credit and money markets. This is in contrast to the unrealistic assumption of a single interest rate in the benchmark New Keynesian framework of Chapter 5.

10.2   Outline of the Results

This chapter introduces the heterogeneus-agent model in the New Keynesian framework by modelling two types of agents, savers and borrowers. Sections 10.3 and 10.4 show that a forced reduction in debt or in loans can be the source of shock that brings the natural real interest rate to negative territory. More generally, movements in the natural rate of interest can be driven by spreads in credit market rates, which depend among other factors on macroeconomic conditions and monetary policy, as Section 10.5 will show. The endogeneity of the natural, frictionless rate of interest to policy gives room to monetary policy in taming the duration of liquidity traps also through the use of unconventional credit-easing policies. A heterogenous-agent model implies a welfare-based objective function that accounts also for variations in consumption across agents, which is why the monetary policy-maker should also care about the distributional consequences of shocks and policy.

10.3 Debt Deleveraging

This chapter refers to Eggertsson and Krugman (2012) in analyzing debt deleveraging, using first a very simplified endowment economy and then adding nominal rigidities and the endogenous output.

Consider an economy inhabited by two agents, each of which obtains a constant endowment $1/2 \cdot Y$ and has preferences represented by

$$E_{t_0} \sum_{t=t_0}^{\infty} (\beta^j)^{t-t_0} \log C_t^j, \tag{10.1}$$

for each $j = s, b$, in which s denotes savers and b denotes borrowers, with savers being more patient than borrowers, that is, $\beta^s > \beta^b$. The flow budget constraint of each agent j is of the form

$$B_t^j = (1 + r_{t-1})B_{t-1}^j - C_t^j + \frac{1}{2}Y, \tag{10.2}$$

in which B_t^j denotes real assets and r_{t-1} is the real interest rate set in period $t - 1$. The debt outstanding at time t, a negative B^j, together with its interest payment, is bounded by a threshold B^{high}, and therefore

$$-(1 + r_{t-1})B_{t-1}^j \leq B^{high} \leq \frac{1}{2}\frac{\beta}{1-\beta}Y.$$

The overall debt outstanding at time t, represented by $-(1 + r_{t-1})B_{t-1}^j$, cannot exceed threshold B^{high}. Moreover, the term after the second inequality represents the natural debt limit, i.e., the maximum amount of debt that the agent can repay with certainty (see Chapter 1). Note that we are setting $\beta^s = \beta$.

The first-order condition for the optimal consumption plan implies the Euler equation

$$\frac{1}{C_t^j} \geq \beta^j (1 + r_t)E_t \left\{ \frac{1}{C_{t+1}^j} \right\}, \tag{10.3}$$

which holds with inequality in the event the borrowing limit is binding at time t.

Let us consider a steady state of the model. Since borrowers are more impatient than savers, they would like to borrow more and, therefore, they will hit the borrowing constraint in the steady state. The Euler equation (10.3) is not binding for borrowers but only for savers, from which we see that the steady state real interest rate is represented by $1 + r = 1/\beta$.

Since borrowers are at their borrowing limit, their steady state consumption is represented by

$$C^b = \frac{1}{2}Y - \frac{r}{1+r}B^{high},$$

while that of the savers is specularly represented by

$$C^s = \frac{1}{2}Y + \frac{r}{1+r}B^{high}.$$

We now consider the following experiment. The economy is in the above steady state. At time t a deleveraging shock occurs that forces debtors to repay their debt. B^{high} goes to a lower threshold B^{low}, with $B^{high} > B^{low}$.

At time $t + 1$, the economy reaches the new steady state, and consumption of borrowers and savers is now

$$C^b_{t+1} = \frac{1}{2}Y - (1 - \beta)B^{low},$$

$$C^s_{t+1} = \frac{1}{2}Y + (1 - \beta)B^{low}.$$

Note that in the short run, i.e., at time t, consumption of the borrowers can be obtained by flow budget constraint (10.2), and therefore

$$C^b_t = \frac{1}{2}Y + \frac{B^{low}}{1+r_t} - B^{high}.$$

We can obtain consumption of savers using short-run goods market equilibrium $C^b_t + C^s_t = Y$, and therefore

$$C^s_t = \frac{1}{2}Y + B^{high} - \frac{B^{low}}{1+r_t}.$$

Inserting the short- and long-run consumption of savers into the Euler equation (10.3) between t and $t + 1$, we can solve for the short-run real rate

$$1 + r_t = \frac{1}{\beta}\frac{\frac{1}{2}Y + B^{low}}{\frac{1}{2}Y + B^{high}} < \frac{1}{\beta},$$

which falls below the initial value, and under a sufficiently high deleveraging shock, i.e., $\beta B^{high} - B^{low} > Y(1 - \beta)/2\beta$, goes below zero.

An economy under debt deleveraging requires a very low real interest rate. The reasoning is that, to deleverage, borrowers are saving to pay off their debt, and this reduces their consumption. In order for markets to clear at full capacity, savers should make up the lower consumption of borrowers. To induce savers to consume more, the real rate should go down. This real rate, in our model, is the frictionless one. When there are nominal rigidities, the market real rate can be different from the one that clears the market. It can be too high. Deleveraging can then be a source of shock that brings the economy to the zero lower bound and creates a slump when there are nominal rigidities, as discussed in Chapter 9.

The model can further be expanded by including endogenous output and sticky prices, as in the benchmark NK model, and can be analyzed also through an *AS-AD* graphical formulation. Let us now consider that the mass of savers is χ while that of borrowers is $1 - \chi$. Intertemporal utility is represented by

$$E_{t_0} \sum_{t=t_0}^{\infty} (\beta^j)^{t-t_0} (U(C_t^j) - H(L_t^j)) \tag{10.4}$$

for $j = b, s$, with b again denoting the borrowers and s the savers; $U(\cdot)$ is the usual concave function of consumption C, and $H(\cdot)$ is a convex function of labor L.

The flow budget constraint is of the form

$$B_t^j = (1 + i_{t-1})B_{t-1}^j - P_t C_t^j + W_t^j L_t^j + \Psi_t - T_t^j, \tag{10.5}$$

in which now B_t^j denotes nominal assets held by consumer of type j.

Wages, W^j, and labor, L^j, are now specific to the type of agent. Firms' profits, Ψ_t, are distributed in equal shares among agents; T_t^j are lumpsum taxes, P_t is the price of goods, and i_t is the risk-free nominal interest rate. As in the simple model outlined above, there is a limit on the amount of real debt that can be borrowed, which can be interpreted as the threshold under which debt can be considered safe:

$$- (1 + r_t)\frac{B_t^j}{P_t} \leq \bar{B}. \tag{10.6}$$

This borrowing limit applies in each period, and r_t is the real interest rate. As before, we assume a deleveraging experiment through a reduction of the threshold $\bar{B}$ from B^{high} to B^{low}.

Households choose consumption and labor to maximize utility (10.4) under flow budget constraint (10.5), taking into account debt limit (10.6).

We now derive the *AD* equation. Consider the Euler equation of savers under perfect foresight,

$$\exp(-zC_t^s) = \beta(1+i_t)\frac{P_t}{P_{t+1}}\exp(-zC_{t+1}^s);$$

taking the logs,

$$C_t^s = C_{t+1}^s - \tilde{\sigma}[\ln(1+i_t) - \pi_{t+1} - \tilde{\beta}], \qquad (10.7)$$

where $\pi_{t+1} = \ln P_{t+1}/P_t$, $\tilde{\beta} = -\ln\beta$, and $\tilde{\sigma} \equiv 1/z$. Notice that C_t^s is in level because we assume exponential utility in consumption, i.e., $u(C^j) = 1 - \exp(-zC^j)$ for some positive parameter z. Using the aggregate resource constraints $Y_t = \chi C_t^s + (1-\chi)C_t^b$ in (10.7), the *AD* equation follows as

$$Y_t = Y_{t+1} - \chi\tilde{\sigma}[\ln(1+i_t) - \pi_{t+1} - \tilde{\beta}] + (1-\chi)(C_t^b - C_{t+1}^b),$$

which can also be written as

$$\hat{Y}_t = \hat{Y}_{t+1} - \chi\sigma[\hat{i}_t - (\pi_{t+1} - \pi)] + (1-\chi)\left(\frac{C_t^b - C_{t+1}^b}{Y}\right), \qquad (10.8)$$

showing that the difference between short- and long-run consumptions of the borrowers acts as a shifter in the *AD* schedule.[1] In particular, if deleveraging sharply reduces short-run consumption for the borrowers, this decreases aggregate demand. To complete the characterization of the *AD* equation, we need to solve for the consumption of the borrowers. We use flow budget constraint (10.5) and make the following assumptions: borrowers are always constrained by their debt limit, B^{high} at time $t-1$ and B^{low} after and including time t; and the real interest rate is at the steady state r after and including time $t+1$. Given these two assumptions and using (10.5), we obtain that consumptions at times t and $t+1$ are respectively represented by

$$C_t^b = -\frac{(1+i_{t-1})}{(1+r_{t-1})}\frac{P_t}{P_{t-1}}B^{high} + \frac{B^{low}}{1+r_t} + Y_t - T_t^b$$

and

$$C_{t+1}^b = -\frac{(1+i_t)}{(1+r_t)}\frac{P_{t+1}}{P_t}B^{low} + \frac{B^{low}}{1+r} + Y_{t+1} - T_{t+1}^b,$$

---

1. Again, variables with a hat are log-deviations with respect to the steady state, whereas $\hat{i}_t = \ln(1+i_t)/\ln(1+i)$. Moreover, note that $\ln(1+i) = \tilde{\beta} + \pi$, where i and π are the steady states of interest rate and inflation. Finally, $\sigma \equiv \tilde{\sigma}/Y = 1/zY$.

where we have anticipated a result that we are going to explain later, i.e., $W_t^j L_t^j + \Psi_t = P_t Y_t$ at any point in time. We can approximate the above two equations around the initial debt position and substitute them in (10.8) to derive the short-run *AD* equation in its final form:

$$\hat{Y}_t = E_t \hat{Y}_{t+1} - \varphi_r[\hat{\imath}_t - (p_{t+1} - p_t - \pi)] + \frac{(1 - \chi)}{\chi}[\hat{b}_t + b(p_t - p^*)]$$

$$- \frac{(1 - \chi)}{\chi}(\hat{T}_t^b - E_t \hat{T}_{t+1}^b), \tag{10.9}$$

where the parameter φ_r is nonnegative and defined as $\varphi_r \equiv [\sigma \chi + (1 - \chi) b\beta]/\chi$. We have used the following definitions: $b \equiv B^{high}/Y$, $\hat{T}_t^b = (T_t^b - T^b)/Y$, and $\hat{b}_t = (B^{low} - B^{high})/Y$, where Y is the steady-state level of output and p_t is the log of the price level at time t, with $\pi_t \equiv p_t - p_{t-1}$.

In general, there are two new channels pushing the slope of the *AD* equation in different directions with respect to the negative one in Chapter 6. On the one hand, an increase in the current price level, with everything else being equal, raises the current real rate, lowering the amount of debt that borrowers can borrow in the short run, and therefore lowering their short-run consumption and decreasing aggregate demand. Through this mechanism the *AD* equation becomes flatter. This channel is reflected by the parameter φ_r on the first line of (10.9), which is now higher than σ because of this additional channel. On the other hand, an increase in the current price level reduces the real value of the current debt and therefore raises the short-run consumption of the borrowers and expands aggregate demand. This is due to the Fisher effect (Fisher, 1933) through which prices affect the real value of nominal debt. This channel is reflected by the positive parameter $(1 - \chi)b/\chi$ on the first line of (10.9). This second channel prevails over the first, since the combined effect $(1 - \chi)b(1 - \beta)/\chi$ is positive. Therefore, for a given σ, the presence of debt-constrained agents makes *AD* steeper than in the previous model. Interestingly, the curve can now slope upward conditional on long-run inflation policies, as we will soon see.

Turning now to the *AS* equation, let us consider the labor supply of households at the point at which the marginal rate of substitution between labor and consumption is equal to the real wage for each type of agent:

$$\frac{H_l(L_t^j)}{U_c(C_t^j)} = \frac{W_t^j}{P_t}. \tag{10.10}$$

First, it is key to observe that the natural rate of output coincides with (5.29) in a log-linear approximation. To this end, consider that there is a continuum of firms, of measure one, producing the differentiated goods with production function $Y = AL$, where now L is the aggregator of the two types of labor, $L = (L^s)^\chi (L^b)^{1-\chi}$, and A is labor productivity. Given this technology, labor compensation for each type of worker is equal to total compensation $W^j L^j = WL$, where the aggregate wage index is appropriately represented by $W = (W^s)^\chi (W^b)^{1-\chi}$, as Benigno, Eggertsson, and Romei (2020) show. Let us assume the isoelastic disutility of working, $H(L^j) = (L^j)^{1+\eta}/(1+\eta)$. Taking a weighted average of (10.10), for $j = s, b$, with weights χ and $1 - \chi$ respectively, it follows that

$$\frac{L_t^\eta}{\exp[-z(\chi C_t^s + (1-\chi)C_t^b)]} = \frac{W_t}{P_t}, \tag{10.11}$$

using the assumption of exponential utility with respect to consumption. Equation (10.11) represents an aggregate labor-supply equation. It can be further simplified by using the production function, $Y_t = A_t L_t$, and the aggregate resource constraint, $Y_t = \chi C_t^s + (1-\chi)C_t^b$, to obtain

$$\frac{(Y_t/A_t)^\eta}{\exp[-zY_t]} = \frac{W_t}{P_t}. \tag{10.12}$$

In the flexible-price allocation, prices are set as a markup (μ) over marginal costs $P_t = \mu_t W_t/A_t$, and therefore the natural level of output is implicitly defined by

$$\frac{(Y_t^n/A_t)^\eta}{\exp[-zY_t^n]} = \frac{A_t}{\mu_t},$$

which in a log-linear approximation coincides with (5.29), having set public expenditure to zero, $G_t = 0$.

Given this result, the AS equation is going to be of the same form as in (5.27). To simplify the analysis, we make assumptions about the economy being in a stationary equilibrium in the long run. Assume that $\pi_T = \pi$ for each $T \geq t + 1$, which through the AS equation implies that output will be at the natural rate for each $T \geq t + 1$. Under these assumptions, the time-t AD equation can be written as

$$\hat{Y}_t = \hat{Y}_{t+1}^n - \varphi_r \hat{\imath}_t - \frac{1-\chi}{\chi}(\hat{T}_t^b - \hat{T}_{t+1}^b) + \frac{1-\chi}{\chi}[\hat{b}_t + b(p_t - p^*)],$$

which again describes a relationship between current output and prices, where now the slope can change in an interesting way because of the presence of

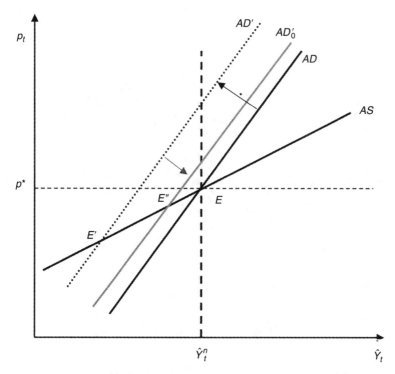

FIGURE 10.1. Deleveraging shock: the AD moves to AD' and equilibrium from E to E'. Lowering the nominal interest rate can bring AD' to AD'_0 and equilibrium to E''.

debt-constrained agents. Given that inflation is anchored at the target after and including period $t+1$, the slope becomes positive.

Here, lower prices unambiguously increase the real value of debt, reducing the consumption of the borrowers and therefore aggregate demand and output.

In Figure 10.1, we plot the AD equation in its new upward-sloping version together with the AS equation.[2] Several interesting implications can be drawn. Deleveraging, interpreted as a reduction in the amount of debt that can be considered safe, acts as a left-shifter of the AD equation, as is shown in (10.9) by a negative $\hat{b}$. This is depicted in the figure with the shift in the AD equation that takes the economy from equilibrium E to E', where it experiences a fall in prices and output.

2. The AS equation is assumed to be flatter than the AD equation for the stability of the equilibrium.

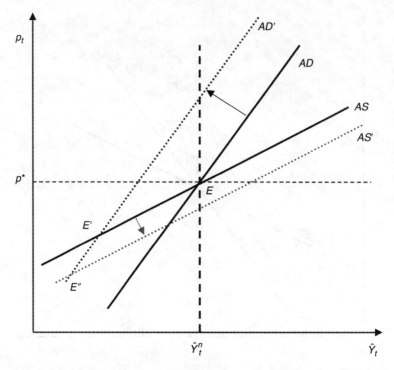

FIGURE 10.2. Paradox of "toil": the deleveraging shock shifts AD upward into AD', the equilibrium moves from E to E'. A downward shift of AS into AS' aggravates the situation and equilibrium move to E''.

The magnitude of the shock can be such as to throw the economy into a liquidity trap, where lowering interest rates to zero does not return the economy to the initial equilibrium, as discussed in Section 9.1 of Chapter 9. At most, conventional monetary policy can push the economy up to equilibrium E''.

Eggertsson and Krugman (2012) identify in this the Keynesian paradox of thrift, for which a higher savings rate for borrowers, which is used to pay off debt, decreases aggregate demand and output and in the end results in lower savings. There is another paradox of "toil," since a downward movement of the AS equation, which in normal conditions would be expansionary, is here contractionary, as shown in Figure 10.2.

This shift can be driven by a temporary increase in productivity or a fall in the markup. After the contraction in aggregate demand, if the AS equation shifts down to AS', then the economy experiences a further contraction.

Finally, there is also the paradox of "flexibility," in which more price flexibility, a steeper AS equation, leads to a larger contraction in output when deleveraging occurs. Indeed, the larger fall in prices depresses demand because it inflates the stock of debt to be repaid.

More insights can also be drawn on how to escape from the liquidity trap. The solution provided in the previous section—raising the future price level—applies here in a reinforced way since the parameter φ_r in (10.9) is larger than before. By increasing the future price level, the real rate falls and savers increase their consumption. At the same time, the fall in the real rate provides a relief for borrowers in the short run, pushing up their consumption. Policies that increase the long-run output level are also expansionary, shifting the AD equation to the right.

10.4 The Credit Crunch

This section discusses the alternative narrative of the aftermath of the 2007–2008 financial crisis, concentrating on turbulences in the banking sector. The crisis originated in the financial sector because of an increase in the riskiness of home borrowers, which resulted in a deterioration of the quality of mortgage-backed securities held by financial intermediaries and sparked doubts on their solvency. In turn, these doubts raised the costs of funding intermediaries in both interbank and bond markets. This shock triggered the need for banks to raise more equity or to lower their leverage. The banks' capital constraint tightened during this period of stress, making banks less willing to lend, and thus triggering a downturn.

The mechanism at work here starts from a shock on the banking sector, which triggers a reduction in lending to the economy. To address this mechanism, we can use the simplified framework presented in Section 10.3.

There are still two agents, borrowers and savers, with preferences (10.1) and budget constraint (10.2). The limit on debt is now amended with an upper bound also on the lending side,

$$L^{high} \geq (1 + r_{t-1})B_{t-1}^j \geq -B^{high} \geq -\frac{1}{2}\frac{\beta}{1-\beta}Y,$$

representing a limit on the maximum amount that lenders are willing to supply, in which now B_t^j denote real assets held by consumer of type j. Let us start from a steady state of the economy, in which this lending limit is not binding, i.e., $L^{high} > B^{high}$. Given the different discount factor in preferences, borrowers are at their borrowing limit. As discussed before, in this steady state, the real interest rate, let's say the savings real rate r^s, is determined by the Euler equation of savers and represented by

$$1 + r^s = \frac{1}{\beta}.$$

It is useful for the analysis that follows to distinguish between the saver's and the borrower's real rates. Although borrowers are not in the Euler equation, we can still use it to characterize a shadow borrowing rate. We insert steady-state consumption of borrowers into (10.3) to obtain the shadow borrowing rate

$$1 + r^b = \frac{1}{\beta^b} > 1 + r^s,$$

which is then higher than the savings rate. In the initial steady state, there is a spread between borrowing and savings rates, which is justified by the different levels of their patience.

Let us assume that due to turbulence in the banking sector, there is a shock at time t driving down the maximum amount of lending from L^{high} to L^{low}, with $L^{low} < B^{high}$. At time $t + 1$, the economy reaches the new steady state. Since now savers are constrained by the maximum amount of lending, given that $L^{low} < B^{high}$, this level also determines debt in the economy. Consumption of borrowers and savers, in the long run, is represented by

$$C_{t+1}^b = \frac{1}{2}Y - (1 - \beta^b)L^{low},$$

$$C_{t+1}^s = \frac{1}{2}Y + (1 - \beta^b)L^{low}.$$

Note that the relevant discount factor to price the real rate in the long run is the discount factor of borrowers, since savers are constrained.[3]

In the short run, i.e., at time t, consumption of savers can be obtained by flow budget constraint (10.2) using their starting asset position B^{high} and the long-run position L^{low},

$$C_t^s = \frac{1}{2}Y - \frac{L^{low}}{1 + r_t^b} + B^{high},$$

3. Note that the Euler equation (10.3) of savers now holds with a reverse inequality sign, i.e., $\leq$ instead of $\geq$. When the constraint on lending is binding, it holds with a strict inequality sign $<$.

while we obtain consumption of borrowers through the short-run equilibrium in the goods market, $C_t^b + C_t^s = Y$, and therefore

$$C_t^b = \frac{1}{2}Y + \frac{L^{low}}{1+r_t^b} - B^{high}.$$

Note that the "market" real rate, in the short run, is that of the borrowers, since their Euler equation is binding. Inserting the short- and long-run consumption of borrowers into the Euler equation (10.3) with equality, between t and $t+1$, we can solve for this short-run real rate:

$$1+r_t^b = \frac{1}{\beta^b}\frac{\frac{1}{2}Y - L^{low}}{\frac{1}{2}Y - B^{high}} > \frac{1}{\beta^b}.$$

Since $L^{low} < B^{high}$, the short-run real rate rises above the initial level. A negative shock on lending leads to an increase in the rate faced by borrowers.

It is interesting to evaluate the "shadow" savings rate, the one implied by the Euler equation of savers. By inserting the consumption of savers at times t and $t+1$ into (10.3), we obtain

$$1+r_t^s = \frac{1}{\beta^s}\frac{\frac{1}{2}Y + L^{low}}{\frac{1}{2}Y + B^{high}} + \frac{1}{\frac{1}{2}Y + B^{high}}\left(\frac{1+r_t^s}{1+r_t^b} - \frac{\beta^b}{\beta^s}\right)L^{low}. \quad (10.13)$$

Note that the right-hand side of the above equation is an increasing function of $(1+r_t^s)$ and is positive when evaluated at $r_t^s = -1$ and less than $1/\beta^s$ when evaluated at $(1+r_t^s) = (\beta^s)^{-1}$. It follows that the time-t "shadow" savings rate is below $1/\beta^s$, and therefore it has fallen below the initial steady state level.

Indeed, while the borrowing rate increases above the initial value $1/\beta^b$, the spread between borrowing and savings rates widens because of the contraction in lending, and therefore the second addendum on the right-hand side of (10.13) becomes negative, consistently with a low savings rate. Savers need to cut their lending to borrowers. They have to save less and consume more. For this to be an equilibrium with a constant aggregate endowment, borrowers should borrow less and consume less. The real rate faced by borrowers should then rise to discourage their borrowing. The key point is to understand that the same exact movements in savings and borrowing rates occurred under the deleveraging shock in Section 10.3. In that case, too, the "shadow" real rate on borrowing was increasing while the market real rate on savings was falling.

Lending or deleveraging shocks are isomorphic. Although the two shocks originate from different mechanisms, they both imply the same widening of the spread between borrowing and lending rates, with the borrowing rate increasing and the savings rate falling. In the case of a large shock, the savings real rate can go below zero and the economy can enter a liquidity trap.

The above stylized model can also be used to discuss some other possible sources of variation in the spread between the rate faced by borrowers and that at which savers are willing to lend. As we have seen, a different rate of time preference between borrowers and savers can itself justify a spread and a variation in the borrowing or lending capacity. Variation in income can also be important for explaining the spread. Suppose that there is a temporary increase in Y affecting both agents equally. If the constraint on borrowers is tight, they will consume all the additional income, whereas savers will like to save more. Since borrowers cannot exceed their borrowing limit, the real rate faced by savers should fall to stimulate their consumption and discourage saving. The shadow borrowing rate will also fall in the same proportion and the spread will remain unchanged. Different is the case in which the variation of income is unequal or when there are zero-sum transfers between the two agents. The spread can change in this case. Suppose that income temporarily rises for borrowers and falls for savers. Borrowers are going to fully consume their income while savers are going to borrow and reduce their asset holdings. To achieve a goods market equilibrium, the savings rate should rise to discourage savers from borrowing. Note also that the borrowing rate falls and therefore the spread decreases.

10.5   A General Framework

The above analysis has shown that in a heterogenous-agent model there can be different interest rates related to borrowing or lending positions in the credit market, which are affected by factors in financial markets or, in general, by macroeconomic variables. In practice, savers and borrowers do not interact directly in credit markets. Instead, financial intermediaries channel funds from savers to borrowers and the spread between the lending and deposit rates measures the marginal profitability of their activity. Before providing more details on this intermediation activity, let us consider a two-agent model in which preferences are still given by (10.4). Savers and borrowers are now no longer constrained by debt or asset limits and therefore the stochastic Euler equations hold with equality,

$$\exp(-zC_t^s) = \beta^s(1 + i_t^s)E_t\left\{\frac{P_t}{P_{t+1}}\exp(-zC_{t+1}^s)\right\}, \qquad (10.14)$$

$$\exp(-zC_t^b) = \beta^b(1 + i_t^b)E_t\left\{\frac{P_t}{P_{t+1}}(1 - \omega_{t+1})\exp(-zC_{t+1}^b)\right\}, \qquad (10.15)$$

in which we have assumed exponential utility of consumption; different rates of time preference, β^b and β^s; and different nominal interest rates between savers and borrowers, i_t^s and i_t^b. The exponential utility is still a convenient assumption for aggregation purposes. The important difference with respect to the previous analysis is that the debt of the borrower is subject to a random rate of default, $\omega_{t+1} \in [\omega_{min}, \omega_{max}]$, with $0 < \omega_{min} < \omega_{max} < 1$, which is therefore incorporated into the Euler equation. Taking a log-linear approximation of the above equations, we obtain two linear Euler equations of the form

$$C_t^s = E_t C_{t+1}^s - \frac{1}{z}(\hat{i}_t^s - E_t(\pi_{t+1} - \pi)),$$

$$C_t^b = E_t C_{t+1}^b - \frac{1}{z}(\hat{i}_t^b - E_t\hat{\omega}_{t+1} - E_t(\pi_{t+1} - \pi)),$$

where all variables have been previously defined, and now $E_t\hat{\omega}_{t+1}$ represents the expected variations of the default rate from a steady-state level. These two equations can now be easily aggregated, noting that $Y_t = \chi C_t^s + (1 - \chi)C_t^b$, where the mass of savers is again χ, while that of borrowers is $1 - \chi$. An aggregate Euler equation follows:

$$\hat{Y}_t = E_t\hat{Y}_{t+1} - \sigma(\hat{i}_t^s - E_t(\pi_{t+1} - \pi)) + (1 - \chi)(\hat{i}_t^b - E_t\hat{\omega}_{t+1} - \hat{i}_t^s)),$$

$$(10.16)$$

where σ has the same definition as in Section 10.3, $\sigma = 1/(zY)$. This aggregate demand equation (10.16) is now isomorphic to the AD equation (5.26) of the benchmark New Keynesian model in Chapter 5, having set $G_t = 0$. The isomorphism follows by noting that the interest rate $\hat{i}_t$ should coincide with $\hat{i}_t^s$ and that the variation in the exogenous preference shock should be set at $E_t\xi_{t+1} - \xi_t = (1 - \chi)(\hat{i}_t^b - E_t\hat{\omega}_{t+1} - \hat{i}_t^s)$, providing an alternative interpretation of the source of shock that can bring the economy to the zero lower bound. An increase in the spread in credit markets, with everything else being equal, lowers aggregate demand and output. The relevant spread is that between the borrowing and savings rates when taking into account the compensation for the expected default.

We can equivalently write the *AD* equation as

$$\hat{Y}_t - \hat{Y}_t^e = E_t(\hat{Y}_{t+1} - \hat{Y}_{t+1}^e) - \sigma(\hat{i}_t^s - E_t(\pi_{t+1} - \pi) - r_t^e), \qquad (10.17)$$

which is the same *AD* equation (7.5) of Chapter 7, using the same definition of efficient level of output, $\hat{Y}_t^e$. The relevant nominal interest rate is the savings rate, which is tied to the policy rate, and the frictionless real rate is now given by

$$r_t^e \equiv E_t \left\{ \frac{1+\eta}{1+\sigma\eta} (\hat{A}_{t+1} - \hat{A}_t) - (1 - \chi)(\hat{i}_t^b - E_t\hat{\omega}_{t+1} - \hat{i}_t^s) \right\}, \qquad (10.18)$$

including the credit spread. An increase in the credit spread leads to a decrease in the frictionless real rate. The fact that financial conditions are included in the determinants of the frictionless rate is an interesting result, in line with recent developments in central banking that aim to define the concept of R-double-star as guidance for monetary policy to account for financial conditions, as seen in Akinci et al. (2020), as opposed to the more popular R-star discussed in Chapter 6.

Another significant innovation in this framework is that the frictionless rate, r^e, might not be entirely exogenous. In general, the credit spread may depend on other features of the model, which we will now outline. Its endogeneity has important implications for the effects of policy on inflation and output, as monetary policy can now influence r^e through the credit spreads, thereby affecting inflation and output.

For now, we will leave the sources of variation in spread unexplained and move to the *AS* equation. Under the assumption of exponential utility and using a Cobb-Douglas aggregator of the two types of labor in the production function, as in Section 10.3, the *AS* equation is exactly of the same form as (5.27) or (7.6):

$$\pi_t - \pi = \kappa(\hat{Y}_t - \hat{Y}_t^e) + \upsilon_t + \beta E_t(\pi_{t+1} - \pi), \qquad (10.19)$$

where κ and υ_t have the same definitions given earlier.

Consider the modelling of financial intermediation. Assume that financial intermediaries live in two periods, in an overlapping way, and focus on a generic intermediary living at time t and $t+1$. At time t, its budget constraint is represented by

$$Z_t = D_t + N_t(1 - \varsigma(Z_t)), \qquad (10.20)$$

in which Z_t is the amount lent to the economy and D_t is its borrowing in the form of risk-free deposits; N_t is equity and $\varsigma(Z_t)$ is an extra cost per unit of equity that may depend on the loans supplied. The function $\varsigma(\cdot)$ is non-decreasing in Z_t.

At time $t+1$, intermediaries' nominal profits are represented by

$$\Psi_{t+1}^I = (1+i_t^b)(1-\omega_{t+1})Z_t - (1+i_t^s)D_t. \tag{10.21}$$

Lending is remunerated at rate i_t^b, set at time t, and is subject to a random default rate ω_{t+1}, consistently with the random default rate faced by borrowers. Deposits are remunerated at savings rate i_t^s. Intermediaries are subject to a limited liability constraint, i.e., $\Psi_{t+1}^I \geq 0$ in all contingencies at time $t+1$. This constraint implies that

$$(1+i_t^b)(1-\omega_{\max})Z_t \geq (1+i_t^s)D_t. \tag{10.22}$$

Using budget constraint (10.20) to substitute for D_t, we can write the limited liability constraint as

$$[(1+i_t^b)(1-\omega_{\max}) - (1+i_t^s)]Z_t \geq -(1+i_t^s)N_t(1-\varsigma(Z_t)),$$

which can be written as a lower bound for equity:

$$N_t \geq \frac{1}{(1-\varsigma(Z_t))}\left[1 - \frac{(1+i_t^b)}{(1+i_t^s)}(1-\omega_{\max})\right]Z_t. \tag{10.23}$$

Intermediaries are owned by savers and maximize rents given by the expected discounted value of profits minus the value of equity, i.e., $\mathcal{R}_t = E_t\left\{\tilde{R}_{t,t+1}^s \Psi_{t+1}^I\right\} - N_t$. The nominal discount factor of savers is represented by

$$\tilde{R}_{t,t+1}^s = \beta^s \frac{\exp(-zC_{t+1}^s)}{P_{t+1}} \frac{P_t}{\exp(-zC_t^s)}.$$

Using (10.21), we can write rents as

$$\mathcal{R}_t = \frac{1+i_t^b}{1+i_t^s}(1 - \tilde{E}_t\omega_{t+1})Z_t - D_t - N_t, \tag{10.24}$$

where we have used the Euler equation of savers (10.14) and defined the expected default rate with respect to the neutral probability distribution as

$$\tilde{E}_t\omega_{t+1} \equiv (1+i_t^s)E_t\left\{R_{t,t+1}^s\omega_{t+1}\right\}, \tag{10.25}$$

which is evaluated by using the nominal discount factor of savers. We can use budget constraint (10.20) to substitute for D_t in (10.24) to write:

$$\mathcal{R}_t = \left(\frac{1 + i_t^b}{1 + i_t^s}(1 - \tilde{E}_t \omega_{t+1}) - 1 \right) Z_t - \varsigma(Z_t) N_t.$$

Using limited liability constraint (10.23) with equality in the above condition to substitute for N_t, we can write it as

$$\mathcal{R}_t = Z_t \left[\left(\frac{1 + i_t^b}{1 + i_t^s}(1 - \tilde{E}_t \omega_{t+1}) - 1 \right) \right.$$
$$\left. - \frac{\varsigma(Z_t)}{(1 - \varsigma(Z_t))} \left(1 - \frac{(1 + i_t^b)}{(1 + i_t^s)}(1 - \omega_{max}) \right) \right]. \qquad (10.26)$$

Competition in the markets of intermediaries reduces all rents to zero; therefore the spread between lending and deposit rates is determined by

$$\frac{1 + i_t^b}{1 + i_t^s} = \frac{1}{(1 - \varsigma(Z_t))(1 - \tilde{E}_t \omega_{t+1}) + \varsigma(Z_t)(1 - \omega_{max})}, \qquad (10.27)$$

which, inserted into (10.23), can be used to obtain the equity-to-loan ratio as

$$\frac{N_t}{Z_t} = \frac{1 + i_t^b}{1 + i_t^s}(\omega_{max} - \tilde{E}_t \omega_{t+1}).$$

The equity-to-loan ratio is increasing in the spread and in the difference between the maximum and average loss on loans. Indeed, intermediaries need to raise equity to cover loan losses in the worst-case scenario.

Consider spread function (10.27). Note that if $\varsigma(\cdot) = 0$, then the spread between the borrowing and savings rates reflects just the expected default rate, and therefore, in a log-linear approximation, it is not a source of perturbation of AD equation (10.16). In general, we can write the spread function as

$$\frac{(1 + i_t^b)}{(1 + i_t^s)} = s(Z_t, \omega_{max}, \tilde{E}_t \omega_{t+1}),$$

in which the function $s(\cdot)$ is nondecreasing in the loans volume through the properties of the function $\varsigma(Z_t)$.

This stylized model is consistent with the more general idea that an increase in the volume of intermediation (higher loans) requires a higher spread to cover the possible losses. Moreover, the maximum default rate,

ω_{max}, which we have kept as exogenous, can instead depend on macroeconomic conditions, such as the current or future income of borrowers, or more broadly can be related to the value of the collateral that borrowers pledge when financing their expenditures. Under favorable conditions, ω_{max} can decrease, lowering the spread. This threshold can also depend on the policy rate set by the central bank and therefore decrease with it. All of these considerations point to the complex interaction between credit spreads, policy, and macroeconomic variables, as well as the need for a more detailed description of the determinants of spreads. Models such as Benigno, Eggertsson, and Romei (2020) and Curdia and Woodford (2010, 2011) provide examples in which the spread function depends on the aggregate level of debt in the economy, and this dynamic can be influenced by monetary policy through adjustments to the nominal interest rate.

Here we will discuss, in more general terms, the implications for policy of the endogeneity of the spread function, starting with *forward guidance*. In Section 9.5 of Chapter 9, we emphasized the importance of providing appropriate guidance regarding future short-term interest rates to navigate out of the liquidity trap in the event of a negative shock to the frictionless real rate, denoted as r^e. However, the situation can differ when the disturbance causing the reduction in the frictionless rate of interest, r^e, and pushing the economy into the zero lower bound, is an increase in credit spreads in financial markets, as indicated in equation (10.18), rather than an exogenous shock.

Credit spreads are influenced by macroeconomic conditions and by policy measures. The interaction between the endogeneity of the spread and the policy response can create scenarios where the exit from zero lower bound policies occurs earlier than when the initial shock is purely exogenous. This is because the policy response aims to decrease the spread and, as a result, the source of the disturbance that pushed the economy into the zero lower bound.

Think about the deleveraging story. When borrowers start to save in order to pay off debt, those savings become much more difficult if the borrowers' incomes fall or if interest payments on their debt increase. Policies that mitigate or offset these effects can improve the deleveraging process and shorten it. In a similar way, if the banking sector is forced to reduce leverage because of an increase in the riskiness of its assets, policies that reduce default probabilities can lower the magnitude of the initial disturbance and dampen its propagation. These effects, in turn, all shorten the stay at the zero lower bound.

Another implication for *forward guidance* in a framework where the credit spread is endogenous is through the sensitivity of output to variations in the

262 DELEVERAGING AND CREDIT CRUNCH

current and future short-term interest rates. As (10.16) shows, the sensitivity of output to the policy rate $\hat{\imath}_t^s$ is unchanged with respect to the benchmark NK model when the credit spread is exogenous, being still characterized by the parameter σ, but it could be lower when the spread is endogenous.[4]

Another dimension of difference with respect to the analysis of Chapter 7 lies in the evaluation of optimal policy. A heterogenous-agent model uncovers an additional objective that the policymaker should follow, if maximizing the welfare of the consumers. In a model similar to that of Section 10.3, a second-order approximation of welfare around the efficient steady state delivers the following quadratic loss function:

$$
L_{t_0}^{CB} = \frac{1}{2} E_t \left\{ \sum_{t=t_0}^{\infty} \beta^{t-t_0} \left[(\hat{Y}_t - \hat{Y}_t^e)^2 + \chi(1-\chi)\Lambda_c(\hat{C}_t^b - \hat{C}_t^s)^2 \right. \right.
$$
$$
\left. \left. + \Lambda_\pi (\pi_t - \pi)^2 \right] \right\}, \tag{10.28}
$$

for positive parameters Λ_c and Λ_π.[5] The additional term in the loss function, compared to equation (7.1) in Section 7.1 of Chapter 7, captures the deviations of consumption of borrowers and savers from their respective efficient steady state. What matters is the difference between borrowers' and savers' consumption, which can be interpreted as a measure of departure from risk sharing in the economy. There is then an additional objective of a welfare-maximizing policy on top of output gap and inflation that accounts for the distributional consequences of stabilization policies. Even in the case of an exogenous credit spread, optimal policy should change to consider this objective, and in general the optimal policy with commitment from a "timeless perspective" will not be characterized by the simple targeting rule (7.3) in Section 7.3 of Chapter 7, but will also consider financial conditions, as discussed in Curdia and Woodford (2016). Furthermore, in the case of the debt-deleveraging or the banking-turbulence story, accounting for the

---

4. The interesting conclusion is that a model with heterogeneous agents is not, by itself, sufficient to alter the implications of *forward guidance*; it requires the endogeneity of the spread. Moreover, it is not even necessary, as demonstrated in Section 9.6 of Chapter 9, where it was shown that the prescriptions of *forward guidance* can differ from those of the benchmark NK model when reserves provide liquidity services in a representative-agent model.

5. In the derivation of (10.28), it is assumed that $\beta^b \to \beta^s = \beta$, as discussed in Benigno, Eggertsson, and Romei (2020).

distributional consequences of stabilization policies induces a more expansionary policy in order to mitigate the fall in borrowers' consumption with respect to that of savers.[6]

The analysis in this chapter can also provide support for the discussion of unconventional monetary policy (see the discussion in Section 9.7 of Chapter 9). In particular, it provides support for credit-easing policies—that is, the central bank's purchases of private risky assets that do not necessarily increase its balance sheet and/or its liabilities. According to the analysis in this chapter, these policies can be effective if they help mitigate the surge in the credit spread during a financial crisis, thereby alleviating the decline in the frictionless real rate.

Under financial stress, interlinkages within financial markets can increase systemic risk, triggering fire sales and putting financial intermediaries at risk of insolvency. The central bank can step in by purchasing impaired assets in the hands of intermediaries, or by supplying them with liquidity at low rates, lowering collateral requirements and also accepting assets under stress. As discussed in Section 9.7 of Chapter 9, these lender-of-last-resort measures have been implemented in several ways during the financial and pandemic crises. This chapter suggests that this lender-of-last-resort role under a systemic crisis also has implications for macroeconomic stabilization. Indeed, through these policies, the central bank can counteract the widening of credit spreads, thereby dampening the effects of the financial crisis on inflation and output. Credit-easing policies can therefore be useful for achieving output and inflation objectives and mitigating the severance and duration of the liquidity trap.

10.6   References

The analysis of deleveraging and its connection with the fall in the frictionless real rate of Section 10.3 is based on Eggertsson and Krugman (2012) and its graphical representation is based on Benigno (2015). Guerrieri and Lorenzoni (2017) analyzed a heterogeneous-agent model with idiosyncratic uncertainty, demonstrating that debt deleveraging exerts an additional depressing effect on the frictionless real rate due to precautionary saving motives. Section 10.4, on the parallel between credit crunch and debt deleveraging, draws from Tsinikos (2018).

6. See Benigno, Eggertsson, and Romei (2020).

The importance of the credit channel in the transmission mechanism of monetary policy was first discussed by Bernanke and Blinder (1988), in addition to the liquidity channel studied in Chapter 9. Bernanke, Gertler, and Gilchrist (1999) emphasized the quantitative importance of the credit channel for the business cycle, and its propagation through a "financial accelerator" mechanism.

In the wake of the 2007–2008 financial crisis, numerous studies incorporated credit market frictions into the standard NK model. These frictions aim to account for the spreads between the loan rate and deposit rate, as well as the unconventional interventions undertaken by central banks worldwide, as discussed by Woodford (2010). Curdia and Woodford (2010, 2011, 2016) introduced a two-agent model with intermediation frictions between saved and borrowed funds, highlighting the significance of credit market spreads in determining output and inflation.

Gertler and Kyotaki (2010) and Gertler and Karadi (2011) expanded the "financial accelerator" framework originally proposed by Bernanke, Gertler, and Gilchrist (1999) by considering defaults on the part of intermediaries, who face constraints on their ability to attract deposits. These studies provided model to analyze the role of uncoventional monetary policies in conditions of financial distress. Gerali et al. (2010) also explored a banking model within a New Keynesian framework, estimating the role of credit factors in business-cycle fluctuations and emphasizing the stickiness in the adjustment of deposit and loan rates in response to changes in the policy rate, similarly to Teranishi (2015). Bianchi and Bigio (2022) developed a tractable model of the interbank market to examine the credit channel and the transmission of monetary policy to lending rates.

Recent literature has delved into the significance of using multi-agent models to provide a more comprehensive understanding of the transmission mechanism of monetary policy. Bilbiie (2008) presents an early example of a two-agent model, wherein one agent does not participate in financial markets. Eggertsson and Krugman (2012) investigate a two-agent model with no restrictions on asset market participation, where one agent, the borrower, is more impatient than the other, the saver. In a similar vein, Benigno, Eggertsson, and Romei (2020) explore the dynamic adjustments to a deleveraging shock, the endogeneity of the frictionless real rate, and optimal monetary policy within the same framework.

Curdia and Woodford (2010, 2011, 2016) categorize agents into two types based on their impatience and allow for random transitions between these types during their lifetime. Piergallini (2006) and Nisticò (2012, 2016) incorporate household heterogeneity by integrating Blanchard's (1985) perpetual youth model into a New Keynesian framework.

McKay, Nakamura, and Steinsson (2016) and Kaplan, Moll, and Violante (2018) embed the New Keynesian model with heterogeneous agents facing idiosyncratic risks, exploring how this alters the transmission mechanism of monetary policy. Debortoli and Galí (2017) and Bilbiie (2019) provide analyses demonstrating how two-agent models can capture features similar to those of heterogeneous-agent models while maintaining analytical tractability.

Bilbiie (2008, 2019), Curdia and Woodford (2016), Nisticò (2016), Benigno, Eggertsson, and Romei (2020), present examples of analyses of optimal monetary policy that utilize a linear-quadratic approach, yielding objective functions for policymakers, as illustrated in (10.28), that take into account the distributional costs of stabilization policies. Woodford (2010) addresses the importance of considering financial stability in the monetary policy framework.

In addition, Dávila and Schaab (2023) provide a general approach for analyzing optimal monetary policy under both discretion and commitment from a "timeless perspective" within a New Keynesian model featuring heterogeneous households.

11

Shortage of "Safe Assets"

11.1 Introduction

"Safe assets" are financial securities that retain their value in terms of the currency over time and possess liquidity properties, as they are used for both transactions and collateral. These liquidity characteristics are reflected in a premium, resulting in these securities carrying lower interest rates. This allows the issuer to secure financing on more favorable terms compared to the broader market.

"Safe assets" can be produced either publicly or privately. The natural producer is the central bank, which, in a "paper" currency system, creates the currency through its liabilities. These liabilities are inherently safe, used for transactions and collateral services. Notably, high-powered money, which comprises the central bank's liabilities, has been limited in supply, unable to fulfill all of the liquidity needs of the economy, and particularly on a global scale for reserve currencies like the dollar.

The lack of supply of "safe assets" is reflected in the liquidity premiums they carry, which incentivizes their creation from alternative sources. Another candidate for the supply of "safe assets" is the sovereign debt; however, this does not apply to every sovereign debt, and it took centuries for a market of sovereign safe debt to develop, as discussed in Gorton (2017).

Hamilton (1947) delves into the origins of sovereign debt in France and England, tracing it back to the thirteenth century in the former case and the seventeenth century in the latter. However, the history is one of repeated defaults before the development of an institutional framework that made the promises to repay credible. Sovereign debt requires the capability to impose sufficient taxes to be deemed safe.

The nuanced relationship between the central bank and the treasury can create implicit conditions under which treasury debt is backed by the central bank's currency issuance. Nevertheless, considering the government as a whole, encompassing both the central bank and treasury, the general equilibrium of our model implies that the overall government liabilities should be matched by an appropriate level of taxes levied or by private assets held by the central bank. The safe or risky nature of the private debt held by the government determines the extent to which a reduction in the tax burden is possible.

Historically, the overall supply of government liquid securities has been limited, notably in the run-up to the 2007–2008 financial crisis, incentivizing the creation of safe securities by the private sector. The ability of financial intermediaries to create safe securities relies on the assets in which they invest and the equity they raise to absorb losses on their investments. Chapter 4 has shown that, in a frictionless and competitive financial market, intermediaries can create safe securities to exploit market rents to the point of completely abating those rents and satiating the economy with all its liquidity needs.

However, the 2007–2008 financial crisis highlighted the existence of money-like securities that provided liquidity services, including several types of liabilities from the so-called shadow banking system. These securities were not completely safe due to a lack of appropriate backing on intermediaries' balance sheets. At the height of the crisis, these securities lost not only their value but also their ability to provide liquidity services, leading to a shortage of "safe assets."

The crisis did not remain confined to the financial sector, but had repercussions on the real economy. Indeed, "disequilibria" in the goods market are the mirror image of "disequilibria" in the asset markets. An excess supply of goods corresponds to a shortage of "safe assets" in financial markets, which can lead to a fall in prices and/or a recession.

This chapter introduces a friction in the private intermediation process, in which it is costly to find safe investments to back the provided liquidity. To offset these costs, intermediaries should rely on the liquidity premium to produce safe assets. Critically, this premium depends on the supply of government liquidity. If that supply is high, the premium is low, and this can completely crowd out the production of "safe assets." However, in these circumstances, a market for creating risky debt securities exists, which can be defaulted on under certain conditions.

The problem arises when these securities are also used for liquidity purposes, essentially becoming "pseudo safe assets." They behave like safe assets under favorable contingencies but turn out to be different under adverse contingencies due to their poor backing. Investors can hold these assets either because they lack enough information to distinguish them from truly "safe assets" or because they can distinguish them but consider the probability of an adverse event to be negligible.

While the supply of purely private "safe assets" can be limited, the supply of risky "pseudo safe assets" can be abundant, even sufficient to satiate all liquidity needs when the economy is running under favorable contingencies. This time things seem different! However, as adverse events materialize and the "pseudo safe assets" lose their backing, they default and cease to provide liquidity services. The economy then experiences a shortage of "safe assets," resulting in rising premiums and costs, including reduced economic activity.

This environment supports prescriptions for monetary policy intervention, which can be summarized as the objective of maintaining nominal spending or some broader form of monetary aggregates on the same trajectory it had before the crisis. This prescription can be viewed in line with Friedman and Schwartz (1963) finding that every economic depression is accounted for by a contraction in money. Maintaining a target on nominal spending, rather than on money aggregates, relieves the monetary policymaker of the responsibility of identifying precisely all sources of money or quasi-money securities.

In response to events like those during the 2007–2008 financial crisis, the U.S. government took various measures. These interventions included the asset purchase programs of the Federal Reserve that expanded the supply of central bank reserves, an increase in the deposit insurance limit, and the Temporary Liquidity Guarantee Program offered by the Federal Deposit Insurance Corporation (FDIC). Additionally, after the crisis, regulations on financial intermediaries were made more stringent, with the objective of making private intermediaries' debt safer and reducing the likelihood and scale of future crises.

The framework presented in this chapter provides a unifying analysis of the interaction between private and public liquidity, along with three key policies implemented in response to the 2007–2008 financial crisis: the central bank's asset purchases and expansion of public liquidity provision, government guarantees of private money, and regulation of financial intermediaries.

11.2   Outline of the Results

In accordance with Chapter 4, Section 11.4 demonstrates that the government can achieve efficient liquidity supply and control the price level when there are no limitations on lumpsum taxes. Similarly, Section 11.5 illustrates that, in the absence of inefficiencies (such as monitoring costs) in the production of privately created "safe assets," there is no liquidity crisis, and the economy is always satiated with liquidity. In this allocation, the government can control the price level at the same values as it would if it had full control over liquidity. Private supply of liquidity, as discussed in Chapter 4, does not pose a challenge to the central bank in controlling the price level.

Section 11.6 shows that with monitoring costs, there is an overall shortage of private "safe assets," and intermediaries also have incentives to create risky debt, on which, however, they default during adverse times, leading to a liquidity crisis. The central bank can still stabilize the price level in this context, but it may need to lower the interest rate on reserves.

Section 11.7 analyzes the government intervention to eliminate the possibility of a liquidity crisis, even when there are limits on the taxes that can be levied. It is possible to achieve efficient liquidity satiation and reduce the tax burden, but only in favorable states of the economy, by investing in risky private debt. However, the supply of safe private debt will be completely crowded out. The same allocation can be implemented with deposit insurance. Regulation of intermediaries to restrict their asset holdings to riskless investments, on the other hand, leads to suboptimal allocation.

11.3   Model

The model is similar to that in Chapter 4, with some modifications and simplifications. First, there are only two periods, t and $t + 1$. The economy still features three sets of actors: households, financial intermediaries, and the government. Aggregate risk is introduced by assuming that there are two states of nature at $t + 1$, high and low. The high state is denoted by h and occurs with probability $1 - \varkappa$, with $0 < \varkappa < 1$. The low state is denoted by l and occurs with probability $\varkappa$. There are two investment opportunities for intermediaries: a safe technology and a risky technology. The key dynamic is that the realization of the low state triggers defaults in the intermediaries that invested in the risky technology, which in turn gives rise to a liquidity crunch.

At time t, households can invest their wealth in three types of securities: safe, riskless private debt issued by intermediaries that invest in safe projects; risky private debt issued by intermediaries that invest in risky projects; and government debt. Riskless debt is backed by safe investments and thus is never defaulted on. Risky debt is instead backed by risky investments that completely lose their value in the low state, in which the debt is fully defaulted on. Government debt is always repaid and therefore always safe.

At $t + 1$, liquidity benefits, via utility, are provided by the debt securities purchased at t. Unlike the model in Chapter 4, here all debt can provide liquidity services, and it provides them at time $t + 1$ rather than immediately, at time t.[1] However, since risky securities are fully defaulted on in the low state, they do not provide any liquidity services in that state. Therefore, this assumption is key to modelling a liquidity crisis that occurs when the economy switches to the low state.

11.3.1   Consumers

Households have the following preference throughout the two periods:

$$C_t + \beta(1 - \varkappa)\left[V\left(\frac{B_t + S_t + D_t}{P_h}\right) + C_h\right] + \beta\varkappa\left[V\left(\frac{B_t + S_t}{P_l}\right) + C_l\right],$$

$$(11.1)$$

where C_t denotes consumption at t; C_h and C_l denote consumption in states h and l at time $t + 1$, respectively; β, with $0 < \beta < 1$, is the discount factor between times t and $t + 1$; and function $V(\cdot)$ is concave, and differentiable, in its argument, with a satiation point at $\bar{q} > 0$, with $V_q(\cdot) = 0$ for its argument at or above the threshold $\bar{q}$, in which $V_q(\cdot)$ is the first-derivative of the function $V(\cdot)$. The securities that provide liquidity services, proxied by function $V(\cdot)$, are: government bonds, B; safe private securities, S; risky private securities D. Government debt and private safe securities are risk-free and thus always pay one unit in both the high and the low states. Risky private debt, however, has a payoff of 1 in state h and 0 in state l because it is fully defaulted on in state l. For this reason, it does not provide liquidity services in state l; P is the price level of the consumption good.

As in Chapter 4, utility $V(\cdot)$ represents the special properties that some debt securities have in the modern financial system because of the liquidity

---

1. The different timing is required since the payoff of the securities is due in period $t + 1$, which is particularly relevant for the defaulted securities.

services they provide. These securities have been broadly labeled "safe assets," and Chapter 4 has modeled them as riskless. However, as discussed by Gorton (2017), historical evidence shows that debt securities that provide liquidity services are not necessarily risk-free. In some countries, such as the U.S. and the U.K., these risky and liquid securities have been issued by private intermediaries, whereas government debt has been essentially risk-free. Throughout the history of financial systems, these private debt securities have taken the form of goldsmith notes, bills of exchange, banknotes, demand deposits, certificates of deposit, commercial paper, money market mutual fund shares, and securitized AAA debt.

At time t, households face the following budget constraint:

$$Q_t^B B_t + Q_t^S S_t + Q_t^D D_t + P_t C_t \le P_t Y_t + B_{t-1}. \tag{11.2}$$

They begin time t with an endowment Y_t of goods and with government bonds B_{t-1}. Households can use the resources on the right-hand side of (11.2) to consume C_t or to invest in a portfolio of securities that includes government bonds B_t traded at price Q_t^B, safe private securities S_t issued by the intermediaries at price Q_t^S, and risky private securities D_t issued by intermediaries at price Q_t^D. Debt is modelled as zero-coupon securities with the face (contractual) value of 1.[2]

Consumption of goods C_h and C_l in period $t+1$ is subject to the following budget constraints:

$$P_h C_h \le P_h Y_h + B_t + S_t + D_t + \Psi_h^A - T_h, \tag{11.3}$$

$$P_l C_l \le P_l Y_l + B_t + S_t + \Psi_l^A - T_l, \tag{11.4}$$

in which T_h and T_l are state-contingent lumpsum taxes and Ψ_h^A, Ψ_l^A are state-contingent intermediaries' aggregate profits. In writing the constraint in state l, as has been the case for the utility (11.1), we have already imposed that debt of type D will experience complete default in this contingency. It is important to note that this outcome is a result of the equilibrium, not a mere assumption.

Consumption and portfolio choices follow from the maximization of (11.1) under constraints (11.2), (11.3), and (11.4). The linearity of utility

---

2. As in Chapter 1, and for tractability, we consider debt securities issued at discount and we express the discount in terms of the price of the security rather than the inverse of the gross interest rate.

with respect to consumption simplifies the analysis since it implies, as in Chapter 4, that the real interest rate is always tied to $1/\beta$.

The demand for government debt and intermediaries' debt is affected by the liquidity value provided by these assets, represented by the random variable ϱ:

$$Q_t^B = \beta \left[(1 - \varkappa) \frac{P_t}{P_h} (1 + \varrho_h) + \varkappa \frac{P_t}{P_l} (1 + \varrho_l) \right], \qquad (11.5)$$

$$Q_t^S \geq \beta \left[(1 - \varkappa) \frac{P_t}{P_h} (1 + \varrho_h) + \varkappa \frac{P_t}{P_l} (1 + \varrho_l) \right], \qquad (11.6)$$

$$Q_t^D \geq \beta \left[\frac{P_t}{P_h} (1 - \varkappa)(1 + \varrho_h) \right], \qquad (11.7)$$

in which

$$\varrho_h = V_q \left(\frac{B_t + S_t + D_t}{P_h} \right)$$

and

$$\varrho_l = V_q \left(\frac{B_t + S_t}{P_l} \right).$$

With the equality sign in (11.5), we are already anticipating the equilibrium result that government bonds, when in positive supply, will always be used for liquidity purposes, while private bonds might not be used. In such cases, (11.6) or (11.7) holds, or both hold, with an equality sign.

Private debt D_t provides liquidity services only in state h when it is not defaulted on. An implication of (11.6) and (11.7) is that $Q_t^S \geq Q_t^D$. Crucially, liquidity services provide benefits not only for households but also for the issuer of the debt security because they lower borrowing costs.

11.3.2   Financial Intermediaries

At time t, there are two types of capital: safe capital K_t^S and risky capital K_t^D. The two types of capital have the same average productivity at $t + 1$, but safe capital requires an extra investment ι for each unit of capital at t. The cost ι can be interpreted as a monitoring cost to control the safety of capital. At $t + 1$, each unit of safe capital K_t^S produces $1/\beta$ unit of output in both state h and state l. By contrast, each unit of risky capital K_t^D produces A_h/β unit of output in state h and zero units in state l. The assumption of equal average productivity of the two types of capital at $t = 1$ can be formalized as $(1 - \varkappa)A_h = 1$.

There is an infinite number of small financial intermediaries that can choose the type of capital (safe capital, K_t^S, or risky capital, K_t^D) in which to invest and therefore the type of debt security to supply, safe or risky. Since intermediaries are small and thus marginal with respect to the supply of each market, they take prices Q_t^S and Q_t^D as a given. Each intermediary can supply only one type of security, although a given security can be supplied by an infinite number of intermediaries.

Intermediaries have limited liability at time $t+1$ and cannot raise equity, unlike in the analysis of Chapter 4. As a result, they default on their own debt if the payoff of capital is not sufficient to cover the debt obligations.

Let us start the analysis with intermediaries issuing safe debt S_t. At time t, they invest in riskless capital K_t^S subject to budget constraint

$$(1 + \iota)P_t K_t^S = Q_t^S S_t. \tag{11.8}$$

As previously discussed, we interpret ι as a cost of monitoring the safe capital. At time $t+1$, their real profits are state-contingent, depending on the realization of the price level:

$$\Psi_h^S = \frac{K_t^S}{\beta} - \frac{S_t}{P_h} \tag{11.9}$$

$$\Psi_l^S = \frac{K_t^S}{\beta} - \frac{S_t}{P_l}. \tag{11.10}$$

Note that the limited liability constraint requires that

$$\min\left\{\Psi_h^S, \Psi_l^S\right\} \geq 0. \tag{11.11}$$

Taking K_t^S from budget constraint (11.8) and inserting it into (11.10), the optimal supply of safe debt is nonnegative insofar as

$$Q_t^S \geq \beta \frac{P_t}{\min\{P_h, P_l\}}(1 + \iota), \tag{11.12}$$

and it is zero otherwise.

Intermediaries issuing risky securities D_t invest in the risky capital at t subject to budget constraint

$$P_t K_t^D = Q_t^D D_t. \tag{11.13}$$

At $t+1$, profits in state h are represented by

$$\Psi_h^D = \frac{A_h}{\beta} K_t^D - \frac{D_t}{P_h},$$ (11.14)

whereas profits in state l are zero because the payoff of risky capital is zero and debt is fully defaulted on, following the limited liability assumption. Using (11.13) to substitute for K_t^D in (11.14) and $(1-\varkappa)A_h = 1$, $\Psi_h^D \geq 0$ implies that the supply of risky debt is nonnegative insofar as

$$Q_t^D \geq \beta \frac{P_t}{P_h} (1 - \varkappa)$$ (11.15)

and is zero otherwise.[3]

   Intermediaries are free to choose which security market to enter, and they make this decision according to the maximum profits that they can obtain. That is, they enter the market of safe securities if the expected profits in that market are higher than those of risky securities, and vice versa.

11.3.3   Government

In the baseline analysis, we consider the simple case in which the balance sheet of the government is composed of only liabilities, that is, zero-coupon bonds. These bonds can be interpreted as treasury debt or central bank reserves and they are risk-free because they define the unit of account of the monetary system, as extensively discussed in Chapter 1. Therefore, they can always provide liquidity services. The budget constraint at time t is

$$Q_t^B B_t = B_{t-1} - T_t,$$ (11.16)

while at time $t+1$ taxes should pay back debt, namely, T_h and T_l in the high and low states of $t+1$. Therefore:

$$T_h = T_l = B_t.$$ (11.17)

We assume the following policies for the government, consistently with the analysis of Chapter 4. The central bank is setting the interest rate on

---

3. Note that intermediaries investing in K^S can also manufacture risky securities because of state-contingent variation in the price level, but we consider them theoretically, since, in the equilibrium analyzed, $P_h = P_l$.

reserves i^X and, for the sake of simplicity, at the rate $1 + i_t^X = 1/\beta$. Therefore, $Q_t^B = \beta$. The treasury follows constant real tax policy at time t and $t + 1$, specified as

$$\frac{T_t}{P_t} = (1 - \beta)b \tag{11.18}$$

and

$$\frac{T_h}{P_h} = \frac{T_l}{P_l} = b, \tag{11.19}$$

for some $b > 0$.

The first implication of the tax policies (11.19), when inserted into the budget constraints (11.17), is that the price level is constant at time $t + 1$ across contingencies, i.e., $P_h = P_l = P^*$, in which $P^* = B_t/b$. Given B_t, the price level is determined at time $t + 1$.

Moreover, we can use the tax policy (11.18) in budget constraint at time t (11.16) to get

$$\frac{B_{t-1} - \beta B_t}{P_t} = (1 - \beta)b, \tag{11.20}$$

noting that it imposes one restriction on B_t and P_t, but is not enough to determine uniquely P_t and B_t, and therefore P^*. The additional restriction for price determination will be obtained through the equilibrium in the market of liquidity.

Section 11.7 expands the analysis by allowing the government to issue more debt at t to purchase privately issued securities, possibly through the central bank, and to guarantee the debt issued by private intermediaries. Moreover, Section 11.7 imposes some restrictions on the government's ability to increase taxes T_h and T_l.

11.4 Equilibrium with the Government Satiating Liquidity

We begin with the simple case in which the government's supply of liquidity is ample enough to satisfy the needs of the economy, rendering the supply of private liquidity irrelevant. This situation is feasible within the framework described so far if the tax policy is sufficiently high, which means that $b \geq \bar{q}$. With full liquidity satiation, $V_q(\cdot) = 0$, and consequently, $\varrho_h = \varrho_l = 0$. Incorporating this into equation (11.5), we get $P_t = P^*$, given the interest rate policy pursued by the central bank, which sets $Q_t^B = \beta$.

By using $P_t = P^* = B_t/b$ in (11.20), we find that $B_t = B_{t-1}$, and therefore P^* is determined by $P^* = B_{t-1}/b$.

The price level remains constant, and the economy is fully supplied with government liquidity. Private liquidity becomes irrelevant for the equilibrium. However, it's worth noting that intermediaries will not produce any safe assets in this context when $\iota > 0$. This is because there is no liquidity premium at full satiation, a situation that doesn't allow them to offset the monitoring cost ι involved in producing safe securities. Only defaulted private securities will be created.

The result reiterates Milton Friedman's proposal (1960), but it is worth emphasizing that it relies on two critical assumptions. First, the government is benevolent. Second, the government does not face any limit on raising taxes. Nonetheless, even with a limit on taxes, Section 11.7.1 shows that other policy interventions allow the government to avoid or at least mitigate liquidity crises.

Interestingly, Section 11.7.1 demonstrates that the same equilibrium price level and liquidity satiation can be achieved with a lower level of taxation in the high state h if the central bank holds risky private securities in its portfolio. The payoff of these securities in the good state enables a reduction in the taxation burden required to produce government liquidity. However, this approach doesn't provide a solution in the bad state, when private debt defaults and taxation must remain high.

In the following sections, we limit the supply of government liquidity below the satiation level, therefore assuming that $b < \bar{q}$.

11.5 Equilibrium with No Frictions in the Supply of Private Safe Assets

This section solves for the equilibrium in the benchmark scenario in which there are no monitoring costs for investing in risk-free projects, that is, $\iota = 0$. The main result is that the same allocation of prices and liquidity of the previous section can be also achieved through private liquidity. Moreover, the economy is immune to any possible liquidity crunch since liquidity is always at the first best $\bar{q}$ in all contingencies. The results of this section revisit those in Chapter 4 with a slightly modified model.

To solve for the equilibrium, we first note that free entry reduces all profits to zero and implies that the supply of safe and risky debt is nonnegative at their respective prices:

$$Q_t^S = \beta \frac{P_t}{P^*}, \tag{11.21}$$

$$Q_t^D = \beta \frac{P_t}{P^*}(1 - \varkappa),$$ (11.22)

which are obtained by imposing an equality sign into (11.12) and (11.15) because of free competition in the liquidity markets.

When $\iota = 0$, the economy achieves the first best because the supply of "safe assets" is sufficiently large. Combining (11.6) and (11.21), we obtain

$$\varrho_h = \varrho_l = V_q \left(\frac{B_t + S_t}{P^*} \right) = 0.$$

When $B_t/P^* = b < \bar{q}$, the safe private money issued by intermediaries is crucial for complementing the supply of public liquidity and achieving the first best. Suppose by contradiction that there is no supply of safe debt. Instead, assume that intermediaries only provide risky assets. As a result, in the low state, risky securities default, and thus consumption can be financed with public liquidity only; therefore

$$\varrho_l = V_q(b) > 0,$$ (11.23)

and thus there is a shortage of liquidity in that state. By contrast, equilibrium in the market of risky securities, which requires both (11.7) and (11.22) to hold, implies that $\varrho_h = 0$. That is, the supply of risky securities is large enough to satiate liquidity needs in the high state, and thus there is no shortage of liquidity in that state.

Now consider a generic intermediary deciding which security to issue. Suppose that the intermediary chooses to issue safe debt, which never defaults. Consumers attach a high value to safe securities because the liquidity premium in the low state is positive; this high value is reflected in the price $Q_t^S = \beta(1 + \varkappa \varrho_l)P_t/P^*$ that they are willing to pay. The high Q_t^S implies that the intermediary can borrow at a lower cost and, thus, its profits are positive in both states: $\Psi_h^S = \Psi_l^S = \varkappa \varrho_l S_t/P^* > 0$. Thus, issuing safe securities S is profitable. This result contradicts the initial conjecture that an equilibrium exists when safe debt is not supplied by any intermediary.

To sum up, intermediaries supply safe private securities up to the point at which the liquidity premium is driven to zero in all states, $\varrho_h = \varrho_l = 0$. That is, free entry into the market ensures that all rents are eliminated. The supply of safe securities is enough to complement the amount of public liquidity and reach the first best, $\bar{q}$. Moreover, the supply of risky securities can be positive in equilibrium, and their price is basically represented by the present discounted value of their expected payoffs. However, the supply of these assets is irrelevant for welfare. Note that, given that $Q_t^B = Q_t^S = \beta P_t/P^*$ in equilibrium and that the central bank sets $Q_t^B = \beta$, the price level is constant at P^* and, using (11.20), $B_t = B_{t-1}$. Therefore, P^* is determined by $P^* = B_{t-1}/b$.

The equilibrium with free competition for private securities reaches the same allocation as in Section 11.4, even if the supply of government liquidity is negligible.

11.6   Equilibrium with Frictions in the Supply of Private Safe Assets

This section analyzes the general model, in which intermediaries face a positive monitoring cost when investing in risk-free projects, $\iota > 0$. The main result is that there is a shortage of privately issued "safe assets," with full satiation of liquidity only in the good state of nature due to an abundant supply of risky debt. The economy is then prone to a liquidity crunch when it is hit by an unfavorable shock.

The first step in characterizing equilibrium is to note that when $\iota > 0$, there must be a positive supply of risky debt securities, that is, $D > 0$. If an equilibrium exists in which intermediaries are active and issue debt, three scenarios are possible: all intermediaries issue safe debt, all intermediaries issue risky debt, or some intermediaries issue safe debt and some issue risky debt. Note, however, that the scenario in which all intermediaries issue only safe debt S is not an equilibrium. We show this by contraction.

Suppose that all intermediaries issue safe debt in equilibrium. In this case, equating demand (11.6) and supply (11.21), it follows that $\varrho_h = \varrho_l = \iota > 0$. To offset the monitoring cost, the liquidity premium on safe debt must be positive; if the liquidity premium were zero, intermediaries would make negative profits because of the cost ι. Note that a positive liquidity premium is associated with a level of liquidity that is below the first best in some states. Furthermore, the fact that there are only safe securities that are equally liquid in both states implies that the overall liquidity is equalized across states. Therefore, $q_h = q_l < \bar{q}$, in which q denotes the overall private and public real liquidity supplied at time $t + 1$; in particular, $q_h < \bar{q}$ and the liquidity premium in state h is positive: $\varrho_h > 0$. We can now identify a profitable deviation that leads us to conclude that the scenario with only safe debt cannot be an equilibrium. Given $\varrho_h > 0$, households are willing to pay a liquidity premium on a security that provides more liquidity in the high state. Now consider an intermediary that issues risky debt D_t. This intermediary earns positive profits in the high state (and zero profits in the low state) because risky securities include a liquidity premium. Therefore $\Psi_h^D = \varrho_h D_t / P^* > 0$, and it is profitable to issue risky debt.

More generally, the previous analysis can be extended to show that any scenario in which $\varrho_h > 0$ cannot be an equilibrium because there would exist profitable deviations to increase the supply of risky securities. Thus, $\varrho_h = 0$. Therefore, liquidity is at the efficient level in state h, $q_h = \bar{q}$.

We have established that risky debt will be supplied. Will private safe debt be supplied as well? The answer is affirmative only if intermediaries can issue them at a premium to offset the monitoring cost. Whether the premium on safe intermediaries' debt is large or not depends in turn on the amount of public liquidity. A large supply of public liquidity implies a low liquidity premium on safe debt (recall that public liquidity is risk-free); thus, issuing safe debt is not profitable for intermediaries. That is, a sufficiently high level of public debt crowds out the production of privately issued safe money by influencing the liquidity premium on default-free obligations. By contrast, a low supply of public liquidity creates a profitable opportunity for intermediaries to issue some safe debt.

Indeed, supply (11.21) requires the price to be $Q_t^S = \beta (1 + \iota) P_t / P^*$. However, investor will not hold safe private debt if the price is too high, and higher than $\tilde{Q}_t^S = \beta (1 + \varkappa \varrho_l) P_t / P^*$. A low value of the liquidity premium in state l makes it harder to supply safe securities. Note that in absence of safe private debt, the premium is governed by the supply of public debt. Therefore, if $V_q(b)$ is smaller than $\iota / \varkappa$, private safe debt will not be supplied because $Q_t^S > \tilde{Q}_t^S$.

It follows that the liquidity premium in state l is determined by

$$\varrho_l = \min \left\{ \frac{\iota}{\varkappa}, V_q(b) \right\}, \tag{11.24}$$

and therefore the overall real supply of public and private liquidity is given by

$$q_l = \max \left\{ V_q^{-1} \left(\frac{\iota}{\varkappa} \right), b \right\} < \bar{q}.$$

In equilibrium, the supply of safe private securities is represented by

$$S = P^* \max \left(V_q^{-1} \left(\frac{\iota}{\varkappa} \right) - b, 0 \right), \tag{11.25}$$

and therefore that of risky debt is given by

$$D \geq P^*(\bar{q} - b) - S > 0, \tag{11.26}$$

at prices $Q^D = (1 - \varkappa) P_t/P^*$.

We need to determine the price level at time t and $t+1$. Since $Q_t^B = \beta (1 + \varkappa \varrho_l) P_t/P^*$ and $Q_t^B = \beta$, it follows that

$$P_t = \frac{P^*}{(1 + \varkappa \varrho_l)} < P^*.$$

We can further use the above result and $P^* = B_t/b$ in (11.20) to obtain

$$\frac{B_t}{B_{t-1}} = \frac{1 + \varkappa \varrho_l}{1 + \beta \varkappa \varrho_l},$$

showing that $B_t > B_{t-1}$. This implies that

$$P_t = \frac{1}{1 + \beta \varkappa \varrho_l} \frac{B_{t-1}}{b}, \qquad P^* = \frac{1 + \varkappa \varrho_l}{1 + \beta \varkappa \varrho_l} \frac{B_{t-1}}{b}.$$

The government, given the tax and interest rate policy, now issues more debt, simply because it can borrow at lower cost than the market rate. This result can be understood by investigating the intertemporal resource constraint of the economy, which in line with equation (4.12) of Chapter 4 is given by

$$\frac{B_{t-1}}{P_t} = \frac{T_t}{P_t} + (Q_t^B - Q_t^f)\frac{B_t}{P_t} + \beta \left(\varkappa \frac{T_h}{P_h} + (1 - \varkappa)\frac{T_l}{P_l} \right), \tag{11.27}$$

in which we have defined with Q_t^f the price at time t of a security that is risk-free but not liquid, with $Q_t^f = \beta P_t/P^*$. This price is lower than Q_t^B, which shows in the above equation extra "revenues" to back the price level. Maintaining fixed the tax policy, these extra revenues lower the price level at time t.

The result that the price level depends on ϱ_l can be seen as a challenge for monetary policy, since relevant variables in the creation of safe securities like ι can influence the price level, and their movements, too. However, this result is a particular feature of the tax policy used rather than a general result. Full government control of the price level can be restored by changing the tax policy at time $t+1$ to

$$\frac{T_h}{P_h} = \frac{T_l}{P_l} = b - (Q_t^B - Q_t^f)\frac{B_t}{P_t},$$

in place of (11.19) while maintaining (11.18). Inserting these policies into (11.27) reveals that the price level at time t will be exactly at the same level, P^*, as in the allocation with no monitoring cost. Prices at time $t + 1$ will be also at P^*, changing the interest rate policy to $1 + i_t^X = \beta^{-1}(1 + \varkappa \varrho_l)^{-1}$. This, in turn, sets the price of government bonds to $Q_t^B = \beta(1 + \varkappa \varrho_l)$, which, combined with equation (11.5), i.e., $Q_t^B = \beta(1 + \varkappa \varrho_l) P_t/P_{t+1}$, implies a constant price level. In this equilibrium, $B_t < B_{t-1}$ to be consistent with the lower taxes levied at time $t + 1$.

That the interest rate policy can still control the inflation rate at a desired target, even when liquidity is not fully satiated, is not a surprising result and is consistent with the analysis in Chapter 3, as demonstrated in equation (3.24). The only difference with respect to the previous analysis is that, in this case, liquidity is also supplied by the private sector, and the central bank should take this into account when setting the interest rate. The interest rate on reserves, to keep prices stable, should be inversely related to the liquidity premium in the low state, ϱ_l, which, in the case of private supply of safe securities, is proportional to the cost of monitoring ι. Sudden variations in the cost of monitoring, increasing it, require a lower interest rate, which could be constrained in its movements by the zero lower bound. There is to note, however, that ϱ_l is bounded above by the supply of government liquidity. A relatively higher supply limits the extent to which the policy rate should be corrected downward.

However, the key result of this section is that the frictions in the supply of safe securities rationalize an equilibrium in which liquidity is at the first-best level $\bar{q}$ in the high state, while it is at a lower level, $q_t < \bar{q}$, in the low state due to a shortage of "safe assets." Therefore, the framework can characterize a liquidity crunch when the economy transitions from the high to the low state. This materializes in a real cost for the economy because it reduces the real value of the securities that provide transaction/collateral services. In a more general framework, this liquidity crunch could lead to a contraction in economic activity, as shown in Benigno and Nisticò (2017). In the next section, we will study the government policies that can prevent this crisis.

11.7 Government Intervention

The possibility of a liquidity crisis that arises in the laissez-faire equilibrium when $\iota > 0$ creates an opportunity for government intervention. The amount of liquidity is large enough only in the high state, whereas the economy experiences a liquidity crunch in the low state.

This section studies general government policies related to debt issuance, the active management of the central bank's balance sheet, and the regulation of financial intermediaries.

Section 11.4 has considered a large supply of public liquidity backed by higher taxes at all times. This intervention entirely crowds out the production of safe private debt but nonetheless achieves the first best. There are two policies that implement the first best even if the government faces a limit on average taxation: asset purchases by the central bank and actuarially fair deposit insurance. These policies exploit the backing provided by intermediaries in good times and, thus, require government backing only in bad times. Crucially, asset purchases and deposit insurance are equivalent, in the spirit of Wallace (1981). The taxes required under the two policies are identical in all contingencies because the consolidated balance sheets of the government and private intermediaries (i.e., of the agents that supply liquidity) are identical under the two policies.

This section also studies regulation that forces all intermediaries to invest in safe projects. This policy reduces welfare because issuing risky securities backed by investments in risky projects allows intermediaries to economize on monitoring costs.

11.7.1   Government Policy with a Limit on Taxes

This section analyzes the supply of public liquidity when the government faces a limit on the average real taxes that it can collect at $t + 1$, when average taxes are $(1 - \varkappa)T_h/P_h + \varkappa T_l/P_l$. To keep the analysis simple and without losing generality, let us assume that the limit on average taxes is

$$(1 - \varkappa)\frac{T_h}{P_h} + \varkappa\frac{T_l}{P_l} \leq b < \bar{q}. \qquad (11.28)$$

Notwithstanding the limit in (11.28), an appropriate policy of asset purchases allows the economy to achieve the first best, $q_h = q_l = \bar{q}$. Under the asset purchase policy, the government supplies a large amount of public money, and purchases private intermediaries' risky debt through the central bank. The risky debt held by the central bank pays a return in the high state, allowing the government to reduce taxes in that contingency. Instead, in the low state, the private risky securities are defaulted on, and thus government debt requires backing through taxes. This policy is related to Friedman's second proposal (1960), which suggests backing the supply of interest-bearing reserves (in our model, B) with the portfolio of assets held by the central bank (in our model, private intermediaries' risky debt).

At time t, the central bank purchases quantity D_t^C of risky securities and finances these purchases by increasing the outstanding debt from the initial level of B_t to $\bar{B}$. Thus, the government's budget constraint at time t is

$$Q_t^B B_t - Q_t^D D_t^C = B_{t-1} - T_t, \qquad (11.29)$$

and therefore can be written as

$$\frac{Q_t^B \bar{B} - Q_t^D D_t^C}{P_t} = \frac{B_{t-1}}{P_t} - (1-\beta)b, \qquad (11.30)$$

in which we have left unchanged the real tax policy at time t as $T_t/P_t = (1-\beta)b$ and used $B_t = \bar{B}$. At time $t+1$, the government repays its debt $\bar{B}$ with the proceeds earned by holding assets D_t^C, if not in default, and taxes:

$$\bar{B} = T_h + D_t^C \qquad (11.31)$$

and

$$\bar{B} = T_l \qquad (11.32)$$

in the high and low states, respectively.

To achieve the first best, the government must issue an amount of real debt equal to $\bar{B}/P_h = \bar{q}$, $\bar{B}/P_l = \bar{q}$. Since there is a bound on overall taxes, to pay back the debt in state l the government should raise real taxes in the maximum amount, $T_l/P_l = \bar{q}$ which together with (11.32) determines $P_l = \bar{B}/\bar{q}$, given $\bar{B}$, which is still an unknown.

In state h taxes are set using the bound of limit (11.28); therefore

$$\frac{T_h}{P_h} = \frac{b - \varkappa\bar{q}}{1 - \varkappa} < \bar{q}.$$

We can use this result in (11.31) to obtain

$$\frac{\bar{B}}{P_h} = \frac{D^C}{P_h} + \frac{b - \varkappa\bar{q}}{1 - \varkappa}, \qquad (11.33)$$

which, for a given $\bar{B} - D^C$, determines the price level P_h at

$$P_h = \frac{1 - \varkappa}{b - \varkappa\bar{q}}(\bar{B} - D^C).$$

To implement the efficient allocation, prices should be equalized across states, which requires asset purchases of the amount

$$D^C = \frac{\bar{q} - b\,\bar{B}}{1 - \varkappa q}.$$

These purchases implement the first best allocation also in state h, with $\bar{B}/P_l = \bar{q}$. By purchasing private assets, the government can indeed reduce the tax burden in state h. Note that if $b < \varkappa\bar{q}$, $D_t^C/P_h > \bar{q}$, and $T_h < 0$, the government is even able to make a positive transfer to the private sector.

In this allocation, liquidity premiums are zero. Considering that $\varrho_l = \varrho_h = 0$ and $Q_t^B = \beta$ in (11.5), we obtain that $P_t = P_h = P_l = P^{**}$. Using all these results in (11.30) together with the equilibrium price for the risky securities $Q^D = \beta(1 - \varkappa)$, we obtain

$$\bar{B} = \frac{\bar{q}}{b}B_{t-1},$$

showing that nominal government debt should increase in this equilibrium financing the purchase of risky assets.[4]

The above analysis has implications for the relevance of unconventional monetary policy in line with the discussion in Section 9.4 of Chapter 9. Section 11.4 showed that, irrespective of the composition of its assets, the central bank can expand the supply of its reserves to avoid a liquidity crisis if there is no limit on taxes. This section has instead shown that it can also economize on taxes by purchasing risky private assets to back the supply of liquidity. This result suggests that, even in normal times, central banks should continue holding private securities for the purpose of fulfilling the economy's liquidity needs and reducing the tax burden, at least in good times. This view is in contrast with the conventional one that prescribes the central banks to hold just treasury bills, an approach in which no reduction in the tax burden would be possible. In any case, to avoid a liquidity crisis, the government should be able to raise taxes in state l. If this is not possible, a liquidity crisis is unavoidable. To reduce the tax burden in state l, safe private debt should be available to back government liquidity. But this is the problem: the private sector is unable to manufacture enough "safe assets," and public liquidity could have a crowding-out effect on private liquidity when the latter is costly to create.

4. Since $\bar{B} > B_{t-1}$, P^{**} is higher than P^* of Sections 11.4 and 11.5.

We discuss an alternative government policy, equivalent to the asset purchase program, that allows the economy to achieve the first best even if the government is subject to the limit on taxes in equation (11.28). This policy can be labelled as deposit insurance, even though it can be interpreted, more generally, as any program that guarantees the liabilities of financial intermediaries.

Let us consider a deposit insurance scheme that is actuarially fair. The government charges intermediaries a fee for the insurance and, on average, the policy does not provide any subsidy to intermediaries. Under a deposit insurance, intermediaries' debt is safe from the households' viewpoint and it therefore always provides liquidity services, even though intermediaries invest in risky projects. In the low state at $t + 1$, when the payoff of intermediaries' investments is zero, the government provides the insurance payment through a transfer to intermediaries, which in turn is used to repay the debt to households in full. In the high state at $t + 1$, when intermediaries' projects produce a positive output, the government charges intermediaries with a proportional fee.

The equilibrium under deposit insurance can be characterized as an equivalence proposition, in the spirit of Wallace (1981). If an equilibrium exists under the asset purchase policy, the same consumption allocation and prices can be sustained under a policy of deposit insurance with the same taxes. The logic of the proof is based on the fact that the consolidated balance sheets of the government and private intermediaries—that is, of the agents that supply liquidity in the economy—are the same under both policies.

Under a more stringent limit on taxes in low states, government policies do not implement the first best, but the equivalence between asset purchases and deposit insurance extends also to this case.[5]

In practice, there is usually a limit on deposit insurance. Nonetheless, during the acute phase of the 2008 crisis, the deposit insurance limit was increased in several countries, and other forms of government guarantees were introduced. In the U.S., the insurance limit was increased from $100,000 to $250,000. Moreover, the Federal Deposit Insurance Corporation (FDIC) set up the Temporary Liquidity Guarantee Program, with the objective of bringing stability to financial markets and the banking industry. The program provided a full guarantee of non-interest-bearing transaction accounts and of the senior unsecured debt issued by a participating entity for about a year.

---

5. See Benigno and Robatto (2019).

Taken together, these two measures dramatically increased the fraction of the liabilities of U.S. financial institutions that were guaranteed by the government. Similar policies were adopted in other countries, including some cases in which the coverage was unlimited, such as in Germany.

Note, finally, that this discussion provides a role for deposit insurance that is different from, although complementary to, the standard role related to bank runs. Following Diamond and Dybvig (1983), bank run literature highlights the importance of deposit insurance as a tool to eliminate bad equilibria driven by panic. In this chapter, crises are driven by fundamental shocks, and deposit insurance plays a key role in reducing the negative impact of such shocks.

11.7.2   Regulation of Intermediaries' Investments

Another policy used in the aftermath of the financial crisis is the regulation of financial intermediaries. This can be implemented in this chapter's model by forcing private intermediaries to invest only in riskless projects, K^S. As a result, all intermediaries issue "safe assets" without the need for the government to provide deposit insurance.

Restricting intermediaries' investments is fundamentally different from the policies studied in Sections 11.4 and 11.7.1. Government provision of liquidity and deposit insurance requires adequate fiscal backing in the low state, even if the government buys assets through the central bank's balance sheet. These policies primarily work by complementing the insufficient private backing of liquidity with public backing. By contrast, the regulation of intermediaries directly affects the private backing of securities issued by intermediaries without requiring any fiscal capacity.

However, regulating intermediaries reduces welfare with respect to laissez-faire.[6] In the unregulated equilibrium, some intermediaries invest in risky technology to economize on the monitoring cost, and thus they issue risky debt that defaults in the low state. Consequently, forcing all intermediaries to invest in safe projects eliminates liquidity crises but results in intermediaries wasting a large amount of resources to pay the monitoring costs. Therefore, welfare is lower in comparison to the laissez-faire equilibrium.

---

6. For a formal proof, note that the laissez-faire equilibrium is constrained-efficient. See Benigno and Robatto (2019).

11.7.3   General Discussion

We discuss the results of this chapter under two headings: control of the price level and supply of liquidity.

CONTROL OF THE PRICE LEVEL

A key result implied by the analysis in this chapter, regarding the potential challenges arising from the expansion of the money supply to financial intermediaries and securities that may not always be safe under all circumstances, is that it does not necessarily lead to indeterminacy in the price level. This holds true when the price level is controlled in accordance with the principles outlined in Chapters 1 and 2.

The results further confirm the findings of Chapter 4 that a frictionless private money market can achieve full liquidity satiation without introducing instability in the control of the price level. However, when there are frictions in the private liquidity market, the path of prices could be influenced by the supply of private liquidity and its determinants. Nonetheless, even in this scenario, the interest rate on reserves should be appropriately adjusted to maintain the desired price level, with the sole constraint being the zero lower bound. This constraint can be mitigated by increasing the supply of government liquidity in adverse states of nature, which can crowd out the supply of completely safe private assets.

However, interest rate policy alone cannot prevent the contraction of real liquidity and the resulting real consequences that impact the economy when it enters unfavorable states of nature, leading to defaults on private risky debt. In a more general model in which the fall in real liquidity endogenously influences production, the stabilization problem of the price level becomes more complex and intertwined with the liquidity crisis. However, it will not change the result that the policy rate should be lowered in a liquidity crisis.

SUPPLY OF LIQUIDITY

The results of this chapter can be used to discuss more broadly the policy implications of the model presented above in comparison with some classic views on the role of private and public liquidity, namely, the free-banking theory, supported also by Hayek (1976); the narrow banking theory of Friedman (1960); and the "real bills" doctrine. It also provides some comparison with regulation of financial intermediaries based on Basel III, introduced in 2010.

The results of the model with costless monitoring ($\iota = 0$) and no limits on taxes are in line with the views of both Hayek (1976) and Friedman (1960), as well as with the discussion in Section 4.4 of Chapter 4. However, the results of the full model with costly monitoring ($\iota > 0$) and limits on taxes suggest that optimal policies represent a mix of the two views.

In Hayek (1976), the process of competition leads the private sector to supply a sufficiently large quantity of the best available type of liquid assets, namely, "safe assets." The competitive market structure in this chapter's model is indeed in the spirit of Hayek's theory (1976, p. 43), when $\iota = 0$. Intermediaries find it worthwhile to supply safe debt because the premium paid by households reduces the intermediaries' financing costs. As a result, the households' interest is perfectly aligned with that of financial intermediaries. Indeed, the premium on "safe assets," which reflects a lack of liquidity from society's point of view, creates incentives for profit-maximizing intermediaries to supply safe securities. Free entry then ensures that there are enough safe securities so that liquidity is fully satiated.

Friedman's proposal (1960) can also achieve the first best. According to this view, the government should have monopoly power in the supply of liquidity. This objective can be reached also under a narrow banking system; that is, intermediaries are forced to satisfy a 100% reserve requirement. In the context of this chapter's model, intermediaries would buy government safe debt B instead of capital. If this were the case, private intermediaries would not create any liquidity because their debt would be backed by liquid government reserves instead of illiquid capital. As a result, the overall supply of liquid assets in the economy would be determined solely by the amount of government debt. Note that the government has to back its debt and interest payments, which is achieved through the collection of taxes. Nevertheless, a benevolent government that implements a narrow banking system and faces no limit on taxes can achieve the first best by supplying government debt in the amount $b \geq \bar{q}$ and by raising enough taxes.

In the more general model with monitoring costs ($\iota > 0$) and limits on taxes ($b < \bar{q}$), neither the private sector nor the government alone can satiate the demand for liquidity. The mechanism of private money creation in a market with frictions leads to an equilibrium that does not implement the first best and can even generate a liquidity crisis because private intermediaries are incentivized to create risky debt. Friedman's proposal (1960) of a narrow banking system does not implement the first best either, if there are costs or limits on taxes in bad states, and therefore cannot help to avert a liquidity crisis and a drop in real liquidity.

In general, however, in terms of both conventional and unconventional instruments, when a crisis of the type described here develops, originating from the poor quality of certain assets, monetary policy should be set to keep the economy on the same trajectory it had before with respect to nominal spending. This can be accomplished by lowering the policy rate, which also pushes down all money market interest rates, and maintaining liquidity as high as possible under adverse conditions, by supplementing the deteriorated assets with high-quality central bank (government) securities.

Finally, Section 11.7.2 warns us about the possible negative consequences of policies that force intermediaries to invest in safer but less productive assets. Historically, these policies can be traced back to the prescription of the "real bills" doctrine, which requires intermediaries to hold essentially risk-free assets (Sargent, 2011). These policies can reduce or help prevent the occurrence of liquidity crises because real liquidity would be limited both in the good and the bad states. Interestingly, this chapter's framework shows that their impact on welfare could be negative with respect to laissez-faire.

11.8 References

The analysis in this chapter is based on Benigno and Robatto (2019). Gorton (2017) describes the historical evolution of the monetary system, emphasizing the creation of private "safe assets" during periods of government debt shortage, and the subsequent financial crises associated with the poor quality of these "safe assets" produced by the financial sector.

Benigno and Nisticò (2017) analyze the macroeconomic consequence of a shock to the liquidity properties of some private securities, showing that it can create a fall in economic activity and a deflation in a model with price rigidity. They also discuss the kind of policies that the central bank can undertake to mitigate the impact of the shock, such as lowering the interest rate on reserves and providing ample public liquidity to replace the privately produced liquidity. Targeting nominal spending during a liquidity crisis due to shortage of safe securities approximates well the optimal policy.

Gorton and Ordonez (2022) also differentiate between "safe assets" supplied publicly, such as government bonds, and those supplied privately, such as asset-backed securities. In their analysis, private assets are not perfect substitutes for public safe assets because they come with heterogeneous and volatile qualities. The extent to which private assets can substitute for public assets depends on their informational content. When there is no information available, they can be considered perfect substitutes for public assets, although they are fundamentally different. However, as more information about their content becomes available, their substitutability decreases, potentially leading to a shortage of "safe assets" and triggering financial crises. It is worth noting that information is endogenous in their context and can be influenced by the supply of government debt, which, in turn, can crowd out the supply of private safe securities. Azzimonti and Yared (2019) also show, in a different context, that an increase in the supply of public debt reduces the production of private safe securities.

Magill, Quinzii, and Rochet (2020) emphasize the increasing production of private securities due to the low supply of public liquidity. Regulation of the banking sector leads to a lower supply of private safe assets, justifying both the central bank's policy of paying interest on reserves and the purchase of risky assets to replace the reduced supply of private safe debt.

Stein (2012) discusses the role of financial stability policy when unregulated banks create too much short-term debt that they have difficulty honoring in a financial crisis without selling assets at fire-sale prices. The possibility of such fire sales may give rise to a negative externality, which can be corrected by conventional open-market operations undertaken by the central bank. Greenwood, Hanson, and Stein (2016) argue that the central bank should use its balance sheet to help reduce the financial instability of the system, as underlined in Stein (2012). It should maintain a large balance sheet even out of zero lower bound policies to provide an ample supply of government liquidity. In doing so, it can crowd out private sector supply of liquidity without compromising the attainment of its inflation target, as in the analysis of Section 11.4.

PART IV

Inflation

Introduction

"... NOT ALL ECONOMISTS ever agree on anything" (Samuelson and Solow, 1960, p. 178). Defining inflation is easier than understanding its causes. It refers to the variation of a well-defined price level over a certain horizon. Since the price level is the inverse of the value of a currency, inflation implies that the currency is losing value. Determining what constitutes high or low inflation is already quite debatable. Cagan (1956) defined hyperinflations as periods with a monthly inflation consistently above 50 percent, while Fisher, Sahay, and Vegh (2002) classify high-inflation episodes as those when the twelve-month inflation rate rises above 100 percent. The causes of inflation are even more debatable, and have been at the root of controversies in macroeconomics.

The introductory Figure 1.1 of this book provides a striking illustration of the worsening of the purchasing power of a dollar in the last 250 years, more so after any linkage, direct or indirect, with tangible assets like gold was relinquished. This could point to the problems in the governing of an intrinsically worthless paper currency. The picture does not do much justice, however, to the early inflationary episodes, given that the escalation of prices after World War II obscures the increases and decreases in prices that occurred before, although clearly less importantly and surely not persistently. The striking difference is, however, between the price anchoring delivered in general by commodity money and the unsatisfactory performance of pure paper money.

It should be generally logically inconceivable that a metallic monetary system experiences inflation unless there are significant discoveries of new sources of metals. However, the power of money and attempts at its manipulation have a long tradition in history. In a conversation with Thomas Sargent and Robert Townsend in 1985, the economic historian Carlo Cipolla invoked the remarkable inflation during the Roman Empire starting at the end of the second century. One possible explanation, he suggested, was the

293

growing expenditure of the administration due to the expansion of the army, bureaucracy, and the welfare state.

It appears that initially there was a stock of metal from which the government minted more coins with the appropriate metal, leading to a rise in prices. Subsequently, deception played a role, with the production of coins containing less metal or even coins that were coated in copper and washed in good silver to give the appearance of silver coins.

The medieval period was also characterized by frequent debasement of coins, which could involve reducing either the fineness or the weight or a combination of both. It could also occur that, for the same weight and fineness, the nominal value was increased. Cipolla explained that changing the weight was considered a "clean" way to debase coins, as opposed to changing the fineness. During that time, Florence had a reputation for never changing the fineness of its coins, and debasement never occurred for financing needs, but rather to maintain a certain supply of currency. Interestingly, there were macroeconomic reasons for this increase in supply, to avoid deflations or the influx of a foreign currency. History has repeated itself several times for what are now called international reserve currencies, as the florin was in its time. In the past century, under Gold Standard regimes, the British pound and the U.S. dollar were subject to deflationary pressures that were resolved with their devaluations with respect to the gold parity.

Disanchoring currency from direct intrinsic metallic content or convertibility with specie, as seen with fiat money, clearly removes any constraints on government manipulation of the currency. The ease of financing needs through a costless printing press makes it tempting option for any government. Hyperinflations are indeed a modern phenomenon, according to the definition given by Cagan (1956), with only a few episodes before the twentieth century, the most notable being during the French Revolution.

Milton Friedman (1970b) once asserted, "Inflation is always and everywhere a monetary phenomenon in the sense that it is and can be produced only by a more rapid increase in the quantity of money than in output" (Friedman 1970b, p. 24).[1] This statement aligns with the analysis in Chapter 1, where we established that monetary policy holds the capability to control the price level in a paper currency system. Consequently, it bears responsibility if prices increase rapidly. Hyperinflation evidence supports unprecedented

---

1. See also Friedman (1963).

money growth rates associated with a skyrocketing increase in prices. However, in line with the discussion in Chapter 1, most, if not all, of these episodes are associated with the subtle linkages between monetary and fiscal policies, which become explicit in the monetary financing of the treasury's deficit. Chapter 13 investigates the theoretical drivers of hyperinflations based on the connection between monetary and fiscal policies and weaknesses in the real backing of the currency.

While hyperinflations exhibit distinct features, as will be explored in Chapter 13, with one notable characteristic being the apparent irrelevance of movements in real activity in comparison to the magnitude of price increases, the causes of inflation in low-inflation environments have sparked major controversies. One principal debate revolves around whether inflation is positively related to economic activity, implying a trade-off between inflation and the unemployment rate. This relationship was first documented in the evidence provided by Phillips (1958), and has since been referred to as the Phillips curve.

The source of the controversy lies in the fundamental questions of whether monetary policy exerts a lasting impact on the real economy and, if so, the duration of such effects. Interpreting the Phillips curve from a policy perspective implies that it is perpetually feasible to leverage monetary policy to enhance the unemployment rate, albeit necessitating a more substantial increase in inflation at low unemployment rates compared to high rates.

Figure 12.1 shows in the top panel the U.S. inflation rate over the past sixty-five years, focusing on the core Consumer Price Index (CPI excluding food and energy items). Additionally, it incorporates the 14-month CPI inflation expectations gathered by the Livingston Survey. The lower panel of the figure illustrates the U.S. unemployment rate, featuring a horizontal line drawn at the 3.7 percent unemployment rate, selected by inspection as a reasonable approximation of a "minimum" unemployment rate. The figure reveals periods during which the unemployment rate fell below this threshold, occurring notably in the late 1960s, sporadically in 2019, and more recently since early 2022.

An intriguing observation emerges from the late 1960s, coinciding with the Vietnam War, and the recent 2022 data, where periods of low unemployment are associated with inflationary surges. While this might suggest evidence supporting a steep trade-off between inflation and unemployment, the narrative is challenged by the events of the 1970s. In that decade, a surge in inflation, alongside periods of price control, coincided with a rise in the unemployment rate.

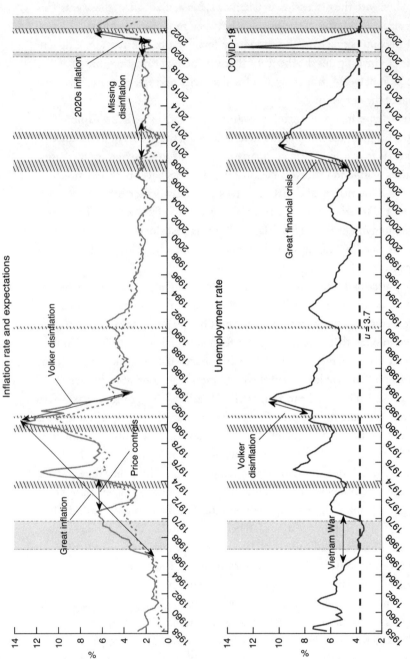

FIGURE 12.1. United States. Top chart: CPI core inflation rate and Livingston Survey 14-month inflation expectations (dotted line). Bottom chart: Unemployment rate, shaded areas: Periods with unemployment rate below or equal to 3.7 percent. Shaded areas with hatching: Periods of significant surge in oil prices. Period: 1958–2023. *Source: U.S. Bureau of Labor Statistics and Federal Reserve Bank of Philadelphia.*

Two other relevant facts deserving attention occured during that period. The world economy suffered a significant increase in oil prices, indicated in the figure by the shaded areas with hatching. This type of shock reignites the longstanding debate between cost-push theories and demand-pull theories of inflation, which were blurred under the Phillips curve.[2] The second notable aspect of the 1970s is the simultaneous rise in inflation expectations alongside peaking inflation. This contrasts sharply with the subdued and controlled expectations of the first part of the 1960s.

This evidence supported theoretical developments early on proposed by Phelps (1967) and Friedman (1968), fundamentally altering the understanding of any trade-off between inflation and unemployment to be a short-run phenomenon. Moreover, it introduced the concept of the natural rate of unemployment, independent of monetary factors, around which the trade-off gravitates. The trade-off inherent in the Phillips curve re-emerged prominently during the Volcker disinflation, when inflation dropped from its peak above 12 percent to almost 3 percent, accompanied by a rise in unemployment from 7 percent to nearly 11 percent. Notably, this period also led to a decline in inflation expectations.

The recent history of inflation and unemployment in the United States tells a remarkable story of achieving a low rate of price increase close to the 2 percent target, a quantitative objective adopted by several central banks and by the Federal Reserve in January 2012. Impressively, the core inflation rate averaged around this target during the first two decades of this century. This stability persisted despite a 145% rise in oil prices from February 2007 to June 2008, followed by a subsequent reversal, and the unprecedented fall of oil prices to zero during the COVID-19 pandemic.

The apparent contradiction lies in the fact that inflation remained stable despite the rise in unemployment to peak levels following the 2007–2008 financial crisis and the dramatic increase during the COVID-19 period. Researchers have coined these episodes as "missing disinflation," raising questions about the existence of a Phillips curve or suggesting that it must be very flat. However, post-COVID, inflation spiked after monetary and fiscal policies engaged in unprecedented expansionary stimuli, coinciding with another energy/oil price shock and supply-constrained capacity.

2. Refer to Samuelson and Solow (1960) for a discussion of the historical content of these theories.

Figure 12.1 illustrates this period with a shaded area, marking times in which the unemployment rate fell around the hypothetical 3.7 threshold, reminiscent of the 1960s.

Chapter 12 will serve as a guide for the reader to interpret Figure 12.1, exploring different versions of the Phillips curve. It will commence with the original formulation, and progress through the evolution of the concept, including the natural rate of unemployment and short-run trade-off theories. Recent developments, as derived in Chapter 5 with the New Keynesian Phillips curve, will be integrated into this comprehensive exploration.

These theories will be complemented by delving into Keynes's perspective on unemployment, emphasizing the resistance of workers to wage reductions and his vision of maximum output during wartime. This perspective suggests a Phillips curve that is predominantly flat, except when maximum capacity is reached, at which point it becomes vertical. This supports the notion that the natural rate of unemployment is not a symmetric concept but is positioned at low values of unemployment, as suggested by the 3.7 percent threshold in Figure 12.1.

12

The Inflation-Unemployment Trade-Off

12.1 Introduction

The most controversial theme in monetary economics concerns the existence and shape of a trade-off between inflation and unemployment and is associated with Alban Phillips and his famous Phillips curve. In 1958, Phillips presented scatter diagrams depicting the rate of change of wages and the percentage of unemployment in the U.K. for the period 1861–1957. To begin with, he showed that during the period 1861–1913, there was a tight negative relationship between the percentage change in wages and the unemployment rate. This relationship, shown in the left-panel of Figure 12.2, was also nonlinear, as wages rose faster when the unemployment rate was reduced from already low levels, compared to when it was elevated. The fit he found for the period 1861–1913 also captured other periods, including the most recent one in his analysis, from 1948–1957.

As Tobin (1972, p. 9) aptly stated, the Phillips curve is "an empirical finding in search of theory, like Pirandello characters in search of an author." Phillips himself offered an explanation for his findings, suggesting that when there are few unemployed individuals, employers compete by bidding wage rates higher to attract the most suitable workforce from other firms. In contrast, when unemployment is high, "workers are reluctant to offer their services at less than the prevailing rates."

This hypothesis reflects Keynes's challenge to the orthodox view of the Great Depression, which saw the observed stickiness of wages as evidence of voluntary unemployment. Keynes argued for an involuntary interpretation of unemployment because workers were willing to accept higher employment

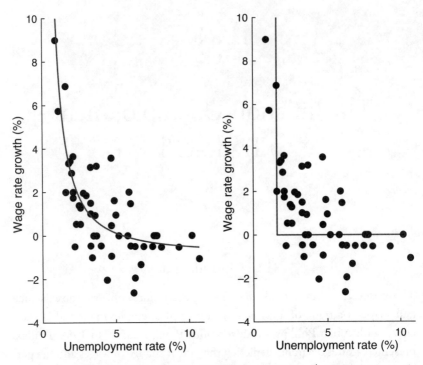

FIGURE 12.2. Phillips Curve (1861–1913, United Kingdom): Wage rate growth (*Source: Brown and Hopkins, 1950*) vs. unemployment rate (*Source: Feinstein, 1972, adjusted by Board of Trade*). Left panel: Phillips's (1958) curve. Right panel: L-curve delimited by wage rate growth at 0% and unemployment rate at 1.6%.

at a lower real wage when it resulted from an increase in prices, rather than from a cut in wages. Keynes viewed money wage rates as "administered prices," meaning they were not set and reset in daily auctions but were posted and fixed for finite periods of time (Tobin, 1972, p. 3). Workers were primarily concerned about their relative wage, leading them to consider quitting a job if their nominal wage fell relative to wages in other firms, but not if the real wage fell uniformly across the economy.

The Phillips curve leads to significant conclusions, and Phillips did not shy away from them. Assuming a 2 percent annual increase in productivity, he observed that "it seems from the relation fitted to the data that if aggregate demand were kept at a value which would maintain a stable level of product prices the associated level of unemployment would be a little under 2.5

percent" (Phillips 1958, p. 299), with Samuelson and Solow (1960) reaching similar conclusions for the U.S.

The critical message from a literal reading of Phillips's analysis is that there is no concept of a full employment level or capacity in the economy. Instead, there is a trade-off along which one must choose between inflation and the unemployment rate. This idea was immediately denied by many economists who, in the tradition of classical analysis, could not conceive of any permanent influence of wage or price inflation on the unemployment rate.

The reactions of Friedman (1968) and Phelps (1967) were to confine the trade-off to the short run, augmenting the Phillips curve with expectations of inflation. This allowed for the possibility of surprise inflation temporarily affecting unemployment. Friedman (1968) theorized, in line with classical analysis, the concept of the natural rate of unemployment as a result of equilibrium in the labor market. This rate is invariant to demand factors and monetary policy. According to this theory, the economy gravitates around the natural rate of unemployment. The concept of gravitation provides the idea of some symmetry between ups and downs.

The original Phillips curve also blurred the distinction between demand and supply factors, although Phillips himself acknowledged in his article the presence of cost-push shock drivers of inflation under some episodes in the U.K. sample. Oil and energy shocks abruptly affected the world economy in the 1970s, causing major shifts in the curve and obscuring it.

In the 1990s, New Keynesian economics revived the Phillips curve by embedding it in micro-founded models of price-setting behavior subject to price frictions, as demonstrated in Chapter 5. This evolution, in comparison to the version augmented with expectations, exhibits more persistence of output deviation following monetary shocks. This persistence results from a staggered price mechanism, where price setters must account for expectations of future demand and, consequently, the future inflation rate, in their decision-making. These developments align the implications of the model with empirical evidence, demonstrating more long-lasting effects of monetary policy on economic activity.

The major controversy surrounding the Phillips curve—whether it is evidence of a short-term or a more medium-term phenomenon—has, however, shifted the focus away from Keynes's primary criticism of the classical analysis of full employment. Keynes did not reject the concept of full employment;

rather, he transformed it into that of maximum aggregate supply, as discussed in Tobin (1972, p. 1). Keynes's perspective aligns with the L function plotted in the right-hand side panel of Figure 12.2, in which the vertical part of the L function indicates a maximum capacity supply in the economy and, consequently, a minimum unemployment rate at which any excess demand would result in price and wage inflation.

Keynes's script, *How to Pay for the War*, published in 1940, describes a price and inflation spiral when the "size of the cake is fixed." In this context, there is a concept of the natural rate of unemployment, positioned asymmetrically like the vertical part of the L function in the right-hand side panel of Figure 12.2, applicable during extraordinary times. During normal times, the economy experiences conditions of involuntary unemployment, where aggregate demand has the leverage to expand the economy without causing significant inflation.

This asymmetric view of the economy surprisingly aligns with Milton Friedman's plucking model. In 1964, Friedman envisions output as occasionally surpassing the ceiling of maximum feasible output, only to be "plucked" down by a cyclical contraction. The difference between Keynes and Friedman lies in the frequency at which maximum output is reached—very rarely under Keynesianism—and in the policies deemed effective for pulling the economy out of a contraction: monetary policy by Friedman and fiscal policy by Keynes.

12.2 Outline of the Results

Section 12.3 initiates the analysis by discussing and deriving the concept of the natural rate of unemployment, demonstrating its independence from monetary policy. Section 12.4 incorporates the assumption of downward nominal wage rigidity to characterize unemployment from a Keynesian perspective. The results are consistent with a natural rate of unemployment only when the labor market is particularly tight; otherwise, unemployment can be critically determined by aggregate demand. Section 12.5 presents a model with information frictions characterized by delays in information, representing a short-run Phillips curve with implications similar to those discussed by Friedman (1968). Section 12.6 contrasts the previous analysis with the persistence effects of monetary policy shocks resulting from the New Keynesian Phillips curve derived in Chapter 5. Section 12.7 merges a labor market characterized by downward nominal wage rigidities into the New Keynesian framework, providing an L-shaped New Keynesian Phillips curve.

12.3 Natural Rate of Unemployment

To understand the inflation/unemployment trade-off, it is useful to start with the concept of the natural rate of unemployment, employing a setting similar to that used in presenting the New Keynesian benchmark model in Chapter 5, with a modelling of the labor market similar to that of Galí (2009).

Consider an economy populated by a large number of identical households. Each household has a continuum of members represented by the unit square and indexed by a pair $(i, z) \in [0, 1] \times [0, 1]$. The first index indicates the type of labor, or age. The second index represents the disutility from work, which is given by z^η in the case the member of the household works, and zero otherwise; η is a parameter with $\eta \geq 0$. The household's per-period utility is given by

$$U_t = \ln C_t - \int_0^1 \left(\int_0^{L_t(i)} z^\eta dz \right) di$$

$$= \ln C_t - \int_0^1 \frac{(L_t(i))^{1+\eta}}{1+\eta} di,$$

in which C_t is a consumption bundle and $L_t(i)$ is the fraction of members of type i who are employed at time t, with $L_t(i) \in [0, 1]$. Each household maximizes the following intertemporal utility:

$$E_{t_0} \left\{ \sum_{t=t_0}^{\infty} \beta^{t-t_0} \left[\ln C_t - \int_0^1 \frac{(L_t(i))^{1+\eta}}{1+\eta} di \right] \right\}, \tag{12.1}$$

in which $E_{t_0} \{\cdot\}$ is the expectation operator at time t_0; β is the rate of time preferences, with $0 < \beta < 1$; and C is a Dixit-Stiglitz aggregator of a continuum of consumption goods produced in the economy

$$C_t = \left[\int_0^1 C_t(j)^{\frac{\theta-1}{\theta}} dj \right]^{\frac{\theta}{\theta-1}},$$

where $\theta > 1$ is the elasticity of substitution across the goods, $(C(j))$, with $j \in [0, 1]$. For the sake of simplicity, special functional forms have been assumed.

At each point in time, households optimize with respect to their consumption and saving choices. In their saving plans, as in Chapter 5, they have access to an ample spectrum of assets to trade in, for we assume that financial markets are complete. Households are subject to a flow budget constraint of the form

$$B_t + P_t C_t = W_t + \int_0^1 W_t(i)L_t(i)di + \Psi_t + \Psi_t^w - T_t, \qquad (12.2)$$

given that B_t is the value of a portfolio with next-period state-contingent payoff W_{t+1} such that

$$B_t = E_t(\tilde{R}_{t,t+1}W_{t+1}),$$

in which $\tilde{R}_{t,t+1}$ is the stochastic nominal discount factor defined in Chapter 5. The right-hand side of (12.2) represents the resources that a household has at time t: namely, the payoff of the portfolio held since time $t-1$, i.e., W_t; labor income $W_t(i)L_t(i)$ for each cohort of workers of type i, in which $(W(i))$ is the nominal wage specific to the type of work done by cohort i; firms' profits (Ψ), less taxes (T); and (Ψ^w), profits of the workers' unions. The resources at time t are spent in purchasing consumption goods C_t, at the price P_t, and the portfolio of value B_t. The household's problem is subject to a standard intertemporal budget constraint, as in Section 5.3 of Chapter 5.

The following set of first-order conditions characterizes the optimal consumption and saving choices at each point in time t:

$$\frac{1}{P_t C_t} = \frac{\beta}{\tilde{R}_{t,t+1}} \frac{1}{P_{t+1}C_{t+1}}.$$

Looking forward from time t, there is a set of first-order conditions (Euler equations) equal to the number of states of nature at time $t+1$. The intertemporal budget constraint of the consumers holds with equality.

The household does not directly determine the fraction of members employed for each type of labor; instead, this responsibility falls to a union. Shifting focus to the problem of determining the employment rate, we start with the firms' problem. The economy is populated by a continuum of measure one of firms. The structure mirrors that of Section 5.3.2 in Chapter 5, with the only difference being the generalization of the framework to a decreasing return technology: $Y_t(j) = A_t(L_t(j))^{\alpha_L}$. Here, A_t represents a technological factor, α_L is a parameter with $0 < \alpha_L \leq 1$, and $L_t(j)$ is an aggregate index of the various types i of labor, which is given by

$$L_t(j) = \left(\int_0^1 (L_t(i))^{\frac{\theta_w - 1}{\theta_w}} di \right)^{\frac{\theta_w}{\theta_w - 1}},$$

in which θ_w is a parameter, with $\theta_w > 1$. Each firm now employs workers from all types i. Given the nominal wage $W_t(i)$ for type i, we can define an appropriate aggregate wage index W as

$$W_t = \left(\int_0^1 (W_t(i))^{1-\theta_w} di \right)^{\frac{1}{1-\theta_w}},$$

and write firm's profits $\Psi_t(j)$ as

$$\Psi_t(j) = (1 - \tau_t)P_t(j)Y_t(j) - W_t L_t(j),$$

considering firm's demand

$$Y_t(j) = \left(\frac{P_t(j)}{P_t} \right)^{-\theta} Y_t,$$

with $\theta > 1$, and in which τ_t is a tax on the firm's revenue and $P(j)$ is the price set by firm j. We are abstracting from public expenditure.

As in Section 5.3 of Chapter 5, the optimal choice of the price $P_t(j)$, which maximizes profits given demand and technology, implies that prices are a mark-up over their marginal costs:

$$P_t(j) = \mu_t \frac{W_t}{A_t} (L_t(j))^{1-\alpha_L},$$

in which the markup μ_t is given by $\mu_t \equiv \theta / [(\theta - 1)(1 - \tau_t)\alpha_L]$. All firms set the same price $P_t(j) = P_t$ for each j. Therefore $L_t(j) = L_t$. The above equation then delivers the following demand of aggregate labor

$$L_t = \left(\frac{\mu_t}{A_t} \frac{W_t}{P_t} \right)^{\frac{1}{\alpha_L - 1}}, \tag{12.3}$$

which is decreasing in the real wage. Note that given the aggregators W_t and L_t, the demand for labor for cohort i is given by

$$L_t(i) = \left(\frac{W_t(i)}{W_t} \right)^{-\theta_w} L_t. \tag{12.4}$$

Unions manage the supply of labor, exercising monopoly power over the labor supply for each type of worker, considering demand (12.4). The union responsible of workers of type i maximizes the following objective:

$$\Psi_t^w = \lambda_t W_t(i) L_t(i) - \frac{L_t(i)^{1+\eta}}{1+\eta}, \tag{12.5}$$

in which the wage bill $W_t(i)L_t(i)$ is converted in units of utility through the marginal utility of nominal income $\lambda_t = 1/(P_t C_t)$. They evaluate the cost of supplying workers considering the household's disutility. The objective in (12.5) is maximized by choosing the wage rate $W_t(i)$ considering demand (12.4). The first-order condition of the optimization problem is

$$\frac{W_t(i)}{P_t} = \mu^w C_t L_t(i)^{\eta},$$

which implies a symmetric choice for all unions such that $W_t(i) = W_t$ and $L_t(i) = L_t$. Note the definition of labor-market markup, $\mu^w \equiv \theta_w/(\theta_w - 1)$.

Accordingly, we can write the above equation as

$$L_t = \left(\frac{1}{\mu^w} \frac{W_t}{P_t C_t} \right)^{\frac{1}{\eta}}, \tag{12.6}$$

describing labor supply as increasing in the real wage and decreasing with respect to aggregate consumption.

Labor demand (12.3) and supply (12.6), as hypothesized by Friedman in several of his works, are critically a function of the real wage. Equilibrium employment is determined at the intersection of these two schedules:

$$L_t^n = \left(\frac{1}{\mu^w} \frac{1}{\mu_t} \right)^{\frac{1}{1+\eta}}.$$

The natural rate of employment, L_t^n, is inversely related to the markup in the goods and labor markets. Critically, it is not influenced by demand factors or the inflation rate.

The framework presented is also suitable to determine and evaluate the unemployment rate, following the insight of Galí (2009). An individual worker of type i, given its utility function and market wages and prices, would be willing to work at time t if and only if

$$\frac{W_t(i)}{P_t} \geq C_t z^{\eta}.$$

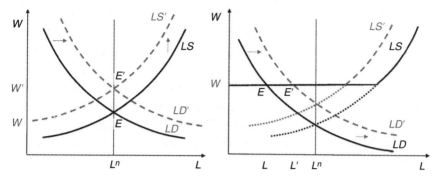

FIGURE 12.3. Equilibrium employment in a diagram with nominal wage (W) on the y-axis and employment (L) on the x-axis. LD = labor demand; LS = labor supply; L^n = natural rate of employment. Left-panel: Labor market with flexible wages. An increase in the price level moves LS and LD upward to LS' and LD', and equilibrium moves from E to E' with employment at the natural rate and an increase in the wage rate. Right panel: Downward wage constraint at W. Labor supply is flat at W and then follows the positively sloped schedule when wages are higher than W. Equilibrium is at E with employment below the natural rate. An increase in the price level shifts LD and LS to LD' and LS', with equilibrium moving to E' with higher employment.

The concept of labor-force participation, $L^s(i)$, can be introduced by considering the "marginal" worker willing to supply labor at the market conditions, and therefore

$$\frac{W_t(i)}{P_t} = C_t(L^s(i))^{\eta}.$$

Since $W_t(i) = W_t$, then $L^s(i) = L^s$, and we can write

$$L_t^s = \left(\frac{W_t}{P_t C_t}\right)^{\frac{1}{\eta}}. \tag{12.7}$$

Comparing with (12.6), we obtain that the (natural) rate of unemployment (u^n) is given by

$$u^n \equiv 1 - \frac{L_t^n}{L_t^s} = 1 - \left(\frac{1}{\mu^w}\right)^{\frac{1}{\eta}}, \tag{12.8}$$

and affected just by the monopolistic distortions in the labor market. While one can introduce time-varying factors, such as a tax on wage bills, to incorporate temporal variations in the natural rate of unemployment, the central point remains unchanged: following Friedman's hypothesis, a natural rate of unemployment exists that is independent of wage or price inflation. The crucial mechanism for this neutrality lies in the dynamics of labor supply and demand. When you depict labor supply and demand on a diagram with nominal wages on the y-axis and employment on the x-axis, as in Figure 12.3, an increase in the price level would shift both the labor supply and the labor demand schedules upward, resulting in a proportional increase in the wage rate without impacting employment. Therefore, the conceptual idea of a trade-off between wage or price inflation and unemployment is flawed from a classical perspective.

12.4   Keynesian Unemployment

As explained by Samuelson and Solow (1960), Keynes's *General Theory* is characterized as "a systematic model that utilizes downward inflexibility of wages and prices to convert any reduction in money spending into a real reduction in output and employment, rather than a balanced reduction in all prices and factor costs." Interestingly, though not contradictorily, Keynes also developed a theory of "demanders" inflation, similar to the neoclassical one, to account for the inflationary surge during the World War II period. This occurred when "government plus investors plus consumers want in real terms . . . more than . . . available producible output," and "in peace time . . . the size of the cake depends on the amount of work done. But in war time the size of the cake is fixed" (Keynes, 1940, p. 4). Even more interestingly, he describes an inflationary price-wage spiral. "Wages and other costs will chase prices upwards, but nevertheless prices will always . . . keep 20 per cent ahead. However much wages are increased, the act of spending these wages will always push prices this much in advance" (Keynes, 1940, p. 66–67). Keynes envisioned an economy running at a "fixed amount of output" during wartime but allowing for fluctuations in employment during peacetime.

To model a Keynesian economy, we can hypothesize that nominal wages are not allowed to fall below a lower bound W due to workers' unwillingness to work at a rate below W. This lower bound is applicable during "normal" times. The original Keynesian norm aims to prevent wages from declining compared to the previous period, but for simplicity, we abstract from dynamics without losing much generality.[1]

---

1. The assumption that the lower bound on wages is a constant greatly simplifies the analysis, transforming it into a static optimization problem. Otherwise, introducing a constraint such

Unions will then maximize (12.5) under labor demand (12.4). The optimal wage choice is to set wages such that

$$W_t(i) = \max\left(W, \mu^w C_t L_t(i)^\eta\right),$$

which again implies a symmetric choice across different cohorts so that $W_t(i) = W$ and $L_t(i) = L$ for each i. The supply schedule resulting from this modified problem exhibits interesting features. It remains flat when the wage is at the lower bound W in a weak labor market. However, as the labor market heats up, workers become more willing to provide additional labor, but they demand higher wages. Equilibrium employment and unemployment now depend on the state of the economy and, critically, on the level of nominal spending.

Figure 12.3, in the right panel, shows this labor supply in a diagram with nominal wages on the y-axis and employment on the x-axis, showing that labor supply is elastic at the wage rate W and increasing when the market wage rises above W.

Labor demand (12.3) still applies to this context and can be rewritten using $Y_t = A_t L_t^{\alpha_L}$ as

$$L_t = \frac{1}{W_t}\frac{\tilde{Y}_t}{\mu_t},$$

in which we have defined nominal spending as $\tilde{Y}_t = P_t Y_t$.

Consider first the conditions under which the level of nominal spending is low. In this case, the downward rigidity constraint binds $W_t = W$, and employment is then determined at

$$L_t = \frac{1}{W}\frac{\tilde{Y}_t}{\mu_t}.$$

This economic state is characterized by low employment, but economic policy, in general, has the potential to boost employment through appropriate measures that increase nominal spending. Figure 12.3 illustrates labor demand for a relatively low level of nominal spending, showing that the equilibrium employment rate is below the natural rate. A right shift of labor demand induced by higher nominal spending has now a positive effect on the employment level.

---

as $W_t \geq W_{t-1}$ would render the optimization problem of the unions dynamic, as shown by Benigno and Ricci (2011).

The model's results can also be expressed in terms of the unemployment rate, using the previous definition. Labor force at the wage rate W is given by

$$L_t^s = \left(\frac{W}{\tilde{Y}_t}\right)^{\frac{1}{\eta}},$$

according to (12.7), using $P_t C_t = P_t Y_t = \tilde{Y}_t$. Unemployment rate is then given by

$$u_t = 1 - \frac{1}{\mu_t}\left(\frac{\tilde{Y}_t}{W}\right)^{1+\frac{1}{\eta}},$$

showing that it is decreasing in nominal spending and increasing in firms' mark-ups.

Transitioning to a state where employment is high and the labor market is tight due to wages being higher than the norm W, we revert to the neoclassical equilibrium, with employment determined by

$$L_t^n = \left(\frac{1}{\mu^w \mu_t}\right)^{\frac{1}{1+\eta}}$$

and unemployment at (12.8).

We can characterize the level of nominal spending, defined as $\tilde{Y}_t^*$, that triggers the economy from one state to the other: it is given by

$$\tilde{Y}_t^* = W \left(\frac{1}{\mu^w u_t}\right)^{\frac{1}{1+\eta}} \mu_t.$$

For values of nominal spending below this threshold, the economy is in the "depressed" state, with the downward rigidity binding and unemployment below the natural rate. For higher values of nominal spending, the economy is at full capacity.

While this framework effectively captures the Keynesian perspective on unemployment determination, relying on the assumption of nominal rigidities, it also offers broader policy implications. Keynes asserted that demand policy stemming from fiscal measures could enhance real allocation and reduce unemployment, but he believed monetary policy to be entirely ineffective. He considered a demand for money, known as the liquidity-preference function, which, in conditions of underemployment, would passively adjust to any change in the money supply, rendering monetary policy entirely ineffective. Furthermore, he posited that underemployment conditions would be prevalent most of the time.

However, the analysis in this section also aligns with a crucial role for monetary policy in controlling nominal spending. This perspective resonates with the views of Friedman and Schwartz in 1963, indicating that depressions are often associated with a decline in the money stock, especially when correlated with nominal spending. The proposed approach advocates for the stabilization of the money stock, emphasizing its importance in stabilizing nominal spending and attaining the natural rate of output.

Interestingly, the conjecture that the model economy is asymmetric with respect to the natural rate of unemployment or potential output is also shared by Friedman's "plucking model." In Friedman (1964, 1993), "output is viewed as bumping above the ceiling of maximum feasible output except that every now and then it is plucked down by a cyclical contraction." (Friedman, 1964, p. 17). And he adds: "Given institutional rigidities in prices, the contraction takes in considerable measure the form of a decline in output. . . . the size of the decline in output can vary widely. When subsequent recovery sets in, it tends to return output to the ceiling; it cannot go beyond." (Friedman, 1964, p. 17). Dupraz, Nakamura, and Steinsson (2019) have indeed recast Friedman's "plucking model" of the business cycle within a labor-market model characterized by downward wage rigidity to characterize the asymmetric behavior of the unemployment rate in the U.S. economy. Along this line of reasoning, the difference between Keynes's and Friedman's views of the cycle is in how frequently the ceiling is reached, very rarely in Keynesian economics.

The next section will delve into another aspect of Friedman's perspective, where he argues for temporary deviations of unemployment with respect to the natural rate, attributing them to informational rigidities. This view offers an interpretation of a more symmetric cycle, with the concept of the natural rate residing somewhere in the middle.

12.5 Short-Run Non-neutralities

It is quite common in the history of economic thought, even from classical economists, to deviate from the notion that the economy is always at the natural rate. We previously discussed, in the introduction to Part II, the perspective of David Hume, the father of the quantity theory, who hypothesized periods of vibrant economic activity following an expansion in the supply of gold before prices would fully adjust. A notable exception to even short-run neutralities is found in the research agenda of real business cycle theories, which relegates monetary policy to unimportant for the real economy even at the short-run frequency.

Following Phillips's findings, scholars did not dismiss the relationship he discovered between inflation and unemployment; instead, they interpreted any trade-off as a short-run phenomenon occurring around the natural rate of unemployment. The key departure from the ideal neoclassical world, however, was not the assumption of wage or price rigidity but the acknowledgment of information frictions leading to relative price distortions and influencing the effects of inflation on economic activity. The assumed short length of these frictions justified only short-run non-neutrality.

To this end, we present a simplified version of a model with informational frictions, which can also be interpreted as a model of wage rigidity. We consider the framework detailed in Section 12.3 and the optimization problem faced by unions. Assume the presence of informational frictions, where unions do not have updated information on the state of the economy. A simple way to model this is to assume that wage setting and labor choices are made based on the information available from the previous period. This convenient assumption aligns the analysis with a scenario in which wages are set one period in advance, albeit in a forward-looking way, resembling a form of nominal rigidity.

The optimal choice of the wage rate, maximizing (12.5) with previous period information, implies, in a symmetric equilibrium, that

$$W_t = \mu^w E_{t-1} \left\{ P_t Y_t L_t^\eta \right\},$$

using $Y_t = C_t$. Labor demand is unchanged and given by:

$$L_t = \frac{1}{\mu_t} \frac{P_t Y_t}{W_t}. \tag{12.9}$$

We can derive a first-order approximation of the above two equations around a non-stochastic steady state to obtain

$$\hat{W}_t = E_{t-1} \left\{ \hat{P}_t + \eta \hat{L}_t + \hat{Y}_t \right\} \tag{12.10}$$

and

$$\hat{L}_t = \hat{P}_t + \hat{Y}_t - \hat{W}_t - \hat{\mu}_t, \tag{12.11}$$

in which a variable with a hat denotes log-deviations with respect to the steady state. We can further take the expectation at time $t-1$ of (12.11) and combine it with (12.10), substituting for $\hat{W}_t$ to obtain

$$E_{t-1}\hat{L}_t = -\frac{E_{t-1}\{\hat{\mu}_t\}}{1+\eta},$$

and therefore the expected employment level settles at the expected value of its natural rate, i.e., $E_{t-1}\hat{L}_t = E_{t-1}\hat{L}_t^n$.

We can further combine (12.10) and (12.11), using the above result, to obtain

$$\hat{L}_t - E_{t-1}\hat{L}_t^n = (\hat{P}_t + \hat{Y}_t) - E_{t-1}(\hat{P}_t + \hat{Y}_t) - (\hat{\mu}_t - E_{t-1}\hat{\mu}_t),$$

showing that unexpected variations in nominal spending, on the right-hand side, correlate positively with changes in the employment level relative to the expected natural rate, on the left-hand side of the equation. It is crucial to note that upward and downward unexpected variations exhibit symmetric effects. From the above equation, using $\hat{L}_t = \alpha_L^{-1}(\hat{Y}_t - \hat{A}_t)$, we can derive a representation in terms of a more canonical Phillips curve, augmented with expectations, as

$$\pi_t = E_{t-1}\pi_t + k(\hat{Y}_t - \hat{Y}_t^n) + v_t, \qquad (12.12)$$

in which π_t is the inflation rate given by $\pi_t = \hat{P}_t - \hat{P}_{t-1} = p_t - p_{t-1}$; $k \equiv (1-\alpha_L)/\alpha_L$ and

$$v_t = \frac{\eta + \alpha_L}{1+\eta}(\hat{\mu}_t - E_{t-1}\hat{\mu}_t) - (\hat{A}_t - E_{t-1}\hat{A}_t);$$

while the natural rate of output is given by

$$\hat{Y}_t^n \equiv \hat{A}_t - \frac{\alpha_L}{1+\eta}\hat{\mu}_t.$$

In the equation (12.12), unexpected variations in the inflation rate positively correlate with deviations of output from the expected natural rate; v_t acts as a supply shifter of the curve, driven by unexpected movements in productivity and in the markup.

We can also express the Phillips curve as a relationship between inflation and unemployment. Note, first, that we can combine (12.7) and (12.9) to obtain the ratio of employment with respect to labor force, given by

$$\frac{L_t}{L_t^s} = \mu_t^{\frac{1}{\eta}} L_t^{1+\frac{1}{\eta}}.$$

Using the definition of the unemployment rate $u_t = 1 - L_t/L_t^s$ and the approximation $u_t \approx -\ln L_t/L_t^s$, which is accurate for small values of u, we can obtain the unemployment rate as

$$u_t = -\frac{1}{\eta} \ln \mu_t - \left(1 + \frac{1}{\eta}\right) \ln L_t$$

or, expressing it in deviations from the steady state,

$$u_t - u^n = -\left(1 + \frac{1}{\eta}\right) (\hat{L}_t - \hat{L}_t^n).$$

Therefore, we can write (12.12) in the following form:

$$\pi_t = E_{t-1}\pi_t - k_u(u_t - u^n) + v_t, \tag{12.13}$$

in which $k_u = [(1 - \alpha_L)\eta]/(1 + \eta)$.

The two versions of the Phillips curve augmented with expectations described in this section, (12.12) and (12.13), differ in the measure of economic slack, respectively, output gap and unemployment. Nonetheless, they share common theoretical underpinnings with relevant policy implications and contribute to the understanding of the evidence on the inflation/unemployment trade-off.

The first important feature is that the length of short-run neutrality is just one period, aligning with Friedman's reasoning that you can't fool all the people all of the time; the Phillips curve can only be transitory. Concerning the duration of this transitory period, Friedman in 1968 also envisioned a relatively long adjustment, considering the fact that adaptive expectations take time to incorporate new information. Friedman (1970a) further adds: "I believe, that full adjustment to monetary disturbances takes very long time and affects many economic magnitudes" (Friedman 1970a, p. 235). With rational expectations, as discussed in the example above and consistently with Lucas (1972, 1973), the transitory path can only last one period.

The second important feature, consistent again with Friedman (1968), is that only unexpected variations in the inflation rate can cause improvements in economic activity. To substantially stimulate the economy, monetary policy has to engineer an accelerating inflation rate, given the catch-up of private sector expectations.

The third feature is symmetry, treating expansions and contractions of output in the same way with respect to the natural rate, creating specular inflationary or disinflationary effects.

It is not clear in this theory what determines the equilibrium inflation rate. It could be the inflation target of the central bank, if any. Unemployment or output is at its natural rate when expectations of inflation are aligned with current inflation, not necessarily at the target inflation the central bank follows.

The analyses of Friedman (1968) and Phelps (1967) were timely in providing an interpretation of the events of the 1970s, specifically the Great Inflation. This period saw the breakdown of the U.S. Phillips curve, as recognized by Samuelson and Solow (1960), into an undecipherable pattern.

As depicted in Figure 12.1, inflation began to rise around 1965 in the aftermath of the Kennedy-Johnson tax cut and initial preparations for the Vietnam War. Unemployment was exceptionally low at that time, reaching historically low values below 4 percent. Inflation increased from 2 percent to 6 percent by the end of 1969.

Under William Martin's chairmanship of the Federal Reserve, the federal funds rate climbed from 4 percent at the beginning of 1965 to 9 percent by the end of 1969. This led to a contraction in economic activity, causing the unemployment rate to rise to 6 percent at the end of 1970.

Notably, the figure illustrates a gradual upward movement of inflation expectations that began oscillating around values close to 4 percent at the beginning of 1970.

Arthur Burns, who assumed the chairmanship of the Federal Reserve in 1970, initiated a reduction in interest rates, bringing them down to 3 percent by the end of 1970. Meanwhile, the Nixon administration sought to stimulate the economy through a tax cut, attempting to address the inflation issue by implementing price and wage controls. These controls were put into effect in August 1971 and concluded through different phases in April 1974.

Despite these efforts, the inflation problem persisted, and the first oil shock of 1973 further aggravated both inflation and inflation expectations. Rather than decreasing, the unemployment rate rose, leading the economy into a period of stagflation—a combination of a high inflation rate and high unemployment. This phenomenon was unprecedented and not anticipated under the Phillips curve. Friedman was correct in arguing that it would fall apart, resulting in more inflation with the same unemployment and output.

The Phillips curve in equation (12.13) supports this view by indicating that as inflation expectations rise, inflation should also increase for the same unemployment rate. Inflation expectations remained elevated, reaching 9 percent as the second oil shock hit the economy in 1979. Moreover, equation (12.13) highlights the role of supply shocks in driving inflation up at the same

316 THE INFLATION-UNEMPLOYMENT TRADE-OFF

unemployment rate, potentially exacerbating the trade-off. While Phillips (1958) did not disregard cost-push shocks in his analysis, before the 1970s they played a minor role.

The schedule (12.13) can also help us understand the successful period of disinflation named after Volcker, who assumed the chairmanship of the Federal Reserve in 1979. While the monetary policy strategy of Burns was characterized by a kind of stop-and-go approach—accommodating when inflation was under control and tightening when it was increasing—Volcker took decisive action to reduce inflation. He adopted control of money aggregates and allowed interest rates to adjust, reaching values as high as 22 percent. As a result, inflation dropped from 13 percent in 1979 to 4 percent in 1982, with inflation expectations decreasing proportionally.[2]

This successful disinflation, as explained in (12.13), can be attributed in part to the substantial rise in unemployment, reaching almost 11 percent at the end of 1982. This not only aligns with the relationship between inflation and unemployment in (12.13), but also reflects how the Fed signaled its determination to bring down inflation, thereby improving credibility and lowering inflation expectations.

12.6 Persistent Monetary Non-neutralities

The new specification of the Phillips curve that emerged in the 1970s does justice to inflation expectations and confines the original Phillips curve trade-off to the short run, centering the relationship symmetrically around the concept of the natural rate of output or unemployment. Assuming the central bank controls nominal spending, a one-time increase in nominal spending would have only a one-period impact on real economic activity under rational expectations. To produce longer-lasting effects, adaptive expectations would be required.

The contentious debate surrounding the duration of the effects of monetary policy on economic activity has garnered new perspectives through empirical evidence that better identifies monetary policy shocks. This evidence suggests prolonged effects on economic activity, indicating a hump-shaped function as a more accurate descriptor of the observed pattern. This function reveals an initial lag or delay, followed by a peak approximately eight

---

2. Goodfriend and King (2005) emphasize the significance of the unemployment cost for the imperfect credibility of the disinflation plan.

quarters after the shock. The effects on economic activity gradually diminish, reaching long-run neutrality.

Inspired by these analyses, the New Keynesian literature that developed in the 1990s provided models for the longer effects of monetary policy shocks on economic activity. These models rely first on the assumption of price rigidities and staggered price mechanisms, enabling them to better fit the empirical evidence.

Chapter 5 has presented the benchmark New Keynesian model, showing one key tenet of the analysis in the AS equation, the so-called New Keynesian Phillips curve, represented here as:

$$\pi_t - \pi = \kappa(\hat{Y}_t - \hat{Y}_t^n) + \beta E_t(\pi_{t+1} - \pi). \tag{12.14}$$

The equation demonstrates a connection between inflation in deviation from the target (π) and the output gap, representing deviations of output from its natural rate $(\hat{Y}^n)$. This relationship closely resembles the second addendum of the neoclassical curve, as shown in (12.12). However, a key difference lies in the additional term on the right-hand side of (12.14). This term captures expectations about future inflation deviations from the target, in contrast to the past-period expectations of current inflation presented in (12.12).

The reason for this significant difference, as discussed in Chapter 5, is in the forward-looking behavior of price setters under Calvo's price-setting model. When price setters are allowed to change their prices, they anticipate that the price set today will remain in place in the future with some probability. As a result, they must assess the future demand for their goods and economic conditions by forming expectations about the general price index and its rate of change.

There is another shared characteristic between the two AS equations, grounded in the central concept of the natural rate of output. When the actual output aligns with the natural rate not only in the current period but also in all future periods, inflation remains on target. Conversely, if inflation hits the target consistently over time, then output is operating at the natural rate. It is important to note, however, that achieving inflation at the target at any given point in time requires all current and future output gaps to be zero.

In contrast to the Phillips curve in (12.12), the closure of the output gap first brings inflation to the target, and subsequently, expectations align. This differs from the scenario where inflation merely equals the previous period's inflation expectations, leaving the inflation rate undetermined. Friedman was arguing that expected inflation was the determinant of actual inflation in his version of the Phillips curve.

The new form of the Phillips curve has important implications for the duration of the non-neutrality of monetary policy. Consider a process for the log nominal spending, $\tilde{y}$, of the form

$$\tilde{y}_t = \pi + \tilde{y}_{t-1} + \varepsilon_t, \tag{12.15}$$

consistent with an inflation target π and in which ε is a white noise process. Note that $\tilde{y}_t = p_t + y_t$, in which p and y are the logs of prices and output. We can write the New Keynesian Phillips curve (12.14)

$$p_t - p_{t-1} - \pi = \kappa(\tilde{y}_t - p_t) + \beta E_t(p_{t+1} - p_t - \pi),$$

abstracting from shocks to the natural rate of output.

We have obtained a second-order stochastic difference equation in p. Using the lag operator L introduced in Chapter 7, we can write it as

$$\left[\mathsf{L}^{-1} - \left(1 + \frac{1}{\beta} + \frac{\kappa}{\beta}\right) + \frac{1}{\beta}\mathsf{L}\right] p_t = -\frac{\kappa}{\beta}\tilde{y}_t - \frac{1-\beta}{\beta}\pi,$$

and therefore

$$\left[\mathsf{L}^{-1} - (\gamma_1 + \gamma_2) + \gamma_1\gamma_2\mathsf{L}\right] p_t = -\gamma_1\gamma_2\kappa\tilde{y}_t - \gamma_1\gamma_2(1-\beta)\pi,$$

in which the eigenvalues γ_1 and γ_2, with $0 < \gamma_1 < 1 < \gamma_2$, associated with the characteristic polynomial of the second-order stochastic difference equation satisfy:

$$\gamma_1 + \gamma_2 = 1 + \frac{1}{\beta} + \frac{\kappa}{\beta}, \tag{12.16}$$

$$\gamma_1\gamma_2 = \frac{1}{\beta}. \tag{12.17}$$

We can then write the previous equation as

$$(1 - \gamma_1\mathsf{L})(1 - \gamma_2^{-1}\mathsf{L}^{-1})p_t = \gamma_1\kappa\tilde{y}_t + \gamma_1(1-\beta)\pi,$$

which can be solved, using similar steps to those in Section 7.3 of Chapter 7, to obtain

$$p_t = \gamma_1 p_{t-1} + \frac{\kappa}{\beta(\gamma_2 - 1)}\tilde{y}_t + \left(\frac{\kappa}{\beta(\gamma_2 - 1)^2} + \frac{1-\beta}{\beta(\gamma_2 - 1)}\right)\pi.$$

The above equation can be further simplified using (12.16) and (12.17) to obtain

$$p_t = \gamma_1 (\pi + p_{t-1}) + (1 - \gamma_1) \tilde{y}_t \tag{12.18}$$
$$= \pi + \gamma_1 p_{t-1} + (1 - \gamma_1)(\tilde{y}_{t-1} + \varepsilon_t),$$

in which we have further used (12.15) to get to the second line.

Equation (12.18) is key to understanding the propagation of a nominal spending shock. A one-time impulse to nominal spending, let's say an increase in ε_t, has an impact effect on p_t equal to $(1 - \gamma_1)$, but then it keeps propagating into future prices decaying at the rate γ_1. The effect on p_{t+j} is given by the factor $(1 - \gamma_1^{j+1})$, which converges to the unitary value in the long run. Considering that output is given by $y_t = \tilde{y}_t - p_t$, its impulse response is specular with respect to that of price, with the largest impact, γ_1, at the time of the shock, and then decaying to zero at the rate γ_1. The key parameter to evaluate the magnitude and persistence of the real effects is γ_1, which is inversely related to the slope of the NK Phillips curve. The flatter the curve, the more persistent is the shock.

The analysis aligns with the concept of persistent monetary non-neutrality, indicating enduring real effects from changes in nominal spending. However, the impulse response does not exhibit the expected hump-shaped pattern. To address this, one might reconsider the example using an autoregressive process of order 1 for nominal spending growth, as outlined by Woodford (2003, Ch. 3). Woodford also discusses how the degree of strategic complementarity in price setting can positively influence the persistence of a monetary shock, enhancing the empirical fit of the NK Phillips curve.

The NK Phillips curve can also be represented by replacing the output gap with the employment gap, defined as the deviation of the employment level from its natural rate. It is important to note that, in this framework, the unemployment rate, as defined in previous sections, remains at the natural rate at all times due to fully flexible wages. Introducing wage rigidities would also lead to deviations of unemployment from the natural rate, as shown in Galí (2009).

Taking a broader perspective, this version of the Phillips curve is also suited to describing the qualitative pattern of inflation and economic activity during the 1970s. It assigns a significant role to inflation expectations and supply shocks, which are embedded in the variations affecting the natural rate of output in (12.14).

12.7   An L-Shaped New Keynesian Phillips Curve

Any type of Phillips curve is subject to challenges and can be easily disproved by the data. The reason is that it is difficult to identify a supply schedule from inflation and economic activity data that accurately reflects the "equilibrium" movements of a complex economic system, especially with demand and supply shifting driven by several perturbations, and monetary and fiscal policies interacting with them.[3]

The events of the 2007–2008 financial crisis and the COVID-19 pandemic provide examples of the relationship between inflation and economic activity that warrant further consideration when explained by the NK Phillips curve. Just before the financial crisis, the world economy experienced a significant surge in oil prices, as highlighted in the hatched shaded area in Figure 12.1. Surprisingly, this surge did not translate into an increase in inflation, thanks to anchored inflation expectations, and the spike in oil prices soon reverted.

Subsequently, the financial crisis witnessed a profound decline in economic activity, with unemployment rising from 4.5 percent to 10 percent in just two years, reaching its peak in October 2009 at levels comparable to those of the Volcker disinflation period. However, unlike that previous episode, this contraction in economic activity did not bring about any significant disinflationary pressures.[4] Core inflation remained at a low 0.6 percent at the same time unemployment peaked, as shown in Figure 12.1.

The intriguing evidence, labeled the "missing disinflation," prompted researchers to question the validity of a traditional Phillips curve. A compelling explanation that supports the continued relevance of the curve posits that it has significantly flattened, accommodating the modest downward shifts in inflation following severe contractions. Hazell et al. (2022) estimated a slope for the curve, suggesting that a 1 percent increase in the unemployment rate resulted in only a 0.34-point decrease in inflation.

Similarly, the sharp increase in the unemployment rate during the COVID-19 pandemic, surpassing 13 percent, did not align with a significant decline in core inflation. Core inflation reached its lowest point at 1.17 in June 2020 on an annual basis, providing another instance of a "missing disinflation."

---

3. Refer to the analysis of McLeay and Tenreyro (2019) for the issues associated with identification strategies of the Phillips curve.

4. To identify correctly the sacrifice ratio during the Volcker disinflation is, however, critical to account for the fall in inflation expectations.

The puzzle arises when considering that the explanation for the missing disinflation does not seem to account for the post-COVID-19 inflationary surge, starting in March 2021, when inflation exceeded the 2-percent target and soared to 6.5 percent a year later. One potential factor was the unprecedented monetary and fiscal accommodation implemented to counteract the pandemic shock, as detailed in Section 9.7 of Chapter 9. However, at first glance, the scale of the expansion does not appear incomparable to the severity of the contraction during the financial crisis. Given the historical precedent of a missing disinflation during that time, one might have expected a corresponding absence of an inflationary surge.

The challenge intensifies when considering that the economy faced negative supply shocks stemming from energy and oil price increases, as well as supply shortages due to the pandemic's resource misallocation and heightened demand for specific goods. Surprisingly, the magnitudes of these shocks, measured by various metrics, did not surpass those seen during the oil shock of the 1970s or those of the substantial fluctuations in oil prices during the financial crisis. Additionally, inflation expectations remained relatively anchored in the 2020s, as illustrated in Figure 12.1.

Benigno and Eggertsson (2023, 2024) provide an explanation for this puzzling evidence by incorporating the Keynesian unemployment theory into the New-Keynesian Phillips curve. In essence, the fiscal and monetary stimuli positioned the economy at the kink point of the L curve, as depicted in Figure 12.4 in the second row's right-hand side panel. At this juncture, and under the conditions of a heated labor market discussed in Section 12.4, where the unemployment rate has reached the natural level, any further increase in demand becomes inherently inflationary. Moreover, they demonstrate that on the vertical segment of the curve, supply shocks have more pronounced effects on inflation, compared to when the labor market is weak.

Figures 12.1 and 12.4 strongly indicate the exceptional nature of episodes over the last 65 years when the natural rate of unemployment is reached. Observationally, this threshold is hypothesized to be at 3.7%. Only during the Vietnam War and after the COVID-19 pandemic was this level reached and slightly surpassed with lower figures. These instances correlate with inflation escalating on the vertical segment of the L-shaped Phillips curve.

Remarkably, the period from 1970 to 1987, as previously discussed, is characterized by a high inflation rate, but unemployment remains far from the natural rate. The scatter plots in the 1970–1987 sample provide explanations supported by supply shocks and the disanchoring of inflation expectations. In the

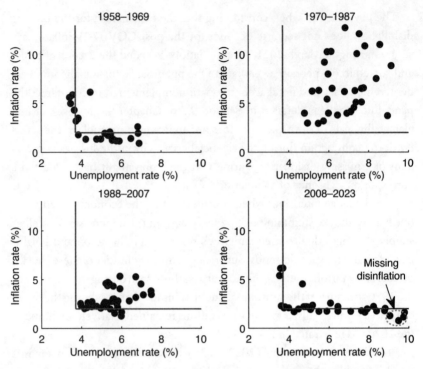

FIGURE 12.4. United States scatter plots of core CPI inflation rate vs. unemployment rate at a semi-annual frequency for different samples, together with L-curve delimited by inflation rate at 2% and unemployment rate at 3.7%. *Source: U.S. Bureau of Labor Statistics.*

last panel on the second row, points within the circle correspond to observations linked to the missing disinflation discussed earlier. However, aside from these points, all inflation and unemployment data align along the 2-percent inflation line, except for those related to the inflationary surge in the 2020s.

To elaborate on this explanation, consider a labor-market model in which workers set wages according

$$W_t = \begin{cases} W_{t-1}(\Pi_t^e)^{\delta_\pi} & \text{if } u_t > u^n \\ W_t^{flex} = \mu^w P_t Y_t L_t^\eta & \text{if } u_t = u^n \end{cases}.$$

The first line considers a slack labor market, when the unemployment rate is above the natural rate. Wages follow the Keynesian norm, according to which they are not falling below the previous period's rate, and they also adjust to expectations of inflation, Π_t^e, through a parameter $\delta_\pi \geq 0$. The case $\delta_\pi = 0$ characterizes complete downward nominal wage rigidity. The second line captures conditions of a tight labor market, when unemployment is at the natural rate. Wages react to economic conditions as in the flex-wage model of Section 12.3.[5]

Considering log-deviations of the above equations with respect to the steady state, we obtain

$$
\hat{w}_t = \begin{cases} \hat{w}_{t-1} - (\pi_t - \pi) + \delta_\pi E_t(\pi_{t+1} - \pi) & \text{if} \quad u_t > u^n \\[2mm] \hat{Y}_t + \eta \hat{L}_t & \text{if} \quad u_t = u^n \end{cases}, \quad (12.19)
$$

expressing the equations in terms of real wages, $\hat{w}_t$.

Considering now the NK Phillips curve derived in Chapter 5 and maintaining the assumption of decreasing return to labor, it can be also expressed in terms of real marginal costs and, in a log-linear approximation, is represented by:

$$
\pi_t - \pi = k_m(\hat{\mu}_t + \hat{w}_t + (1 - \alpha_L)\hat{L}_t - \hat{A}_t) + \beta E_t(\pi_{t+1} - \pi),
$$

for some parameter $k_m > 0$, or, equivalently, by

$$
\pi_t - \pi = k_m(\hat{\mu}_t + \hat{w}_t + \hat{L}_t - \hat{Y}_t) + \beta E_t(\pi_{t+1} - \pi), \quad (12.20)
$$

using the production function $\hat{Y}_t = \hat{A}_t + \alpha_L \hat{L}_t$.

Let us focus first on the conditions in which the labor market is tight and wages are characterized by the second line in (12.19). Then substituting this expression into (12.20) for $\hat{w}_t$, we obtain

$$
\pi_t - \pi = k_m[(1 + \eta)\hat{L}_t + \hat{\mu}_t] + \beta E_t(\pi_{t+1} - \pi). \quad (12.21)
$$

Similarly, when the labor market is loose, using the first line of (12.19), we obtain

$$
\pi_t - \pi = \tilde{k}_m[\hat{w}_{t-1} + (1 - \alpha_L)\hat{L}_t + \hat{\mu}_t - \hat{A}_t] + \tilde{k}_\pi E_t(\pi_{t+1} - \pi), \quad (12.22)
$$

in which $\tilde{k}_m = k_m/(1 + k_m)$ and $\tilde{k}_\pi = (\beta + k_m \delta_\pi)/(1 + k_m)$.

The comparison between (12.21) and (12.22) carries interesting implications. Firstly, the slope of the curve concerning employment and, similarly, the

---

5. As discussed in Section 12.4, we can also express the wage equations by using the triggering unemployment rate, the point at which the flexible wage rate exceeds the norm. This adjustment does not alter the qualitative results that will be obtained.

curve expressed in terms of output indicate a flatter curve under loose labor market conditions (where $\tilde{k}_m < k_m$) than under tight conditions. Secondly, and similarly, the response to the markup shock, which in a more general model is isomorphic to an energy price or an oil price shock, is also lower under a loose labor market than under a tight one. The third implication is the incorporation of past real wages into (12.22), creating a much more sluggish behavior of inflation than under a tight labor market. Finally, $\tilde{k}_\pi$ can be larger or smaller than β, depending critically on the degree of wage indexation, with δ_π being larger or smaller.[6]

Drawing implications for the unemployment rate is straightforward under conditions of a tight labor market, where wages are perfectly flexible, and thus, unemployment is at the natural rate. However, this does not align with conditions where output or employment is at its natural rate. As shown in equation (12.21), inflation will be determined by demand and supply shocks on a steep short-run Phillips curve.

In contrast, when the labor market is not tight, we can also express the short-run Phillips curve in terms of the unemployment rate. To this end, consider that in a log-linear approximation, labor-force participation (12.7) is given by:

$$\hat{L}_t^s = \frac{1}{\eta}(\hat{w}_t - \hat{Y}_t). \tag{12.23}$$

We can use (12.23) in (12.20), to obtain

$$\hat{L}_t^s = \frac{1}{\eta}(\Omega_t - \hat{\mu}_t - \hat{L}_t),$$

having defined

$$\Omega_t \equiv \frac{\pi_t - \pi - \beta E_t(\pi_{t+1} - \pi)}{k_m}.$$

Using the above equations, it follows that the unemployment gap is given by

$$u_t - u^n = \hat{L}_t^s - \hat{L}_t = \frac{1}{\eta}\Omega_t - \frac{1}{\eta}\hat{\mu}_t - \left(1 + \frac{1}{\eta}\right)\hat{L}_t,$$

6. Note also that equation (12.22) is influenced by the productivity shock. When both equations are expressed in terms of output, they will each display this term, albeit with different coefficients.

through which we can express employment as a function of the unemployment gap

$$\hat{L}_t = -\frac{\eta}{1+\eta}(u_t - u^n) + \frac{1}{1+\eta}(\Omega_t - \hat{\mu}_t).$$

We can substitute the above expression in (12.22) for $\hat{L}_t$ to obtain:

$$\pi_t - \pi = \tilde{k}_u(\hat{w}_{t-1} - \gamma_u(u_t - u^n) + \gamma_\mu \hat{\mu}_t - \hat{A}_t) + \tilde{k}'_\pi E_t(\pi_{t+1} - \pi),$$
$$(12.24)$$

which applies when $u_t > u^n$ for positive parameters $\tilde{k}_u$, $\tilde{k}'_\pi$ and γ_u, γ_μ.

It is key to note that the following inequalities hold: $\tilde{k}_u < \tilde{k}$ and $\gamma_u < 1$, implying a relatively flat slope of the inflation/unemployment trade-off.[7] As long as unemployment is above the natural rate, variations in the unemployment rate could have a smaller impact on inflation. Once the unemployment rate reaches the natural rate, any relationship between inflation and unemployment ceases to exist, as inflation becomes driven by excess output or employment above its natural rate.

Within the framework of the Keynesian unemployment theory, this configuration would be consistent with economies frequently operating below their potential. This perspective finds visual support in Figures 12.1 and 12.4, indicating that the U.S. economy rarely reached conditions of very low unemployment rates and tight labor markets, except under specific circumstances. In these instances, inflation tends to rise rapidly as the economy approaches full employment.

However, as already discussed, it is noteworthy that inflation also surged in the 1970s. According to this theory, the driving forces behind the inflation during that period occurred under a loose labor market, influenced by adverse supply shocks combined with disanchored inflation expectations. Note that if wages more closely follow inflation expectations, i.e., a higher value of δ_π, then this implies a larger $\tilde{k}'_\pi$ in (12.24) and, therefore, a greater impact of inflation expectations on inflation.

In contrast, the inflationary surge in the 2020s occurred under conditions of a very tight labor market, where demand stimuli and supply shocks interacted with a steeper aggregate-supply equation. Episodes of tight labor markets are extraordinary in the last century, primarily associated with periods of wars, such as World Wars I and II, the Korean War, and the Vietnam

---

7. Note that $\tilde{k}_u = k_m(1+\eta)/[(1+k_m)(1+\eta) + (1-\alpha_L)]$ and is lower than $\tilde{k}_m$ provided $\alpha_L < 1$. Moreover, $\gamma_u = (1-\alpha_L)/(1+\eta)$.

War, or catastrophes, such as the recent COVID-19 pandemic. Benigno and Eggertsson (2023) similarly describe conditions of a tight labor market associated with a vacancy-to-unemployed ratio consistently exceeding the unitary value, which characterizes such episodes.

A reading of events through a steep Phillips curve rather than a flat one has different policy implications, given the same other drivers of the curve. Regarding the increase in unemployment necessary to tame inflation, it is smaller in the first case and larger in the second.

12.8   References

The seminal analysis of the Phillips curve is found in the work of Phillips (1958). Since then, the curve has attracted considerable attention from researchers, sparking important debates and controversies. Samuelson and Solow (1960) were the first to label the Phillips curve and analyze a similar scatter plot for the U.S. economy. They also suggested that it is the kind of relationship that depends heavily on "remembered experience," emphasizing the importance of incorporating past observations on inflation into the actual relationship.

Phelps (1967) formulated a Phillips curve that incorporated the expected rate of inflation, questioning the validity of any curve lacking this element. He also defined the equilibrium utilization ratio as the point when the actual rate of inflation equals its expected value. In his 1968 presidential address to the American Economic Association, Friedman introduced the concept of the natural rate of unemployment, viewing it as independent of money wages and arising from equilibrium in the labor market. He further explored the real effects of an unexpected increase in the rate of money growth.

Expanding on Phelps's economic hypothesis (1970), which envisions goods being produced on different "islands" that capture the barriers to information faced by producers, Lucas (1972, 1973) introduced Phillips curves that depict a short-run relationship between inflation and economic activity. His model is grounded in agents' imperfect information, where they are unable to distinguish between changes in relative prices and those in the general price index. Subsequently, Woodford (2001a) further elaborated on the concept of information frictions inspired by Phelps's parable, introducing imperfect knowledge of others' expectations. In this context, non-neutrality extends beyond the short run and aligns with the effects of monetary policy shocks, as identified in structural VAR analysis.

The conclusive section of Chapter 5 has already outlined some of the relevant references with respect to the New Keynesian Phillips curve. De Vroey (2016) provides a thorough perspective on the evolution of the Phillips curve.

The labor-market model presented in this chapter is quite stylized and draws from the analysis of Galí (2009). Extensive literature has incorporated models with more detailed frictions in the labor market, following the approach of Mortensen and Pissarides (1994), into the New Keynesian framework. Notable examples in this vast literature, such as Blanchard and Galí (2010), Gertler and Trigari (2009), and Michaillat (2014), have formulated Phillips curves in terms of the unemployment rate. A recent alternative approach has been taken by Benigno and Eggertsson (2023), who express the New Keynesian Phillips curve as a relationship between inflation and the vacancy-to-unemployed ratio. Erceg, Henderson, and Levin (2000) have introduced symmetric wage rigidities in the New Keynesian model, analyzing optimal monetary policy in that context.

Tobin (1972) underscored the relevance of downward nominal wage rigidities in explaining the relationship found by Phillips. Extensive empirical literature, including studies by Barattieri, Basu, and Gottschalk (2014) and Dickens et al. (2007), has supported this evidence. Models rationalizing nonlinear Phillips curves based on the downward nominal wage rigidity constraint have been put forth by Benigno and Ricci (2011) and Eggertsson, Mehrotra, and Robbins (2019). Benigno and Eggertsson (2023, 2024) incorporated a downward rigidity constraint into a New Keynesian Phillips curve for price inflation. This addition introduces nonlinearity into the curve, offering an explanation for various phenomena associated with the co-movements between inflation and labor-market tightness in the U.S. economy. Dupraz, Nakamura, and Steinsson (2019) developed a microfounded "plucking model" of the business cycle, relying on downward nominal wage rigidity. Harding, Lindé, and Trabandt (2023) characterized a nonlinear Phillips curve due to a quasi-kinked demand schedule for goods produced by firms.

Empirical studies on the Phillips curve are extensive and varied. Some recent works, including those by Ball, Leigh, and Mishra (2022), Barnichon and Shapiro (2022), Gordon (1977, 2013), Hazzell et al. (2022), and McLeay and Tenreyro (2019), employ various identification strategies.

Coibion and Gorodnichenko (2015) and Coibion, Gorodnichenko, and Kamdar (2018) argue that the use of survey data on inflation expectations can address the puzzling shortcoming of the New Keynesian Phillips curve under rational expectations, such as the 2008–2009 "missing disinflation." Bernanke and Blanchard (2023) and Gagliardone and Gertler (2023) explain the 2020s inflationary surge emphasizing the importance of supply shocks, whereas Comin, Johnson, and Jones (2023) highlight the relevance of capacity constraints.

13

Hyperinflation

13.1 Introduction

Hyperinflations are a modern phenomenon. Cagan (1956) defined them as periods with a monthly inflation consistently above 50 percent. History accounts for really few episodes before the twentieth century. The first that would qualify according to Cagan's definition occured during the French Revolution, in which, between 1795 and 1796, there were five months of monthly inflation above 50 percent (see Capie, 1991). Cagan (1956) studied seven of the eight episodes between 1920 and 1946. Fisher, Sahay, and Vegh (2002) classify fifteen other episodes during 1956–1996. Since then, Zimbabwe and Venezuela have also experienced hyperinflations. The highest rate of inflation was recorded in Hungary after World War II with a 42,000,000,000,000,000 percent inflation in the month of July 1946. During that episode, the price index rose from 1 to 3.8×10^{27}, while during the French Revolution it rose from 1 to "only" 18.

High-inflation episodes look tiny with respect to hyperinflations, but should not at all be disregarded. For the period 1960–1996, Fisher, Sahay, and Vegh (2002) found 45 episodes involving 25 countries with twelve-month inflation rates above 100 percent. There are 212 episodes with annualized inflation of 25 percent involving 92 of the 133 countries in their analysis.

The fact that high inflations and hyperinflations are recent phenomena suggests that the advent of paper currency could have played a role in their causes. Part I of this book has emphasized that in a paper currency system the currency is defined as a unit of the central bank's liabilities, which empowers the central bank with the authority to print bills at will. However, it is exactly this freedom that might result in a high-inflation episode. High-inflation rates have to be associated, in one way or another, with an increase of central bank's liabilities or other liabilities, such as those of the treasury, backed by the central bank. "Earlier extreme inflations were rare because of the prevalence of commodity monies and convertibility. Only inconvertible paper currencies can be expanded rapidly without limit to generate hyperinflation" (Cagan, 1989a, p. 179).

Inflation and money growth are found to be highly correlated in hyperinflations and high-inflation episodes, supporting Milton Friedman's view that "inflation is always and everywhere a monetary phenomenon" (see Friedman, 1963, 1970b). Hyperinflations are the appropriate laboratory for studying this connection, since, as argued by Cagan (1956), one can abstract from the movements in output, for they are so small with respect to the movements in prices. In hyperinflations, prices run even faster than money supply, so that real money balances fall, showing a link between real money balances and the expected inflation rate, as in the famous money demand equation in Cagan (1956).

Figure 13.1 shows data from the Zimbabwe hyperinflation of 2007–2008, in which the monthly inflation rate was consistently above 50%. The correlation between money growth and inflation is evident.

Blaming monetary policy does not end the analysis of the causes of high-inflation episodes. In many cases, the rampant growth of money supply is the result of a coordinated effort between monetary and fiscal policies. Hyperinflation episodes, dating back to the first during the French Revolution, are often driven by the government's need to finance wartime or postwar expenditures. Printing bills to cover these expenses is not only an easy solution but, in certain circumstances, may be the only viable option.

In some other cases, the link between monetary and fiscal policies are blurred and subtler, for there is no direct monetary financing of the deficit, but a guarantee on the treasury's debt could be understood to be in place. Fiscal policy then becomes important for backing the value of the currency, as Section 1.4 of Chapter 1 has shown, with the drawback that if the policy is deemed insufficient for this backing, high inflation and hyperinflation could then be triggered. The treasury does not even have to run a deficit for this to happen; all that is needed is insufficient fiscal capacity. Hyperinflation can then be fueled by monetary policy counteracting inflation with ever higher interest rates. Loyo (1999) argues that Brazil's experience in the late 1970s can be narrated along these lines, not finding justification in any direct seigniorage target.

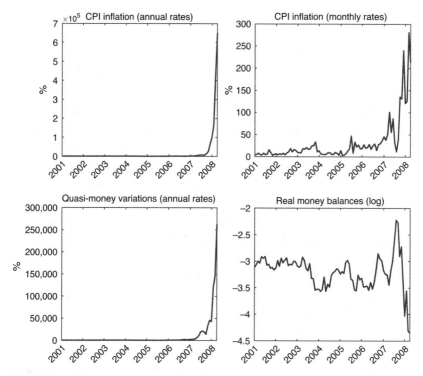

FIGURE 13.1. Zimbabwe hyperinflation. Period: January 2001–October 2008. *Source: Reserve Bank of Zimbabwe.*

The preceding discussion suggests that the causes of inflation can often be traced to the explicit or implicit interconnections between monetary and fiscal policies. While it might be tempting to assume that severing these connections would completely eliminate inflation, this is not the case.

As highlighted in Section 1.4.2 of Chapter 1, supporting the value of a currency requires more than just policy disconnection. The central bank should have a form of backing. In the absence of backing from the treasury through taxes, the alternative is to rely on the assets held in the central bank's portfolio. Investing in default-free securities can help maintain the currency's value.

However, when conditions arise where the central bank's liabilities exceed its assets, often due to portfolio losses, it can lead to inflation and, in extreme cases, hyperinflation.

Stella (2008) conducted cross-country comparisons that provide compelling evidence of a negative correlation between the financial strength of central banks and inflation rates. Additionally, his research sheds light on intriguing cases where relatively high inflation was associated with central banks having negative net worth. For instance, in 1997, Hungary faced a high inflation rate of 23 percent, which significantly decreased to 11 percent following the recapitalization of the central bank. A similar situation occurred in Jamaica after a recapitalization effort in 1995. On the other hand, the Central Bank of Peru has achieved single-digit inflation rates since it bolstered its financial position by turning profits into a positive value in 1996.[1]

In many of these cases, central bank losses can be attributed to non-performing loans provided to the banking sector with relative ease. History seems to repeat itself in this regard.

A noteworthy historical example is narrated by Quinn and Roberds (2014), who describe the challenges faced by the Central Bank of Amsterdam during the time when the Dutch florin was the dominant currency in Europe, throughout much of the seventeenth and eighteenth centuries. This dominance was lost due to substantial losses on loans extended to the Dutch East India Company, which left the central bank in an insolvent state.

The models presented in this book serve as a valuable laboratory for the study of inflation and hyperinflation episodes. This chapter's analysis is organized into three distinct blocks, each addressing a distinct underlying cause of inflation.

In the first framework, the connection between the central bank and the treasury is explicit, with the central bank resorting to money printing to finance the treasury's persistent deficit.

In the second framework, the link between the central bank and the treasury is more subtle, not directly tied to deficit financing but involving implicit backing of the treasury's liabilities. This scenario aligns with what has been termed "unpleasant monetaristic arithmetic," where the resource constraints shared by the central bank and the treasury can impose limits on monetary policy, potentially leading to inflationary equilibria.

---

1. A notable exception is the Central Bank of Chile—see Stella (2005)—which has been running a negative net worth since 1997 without any consequences for the achievement of low inflation rates. It is worth mentioning that during these periods the Chilean Treasury has often run fiscal surpluses that have reduced the outstanding Treasury debt to the point that it reached only 4 percent of GDP in 2007. This could suggest that the strong fiscal capacity has compensated for the poor backing provided by the central bank's assets, from the perspective of a consolidated intertemporal resource constraint.

The third framework considers a complete disconnection between the treasury and the central bank. Nevertheless, even in this scenario, episodes of inflation can be triggered by a lack of sufficient backing for the central bank's liabilities, stemming from balance sheet losses due to easy financing extended to the banking or private sector.

13.2   Outline of Results

Financing the treasury's deficit through money printing places significant constraints on the nature of monetary policy that the central bank can implement, as will be detailed in Section 13.3. In such scenarios, seigniorage revenues are essential for funding the deficit.

Under these circumstances, hyperinflationary equilibria may emerge, characterized by connections between real money balances, inflation, and money growth, as observed in the data.

In the absence of direct treasury financing but with the central bank providing backing to treasury debt, hyperinflation and high-inflation episodes may not appear significantly different, often triggered by an insufficient fiscal capacity. This situation can also give rise to the possibility of multiple equilibria. Section 13.4 discusses these cases under the heading of "unpleasant monetaristic arithmetic."

Finally, when the central bank is completely independent of the treasury, maintaining a positive net worth for the central bank can serve as a safeguard against undesired inflation dynamics. Conversely, the potential for inflation arises when the central bank incurs substantial balance sheet losses, as demonstrated in Section 13.5.

13.3   Deficit Financing and Inflation

One of the most popular narratives of hyperinflation or high-inflation episodes is rooted in the central bank's financing of treasury deficit. Treasuries can finance deficits by borrowing on markets and/or raising taxes. It can happen that under certain circumstances market access is precluded and taxes are difficult to raise. The central bank's financing through seigniorage could represent an "easy" way to provide resources, which then becomes the precise reason that inflation gets ignited.

A model suitable for characterizing the implications of money-financing of deficit is that of Chapter 2, in which the central bank issues reserves and cash.

Let's outline the main equilibrium conditions of the model. Consider, first, the Fisher equation,

$$1 + i_t = \frac{1}{\beta} \frac{P_{t+1}}{P_t}, \tag{13.1}$$

relating the nominal interest rate, i, to the real rate, $1/\beta$, and the inflation rate, P_{t+1}/P_t, in which P is again the price level. We still maintain the assumption that output is constant, which in high-inflation episodes would have variations that will look insignificant with respect to those of prices. As Cagan (1956) argued, "relations between monetary factors can be studied, therefore, in what almost amounts to isolation from the real sector of the economy."

Consider the equilibrium in the money market, which links real money balances to interest rates through the equation

$$\frac{M_t}{P_t} = L(i_t), \tag{13.2}$$

which omits the dependence of output for the same reasons underlined above; M is money and $L(\cdot)$ is a nondecreasing function of its argument. Combining (13.1) and (13.2), we obtain a classical relationship, consistent with the analysis in Cagan (1956),

$$\frac{M_t}{P_t} = \tilde{L}\left(\frac{P_t}{P_{t+1}}\right), \tag{13.3}$$

for some function $\tilde{L}(\cdot)$, in which real money balances are inversely related to the gross future inflation rate.

To complete the set of equilibrium conditions, we consider the flow budget constraint of the treasury and the central bank, which are, respectively,

$$\frac{B_t^F}{1 + i_t} = B_{t-1}^F + \mathcal{D}_t - T_t^C \tag{13.4}$$

and

$$\frac{B_t^C - X_t}{1 + i_t} - M_t = B_{t-1}^C - X_{t-1} - M_{t-1} - T_t^C, \tag{13.5}$$

with B^F denoting, as in previous chapters, treasury debt; $\mathcal{D}_t$ representing the overall treasury primary deficit, when positive, and surplus, when negative; T^C, the remittances received from the central bank; X, the central bank's reserves; and B^C, holdings of short-term assets.

The model is closed by the intertemporal resource constraint,

$$\sum_{t=t_0}^{\infty} \beta^{t-t_0} \left(\frac{i_t}{1+i_t} \frac{M_t}{P_t} - \frac{\mathcal{D}_t}{P_t} \right) = \frac{B_{t_0-1} + X_{t_0-1} + M_{t_0-1}}{P_{t_0}}, \qquad (13.6)$$

which, following the discussion of equation (2.18) in Section 2.3.3 of Chapter 2, is the mirror image of the intertemporal budget constraint of the consumers, using goods and asset market equilibrium.

To characterize inflations driven by money-financed fiscal deficits, we distinguish two cases that have different implications and depend on whether the deficit to be financed is specified in nominal rather than in real terms. We start with the latter, which is often the one analyzed in the literature.

13.3.1   Money-Financed Real Fiscal Deficit

We assume that the treasury runs a fiscal deficit in real terms, modelled by setting an exogenous positive sequence $\{d_t\}_{t=t_0}^{\infty}$, with $d_t \equiv \mathcal{D}_t/P_t$.

With regard to the path of the real deficits during hyperinflations, empirical analysis show that fiscal revenues may fall due to the lags in collecting taxes (Keynes-Tanzi effect). For a given path of real government expenditures, a fall in fiscal revenues leads to an increase of the deficit evaluated in real terms. On the contrary, if spending is fixed in nominal terms, it falls once evaluated in real terms during episodes of high inflation (Patinkin effect). In this case, were taxes indexed, deficits could fall rather than increase.[2]

We assume that all treasury debt is held by the central bank, therefore $B_t^F = B_t^C$ and $B_t = 0$. Given the sequence $\{d_t\}_{t=t_0}^{\infty}$, we assume that each-period deficit and the maturing debt are financed by the new debt held by the central bank plus the remittances received from the central bank, according to:

$$P_t d_t + B_{t-1}^C = \frac{B_t^C}{1+i_t} + T_t^C.$$

Substituing in the right-hand side of the above expression the flow budget constraint of the central bank, equation (13.5) with $X_t = 0$ at all times, we obtain

$$d_t = \frac{M_t - M_{t-1}}{P_t}. \qquad (13.7)$$

---

2. See Cardoso (1998). During periods of high inflation, the government could delay the payment of salaries and purchases, which leads to a fall of real expenditure.

The deficit is financed, in the end, by an increase in the money stock.[3]

In this section, we assume that monetary policy is set in terms of money supply, but the key aspect is that the monetary-fiscal interconnection imposes restrictions on the type of monetary policy that can be set. Consider a constant growth rate of money such that $M_t = (1+\vartheta)M_{t-1}$ with $\vartheta \geq 0$. The first restriction imposed by (13.7) is that ϑ should be strictly positive. Additional restrictions follow.

First, use equation (13.3) under a simplifying functional form for $\tilde{L}(\cdot)$ such that

$$\frac{M_t}{P_t} = (\Pi_{t+1})^{-\lambda_\pi} \tag{13.8}$$

for a positive parameter λ_π, with $\Pi_{t+1} \equiv P_{t+1}/P_t$. The chosen functional form is consistent with the estimates of Cagan (1956), showing a negative relationship between the log of real money balances and expected inflation.[4] Using $M_t = (1+\vartheta)M_{t-1}$, we can write (13.8) as

$$m_t = \left(\frac{m_t}{m_{t+1}}(1+\vartheta)\right)^{-\lambda_\pi},$$

with $m_t \equiv M_t/P_t$, which implies:

$$m_{t+1} = m_t^{1+\frac{1}{\lambda_\pi}}(1+\vartheta). \tag{13.9}$$

The above is a nonlinear difference equation in real money balances that is plotted in Figure 13.2, showing a stationary solution in which $m_t = m = (1+\vartheta)^{-\lambda_\pi}$. In this solution, real money balances are constant and prices grow at the same rate as money supply. However, on the left, there are also solutions in which real money balances fall over time and inflation keeps rising above the money growth rate. In such solutions, interest rates are increasing, making it more costly to hold real money balances.

Equation (13.7) is key in determining which type of solution prevails as an equilibrium. In line with the literature (see Bruno and Fischer, 1990), we assume that the real deficit is constant at $d_t = d$. Using this assumption, the definition of real money balances, and the fact that $M_{t-1} = (1+\vartheta)^{-1}M_t$, we

---

3. The assumption $X_t = 0$ is done to make the analysis comparable with the assumptions made in the literature; see Bruno and Fisher (1990).

4. Benati et al. (2021) support, instead, a relationship between log real money balances and the log of the inflation rate, which has different implications for the equilibrium inflation rate and seigniorage dynamics.

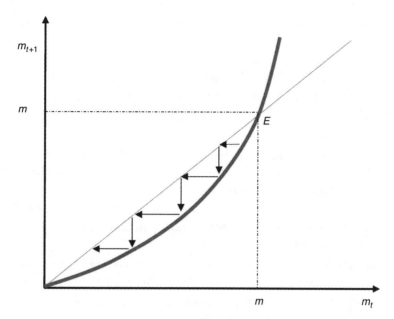

FIGURE 13.2. Plot of difference equation (13.9). Point E is the stationary solution. On the left, hyperinflationary paths with falling real money balances.

can write (13.7) as

$$d = \frac{\vartheta}{1 + \vartheta} m_t,$$

which implies that in equilibrium real money balances should also be constant, $m_t = m$, given the constant deficit and the constant growth rate of money supply.

   This framework cannot account for the fall in real money balances often observed in hyperinflation episodes. To this end, we should allow for time-varying deficit and money growth rate in particular combinations. The only equilibrium, using (13.9), is therefore $m_t = m = (1 + \vartheta)^{-\lambda_\pi}$, which, substituted in the above equation, imposes further restriction on ϑ, represented by

$$d = \vartheta (1 + \vartheta)^{-\lambda_\pi - 1}. \tag{13.10}$$

Note, first, that the right-hand side of the above equation is zero when $\vartheta = 0$ and when ϑ goes to infinity. Therefore, it is a hump-shaped function of ϑ. Moreover, it is maximized at $\vartheta = 1/\lambda_\pi$, taking the value of $d_{max} = \lambda_\pi^{\lambda_\pi}$ $(1 + \lambda_\pi)^{-(1+\lambda_\pi)}$. Note that according to Cagan's estimates, λ_π is around 4.68

on monthly data; therefore the maximum ϑ could be as high as 20 percent at monthly rates. Whenever d exceeds d_{max}, there is no equilibrium. For values of d below d_{max}, there are two values of ϑ that can finance the same deficit and be compatible with equilibrium, ϑ_H and ϑ_L, with $\vartheta_H > \vartheta_L > 0$.

This result should be interpreted not as saying that there are multiple equilibria, but, rather, that given d there are only two possible values for the growth rate of money consistent with equilibrium.[5] Since ϑ is a monetary-policy choice, once the central bank selects which among ϑ_H and ϑ_L to follow, there is only one equilibrium. Moreover, considering that inflation is determined by money growth, $\Pi = 1 + \vartheta$, the choice of ϑ implies whether the equilibrium is with a relatively high or low inflation rate. But, again, there are no multiple equilibria here and the central bank, though constrained by fiscal policy, may choose the low inflation equilibrium.

The above analysis says something about the causes of inflation, although it cannot account for the dynamic adjustment of inflation and real money balances observed during hyperinflation episodes. The model is consistent with the observation that money supply grows and that inflation is positively correlated with this growth. Some critical questions arise on the causality nexus.

Are inflation and hyperinflation monetary phenomena? Does this imply a causal relationship from money to inflation? The answer is twofold. On the one hand, the cause of inflation is in the irresponsible fiscal policy that runs permanent deficits without any attempt of a correction. On the other hand, monetary policy is completely subordinated to fiscal policy because of deficit financing, which is a choice rather than a restriction on the governing of its money supply. The cause of inflation is in the interconnection between monetary and fiscal authorities. Were the central bank completely independent of the treasury, it could have set a different monetary policy and let the treasury correct its deficit or left it to the only other possibility, which is default on its obligations. Inflation, in the above examples, is then caused by money supply financing of the fiscal deficit.

13.3.2 Money-Financed Nominal Fiscal Deficit

We consider a variation of the above framework in which the treasury's deficit is specified in nominal terms, a positive sequence $\{D_t\}_{t=t_0}^{\infty}$, which is financed

---

5. Multiple equilibria arise if central bank policy is explicated in terms of transfers to the treasury rather than in terms of money supply; see Gersbach (1999).

through the remittances received from the central bank and/or issuing bonds held only by the central bank. In this case,

$$\mathcal{D}_t + B_{t-1}^C = \frac{B_t^C}{1+i_t} + T_t^C,$$

which, using the flow budget constraint of the central bank assuming $X_t = 0$, implies that the time-variation of money supply is directly determined by the nominal fiscal deficit as

$$M_t = \mathcal{D}_t + M_{t-1}.$$

To keep things simple, we assume that $\mathcal{D}_t/M_{t-1} = \vartheta$ for a positive constant ϑ. Therefore, $M_t = (1+\vartheta)M_{t-1}$. Note that ϑ is now determined in a unique way by the fiscal policy, differently from the previous section.

We can still combine the money supply rule with the equilibrium in the money market (13.8) to obtain the same nonlinear difference equation (13.9) in real money balances,

$$m_{t+1} = m_t^{1+\frac{1}{\lambda_\pi}}(1+\vartheta),$$

which is plotted in Figure 13.2.

There are two novel results with respect to the previous section. First, there is always an equilibrium for a positive ϑ, which is determined by the direct financing of the nominal deficit. Second, for a given ϑ, there are multiple equilibria. There is a stationary equilibrium with constant real money balances, $m_t = m = (1+\vartheta)^{-\lambda_\pi}$, in which case prices grow at the same rate as money supply. Treasury deficit and seigniorage are constant in real terms. Differently from the previous section, there are, however, also hyperinflationary equilibria displaying features consistent with empirical evidence, such as real money balances falling over time, pushed by an inflation rate higher than the growth rate of money.[6] In such equilibria, interest rates keep increasing, thereby making it more costly to hold real money balances. Real deficits also decrease over time, following the path of real money balances, since

$$d_t = \frac{\vartheta}{1+\vartheta}m_t.$$

---

6. Note, moreover, that (13.9) also has solutions in which real money balances grow over time. These solutions are not equilibria since they would violate the transversality condition of households. Indeed, with increasing real money balances, nominal interest rates would fall to zero and prices would decrease at the rate β so that $\lim_{t\to\infty}\beta^{t-t_0}M_{t-1}/P_t > 0$.

13.3.3 ... with Interest Rate Policies

The previous analysis assumed a monetary policy set in terms of money supply. Things are not much different when it specifies the interest rate on reserves, following more modern central banking practices. The key feature, which unites both cases, is that fiscal policy commands monetary policy.

Consider central bank flow budget constraint (13.5) and note, as in Section 2.3 of Chapter 2, that given the net worth definition,

$$N_t^C \equiv \frac{B_t^C - X_t}{1 + i_t} - M_t,$$

constraint (13.5) can be written as

$$N_t^C = N_{t-1}^C + \Psi_t^C - T_t^C,$$

with the central bank's profits represented by

$$\Psi_t^C = i_{t-1}(N_{t-1}^C + M_{t-1}).$$

Assume zero initial net worth, $N_{t_0-1}^C = 0$, and that the central bank's profits are rebated to the treasury, i.e., $T_t^C = \Psi_t^C$; therefore the net worth is always zero. Assets and liabilities exactly match as

$$\frac{B_t^C}{1 + i_t} = \frac{X_t}{1 + i_t} + M_t, \tag{13.11}$$

and remittances are represented by $T_t^C = i_{t-1}M_{t-1}$.

Consider now the treasury and assume, as before, that a constant real deficit d is financed through the remittances received from the central bank and by issuing debt held only by the central bank. Therefore:

$$P_t d + B_{t-1}^C = \frac{B_t^C}{1 + i_t} + T_t^C.$$

Using (13.11) and the remittances policy, we can write the above equation as

$$P_t d + X_{t-1} + M_{t-1} = \frac{X_t}{1 + i_t} + M_t, \tag{13.12}$$

showing that, in the end, the deficit is fully financed by the central bank's liabilities, which is high-powered money.

Another way to write (13.12) considering (13.6) is

$$\frac{b^g_{t_0-1}}{\Pi_{t_0}} + d = (1-\beta) \sum_{t=t_0}^{\infty} \beta^{t-t_0} \left(\frac{i_t}{1+i_t} \frac{M_t}{P_t} \right),$$

(13.13)

in which we have defined $b^g_{t_0-1} \equiv (1-\beta)(X_{t_0-1}+M_{t_0-1})/P_{t_0-1}$. The central bank's outstanding real liabilities plus the treasury's deficits should be equal in equilibrium to the current and future seigniorage revenues. Equilibrium condition (13.13) then becomes a constraint on monetary policy, for it imposes restrictions on Π_{t_0} and on current and future interest rate policies. Consider now a constant interest rate policy $i_t = i$ for each $t \geq t_0$. Using (13.1), inflation is found to be constant at $\Pi = \beta(1+i)$ for each $t > t_0$. Using the latter result together with (13.8) in (13.13), we obtain

$$\frac{b^g_{t_0-1}}{\Pi_{t_0}} = \left(\frac{\Pi - \beta}{\Pi} \right) \Pi^{-\lambda_\pi} - d.$$

(13.14)

The first equilibrium restriction is that the right-hand side should be positive given that $b^g_{t_0-1} > 0$, which imposes constraints on the interest rate policy and the future inflation rate. Note that the first term on the right-hand side is hump-shaped with respect to Π, zero when $\Pi = \beta$ and when $\Pi \to \infty$, and reaches a maximum at $\Pi = \beta(1+\lambda_\pi^{-1})$. Using again the estimates of λ_π provided by Cagan (1956), this maximum corresponds approximately to a 20 percent monthly inflation rate.

The implication of equation (13.14) is that the central bank is forced to set an appropriate i so that the right-hand side of (13.14) is positive: seigniorage revenues should compensate at least for the deficit. Given the chosen policy, inflation at time t_0, Π_{t_0}, adjusts to equilibrate the equation. The more the seigniorage revenues extracted, the lower the inflation at time t_0. Under certain conditions, there are also equilibria in which inflation is always constant at the same level and, in this case, there can be two values that solve equation (13.14). This, again, is not a result of multiplicity of equilibria. It only means that there are two values for the nominal interest rate, so that there is an equilibrium with constant inflation.

Whether the central bank formulates its policy based on money supply or on interest rates does not significantly alter the outcome. The crucial factor limiting monetary policy is the subordination to fiscal policy.

All three models in this section share a common cause of inflation: the connection between deficits and seigniorage. These models are consistent with the observed correlation between money supply growth and inflation in empirical data. In cases of hyperinflation, they also demonstrate the phenomenon of falling real money balances and increasing nominal interest rates.

13.4   Some Unpleasant Monetarist Arithmetic

The previous section showed that the central bank's control of inflation depends on the way fiscal and monetary policies are coordinated. In particular, coordination was very explicit because the central bank was completely subordinated to financing the treasury's deficit. The connection between monetary and fiscal policy could be subtler and less direct, as in Section 1.4 of Chapter 1, where there is an implicit central bank backing of the treasury's liabilities. If it is understood that the treasury's liabilities have the same default-free properties as the central bank's liabilities, then there is no limit to the treasury's borrowing, except that it is inflationary. This implicit backing could be made more explicit by having the central bank purchase the treasury debt at some point in time.[7] Even when the backing is not so explicit but understood to be in place, sooner or later the inflationary consequences of deficits or insufficient fiscal capacity will manifest themselves. What is more striking is that once the central bank's implicit guarantee is in place, there is no hope that it can set an independent monetary policy and control the inflation rate, even if there is no direct deficit financing.

To support this view, we model the treasury to run a constant real deficit of type $d_t = d$, which, used in equilibrium condition (13.6), implies

$$(1-\beta)\sum_{t=t_0}^{\infty}\beta^{t-t_0}\left(\frac{i_t}{1+i_t}\frac{M_t}{P_t}\right)-d=(1-\beta)\frac{B_{t_0-1}+X_{t_0-1}+M_{t_0-1}}{P_{t_0}},$$

and therefore, using (13.1), that

$$(1-\beta)\sum_{t=t_0}^{\infty}\beta^{t-t_0}\left(\frac{M_t-M_{t-1}}{P_t}\right)-d=\frac{b_{t_0-1}^G}{\Pi_{t_0}}, \tag{13.15}$$

7. Treasury debt can be purchased by issuing reserves and not necessarily by increasing money supply.

in which we have defined the overall government real liabilities with respect to the private sector, net of money holdings, as $b_{t_0-1}^G \equiv (1-\beta)(B_{t_0-1} + X_{t_0-1})/P_{t_0-1}$.[8]

Equation (13.15) is an equilibrium condition, not a solvency constraint—since the treasury's and the central bank's liabilities are default-free—for the implicit backing of the central bank, as discussed in Section 1.4.1 of Chapter 1. However, equation (13.15) imposes restrictions on policies and on equilibrium inflation. The treasury runs its fiscal policy, which constrains in any case monetary policy, although there is no direct financing of the deficit.

The first result, in line with the analysis of the previous section, is that there is no equilibrium in which money supply remains constant at all times, considering $b_{t_0-1}^G > 0$ and $d > 0$. At some point in time, sooner or later, monetary policy is forced to increase the money supply. Let us consider first an equilibrium in which the growth rate of money is constant, i.e., $M_t = (1+\vartheta)M_{t-1}$ for some ϑ and for each $t \geq t_0$. We can write (13.15) as

$$\frac{\vartheta(1-\beta)}{(1+\vartheta)}\left(\sum_{t=t_0}^{\infty} \beta^{t-t_0} m_t\right) = d + \frac{b_{t_0-1}^G}{\Pi_{t_0}}. \qquad (13.16)$$

Note, moreover, that we again obtain from (13.8) that

$$m_{t+1} = m_t^{1+\frac{1}{\lambda_\pi}}(1+\vartheta) \qquad (13.17)$$

for each $t \geq t_0$, which, as before, admits a stationary solution, $m_t = m = (1+\vartheta)^{-\lambda_\pi}$, and other solutions in which real money balances decrease over time, with $m_t < m$. First, we discuss under which conditions the stationary solution is an equilibrium. Substitute $m_t = m = (1+\vartheta)^{-\lambda_\pi}$ for each $t \geq t_0$ in (13.16) to obtain

$$\frac{b_{t_0-1}^G}{\Pi_{t_0}} + d = \vartheta(1+\vartheta)^{-(\lambda_\pi+1)}. \qquad (13.18)$$

Equation (13.18) could be seen as a generalization of (13.10), but it is not. There, the central bank was directly financing the treasury's real deficit. Here, it is only implicitly backing the treasury's debt, though similar restrictions arise on its policy.

To see these restrictions, first consider that if $m_{t_0} = (1+\vartheta)^{-\lambda_\pi}$, and by identity $m_{t_0} = m_{t_0-1}(1+\vartheta)/\Pi_{t_0}$, it follows that $\Pi_{t_0} = (1+\vartheta)^{\lambda_\pi+1}m_{t_0-1}$,

---

8. In writing equation (13.15) from the previous one, we are assuming that $\lim_{t\to\infty}\beta^{t-t_0}M_{t-1}/P_t = 0$, which is the case on non-deflationary equilibria.

which, used in the above equation, implies

$$\vartheta = \mathsf{d}(1+\vartheta)^{(\lambda_\pi+1)} + \frac{b_{t_0-1}^G}{m_{t_0-1}}. \qquad (13.19)$$

The right-hand side of (13.19) is positive when $\vartheta = 0$ and is a strictly concave function of ϑ. Therefore, equation (13.19) admits two solutions, for relatively low values of d and $b_{t_0-1}^G$, with $\mathsf{d} > 0$ and $b_{t_0-1}^G > 0$. Let's define the solutions as ϑ_H and ϑ_L, with $\vartheta_H > \vartheta_L > 0$. Corresponding to these two values, two respective inflation rates are associated, since, in equilibrium, $\Pi = (1+\vartheta)$. For relatively high deficit d and government liabilities $b_{t_0-1}^G$, there is no equilibrium. Similarly to Section 13.3.1, fiscal policy is leading and forces the "equilibrium" monetary policy, which is the result of the arithmetic of the intertemporal resource constraints of the economy.[9]

A first important difference with respect to the analysis in Section 13.3.1 is that it is not just the deficit that matters but also the outstanding government liabilities. Even if $\mathsf{d} < 0$, there could be a positive inflation for a relatively high $b_{t_0-1}^G/m_{t_0-1}$. This happens whenever $-\mathsf{d} < b_{t_0-1}^G/m_{t_0-1}$, i.e., the fiscal capacity is not sufficient to back the overall government liabilities. Indeed, when $-\mathsf{d} = b_{t_0-1}^G/m_{t_0-1}$, there can be an equilibrium with zero money growth.

The second important difference is that there are also equilibria with hyperinflation, for the same and other values of ϑ. Note that solutions of (13.17) with falling real money balances are such that $m_t < (1+\vartheta)^{-\lambda_\pi}$ for each $t \geq t_0$. Provided the left-hand side of (13.16) is positive, these inflationary paths can be equilibria for an initial inflation rate Π_{t_0} that jumps above $(1+\vartheta)^{\lambda_\pi+1} m_{t_0-1}$ and puts in equilibrium (13.16). Although monetary policy is not directly financing the treasury, there is no hope of containing inflation once it is understood that the central bank guarantees the treasury debt.

In this environment, we can run another experiment in the spirit of Sargent and Wallace (1981), postulating a case in which the central bank tries to resist any inflationary pressure by tightening money, with the result that sooner or later it has to succumb. This experiment underlines the fact that forces linking monetary and fiscal policies can be hidden and implicit.

Consider a monetary policy in which the central bank keeps money constant until time T, i.e., $M_t = M_{t_0-1}$ for each $t_0 \leq t \leq T$, and lets it grow at the

---

9. There is no issue, again, of multiple equilibria, because the central bank can have freedom in choosing between ϑ_H and ϑ_L.

constant rate ϑ', i.e., $M_{t+1} = (1 + \vartheta')M_t$ for each $t \geq T$.[10] Correspondingly, we look for an equilibrium in which real money balances remain constant after and including period T; therefore $m_t = m_T = (1 + \vartheta')^{-\lambda_\pi}$ for $t \geq T$. Instead, for $t_0 \leq t < T$, the path for real money balances is represented by

$$m_{t+1} = m_t^{1 + \frac{1}{\lambda_\pi}}, \tag{13.20}$$

since $\vartheta = 0$ in (13.17). Equation (13.20) can be solved backward from time T to obtain all the path of real money balances until time t_0. Since $m_T < 1$, equation (13.20) implies that $m_{t_0} > m_T$, but still $m_{t_0} < 1$. Real money balances fall over time until time T to reach m_T, even if money supply is constant, because inflation is positive during this period. Moreover, using these results in (13.15), we obtain

$$\beta^{T+1-t_0} \frac{\vartheta'(1 + \vartheta')^{-(\lambda_\pi + 1)}}{1 - \beta} - \mathsf{d} = \frac{b_{t_0-1}^G}{\Pi_{t_0}'}. \tag{13.21}$$

The comparison between equations (13.18) and (13.21) is informative on how the effects of tight money today are either to increase seigniorage in the future and/or inflation today. Sooner or later tight money leads to inflation.[11] Monetary policy has to surrender to an irresponsible fiscal policy, though in the end this irresponsability reflects the implicit backing of monetary policy.

13.4.1   Tight Money Paradox

Monetary policy can try to fight inflation with the unfavorable outcome that it can create more of it. We present here another paradox of tight money, with monetary policy now setting an interest rate policy that reacts aggressively to inflation (see Loyo, 1999). A hyperinflation dynamic can arise in a vicious circle of ever higher interest rates and higher inflation. This escalation can be triggered either by an inadequate fiscal capacity or by self-fulfilling expectations, but in the background there are still the subtler links between monetary and fiscal policies.

Consider a central bank that follows an interest rate policy of the type $1 + i_t = \Pi_t^{\phi_\pi}/\beta$, with $\phi_\pi > 1$. A reaction to a zero inflation target is implicit in this policy, i.e., $\Pi_t = 1$. If inflation rises above the target, the interest rate

---

10. Note that a policy of constant money supply is not feasible at all.

11. We are implicitly assuming that for seigniorage we are on the left-hand side of the Laffer curve, and therefore $\vartheta' > \vartheta$.

increases more than proportionally, given that ϕ_π is above the unitary value. Using the interest rate policy in (13.1), we obtain

$$\Pi_{t+1} = \Pi_t^{\phi_\pi} \tag{13.22}$$

for each $t \geq t_0$, which is consistent with an increasing inflation path when $\Pi_{t_0} > 1$, and with constant prices whenever $\Pi_{t_0} = 1$. To determine which path is going to prevail in equilibrium, it is again important to understand how the inflation rate is determined at time t_0. The key equation is (13.6):

$$(1-\beta) \sum_{t=t_0}^{\infty} \beta^{t-t_0} \left(\frac{i_t}{1+i_t} \frac{M_t}{P_t} \right) + \tau = \frac{b_{t_0-1}^g}{\Pi_{t_0}}, \tag{13.23}$$

in which we have now defined $b_{t_0-1}^g \equiv (1-\beta)(B_{t_0-1} + X_{t_0-1} + M_{t_0-1})/P_{t_0-1}$, and set a policy of fiscal surplus such that $-\mathcal{D}_t/P_t = \tau$, with $\tau > 0$. Using the Fisher's equation (13.1) and (13.8), we can further write it as

$$(1-\beta) \sum_{t=t_0}^{\infty} \beta^{t-t_0} \left(1 - \beta \Pi_{t+1}^{-1} \right) \Pi_{t+1}^{-\lambda_\pi} + \tau = \frac{b_{t_0-1}^g}{\Pi_{t_0}},$$

and therefore

$$(1-\beta) \sum_{t=t_0}^{\infty} \beta^{t-t_0} \left(1 - \beta \Pi_{t_0}^{-\phi_\pi^{(t-t_0)+1}} \right) \Pi_{t_0}^{-\lambda_\pi \phi_\pi^{(t-t_0)+1}} + \tau = \frac{b_{t_0-1}^g}{\Pi_{t_0}}, \tag{13.24}$$

using $\Pi_{t+1} = \Pi_t^{\phi_\pi}$ recursively until time t_0.

Hyperinflation can arise under certain conditions. The first case is when the fiscal capacity τ is not enough to support an initial price level consistent with price stability. For this to be the case, τ should be such that $\tau < b_{t_0-1}^g - (1-\beta)$. The inequality excludes that $\Pi_{t_0} = 1$ is a solution of (13.24), and, instead, implies that the only equilibrium is with $\Pi_{t_0} > 1$. Therefore, through (13.22) there is an escalating inflation path. To get the result, it is not even necessary that fiscal policy run a permanent deficit provided $b_{t_0-1}^g > (1-\beta)$, which allows τ to be even positive. The insufficient fiscal capacity is measured by the present-discounted value of surpluses that are not enough to back the outstanding liabilities; therefore, via an intertemporal mismatch.[12]

---

12. Since we have normalized output to the unitary value, real debt over output should be above the unitary value in order for $b_{t_0-1}^g > (1-\beta)$ given the definition $b_{t_0-1}^g$. Recall indeed that $b_{t_0-1}^g \equiv (1-\beta)(B_{t_0-1} + X_{t_0-1} + M_{t_0-1})/P_{t_0-1}$. Note, however, that debt is a stock

The hyperinflation dynamic that follows is a joint fiscal and monetary responsibility for the following reasons. First, it is implicit in the above setting that fiscal policy is fully backed by monetary policy, for it is understood that the treasury's liabilities are similar to the central bank's liabilities and do not face any solvency constraint. Second, the kickoff of the hyperinflation spiral originates from the insufficient fiscal capacity. Finally, monetary-policy overreaction is critical to fueling inflation rather than curbing it. Higher interest rates imply higher interest payments on the treasury debt and therefore growing nominal government liabilities.[13] The increase in nominal liabilities fuels inflation through wealth effects on the securities' holders. Note that a less aggressive policy rule with $\phi_\pi < 1$ would not lead to escalating inflation, but rather to taming it.

The next result we show is that high inflations can also arise due to self-fulfilling equilibria, even if fiscal policy is "adequate." To this end, consider a fiscal policy that supports price stability, i.e., $\tau = b^g_{t_0-1} - (1 - \beta)$, and, for the sake of illustration, focus on the simple case in which $\phi_\pi = 1$. Using these assumptions, equation (13.24) implies

$$\left(\frac{\Pi_{t_0} - \beta}{\Pi_{t_0}}\right) \Pi_{t_0}^{-\lambda_\pi} = (1 - \beta) + b^g_{t_0-1}\left(\frac{1}{\Pi_{t_0}} - 1\right),$$

which displays an equilibrium with price stability, since $\Pi_{t_0} = 1$ is a solution. Consider the realistic case of $\lambda_\pi > 1$; then there is also another equilibrium in which $\Pi_{t_0} > 1$ provided $b^g_{t_0-1} < (1 - \beta)$. Note, indeed, that under the latter assumption, the limit for Π_{t_0} that goes to infinity on the left-hand side is zero, while in the same limit the right-hand side is positive, assuming $b^g_{t_0-1} < (1 - \beta)$. Left- and right-hand sides as a function of Π_{t_0} cross two times, once at $\Pi_{t_0} = 1$ and once with positive inflation at $\Pi_{t_0} > 1$.

The intuition for this result is in the interplay between seigniorage revenues and the initial inflation rate. According to (13.23), if seigniorage revenues are expected to be lower, for the same fiscal capacity, an increase in inflation at time t_0 is needed for the equation to hold with equality, fulfilling then the lower expected seigniorage revenues. Seigniorage is the cost for households to hold real money balances that, once lowered, increase their wealth. In turn, this stimulates consumpion and results in higher current inflation. A similar

---

and output is a flow. If the model is quarterly, a 25-percent debt-to-output ratio, when output is yearly, corresponds to a value of debt equal to 1 when output is quarterly and not annualized.

13. Note that real liabilities remain bounded in equilibrium and decrease in the limit.

argument can be made for the case $\phi_\pi > 1$, rationalizing then self-fulfilling hyperinflation.

The multiplicity of equilibria can be eliminated in a simple way: have fiscal policy rebate also seigniorage to the private sector, in which case only the fiscal capacity net of seigniorage revenues matters for determining the equilibrium inflation rate at time t_0.[14] This, however, does not rule out the hyperinflation triggered by inadequate fiscal capacity, fueled by the run between interest rates and the inflation rate.

To summarize the cases discussed under the heading "unpleasant monetaristic arithmetic," the takeaway is that they all share the source of high inflation or hyperinflation, which is in the subtle link between monetary and fiscal policy.

13.5 Central Bank's Balance Sheet and Inflation

The source of inflation and hyperinflation in the previous sections was rooted in a fiscal imbalance, which was explicit in the case the central bank was directly financing the treasury and less explicit when the central bank was just backing the treasury's liabilities. One might wonder whether a solution that avoids hyperinflationary spirals is to break the link with the treasury so that it addresses its solvency problems without the central bank's backing. The proposal is even more legitimate since we have argued in Chapters 1 and 2 that the central bank can control the price level without any support from the treasury.

Consider the above framework but with the treasury satisfying solvency condition (1.12), with equality, for its debt to be default-free, here restated as

$$\frac{B^F_{t_0-1}}{P_{t_0}} = \sum_{t=t_0}^{\infty} \beta^{t-t_0} \left(\frac{T_t}{P_t} + \frac{T^C_t}{P_t} \right), \tag{13.25}$$

requiring taxes to appropriately adjust to pay the debt.

Equilibrium conditions (13.1) and (13.8) still apply, while (13.6) using (13.25) is replaced by

$$\sum_{t=t_0}^{\infty} \beta^{t-t_0} \left(\frac{T^C_t}{P_t} \right) = \sum_{t=t_0}^{\infty} \beta^{t-t_0} \left(\frac{i_t}{1+i_t} \frac{M_t}{P_t} \right) + \frac{1}{\Pi_{t_0}} \frac{(1+i_{t_0-1})N^C_{t_0-1}}{P_{t_0-1}}, \tag{13.26}$$

with the central bank's net worth defined by $N^C_t = (B^C_t - X_t)/(1+i_t) - M_t$.

14. Note indeed that, in this case, the summation on the left-hand side of (13.24) will cancel out.

Equal treatment requires that, when the treasury is not backed or supported by the central bank, the central bank remain financially independent from the treasury. The latter requirement imposes a nonnegative remittances policy, i.e., $T_t^C \geq 0$ for each $t \geq t_0$.

In this context, the initial finding aligns with the content presented in Chapters 1 and 2. It emphasizes that a central bank can exercise full control over the inflation rate when its net worth remains positive, regardless of whether the policy is formulated in terms of the money supply or interest rates. A positive net worth empowers the central bank to manage inflation effectively without requiring support from the treasury.

Instead, a negative net worth can make the constraint $T_t^C \geq 0$ binding and be the trigger of inflation, as discussed in Del Negro and Sims (2015). To see this result, consider $N_{t_0-1}^C < 0$ and a zero remittances policy. Equation (13.26) implies

$$-\frac{n_{t_0-1}^C}{\Pi_{t_0}} = \sum_{t=t_0}^{\infty} \beta^{t-t_0} \left(\frac{i_t}{1+i_t} \frac{M_t}{P_t} \right),$$

in which we have defined $n_{t_0-1}^C \equiv (1+i_{t_0-1})N_{t_0-1}^C/P_{t_0-1}$. In equilibrium, the negative real net worth of the central bank should be equal to the seigniorage revenues. Substituting (13.1) and (13.8) in the above equation, we obtain

$$-\frac{n_{t_0-1}^C}{\Pi_{t_0}} = \sum_{t=t_0}^{\infty} \beta^{t-t_0} \left(1 - \beta\Pi_{t+1}^{-1} \right) \Pi_{t+1}^{-\lambda_\pi}, \qquad (13.27)$$

which becomes a restriction on current and future inflation rates. The equilibrium inflation rate depends on the type of policy followed by the central bank, whether it is an interest rate rule or money rule, and whether or not these rules are time-varying. Let us consider an interest rate policy in which the central bank targets a constant interest rate, fixing a constant inflation rate, i.e., $1+i_t = 1+i = \beta^{-1}\Pi$, for each $t \geq t_0$. Using this policy rule in (13.1) implies $\Pi_t = \Pi$ for each $t \geq t_0 + 1$. Substituting this result in (13.27), we can determine the inflation rate at time t_0:

$$-(1-\beta)\frac{n_{t_0-1}^C}{\Pi_{t_0}} = \left(1 - \beta\Pi^{-1}\right) \Pi^{-\lambda_\pi}. \qquad (13.28)$$

The higher the seigniorage revenues, which is the term on the right-hand side of the above equation, the lower the inflation rate at time t_0. A larger and

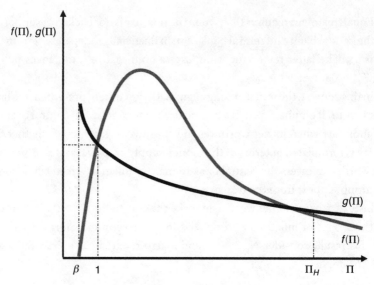

FIGURE 13.3. Solutions of equation (13.28) when $n_{t_0-1}^C = -1$, in which $g(\Pi) = (1 - \beta)/\Pi$ and $f(\Pi) = \left(1 - \beta\Pi^{-1}\right)\Pi^{-\lambda_\pi}$.

negative net worth requires either higher seigniorage in the future or a higher inflation rate today.

We study equilibria with a constant inflation rate at all times, $\Pi_{t_0} = \Pi$, which requires an appropriate choice of the target i and Π so that the above equation is satisfied. Consider first the case $n_{t_0-1}^C = -1$: price stability, $\Pi = 1$, is a solution of equation (13.28) and, therefore, an equilibrium, showing that even a negative net worth is not necessarily inflationary. However, under the assumption $\lambda_\pi > 1$, the above equation also has another solution with high inflation, as shown in Figure 13.3. Note that there are no multiple equilibria here since, as before, the policymaker sets the interest rate policy and therefore can choose at will the inflation rate among the two solutions. With $n_{t_0-1}^C$ decreasing below -1, there are still two solutions with a positive inflation rate. For larger values of $n_{t_0-1}^C$, there are no solutions and, therefore, no equilibria with a constant inflation rate. There can still be equilibria with a different inflation rate between time t_0 and later.

An inflation dynamic that escalates is also possible, provided the interest-rate policy reacts aggressively to inflation with a coefficient ϕ_π above the unitary value, in which case inflation dynamics are represented by (13.22) and Π_{t_0} is determined by (13.27).

Negative net worth can then be responsible for inflation or hyperinflation dynamics even in a context in which the central bank is completely independent of the treasury. The reason is that the central bank needs some form of backing to maintain the value of money, and absent any treasury support, this backing can only be provided by the value of its assets. If the central bank's assets lose their value because they are defaulted on, and the loss is significant enough to bring the net worth to a very negative value, then the central bank faces an inflation risk and, depending on its interest rate policy, can even experience hyperinflation. The composition of the asset portfolio then becomes important for conducting monetary policy and controlling inflation even if there is disconnection with the treasury. Holding gold, and selling it, could also provide additional revenues that can offset at some point in time losses on nominal assets, avoiding the inflationary outcome. In the above framework, this might be captured by a higher $n_{t_0-1}^C$.

13.6 References

Bresciani-Turroni (1931) and Cagan (1956) are classical studies on hyperinflations.[15] Cagan (1956) estimated the demand for real money balances during hyperinflation as inversely dependent on the expected rate of inflation. He posits a linear relationship between the logarithm of real money balances and expected inflation, similar to the approach in this Chapter.

Benati et al. (2021) provide evidence based on a sample of 44 countries since World War I, suggesting that the specification should be linear between the logarithm of real money balances and the logarithm of the expected inflation rate, as initially proposed by Meltzer (1963). This implies a significant difference in the relationship between seigniorage and money growth. In Cagan's case, it resembles a Laffer-curve type relationship, while in the log-log case, it remains consistently positive, as discussed in Benati (2023).

Bruno and Fisher (1990) discuss the multiplicity of equilibria, and their stability properties, which can arise when the seigniorage curve is of Laffer type.

Fisher, Sahay, and Vegh (2002) study very high inflation episodes, with rates above 100 percent per annum, since 1947, showing that the relationship between the fiscal balance and seigniorage is strong also in these cases.

---

15. See also the review in Cagan (1989a).

Sargent (1982), in discussing four hyperinflation episodes, shows that, regardless of their severity, they were effectively brought to an end without much economic disruption. The key lies in terminating monetary support and implementing a well-structured reform program. Importantly, they can help restore public confidence in the currency, leading to a noticeable increase in real money balances.

Sargent and Wallace (1981) introduced what they termed "unpleasant monetarist arithmetic." This concept highlights a complex relationship between monetary and fiscal policies. Specifically, in cases where fiscal policy is set independently, a decision to adopt a tight monetary policy today can surprisingly result in higher inflation, either in the future or immediately. Loyo (1999), in discussing the inflationary episodes of Brazil in the 1970s and 1980s, suggests that hyperinflation may not necessarily be the result of direct seigniorage financing of the deficit. Instead, it could be a consequence of the fiscal effects of a tight monetary policy, which increases the cost of government liabilities.

Del Negro and Sims (2015) discuss the inflationary consequences of capital losses for the central bank when there is no support from the treasury. Stella (2005, 2008) shows cross-country comparisons supporting the view that the central bank's financial strength is negatively correlated with inflation.

PART V

Conclusion

14

The Future of Monetary Policy

The complex nature of the multifaceted governance of a currency, as revealed through the analysis in this book, cautions one against making definitive conclusions. Attempting to do so could inevitably lead to contradictory statements. Nevertheless, after having been presented the analysis within a unitary framework, one may be tempted to form a preliminary comprehensive view about which characteristics could be part of a "stable monetary framework," along the lines of Friedman (1960) and Friedman and Schwartz (1986).

Immersed as we are in the latest developments of technology, we often tend to overlook those of the past, and money is undoubtedly one such example. An economy based on the coincidence of wants, as seen in barter, represented a significant limitation to economic development, confining exchange to the proximity of the two parties involved.

The Dark Ages of medieval Europe were not far removed from barter economies, as highlighted by Cipolla (1967). The demand for coins was greatly depressed, and coins served merely as one method among many for settling payments, with any commodity considered a medium of exchange. Even debts stipulated in units of coins were frequently settled with items such as vases, clothes, and even horses. One reason for this was the inefficient functioning of the market; hence, "people could not rely confidently on the market's having what they wanted" (Cipolla, 1967, p. 11). There was no incentive to trade in coins with the expectation of a future transaction involving a third party.

If, in an ideal scenario, we could gather the entire world population, encompassing both current and future generations, in a "virtual room" where everyone expresses their current and future economic plans, a virtual Walrasian auctioneer could make them compatible by adjusting relative intratemporal

355

and intertemporal prices—without the need for any intermediation through a currency. While this ideal "virtual room" may never exist, given the challenges, including the need for knowledge of the plans of future unborn generations, it can serve as an intriguing benchmark to evaluate the desiderata of a currency system. One of these that emerges is that the currency be essentially neutral, meaning it not distort the economic plans that would be settled in that ideal "virtual room," for the reason that it would be hard to imagine in that ideal world that a worthless currency could improve for some or all agents their real economic plans.

Given the current challenge in envisioning how that "virtual room" could actually exist, a currency system and a market economy might be the best approximation we can get to that "virtual room."

Moving away from a barter economy through an agreement on a specific commodity to facilitate exchanges already introduces the potential for manipulation. Granting favored status to this commodity endows it with additional purchasing power not present before, creating a distortion in the allocation that disproportionately benefits those holding more of that commodity. While commodity currency offers advantages by overcoming the double coincidence of wants, historical instances reveal practices such as the retrieving of seigniorage revenues and the deceptive debasing of its intrinsic value. These practices, often by sovereign entities in the monopolistic management of metallic coin issuance and verification, aimed at appropriating real resources, contributing to overall distortion.

Moving to a currency system with inconvertible paper currency has only heightened the temptation to manipulate real allocations, as currency becomes nothing more than what can be printed at will. Indeed, central banks within sovereign states have not refrained from doing so over the relatively short history of inconvertible paper currency. The modern-era establishment of central banks originated from the urgent needs of the state for money or to avert banking liquidity crises. These endeavors, in one way or another, aim to distort real allocations in favor of the state, consequently benefiting certain groups, or the banking sector.

The global economy has witnessed such events even recently, notably during the 2007–2008 financial crisis and the COVID-19 pandemic, where central banks assumed the role of buyers of last resort for almost everything. Whether this constitutes appropriate governance of money is highly disputable, especially considering the dilemmas and decisions of policymakers. For instance, the decision to let Lehman Brothers fail on September 15, 2008, followed by the immediate shift to purchasing nearly everything the next day, underscores the complexities involved.

Turning to Europe, a new era of central bank backing national fiscal authorities is evident, marked by the renowned "whatever it takes" statement from the president of the European Central Bank, Mario Draghi, on July 26, 2012. The shift, at the onset of the pandemic, in President Christine Lagarde's stance, i.e., the transitioning from "we are not here to close spreads" to instigating an unprecedented national debt purchase program motivated by the pandemic further highlights the evolving dynamics in central bank policies.

Assessing the outcomes and observing the nature of fiscal interventions by national states, enabled by generous budgets with a lower degree of sustainability constraints, prompts contemplation on whether the resulting distortions in real allocation would be agreed upon by all citizens, or even by the ones gathered in that hypothetical "virtual room." These distortions have contributed to the post-COVID-19 inflationary surge.

Examining this scenario from the perspective of that "virtual room," the desirable goal of a neutral currency appears challenging to achieve, even in the second-best world. This predicament seems to consign citizens to the inevitable fate of residing in currency jurisdictions that are always susceptible to manipulation, as witnessed in both past and recent history.

The emergence during the last decade of private digital currencies, commonly known as cryptocurrencies, could represent a watershed event in the history of monetary economics for at least two reasons.

The first and most significant reason is that they introduce competition in the adoption and use of currencies, providing systems that transcend national borders and enabling world citizens to enter into a different currency system without changing their location.[1] This allows them to choose a currency that best serves their needs and preferences in a world that is becoming more integrated in the exchange of goods and services. Competition could be a powerful force in producing better currencies or, at the very least, providing options from which to choose.

---

1. A single currency within national borders is a relatively recent phenomenon. In metallic currency systems, competition among different coins with varying metallic content was frequent. This competition often gave rise to cases of Gresham's law, where the "good" coins, in terms of intrinsic value, were hoarded rather than used in exchanges, leading to the prevalence of "bad" coins.

In his argument for the denationalization of money, Hayek believes that competition could represent "a more effective constraint forcing the issuing institutions to keep the value of their currency constant (in terms of a stated collection of commodities) than would any obligation to redeem the currency in those commodities (or in gold)" (Hayek, 1976, p. 48). He envisions the dominance of a currency that maintains its real value, a "real dollar," and suggests that different definitions of purchasing power appropriate to different groups would require the coexistence of several currency systems. It is important to add that inherent in the dominance of a currency able to keep its purchasing power stable could be also the idea of its being shielded from any form of fiscal and financial dominance experienced so far. Or, at least, it could be an additional desideratum that people will seek in their free choices.

In contrast, Friedman and Schwartz (1986) in commenting on Hayek's proposal say: "We continue to believe that the possibility that private issuers can (in either sense of that term) provide competing, efficient and safe fiduciary currencies with no role for governmental monetary authorities remains to be demonstrated" (Friedman and Schwartz, 1986, p. 58). One should adopt an agnostic stance regarding which currency—government-issued or private—is likely to prevail and recognize that we are only at the beginning of the process. As such, current private currencies may be not suitable in serving the role of dominant currencies. However, competition poses a challenge to the government to ensure that its currency retains its role, and incentivizes the government to provide a better currency. In the same article, Friedman and Schwartz (1986, p. 39) say: "Even granted the market failures that we and many other economists had attributed to a strictly laissez-faire policy in money and banking, the course of events encouraged the view that turning to government as an alternative was a cure that was worse than the disease, at least with existing government policies and institutions. Government failure might be worse than market failure."

The second important feature of the innovations brought about by cryptocurrency is the decentralized system of verifying the legitimacy of transactions based on cryptography. This system grants no particular privilege to anyone, except for mathematical consensus. This represents a significant departure from the current financial system, which relies on third-party verification and subjective judgments when it involves court decisions on dispute. Through the new technology, it could be possible to transition from a financial system based on "subjective-paper guarantee" to one characterized by a "cryptography guarantee." This shift would address the problem emphasized by Friedman and Schwartz regarding "the peculiar difficulty of enforcing contracts involving promises to pay that serve as a medium of exchange and of preventing fraud in respect of them" (Friedman and Schwartz, 1986, p. 58). The recent developments in decentralized finance, enabling the execution of "smart" contracts on blockchains, align with the goal of overcoming such difficulties.

Considering the distortions experienced in past and current monetary systems and the new developments arising from the competition among private currencies, what does the future hold for monetary policy, or for a more optimal design of it? This book aids in comprehending certain dimensions, such as anchoring the value of an intrinsically worthless currency, supplying liquidity to the system, achieving macroeconomic stabilization, and intervening to prevent macroeconomic crises.

Chapters 1 and 2, along with Chapter 13, provide arguments for the complete separation of monetary and fiscal policies. Offering a special guarantee to the treasury's liabilities or directly financing the state can be detrimental to the stability of the currency's value, unnecessarily giving prominence to fiscal policy in determining it. The reason for this disconnection becomes clear once one recognizes that there is not even a need for a fiscal authority to provide real backing for the currency.

The control of the currency's value can indeed be put into operation by utilizing a diverse set of instruments available to the central bank, as exemplified in Chapters 1 and 2. Disregarding seigniorage resources that might be diminished through competition with other currencies, effective control of the price level hinges on possessing high-quality assets to support liabilities or investing in tangible real assets like gold. While the establishment of a security market of safe assets denominated in newly created currencies may take time, the immediate availability of gold or any other tangible asset can offer a straightforward means to implicitly anchor the value of a nascent currency. It is worth noting that even the currency of the Mediterranean area during the Middle Ages, specifically the gold coins of the Italian republics, initially faced challenges in gaining acceptance, as reported by Cipolla (1967, p. 20): "e non n'era quasi chi il volesse" (and there were hardly any who wanted it).

Other crucial factors for controlling the currency's value involve appropriately determining the quantity of currency to issue or any interest payment on it. The selected operational framework from the available array of instruments should be designed to uphold the stability of the currency's value. As highlighted in Chapter 7, the concept of currency value stability can be encoded in terms of an inflation or price level targeting framework. Targeting a specific path for nominal spending could also effectively serve the purpose. In such a framework, a positive but low growth rate of prices is allowed as a buffer to partly offset certain distortions we have highlighted. The distortion resulting from the zero lower bound constraint might become less relevant with the increasing digitization of currency, and other distortions could potentially play a diminished role in the future.

There should not be any doubt that to provide a "stable monetary framework," the issuer of the unit of account in a competitive environment should assume the sole responsibility of maintaining the stability of the value of its currency in terms of the purchasing power of certain commodities, playing a "neutral" role in the currency system to avoid distorting real allocations.

The next issue to address is whether the provider of the unit of account should also supply the medium of exchange, or the liquidity of the system, or more broadly, the so-called safe assets. Chapters 4 and 11 provide contradictory statements but useful information for drawing conclusions. Frictionless markets of private money creation under unfettered competition can satisfy the liquidity needs of the economy, grounded in the private incentive to exploit low financing costs by supplying safe securities, as Chapter 4 has shown. This does not create any interference with the control of the value of currency undertaken by the supplier of the unit of account. Chapter 11 has instead provided a different picture when there are frictions in private money creation, together with the possibility that some pseudo-safe securities could be used for liquidity purposes. This environment can rationalize periods of economic contraction due to the poor performance of the pseudo-safe securities used for liquidity purposes, as witnessed during the recent 2007–2008 financial crisis and throughout history, and as also evidenced by the analysis of Friedman and Schwartz in 1963.

These events, as detailed in Chapter 11, may impact the control of the unit of account's value by its supplier, creating disinflationary or deflationary pressures. In response, the supplier must promptly substitute low-quality private liquidity with its high-quality, safe liquidity.

In general, the failure of private liquidity creation suggests that, even beyond such crises, the supplier of the unit of account should also fulfill all liquidity needs in the economy, aligning with Friedman's proposal. However, the provision of abundant liquidity must be matched by the issuer holding an equivalent amount of high-quality private assets on the balance sheet. Alternatively, within a government-integrated framework where currency issuers back the treasury, the supplied liquidity should correspond to an equivalent amount of current and future taxes levied by the government. These two possibilities, however, could create subtle linkages between the currency issuer and the private sector in one case, or between the issuer and the treasury in the other case, potentially leading to instances of financial or fiscal dominance that could, at some point, impact the control of the value of the currency.

While historical trends indicate that currency issuers have traditionally supplied the medium of exchange, albeit in limited quantities, it is crucial to recognize that the breakdown of private money creation stems from an underdeveloped intermediation process for two reasons.

One critical issue is the opacity of the intermediation activity, characterized by a limited assessment of intermediaries' balance sheets, especially concerning their assets. In this context, the potential of innovations like cryptographic guarantees for securities and financial transactions, operational under a decentralized blockchain system, could significantly enhance the fair evaluation of risk and liquidity characteristics of various financial instruments, including money securities. Once prices accurately reflect the inherent characteristics of securities, competition could effectively guide the market in determining the appropriate amount of liquidity.

Another critical consideration is the maturity transformation process, historically a defining feature of the banking sector, which has been regarded as the primary provider of money claims. However, this process is indicative of an underdeveloped intermediation system rather than being an inherent characteristic of a money-like provider.

Recent developments in alternative forms of intermediation, such as private equity, demonstrate that funds can easily flow toward the long-term financing needs of the economy, and be secured for a similar duration without involving maturity transformation. A developed financial system could naturally lead to a separation between money and credit markets, where the issuer of the unit of account refrains from any implicit guarantee in private money markets, thus avoiding the encouragement of risk-taking behavior.

The potential exists for more advanced financial markets incorporating new technologies to serve as the inherent providers of the medium of exchange within the currency system. Incentives are propelled by the advantages of obtaining lower-cost financing through money claims, while competition works to diminish all rents in the market, resulting in the convenience yield on these money claims eventually becoming zero. In such a framework, as previously stated, the unit of account supplier should have the sole and important responsibility of keeping stable the value of the currency, and this control can happen with the principles discussed in Chapter 1, as shown in Chapter 4.

In the current financial framework, it is challenging to envision dispensing with a lender of last resort agent, as, for example, discussed in Goodhart (1999). However, in the more developed financial framework discussed above, no need for such a role arises. It is uncontroversial that a lender of last resort should not address solvency problems. Therefore, there is no role to be taken in a private equity market in which projects do not deliver a pay-off in certain contingencies, as those losses should be borne by the financiers and equity holders, who have appropriately taken the risk. Similarly, there is no such role to be taken in the money markets, since money or money-like claims are appropriately priced, being the assets and balance sheets of providers accurately ascertained through new technologies.

A "stable monetary framework" can be envisioned where the issuer of the unit of account ensures a stable currency value, while the private sector handles the medium of exchange. In this setup, the treasury is one among many agents, lacking a specific connection to the unit of account. I believe that this framework serves as the best approximation for a neutral currency system when viewed from the perspective of that "virtual room," avoiding distortions in favor of any particular group's or agents' economic plans. In a second-best world, this approach would best facilitate the coexistence of economic plans, promoting macroeconomic stability.

In the near future, there is hope that competition among currencies might give rise to a "stable monetary framework" capable of transcending national borders—something to which world citizens could readily and freely adhere. This vision holds the promise of consigning currency manipulations to the pages of history.

PART VI

Appendix

Appendix

Appendix to Chapter 1

A Derivation of Equation (1.5)

We show that (1.2) and (1.4) imply (1.5).

Consider budget constraint (1.2), setting $i_t = i_t^X$, $M_t = 0$ and dividing it by P_t,

$$\frac{B_t + X_t}{P_t(1 + i_t)} = \frac{B_{t-1} + X_{t-1}}{P_t} + Y - C_t - \frac{T_t}{P_t}.$$

Multiply it by discount factor $R_{t_0,t}$ and sum all the constraints from time t_0 to time k, obtaining

$$R_{t_0,k}\frac{B_k + X_k}{P_k(1 + i_k)} = \frac{B_{t_0-1} + X_{t_0-1}}{P_{t_0}} + \sum_{t=t_0}^{k} R_{t_0,t}\left(Y_t - C_t - \frac{T_t}{P_t}\right)$$

and therefore

$$R_{t_0,k+1}\frac{B_k + X_k}{P_{k+1}} + \sum_{t=t_0}^{k} R_{t_0,t}C_t = \frac{B_{t_0-1} + X_{t_0-1}}{P_{t_0}} + \sum_{t=t_0}^{k} R_{t_0,t}\left(Y_t - \frac{T_t}{P_t}\right).$$

$$(\text{A.1})$$

Use (1.4) at time k as a substitute for $(B_k + X_k)/P_{k+1}$ on the left-hand side of the above equation to obtain

$$\sum_{t=t_0}^{k} R_{t_0,t}C_t \leq \frac{B_{t_0-1} + X_{t_0-1}}{P_{t_0}} + \sum_{t=t_0}^{\infty} R_{t_0,t}\left(Y_t - \frac{T_t}{P_t}\right).$$

Note first that the right-hand side is bounded by assumption—see (1.4)—and that the left-hand side as a function of k is a monotone nondecreasing sequence since $R_{t_0,t}$ is positive and $C_t \geq 0$. Therefore, this bounded mono-tone nondecreasing sequence has a limit as $k \to \infty$, which satisfies the bound. Therefore, equation (1.5) follows.

$$\sum_{t=t_0}^{\infty} R_{t_0,t} C_t \leq \frac{B_{t_0-1} + X_{t_0-1}}{P_{t_0}} + \sum_{t=t_0}^{\infty} R_{t_0,t} \left(Y_t - \frac{T_t}{P_t} \right), \qquad \text{(A.2)}$$

completing the proof.

The converse is also true. Equations (1.2) for each $t \geq t_0$ and (1.5) imply that (1.4) holds for each $t \geq t_0$. Consider first (1.5), which is exactly (A.2); then (1.4) holds at time t_0 since consumption is nonnegative. Combine (1.4) at time t_0 with (A.2) to obtain

$$\sum_{t=t_0+1}^{\infty} R_{t_0,t} C_t \leq \frac{B_{t_0} + X_{t_0}}{P_{t_0}(1 + i_{t_0})} + \sum_{t=t_0+1}^{\infty} R_{t_0,t} \left(Y_t - \frac{T_t}{P_t} \right),$$

or, equivalently,

$$\sum_{t=t_0+1}^{\infty} R_{t_0+1,t} C_t \leq \frac{B_{t_0} + X_{t_0}}{P_{t_0+1}} + \sum_{t=t_0+1}^{\infty} R_{t_0+1,t} \left(Y_t - \frac{T_t}{P_t} \right).$$

Therefore (1.4) also holds at time $t_0 + 1$, since the left-hand side of the above inequality is nonnegative. Following similar steps, it can be shown that (1.4) holds at all future times, completing the proof.

We show, now, that (1.2) and (1.4) imply (1.6). We have shown that $\sum_{t=t_0}^{\infty} R_{t_0,t} C_t$ is finite and bounded above as in (A.2). We take the limit for $k \to \infty$ in (A.1), and comparing with (A.2) we obtain (1.6), i.e.,

$$\lim_{k \to \infty} R_{t_0,k+1} \frac{B_k + X_k}{P_{k+1}} \geq 0.$$

The converse, that (1.2) and (1.6) imply (1.4), is also true. Use (1.2) to obtain (A.1) and consider that

$$\sum_{t=t_0}^{k} R_{t_0,t} C_t \geq 0,$$

and therefore

$$R_{t_0,k+1} \frac{B_k + X_k}{P_{k+1}} \leq \frac{B_{t_0-1} + X_{t_0-1}}{P_{t_0}} + \sum_{t=t_0}^{k} R_{t_0,t} \left(Y_t - \frac{T_t}{P_t} \right).$$

Taking the limit on both sides of the above inequality for $k \to \infty$ and using (1.6), the borrowing limit (1.4) follows.

Appendix to Chapter 2

B   Derivation of Equation (2.4)

We show that (2.2) and (2.3) imply (2.4). Consider budget constraint (2.2) and divide it by P_t:

$$\frac{B_t + X_t}{P_t(1 + i_t)} + \frac{M_t}{P_t} = \frac{B_{t-1} + X_{t-1} + M_{t-1}}{P_t} + Y - C_t - \frac{T_t}{P_t}.$$

Write it as

$$\frac{B_t + X_t + M_t}{P_t(1 + i_t)} + \frac{i_t}{1 + i_t}\frac{M_t}{P_t} = \frac{B_{t-1} + X_{t-1} + M_{t-1}}{P_t} + Y - C_t - \frac{T_t}{P_t}.$$

Multiply it by discount factor $R_{t_0,t}$ and sum all the constraints from time t_0 to time k, obtaining

$$R_{t_0,k}\frac{B_k + X_k + M_k}{P_k(1 + i_k)} = \frac{B_{t_0-1} + X_{t_0-1} + M_{t_0-1}}{P_{t_0}}$$

$$+ \sum_{t=t_0}^{k} R_{t_0,t}\left(Y_t - C_t - \frac{T_t}{P_t} - \frac{i_t}{1 + i_t}\frac{M_t}{P_t}\right)$$

and, therefore,

$$R_{t_0,k+1}\frac{B_k + X_k + M_k}{P_{k+1}} + \sum_{t=t_0}^{k} R_{t_0,t}\left(C_t + \frac{i_t}{1 + i_t}\frac{M_t}{P_t}\right)$$

$$= \frac{B_{t_0-1} + X_{t_0-1} + M_{t_0-1}}{P_{t_0}} + \sum_{t=t_0}^{k} R_{t_0,t}\left(Y_t - \frac{T_t}{P_t}\right).$$

Use (2.3) at time k as a substitute for $(B_k + X_k + M_k)/P_{k+1}$ on the left-hand side of the above equation to obtain

$$\sum_{t=t_0}^{k} R_{t_0,t}\left(C_t + \frac{i_t}{1 + i_t}\frac{M_t}{P_t}\right) \leq \frac{B_{t_0-1} + X_{t_0-1} + M_{t_0-1}}{P_{t_0}}$$

$$+ \sum_{t=t_0}^{\infty} R_{t_0,t}\left(Y_t - \frac{T_t}{P_t}\right).$$

Note first that the right-hand side is bounded by assumption—see (2.3)—and that the left-hand side as a function of k is a monotone nondecreasing sequence since $R_{t_0,t}$ is positive and $C_t \geq 0$, $i_t \geq 0$, $M_t \geq 0$. Therefore, this bounded monotone nondecreasing sequence has a limit as $k \to \infty$, which satisfies the bound. Therefore, equation (2.4) follows,

$$\sum_{t=t_0}^{\infty} R_{t_0,t}\left(C_t + \frac{i_t}{1+i_t}\frac{M_t}{P_t}\right) \leq \frac{B_{t_0-1} + X_{t_0-1} + M_{t_0-1}}{P_{t_0}}$$

$$+ \sum_{t=t_0}^{\infty} R_{t_0,t}\left(Y_t - \frac{T_t}{P_t}\right),$$

completing the proof.

The converse is also true, and other equivalence results follow the same steps as in Appendix A.

Appendix to Chapter 3

C Derivation of Equation (3.4)

The derivation follows the same steps as in Appendix A. Just note that budget constraint (3.2) can be written by dividing it by P_t and setting $M_t = M_{t-1} = 0$ as

$$\frac{B_t}{P_t} + \frac{X_t}{P_t} + C_t + \frac{T_t}{P_t} = \frac{(1+i_{t-1})B_{t-1} + (1+i_{t-1}^X)X_{t-1}}{P_t} + Y.$$

Denote

$$\mathcal{W}_{t-1} = (1+i_{t-1})B_{t-1} + (1+i_{t-1}^X)X_{t-1}$$

and observe that

$$B_t = \frac{\mathcal{W}_t}{1+i_t} - \frac{1+i_t^X}{1+i_t}X_t.$$

It follows that

$$\frac{\mathcal{W}_t}{P_t(1+i_t)} + \frac{(i_t - i_t^X)X_t}{(1+i_t)P_t} + C_t + \frac{T_t}{P_t} = \frac{\mathcal{W}_{t-1}}{P_t} + Y.$$

Starting from the above equation, equation (3.4) can be derived following steps similar to those in Appendix A.

Appendix to Chapter 5

D   Derivation of Equations (5.3) and (5.4)

The price index (P) is defined as the minimum expenditure needed to purchase one unit of consumption good (C). The total expenditure is represented by

$$T_t = \int_0^1 P_t(j)C_t(j)dj,$$

and P_t is such that

$$P_t = \min_{\{C_t(j)\}} T_t$$

subject to

$$C_t = \left[\int_0^1 C_t(j)^{\frac{\theta-1}{\theta}} dj\right]^{\frac{\theta}{\theta-1}} = 1.$$

The Lagrangian of the problem is represented by

$$\mathcal{L} = \int_0^1 P_t(j)C_t(j)dj - \lambda\left[\left(\int_0^1 C_t(j)^{\frac{\theta-1}{\theta}} dj\right)^{\frac{\theta}{\theta-1}} - 1\right],$$

whose first-order conditions are

$$P_t(j) = \lambda \left(\int_0^1 C_t(j)^{\frac{\theta-1}{\theta}} dj\right)^{\frac{\theta}{\theta-1}-1} C_t(j)^{-\frac{1}{\theta}}$$

$$= \lambda C_t^{\frac{1}{\theta}} C_t(j)^{-\frac{1}{\theta}} \tag{D.1}$$

for each j. Inserting this result into the expenditure function, we obtain

$$T_t = \int_0^1 P_t(j)C_t(j)dj = \lambda C_t^{\frac{1}{\theta}} \int_0^1 C_t(j)^{1-\frac{1}{\theta}} dj = \lambda C_t.$$

Therefore, given that P_t is defined as the minimum expenditure T_t to purchase one unit of C_t, and setting $P_t = T_t$ and $C_t = 1$ in the above equation, it follows that $P_t = \lambda$. Taking $C_t(j)$ from (D.1) and inserting it into the expenditure function and using $P_t = \lambda$ and $C_t = 1$, it follows that

$$P_t = \left(\int_0^1 P_t(j)^{1-\theta} dj\right)^{\frac{1}{1-\theta}},$$

which is (5.4). Demand (5.3) can be obtained from (D.1) using $P_t = \lambda$.

E Derivation of the Log-linear Approximations of Section 5.5.2 of Chapter 5

We derive the first-order approximation of the AD equation (5.24):

$$\xi_t U_c(Y_t - G_t) = \beta(1 + i_t)E_t\left\{\frac{P_t}{P_{t+1}}\xi_{t+1}U_c(Y_{t+1} - G_{t+1})\right\}. \quad (E.1)$$

Assume isoelastic utility of the form

$$U(C) = \frac{C^{1-\tilde{\sigma}^{-1}}}{1 - \tilde{\sigma}^{-1}},$$

with $\tilde{\sigma} > 0$, and recall that $C_t = Y_t - G_t$.

Take logs of (E.1) to obtain

$$\ln \xi_t - \tilde{\sigma}^{-1}\ln C_t = \ln \beta + \ln(1 + i_t) + \ln E_t\left\{\frac{P_t}{P_{t+1}}\xi_{t+1}U_c(C_{t+1})\right\}. \quad (E.2)$$

Note that in a log-linear approximation

$$\ln E_t\left\{\frac{P_t}{P_{t+1}}\xi_{t+1}U_c(C_{t+1})\right\} = \ln\left\{\frac{1}{\Pi}\xi C^{-\tilde{\sigma}^{-1}}\right\} + E_t\left\{\ln \xi_{t+1}/\xi + \right.$$
$$\left. -\tilde{\sigma}^{-1}\ln C_{t+1}/C - \ln \Pi_{t+1}/\Pi\right\}$$
$$= \ln \xi - \tilde{\sigma}^{-1}\ln C - \pi + E_t\left\{\hat{\xi}_{t+1} - \tilde{\sigma}^{-1}\hat{C}_{t+1}\right.$$
$$\left. - (\pi_{t+1} - \pi)\right\}, \quad (E.3)$$

using the definitions $\pi_t \equiv \ln \Pi_t$ and $\pi \equiv \ln \Pi$, where variables with hats denote log deviations of the respective variables from the steady state. Combining (E.2) and (E.3), we can write

$$\hat{\xi}_t - \tilde{\sigma}^{-1}\hat{C}_t = \hat{i}_t + E_t\left\{\hat{\xi}_{t+1} - \tilde{\sigma}^{-1}\hat{C}_{t+1} - (\pi_{t+1} - \pi)\right\} \quad (E.4)$$

using definition $\hat{i}_t = \ln(1 + i_t)/\ln(1 + i)$ and noting that $\ln(1 + i) = -\ln \beta + \ln \Pi$. Consider now equilibrium condition $C_t = Y_t - G_t$; it can be written as

$$\frac{C}{Y}\frac{C_t - C}{C} = \frac{Y_t - Y}{Y} - \frac{G_t - G}{Y},$$

and therefore

$$\frac{C}{Y}\hat{C}_t = \hat{Y}_t - \hat{G}_t, \quad (E.5)$$

noting that up to a first-order approximation $\hat{C}_t = \ln C_t/C = (C_t - C)/C$ and $\hat{Y}_t = \ln Y_t/Y = (Y_t - Y)/Y$, and using definition $\hat{G}_t = (G_t - G)/Y$. Using (E.5) in (E.4), we obtain AD equation (5.26),

$$\hat{Y}_t = \hat{G}_t + E_t(\hat{Y}_{t+1} - \hat{G}_{t+1}) - \sigma \left(\hat{i}_t - E_t(\pi_{t+1} - \pi) + E_t \hat{\xi}_{t+1} - \hat{\xi}_t \right),$$

in which $\sigma = \tilde{\sigma} Y/C$.

We derive now the first-order approximation of the AS block represented by

$$\left(\frac{1 - \alpha \left(\frac{\Pi_t}{\Pi} \right)^{\theta - 1}}{1 - \alpha} \right)^{\frac{1 + \theta\eta}{\theta - 1}} = \frac{F_t}{J_t}, \tag{E.6}$$

where F_t and J_t satisfy:

$$F_t = \xi_t(Y_t - G_t)^{-\frac{1}{\sigma}} \frac{Y_t}{\mu_t} + \alpha\beta E_t \left\{ F_{t+1} \left(\frac{\Pi_{t+1}}{\Pi} \right)^{\theta - 1} \right\}, \tag{E.7}$$

$$J_t = \xi_t \left(\frac{Y_t}{A_t} \right)^{(1+\eta)} + \alpha\beta E_t \left\{ J_{t+1} \left(\frac{\Pi_{t+1}}{\Pi} \right)^{\theta(1+\eta)} \right\}. \tag{E.8}$$

Take logs of equation (E.6) to obtain

$$\log \left(\frac{1 - \alpha \left(\frac{\Pi_t}{\Pi} \right)^{\theta - 1}}{1 - \alpha} \right) = -\frac{\theta - 1}{1 + \theta\eta}(\log J_t - \log F_t), \tag{E.9}$$

and also define

$$f_t \equiv \xi_t(Y_t - G_t)^{-\frac{1}{\sigma}} Y_t \mu_t^{-1},$$

$$j_t \equiv \xi_t \left(\frac{Y_t}{A_t} \right)^{(1+\eta)}.$$

A first-order Taylor approximation of the left-hand side of (E.9) implies that

$$\log \left(1 - \frac{\alpha \left(\frac{\Pi_t}{\Pi} \right)^{\theta - 1}}{1 - \alpha} \right) = -\frac{\alpha}{1 - \alpha}(\theta - 1)(\pi_t - \pi). \tag{E.10}$$

We must still derive a first-order approximation for $\log J_t$ and $\log F_t$ on the right-hand side of equation (E.9).

The definitions of J_t and F_t imply first-order expansions:

$$\hat{F}_t = (1 - \alpha\beta)\hat{f}_t + \alpha\beta E_t\{\hat{F}_{t+1} + (\theta - 1)(\pi_{t+1} - \pi)\}, \tag{E.11}$$

$$\hat{J}_t = (1 - \alpha\beta)\hat{j}_t + \alpha\beta E_t\{\hat{J}_{t+1} + \theta(1 + \eta)(\pi_{t+1} - \pi)\}. \tag{E.12}$$

Moreover, note that

$$\frac{\alpha(1 + \theta\eta)}{1 - \alpha}(\pi_t - \pi) = (\hat{J}_t - \hat{F}_t), \tag{E.13}$$

using (E.9) and (E.10). Therefore,

$$
\begin{aligned}
(\pi_t - \pi) &= \frac{1 - \alpha}{\alpha(1 + \theta\eta)}((1 - \alpha\beta)(\hat{j}_t - \hat{f}_t) + \alpha\beta E_t\{\hat{J}_{t+1} - \hat{F}_{t+1} \\
&\quad + (1 + \theta\eta)(\pi_{t+1} - \pi)\}) \\
&= \frac{1 - \alpha}{\alpha(1 + \theta\eta)}(1 - \alpha\beta)(\hat{j}_t - \hat{f}_t) + \beta E_t\{\pi_{t+1} - \pi\}.
\end{aligned}
$$

Note that

$$\hat{f}_t = \hat{\xi}_t - \sigma^{-1}(\hat{Y}_t - \hat{G}_t) + \hat{Y}_t - \hat{\mu}_t,$$

$$\hat{j}_t = \hat{\xi}_t + (1 + \eta)(\hat{Y}_t - \hat{A}_t).$$

We can finally derive the AS equation (5.27),

$$\pi_t - \pi = \kappa(\hat{Y}_t - \hat{Y}_t^n) + \beta E_t(\pi_{t+1} - \pi),$$

where

$$\kappa = \frac{(1 - \alpha)(1 - \alpha\beta)(\sigma^{-1} + \eta)}{\alpha(1 + \theta\eta)},$$

given the definition of the natural level of output,

$$\hat{Y}_t^n = \frac{1 + \eta}{\sigma^{-1} + \eta}\hat{A}_t + \frac{\sigma^{-1}}{\sigma^{-1} + \eta}\hat{G}_t - \frac{1}{\sigma^{-1} + \eta}\hat{\mu}_t.$$

Appendix to Chapter 7

F   Derivations of the Loss Function (7.1)

Consider the expected utility of the consumers (5.1) and write it as

$$U_{t_0} = E_{t_0} \left\{ \sum_{t=t_0}^{+\infty} \beta^{t-t_0} \xi_t \left[(U(C_t) - H(L_t) \Delta_t) \right] \right\},$$

in which

$$U(C_t) = \frac{C_t^{1-\frac{1}{\sigma}}}{1 - \frac{1}{\sigma}},$$

$$H(L_t) = \frac{L_t^{1+\eta}}{1 + \eta},$$

and

$$\Delta_t \equiv \int_0^1 \left(\frac{p_t(j)}{P_t} \right)^{-\theta(1+\eta)} dj.$$

Observe, indeed, that

$$L_t(j) = \frac{Y_t(j)}{A_t} = \left(\frac{p_t(j)}{P_t} \right)^{-\theta} \frac{Y_t}{A_t} = \left(\frac{p_t(j)}{P_t} \right)^{-\theta} L_t.$$

Note the second-order Taylor approximation

$$\frac{C_t^{1-\frac{1}{\sigma}}}{1 - \frac{1}{\sigma}} = \frac{C^{1-\frac{1}{\sigma}}}{1 - \frac{1}{\sigma}} + C^{-\frac{1}{\sigma}}(C_t - C) - \frac{1}{2}\frac{1}{\sigma}C^{-\frac{1}{\sigma}-1}(C_t - C)^2 + \mathcal{O}(||\xi||^3)$$

$$= \frac{C^{1-\frac{1}{\sigma}}}{1 - \frac{1}{\sigma}} + C^{1-\frac{1}{\sigma}}\hat{C}_t + \frac{1}{2}\left(1 - \frac{1}{\sigma}\right)C^{1-\frac{1}{\sigma}}\hat{C}_t^2 + \mathcal{O}(||\xi||^3), \quad \text{(F.1)}$$

where $\mathcal{O}(||\xi||^3)$ collects terms of order higher than the second and where, in the second line, we have used the following approximation:

$$\left(\frac{C_t - C}{C} \right) = \hat{C}_t + \frac{1}{2}\hat{C}_t^2 + \mathcal{O}(||\xi||^3).$$

Similarly, we can write

$$H(L_t)\Delta_t = H(L) + H_l(L_t - L) + \frac{1}{2}H_{ll}(L_t - L)^2 +$$

$$+ H(L)(\Delta_t - 1) + \mathcal{O}(\|\xi\|^3)$$

$$= H(L) + H_l L\hat{L}_t + \frac{1}{2}H_l L(1 + \eta)\hat{L}_t^2 +$$

$$+ H(L)(\Delta_t - 1) + \mathcal{O}(\|\xi\|^3), \qquad (\text{F.2})$$

using $\eta = H_{ll}Y/H_l$ and the fact that the expansion of Δ_t is of second-order magnitude, as will be shown.

Combining (F.1) and (F.2), we obtain

$$U(C_t) - H(L_t)\Delta_t$$

$$= U(C) - H(L)\Delta + U_c\hat{C}_t + \frac{1}{2}U_cC\left(1 - \frac{1}{\tilde{\sigma}}\right)\hat{C}_t^2 - H_l L\hat{L}_t +$$

$$- \frac{1}{2}H_l L(1 + \eta)\hat{L}_t^2 - H(L)(\Delta_t - 1) + \mathcal{O}(\|\xi\|^3). \qquad (\text{F.3})$$

Note that, given $Y_t = A_t L_t$, it holds exactly that

$$\hat{L}_t = \hat{Y}_t - \hat{A}_t, \qquad (\text{F.4})$$

whereas a second-order expansion of the equilibrium in the goods market $Y_t = C_t + G_t$ implies

$$Y_t - Y = C_t - C + G_t - G$$

and, therefore,

$$\hat{Y}_t + \frac{1}{2}\hat{Y}_t^2 = \frac{C}{Y}\left(\hat{C}_t + \frac{1}{2}\hat{C}_t^2\right) + \hat{G}_t + \mathcal{O}(\|\xi\|^3),$$

using definition $\hat{G}_t = (G_t - G)/Y$. We can then write

$$\hat{C}_t = \frac{Y}{C}\left(\hat{Y}_t - \hat{G}_t\right) + \frac{1}{2}\frac{Y}{C}\hat{Y}_t^2 - \frac{1}{2}\hat{C}_t^2 + \mathcal{O}(\|\xi\|^3)$$

and, therefore,

$$\hat{C}_t = \frac{Y}{C}\left(\hat{Y}_t - \hat{G}_t\right) + \frac{1}{2}\frac{Y}{C}\hat{Y}_t^2 - \frac{1}{2}\frac{Y^2}{C^2}\left(\hat{Y}_t - \hat{G}_t\right)^2 + \mathcal{O}(\|\xi\|^3). \qquad (\text{F.5})$$

We can combine (F.4) and (F.5) in (F.3) to obtain

$$U(C_t) - H(L_t)\Delta_t = C^{1-\frac{1}{\tilde\sigma}} \left[\frac{Y}{C}\left(\hat{Y}_t - \hat{G}_t\right) + \frac{1}{2}\frac{Y}{C}\hat{Y}_t^2 - \frac{1}{2}\frac{Y^2}{C^2}\left(\hat{Y}_t - \hat{G}_t\right)^2 \right]$$

$$- L^{1+\eta}(\hat{Y}_t - \hat{A}_t) + \frac{1}{2}\left(1 - \frac{1}{\tilde\sigma}\right)C^{1-\frac{1}{\tilde\sigma}}\frac{Y^2}{C^2}\left(\hat{Y}_t - \hat{G}_t\right)^2$$

$$- \frac{1}{2}(1+\eta)L^{1+\eta}(\hat{Y}_t - \hat{A}_t)^2 - H(L)(\Delta_t - 1)$$

$$+ \mathcal{O}(||\xi||^3)$$

by neglecting constant terms. Note that in the steady state $C^{-\frac{1}{\tilde\sigma}}/L^\eta = 1/A = L/Y$, implying $C^{-\frac{1}{\tilde\sigma}}Y = L^{1+\eta}$. We can then simplify the above equation by also neglect all terms independent of policy to

$$U(C_t) - \Delta_t H(L_t) = L^{1+\eta}\left\{ -\frac{\hat{\Delta}_t}{(1+\eta)} + \frac{1}{2}\hat{Y}_t^2 - \frac{1}{2}\frac{1}{\tilde\sigma}\frac{Y}{C}\left(\hat{Y}_t - \hat{G}_t\right)^2 \right.$$

$$\left. -\frac{1}{2}(1+\eta)(\hat{Y}_t - \hat{A}_t)^2 \right\} + \mathcal{O}(||\xi||^3).$$

Use now definition $\sigma \equiv \tilde\sigma C/Y$ and that of efficient level of output,

$$\hat{Y}_t^e = \frac{1+\eta}{\sigma^{-1}+\eta}\hat{A}_t + \frac{\sigma^{-1}}{\sigma^{-1}+\eta}\hat{G}_t,$$

to write

$$U(C_t) - \Delta_t H(L_t) = L^{1+\eta}\left\{ -\frac{\hat{\Delta}_t}{(1+\eta)} - \frac{\sigma^{-1}+\eta}{2}(\hat{Y}_t - \hat{Y}_t^e)^2 \right\}$$

$$+ \mathcal{O}(||\xi||^3). \tag{F.6}$$

Consider now the following approximation

$$\xi_t[U(C_t) - \Delta_t H(L_t)] = (\xi_t - \xi)[U(C) - \Delta H(L)] + \xi[U(C_t) - \Delta_t H(L_t)]^{2^{nd}}$$

$$+ (\xi_t - \xi)[U_c(C_t - C) - H_l(L_t - L)] + \mathcal{O}(||\xi||^3),$$

in which the second addendum on the right-hand side of the first line is meant to represent the second-order approximation found above. Given the steady-state assumptions made above, it follows that

$$\xi_t[U(C_t) - \Delta_t H(L_t)] = [U(C_t) - \Delta_t H(L_t)]^{2^{nd}} + \text{t.i.p.} + \mathcal{O}(||\xi||^3),$$

in which t.i.p. represents terms independent of policy.

Therefore, using (F.6), we can write a second-order approximation of the expected discounted utility as

$$
U_{t_0} = -L^{1+\eta} E_{t_0} \left\{ \sum_{t=t_0}^{+\infty} \beta^{t-t_0} \left[-\frac{\hat{\Delta}_t}{(1+\eta)} - \frac{\sigma^{-1}+\eta}{2}(\hat{Y}_t - \hat{Y}_t^e)^2 \right] \right\}
$$
$$
+ \text{ t.i.p. } + \mathcal{O}(\|\xi\|^3). \tag{F.7}
$$

Recall the definition of Δ_t,

$$
\Delta_t \equiv \int_0^1 \left(\frac{p_t(j)}{P_t} \right)^{-\theta(1+\eta)} dj,
$$

which can be written recursively as

$$
\Delta_t = \alpha \Delta_{t-1} \left(\frac{\Pi_t}{\Pi} \right)^{\theta(1+\eta)} + (1-\alpha) \left(\frac{P_t^*}{P_t} \right)^{-\theta(1+\eta)}.
$$

Using (5.20) to substitute for $\mathcal{P}_t^*/P_t$, we obtain

$$
\Delta_t = \alpha \Delta_{t-1} \left(\frac{\Pi_t}{\Pi} \right)^{\theta(1+\eta)} + (1-\alpha) \left(\frac{1-\alpha \left(\frac{\Pi_t}{\Pi} \right)^{\theta-1}}{1-\alpha} \right)^{\frac{\theta(1+\eta)}{\theta-1}}. \tag{F.8}
$$

Take a second-order Taylor expansion around the steady state in which $\Delta_t = 1$ and $\Pi_t = \Pi$ to obtain

$$
\Delta_t - 1 = \alpha(\Delta_{t-1} - 1) + \alpha\theta(1+\eta) \left(\frac{\Pi_t - \Pi}{\Pi} \right) +
$$
$$
+ \frac{1}{2}\alpha\theta(1+\eta)(\theta(1+\eta)-1) \left(\frac{\Pi_t - \Pi}{\Pi} \right)^2 +
$$
$$
- \alpha\theta(1+\eta) \left(\frac{\Pi_t - \Pi}{\Pi} \right) +
$$
$$
+ \frac{1}{2}\frac{\alpha\theta(1+\eta)}{(\alpha-1)} (\theta + \alpha - \theta(1+\eta)\alpha - 2) \left(\frac{\Pi_t - \Pi}{\Pi} \right)^2 +
$$
$$
+ \mathcal{O}(\|\xi\|^3),
$$

which can be written as

$$\hat{\Delta}_t = \alpha \hat{\Delta}_{t-1} + \frac{1}{2}\alpha\theta(1+\eta)(\theta(1+\eta)-1)(\pi_t - \pi)^2 +$$

$$\frac{1}{2}\frac{\alpha\theta(1+\eta)}{(\alpha-1)}(\theta + \alpha - \theta(1+\eta)\alpha - 2)(\pi_t - \pi)^2 +$$

$$+ \mathcal{O}(||\xi||^3),$$

using

$$\Pi_t = \Pi\left[1 + (\pi_t - \pi) + \frac{1}{2}(\pi_t - \pi)^2\right] + \mathcal{O}(||\xi||^3).$$

We can simplify the above equation to

$$\hat{\Delta}_t = \alpha \hat{\Delta}_{t-1} + \frac{\alpha}{1-\alpha}\theta(1+\eta)(1+\eta\theta)\frac{(\pi_t - \pi)^2}{2} + \text{t.i.p.} + \mathcal{O}(||\xi||^3).$$

Now note that

$$\hat{\Delta}_t = \alpha^{t-t_0+1}\hat{\Delta}_{t_0-1} + \frac{1}{2}\frac{\alpha\theta}{(1-\alpha)}(1+\eta)(1+\eta\theta)\sum_{s=t_0}^{t}\alpha^{t-s}(\pi_s - \pi)^2$$

$$+ \text{t.i.p.} + \mathcal{O}(||\xi||^3)$$

and, therefore,

$$\sum_{t=t_0}^{\infty}\beta^{t-t_0}\hat{\Delta}_t = \frac{1}{2}\frac{\alpha\theta(1+\eta)(1+\eta\theta)}{(1-\alpha)(1-\alpha\beta)}\sum_{t=t_0}^{\infty}\beta^{t-t_0}(\pi_t - \pi)^2$$

$$+ \text{t.i.p.} + \mathcal{O}(||\xi||^3), \tag{F.9}$$

neglecting initial condition $\hat{\Delta}_{t_0-1}$.

Combining and inserting this result into the expected discounted value of the approximated utility flow, (F.7), we finally obtain

$$U_{t_0} = -(\sigma^{-1}+\eta)L^{1+\eta}E_{t_0}\left\{\sum_{t=t_0}^{+\infty}\beta^{t-t_0}\left[\frac{1}{2}(\hat{Y}_t - \hat{Y}_t^*)^2 + \frac{1}{2}\frac{\theta}{\kappa}(\pi_t - \pi)^2\right]\right\}$$

$$+ \text{t.i.p.} + \mathcal{O}(||\xi||^3),$$

from which loss function (7.1) follows.

G Conditions for Determinacy

This appendix discusses the conditions under which a system of stochastic linear difference equations has a unique and stable solution. Blanchard-Kahn conditions require that the number of predetermined variables of the system be equal to the number of eigenvalues within the unit circle.[1] We provide a very informal reasoning for this result by discussing a simple example of linear stochastic difference equations. There are four cases to consider.

G.1 CASE I

Consider a linear stochastic difference equation in the variable x_t of the form

$$E_t x_{t+1} = \lambda x_t, \tag{G.1}$$

where λ, which is the eigenvalue, is outside the unit circle, i.e., $|\lambda| \geq 1$. The solutions of (G.1) are of the form

$$x_t = c \xi_t \lambda^t \tag{G.2}$$

for some $c \in \mathcal{R}$, with ξ_t being a martingale process, i.e., $E_t \xi_{t+1} = \xi_t$. Indeed, it can be verified that solutions (G.2) satisfy the difference equation (G.1) by inserting them into (G.1). There is no predetermined variable in equation (G.1), meaning that there is no initial condition for variable x_t. Since the eigenvalue is outside the unit circle, the Blanchard-Kahn conditions are satisfied. There is then a unique and bounded solution. Indeed, just set $c = 0$ in (G.2). Solution $x_t = 0$ is the only one that is stable, since the others diverge, given that $|\lambda| \geq 1$.

G.2 CASE II

Consider again the same stochastic linear difference equation (G.1), but now $|\lambda| < 1$. The solutions are again of the form (G.2). However, $x_t = 0$ is no longer a unique and stable solution since even the solutions with $c \neq 0$ converge to it. Therefore, when the number of eigenvalues within the unit circle is higher than the number of predetermined variables, there are multiple stable solutions.

---

1. See Blanchard and Kahn (1980).

G.3   CASE III

Consider a linear stochastic difference equation in the variable x_t of the form

$$x_t = \lambda x_{t-1} + \varepsilon_t, \tag{G.3}$$

where λ, which is the eigenvalue, is inside the unit circle, i.e., $|\lambda| < 1$. There is one predetermined variable and one eigenvalue within the unit circle. The Blanchard-Kahn conditions are satisfied. Indeed, (G.3) is already the stable and unique solution.

G.4   CASE IV

Consider again linear stochastic difference equation (G.3), but now with $|\lambda| \geq 1$. The number of eigenvalues inside the unit circle is lower than the number of predetermined variables. In this case there is no stable solution. Indeed, solution (G.3) is now unstable.

Appendix to Chapter 8

H   Derivations of Approximations (8.22) and (8.23)

Equation (8.22) represents a log-linear approximation of equation (8.6),

$$(1 + i_t^D) = \rho(1 + i_t^X) + (1 - \rho)(1 + i_t), \tag{H.1}$$

which can be written as

$$i_t^D - i^D = \rho(i_t^X - i^X) + (1 - \rho)(i_t - i_t)$$

and, therefore,

$$\frac{i_t^D - i^D}{1 + i^D} = \rho \frac{1 + i^X}{1 + i^D} \frac{i_t^X - i^X}{1 + i^X} + (1 - \rho) \frac{1 + i}{1 + i^D} \frac{i_t - i_t}{1 + i}.$$

The above equation can be written as

$$\hat{i}_t^D = \rho \frac{1 + i^X}{1 + i^D} \hat{i}_t^X + (1 - \rho) \frac{1 + i}{1 + i^D} \hat{i}_t, \tag{H.2}$$

in which $\hat{\imath}_t = \ln(1+i_t)/(1+i)$ is the first-order log-linear approximation of the respective variable. Define ν such that

$$\nu = 1 - \frac{1+i^D}{1+i}.$$

Therefore, using (H.1) evaluated at the steady state, we obtain

$$\frac{1+i^X}{1+i^D} = \frac{\rho-\nu}{1-\nu}\frac{1}{\rho}.$$

We can then write (H.2) as

$$\hat{\imath}_t^D = \frac{\rho-\nu}{1-\nu}\hat{\imath}_t^X + \frac{1-\rho}{1-\nu}\hat{\imath}_t,$$

from which (8.22) follows.

Equation (8.23) represents a log-linear approximation of equation (8.11), here restated:

$$\frac{(1+i_t^D)}{(1+i_t)} = \left(1 - \frac{V_d(d_t)}{U_c(Y_t)}\right). \tag{H.3}$$

Taking a first-order approximation, we obtain

$$\frac{(1+i^D)}{(1+i^B)}\frac{(i_t^D-i^D)}{(1+i^D)} - \frac{(1+i^D)}{(1+i)}\frac{(i_t-i)}{(1+i)} = -\frac{U_cV_{dd}(d_t-d) - V_dU_{cc}(Y_t-Y)}{(U_c)^2},$$

which can be written as

$$(1-\nu)(\hat{\imath}_t^D - \hat{\imath}_t) = -\frac{V_{dd}d}{V_d}\frac{V_d}{U_c}\hat{d}_t - \frac{U_{cc}Y}{U_c}\frac{V_d}{U_c}\hat{Y}_t.$$

Noting that $V_d/U_c = \nu$ and using the definitions $\sigma_d \equiv -V_d/(V_{dd}d)$ and $\sigma \equiv -U_c/(U_{cc}C)$, equation (8.23) follows, in which $d_y = \sigma_d/\sigma$ and $d_i = \sigma_d(1-\nu)/\nu$.

I Derivations of the Loss Function (8.27)

The derivation of the loss function (8.27) as a second-order approximation of equation (8.7) follows similar steps as the derivation of (7.1) for what concerns the utility of consumption and the disutility of labor, considering that $G_t = 0$. We just need to expand the term $V(d_t)$ in (8.7). We assume that in the steady state the economy is close to the satiation level, i.e., V_d is nonzero but of a small order ($V_d = \mathcal{O}(||\xi||)$). This corresponds to an economy in which the parameter ν is of a small order. We also assume that as d_t approaches from below the satiation level $\bar{d}$, the limiting value V_{dd} from below is negative. In the limit in which V_q becomes small, the demand for liquidity will still be of the same form as (8.23), with parameters $d_y = 0$ and $d_i = -U_c/(V_{dd}d)$.

Consider a second-order approximation of the term $V(d_t)$ as

$$V(d_t) = V(d) + V_d(d_t - d) + \frac{1}{2}V_{dd}(d_t - d)^2 + \mathcal{O}(||\xi||^3),$$

which can be written as

$$V(d_t) = V(d) + V_d d \hat{d}_t + \frac{1}{2}(V_d d + V_{dd}d^2)\hat{d}_t^2 + \mathcal{O}(||\xi||^3),$$

using

$$(d_t - d) = d\left(\hat{d}_t + \frac{1}{2}\hat{d}_t^2\right) + \mathcal{O}(||\xi||^3).$$

We can further write it as

$$V(d_t) = U_c Y\left[\frac{V_d d}{U_c Y}\hat{d}_t + \frac{1}{2}\left(\frac{V_d d}{U_c Y} + \frac{V_{dd}d^2}{U_c Y}\right)\hat{d}_t^2\right] + \mathcal{O}(||\xi||^3),$$

neglecting terms that are independent of policy. Note that $V_d = \mathcal{O}(||\xi||)$; therefore

$$V(d_t) = U_c Y\left[\frac{V_d d}{U_c Y}\hat{d}_t + \frac{1}{2}\left(\frac{V_{dd}d^2}{U_c Y}\right)\hat{d}_t^2\right] + \mathcal{O}(||\xi||^3),$$

which we can write it as

$$V(d_t) = U_c Y\frac{d}{Y}\left[v\hat{d}_t - \frac{1}{2}\frac{1}{d_i}\hat{d}_t^2\right] + \mathcal{O}(||\xi||^3),$$

since $v = V_d/U_c$, $d_i = -U_c/(V_{dd}d)$. Therefore, we can conclude that

$$V(d_t) = -\frac{1}{2}\frac{U_c d}{d_i}(\hat{d}_t - d^*)^2 + \mathcal{O}(||\xi||^3),$$

in which $d^* \equiv vd_i$. The loss function (8.27) follows combining the results of Appendix F, defining $\Lambda \equiv d/(Yd_i)$.

BIBLIOGRAPHY

Adam, Klaus and Henning Weber. 2019. "Optimal Trend Inflation." *American Economic Review* 109(2): 702–37.

Afrouzi, Hassan, Marina Halac, Kenneth Rogoff, and Pierre Yared. 2023. "Monetary Policy without Commitment." NBER Working Paper No. 31207.

Akinci, Ozge, Gianluca Benigno, Marco Del Negro, and Albert Queralto. 2020. "The Financial (In)Stability Real Interest Rate R^{**}." Federal Reserve Bank of New York Staff Report (946).

Alvarez, Fernando, Hervé Le Bihan, and Francesco Lippi. 2016. "The Real Effects of Monetary Shocks in Sticky Price Models: A Sufficient Statistic Approach." *American Economic Review* 106(10): 2817–2851.

Angeletos, Marios, Fabrice Collard and Harris Dellas. 2023. "Public Debt as Private Liquidity: Optimal Policy." *Journal of Political Economy* 131(11): 3233–3264.

Aoki, Kosuke. 2001. "Optimal Monetary Policy Responses to Relative-Price Changes." *Journal of Monetary Economics* 48(1): 55–80.

Aoki, Kosuke. 2015. "Relative Prices and Inflation Stabilization." *The Japanese Economic Review* 66: 35–59.

Arce, Oscar, Galo Nuno, Dominik Thaler, and Carlos Thomas. 2020. "A Large Central Bank Balance Sheet? Floor vs. Corridor Systems in a New Keynesian Environment." *Journal of Monetary Economics* 114: 350–367.

Arias, Jonas E., Dario Caldara, and Juan F. Rubio-Ramirez. 2019. "The Systematic Component of Monetary Policy in SVARs: An Agnostic Identification Procedure." *Journal of Monetary Economics* 101: 1–13.

Ascari, Guido and Argia M. Sbordone. 2014. "The Macroeconomics of Trend Inflation." *Journal of Economic Literature* 52(3): 679–739.

Auclert, Adrien, Rodolfo Rigato, Matthew Rognlie, and Ludwig Straub. 2024. "New Pricing Models, Same Old Phillips Curve." *Quarterly Journal of Economics* 139(1): 121–186.

Azzimonti, Marina and Pierre Yared. 2019. "The Optimal Public and Private Provision of Safe Assets." *Journal of Monetary Economics* 102: 126–144.

Bagehot, Walter. 1873. *Lombard Street: A Description of the Money Market*. London: Henry S. King.

Ball, Laurence and David Romer. 1990. "Real Rigidities and the Non-neutrality of Money." *Review of Economic Studies* 57: 183–203.

Ball, Laurence, Daniel Leigh, and Prachi Mishra. 2022. "Understanding U.S. Inflation During the COVID Era." *Brookings Papers on Economic Activity*.

Barattieri, Alessandro, Susanto Basu, and Peter Gottschalk. 2014. "Some Evidence on the Importance of Sticky Wages." *American Economic Journal: Macroeconomics* 6(1): 70–101.

Barnichon, Regis and Adam Hale Shapiro. 2022. "What's the Best Measure of Economic Slack?" *FRBSF Economic Letter* 2022-04.

Barro, Robert J. 1979. "Money and the Price Level under the Gold Standard." *Economic Journal* 89: 13–33.

Barsky, Robert B. and Lawrence H. Summers. 1988. "Gibson's Paradox and the Gold Standard." *Journal of Political Economy* 96(3): 528–550.

Bassetto, Marco. 2008. "Fiscal Theory of the Price Level." *The New Palgrave Dictionary of Economics*: 1–5.

Bassetto, Marco and Thomas Sargent. 2020. "Shotgun Wedding: Fiscal and Monetary Policy." *Annual Review of Economics* 12(1): 659–690.

Bauer, Michael D. and Eric T. Swanson. 2023. "A Reassessment of Monetary Policy Surprises and High-Frequency Identification." *NBER Macroeconomics Annual* 37.1: 87–155.

Belongia, Michael and Peter N. Ireland. 2006. "The Own-Price of Money and the Channels of Monetary Transmission." *Journal of Money, Credit and Banking* 38(2): 429–445.

Belongia, Michael and Peter N. Ireland. 2012. "The Barnett Critique after Three Decades: A New Keynesian Analysis." NBER Working Paper No. 17885.

Benati, Luca. 2023. "The Monetary Dynamics of Hyperinflation Reconsidered." University of Bern, Discussion Paper No. 2305.

Benati, Luca and Pierpaolo Benigno. 2023. "Gibson's Paradox and the Natural Rate of Interest." CEPR Discussion Paper No. 17959.

Benati, Luca, Robert E. Lucas, Juan Pablo Nicolini, and Warren Weber. 2021. "International Evidence on Long-Run Money Demand." *Journal of Monetary Economics* 117: 43–63.

Benhabib, Jess, Stephanie Schmitt-Grohé and Martín Uribe. 2001a. "The Perils of Taylor Rules." *Journal of Economic Theory* 96: 40–69.

Benhabib, Jess, Stephanie Schmitt-Grohé, and Martin Uribe. 2001b. "Monetary Policy and Multiple Equilibria." *American Economic Review* 91: 167–186.

Benhabib, Jess, Stephanie Schmitt-Grohé, and Martin Uribe. 2002. "Avoiding Liquidity Traps." *Journal of Political Economy* 110: 535–563.

Benigno, Gianluca and Pierpaolo Benigno. 2022. "Managing Monetary Policy Normalization." CEPR Discussion Paper No. 17290.

Benigno, Gianluca and Luca Fornaro. 2018. "Stagnation Traps." *Review of Economic Studies* 85(3): 1425–1470.

Benigno, Pierpaolo. 2015. "New-Keynesian Economics: An AS-AD View." *Research in Economics* 69: 503–524.

Benigno, Pierpaolo. 2020. "A Central-Bank Theory of the Price Level." *American Economic Journal: Macroeconomics* 12(3): 258–283.

Benigno, Pierpaolo. 2023. "Monetary Policy in a World of Cryptocurrencies." *Journal of the European Economic Association* 21(4): 1363–1396.

Benigno, Pierpaolo and Gauti Eggertsson. 2023. "It's Baaack: The Surge in Inflation in the 2020s and the Return of the Non-linear Phillips Curve." NBER Working Paper No. 31197.

Benigno, Pierpaolo and Gauti Eggertsson. 2024. "The Slanted-L Phillips Curve." AEA Papers and Proceedings 114: 84–89.

Benigno, Pierpaolo and Salvatore Nisticò. 2017. "Safe Assets, Liquidity and Monetary Policy." *American Economic Journal: Macroeconomics* 9(2): 182–227.

Benigno, Pierpaolo and Salvatore Nisticò. 2020. "Non-neutrality of Open Market Operations." *American Economic Journal: Macroeconomics* 12(3): 175–226.

Benigno, Pierpaolo and Salvatore Nisticò. 2022. "The Economics of Helicopter Money." Unpublished manuscript, University of Bern.

Benigno, Pierpaolo and Luca Antonio Ricci. 2011. "The Inflation-Output Trade-off with Downward Wage Rigidities." *American Economic Review* 101(4): 1436–1466.

Benigno, Pierpaolo and Roberto Robatto. 2019. "Private Money Creation, Liquidity Crises, and Equilibrium Liquidity." *Journal of Monetary Economics* 106: 42–58.

Benigno, Pierpaolo and Michael Woodford. 2005. "Inflation Stabilization and Welfare: The Case of a Distorted Steady State." *Journal of the European Economic Association* 3: 1–52.

Benigno, Pierpaolo and Michael Woodford. 2012. "Linear-Quadratic Approximation of Optimal Policy Problems." *Journal of Economic Theory* 147: 1–42.

Benigno, Pierpaolo, Gauti Eggertsson, and Federica Romei. 2020. "Dynamic Debt Deleveraging and Optimal Monetary Policy." *American Economic Journal: Macroeconomics* 12: 310-50.

Benigno, Pierpaolo, Linda Schilling, and Harald Uhlig. 2022. "Cryptocurrencies, Currency Competition and The Impossible Trinity." *Journal of International Economics* 136.

Bernanke, Ben S. 1983. "Nonmonetary Effects of the Financial Crisis in the Propagation of the Great Depression." *American Economic Review* 73(3): 257–76.

Bernanke, Ben S. 2002. "Deflation: Making Sure 'It' Doesn't Happen Here." Remarks at the National Economists Club. Board of Governors of the Federal Reserve System, Washington, D.C.

Bernanke, Ben S. 2022. *21st Century Monetary Policy.* W. W. Norton & Company: New York.

Bernanke, Ben S. and Olivier Blanchard. 2023. "What Caused the US Pandemic-Era Inflation?" Hutchins Center Working Papers.

Bernanke, Ben S. and Alan S. Blinder. 1988. "Credit, Money, and Aggregate Demand." *American Economic Review* 78(2): 435–39.

Bernanke, Ben S., and Harold James. 1991. "The Gold Standard, Deflation, and Financial Crisis in the Great Depression: An International Comparison." In: Hubbard (ed.) *Financial Markets and Financial Crisis.* Chicago: University of Chicago Press.

Bernanke, Ben S. and Frederic S. Mishkin. 1997. "Inflation Targeting: A New Framework for Monetary Policy?" *Journal of Economic Perspectives* 11(2): 97–116.

Bernanke, Ben S., Mark Gertler, and Simon Gilchrist. 1999. "The Financial Accelerator in a Quantitative Business Cycle Framework." *Handbook of Macroeconomics* 1: 1341–1393.

Berriel, Tiago C. and Saroj Bhattarai. 2009. "Monetary Policy and Central Bank Balance Sheet Concerns." *The B. E. Journal of Macroeconomics* 9, Contributions, Article 1.

Bhattarai, Saroj, Gauti Eggertsson, and Bulat Gafarov. 2023. "Time Consistency and Duration of Government Debt: A Model of Quantitative Easing." *Review of Economic Studies* 90(4): 1759–1799.

Bianchi, Francesco and Cosmin Ilut. 2017. "Monetary/Fiscal Policy Mix and Agent's Beliefs." *Review of Economic Dynamics* 26: 113–139.

Bianchi, Francesco and Leonardo Melosi. 2019. "The Dire Effects of the Lack of Monetary and Fiscal Coordination." *Journal of Monetary Economics* 104: 1–22.

Bianchi, Francesco, Renato Faccini, and Leonardo Melosi. 2023. "A Fiscal Theory of Persistent Inflation." *Quarterly Journal of Economics* 138(4): 2127–2179.

Bianchi, Javier and Saki Bigio. 2022. "Banks, Liquidity Management, and Monetary Policy." *Econometrica* 90(1): 391–454.

Bigio, Saki and Yuliy Sannikov. 2021. "A Model of Credit, Money, Interest, and Prices." NBER Working Paper No. 28540.

Bilbiie, Florin. 2008. "Limited Asset Markets Participation, Monetary Policy and (Inverted) Aggregate Demand Logic." *Journal of Economic Theory* 140.1: 162–196.

Bilbiie, Florin. 2019. "Monetary Policy and Heterogeneity: An Analytical Framework." Unpublished manuscript, University of Lausanne.

Bilbiie, Florin, Ippei Fujiwara, and Fabio Ghironi. 2014. "Optimal Monetary Policy with Endogenous Entry and Product Variety." *Journal of Monetary Economics* 64: 1–20.

Blanchard, Olivier. 1985. "Debt, Deficits, and Finite Horizon." *Journal of Political Economy* 93, 223–247.

Blanchard, Olivier and Jordi Galí. 2010. "Labor Markets and Monetary Policy: A New Keynesian Model with Unemployment." *American Economic Journal: Macroeconomics* 2(2): 1–30.

Blanchard, Olivier and Charles Kahn. 1980. "The Solution of Linear Difference Models under Rational Expectations." *Econometrica* 48: 1305–1311.

Blanchard, Olivier and Nobuhiro Kiyotaki. 1987. "Monopolistic Competition and the Effect of Aggregate Demand." *American Economic Review* 77(4): 647–666.

Blinder, Alan S. 2022. *A Monetary and Fiscal History of the United States 1961–2021*. Princeton University Press, Princeton, NJ.

Bordo, Michael D. 1981. "The Classical Gold Standard—Some Lessons for Today." *Federal Reserve Bank of St. Louis Review* 63(5): 2–17.

Bresciani-Turroni, Constantino. 1931. *The Economics of Inflation: A Study of Currency Depreciation in Post-war Germany, 1914–1923*. Routledge, 2013.

Brock, William A. 1974. "Money and Growth: The Case of Long Run Perfect Foresight." *International Economic Review*, 15(3): 750–777.

Brown, E. H. Phelps and Sheila V. Hopkins. 1950. "The Course of Wage-Rates in Five Countries, 1860–1939." *Oxford Economic Papers* 2.2: 226–296.

Brunner, Karl. 1989. "High-Powered Money and the Monetary Base." In: Eatwell, J., Milgate, M., Newman, P. (eds.) *Money*. The New Palgrave. Palgrave Macmillan, London, 175–178.

Bruno, Michael and Stanley Fisher. 1990. "Seigniorage, Operating Rules, and the High Inflation Trap." *Quarterly Journal of Economics* 105(2): 353–374.

Buiter, Willem H. 1999. "The Fallacy of the Fiscal Theory of the Price Level." NBER Working Paper No. 7302.

Buiter, Willem H. 2002. "The Fiscal Theory of the Price Level: A Critique." *Economic Journal* 112.481: 459–480.

Buiter, Willem H. 2014. "The Simple Analytics of Helicopter Money: Why It Works Always." *Economics E-Journal* 8: 1–51.

Cagan, Phillip. 1956. "The Monetary Dynamics of Hyperinflation." In: Friedman, Milton (ed.) *Studies in the Quantity Theory of Money*. Chicago: University of Chicago Press.

Cagan, Phillip. 1989a. "Hyperinflation." In: Eatwell, J., Milgate, M., Newman, P. (eds.) *Money*. *The New Palgrave*. Palgrave Macmillan, London, 179–184.

Cagan, Phillip. 1989b. "Monetarism." In: Eatwell, J., Milgate, M., Newman, P. (eds.) *Money*. *The New Palgrave*. Palgrave Macmillan, London, 195–205.

Calvo, Guillermo. 1978. "On the Time-Consistency of Optimal Policy in a Monetary Economy." *Econometrica* 46(6): 1411–1428.

Calvo, Guillermo. 1983. "Staggered Prices in a Utility-Maximizing Framework." *Journal of Monetary Economics* 12: 383–398.

Canzoneri, Matthew B. and Behzad T. Diba. 2005. "Interest Rate Rules and Price Determinacy: The Role of Transactions Services on Bonds." *Journal of Monetary Economics* 52(2): 329–343.

Canzoneri, Matthew B., Robert E. Cumby, and Behzad T. Diba. 2001. "Is the Price Level Determined by the Needs of Fiscal Solvency?" *American Economic Review* 91: 1221–1238.

Canzoneri, Matthew B., Robert E. Cumby, and Behzad T. Diba. 2002. "Should the European Central Bank and the Federal Reserve Be Concerned about Fiscal Policy?" In: *Rethinking Stabilization Policy*, Federal Reserve Bank of Kansas City.

Canzoneri, Matthew B., Robert E. Cumby, and Behzad T. Diba. 2017. "Should the Federal Reserve Pay Competitive Interest on Reserves?" *Journal of Money, Credit and Banking*, 49(4): 663–693.

Canzoneri, Matthew B., Robert E. Cumby, Behzad T. Diba, and David Lopez-Salido. 2008. "Monetary Aggregates and Liquidity in a Neo-Wicksellian Framework." *Journal of Money Credit and Banking* 40(8): 1667–1698.

Canzoneri, Matthew B., Robert Cumby, Behzad T. Diba, and David Lopez-Salido. 2011. "The Role of Liquid Government Bonds in the Great Transformation of American Monetary Policy." *Journal of Economic Dynamics and Control* 35(3): 282–294.

Capie, Forrest H. (ed.). 1991. *Major Inflations in History*. Aldershot, Hants. England: Edgard Publishing.

Cardoso, Eliana. 1998. "Virtual Deficits and the Patinkin Effect." *IMF Economic Review* 45: 619–646.

Carlin Wendy and David Soskice. 2005. "The Three-Equation New Keynesian Model: A Graphical Exposition." *Contributions to Macroeconomics* 5(1) Article 13.

Christiano, Lawrence J., Martin Eichenbaum, and Charles L. Evans. 1999. "Monetary Policy Shocks: What Have We Learned and to What End?" In: J. B. Taylor and M. Woodford (eds.) *Handbook of Macroeconomics*, Vol. 1A: 65–148.

Christiano, Lawrence J., Martin Eichenbaum, and Charles L. Evans. 2005. "Nominal Rigidities and the Dynamic Effects of a Shock to Monetary Policy." *Journal of Political Economy* 113(1): 1–45.

Cipolla, Carlo Maria. 1967. *Money, Prices, and Civilization in the Mediterranean World*. Gordian Press, INC, New York.

Cipolla, Carlo Maria. 1982. *The Monetary Policy of Fourteenth-Century Florence*. University of California Press, Berkeley, CA.

Cipolla, Carlo Maria. 1990. *Il governo della moneta a Firenze e a Milano nei secoli XIV–XVI*. Il Mulino, Bologna.

Clarida, Richard, Jordi Galí, and Mark Gertler. 1999. "The Science of Monetary Policy: A New Keynesian Perspective." *Journal of Economic Literature*, 37(4): 1661–1707.

Clarida, Richard, Jordi Galí, and Mark Gertler. 2000. "Monetary Policy Rules and Macroeconomic Stability: Evidence and Some Theory." *Quarterly Journal of Economics* 115(1): 147–180.

Cochrane, John. 2005. "Money as Stock." *Journal of Monetary Economics* 52: 501–528.

Cochrane, John. 2023. *The Fiscal Theory of the Price Level.* Princeton University Press, Princeton.

Coibion, Olivier and Yuriy Gorodnichenko. 2015. "Is the Phillips Curve Alive and Well After All? Inflation Expectations and the Missing Disinflation." *American Economic Journal: Macroeconomics* 7(1): 197–232.

Coibion, Olivier, Yuriy Gorodnichenko, and Rupal Kamdar. 2018. "The Formation of Expectations, Inflation, and the Phillips Curve." *Journal of Economic Literature*, 56(4): 1447–1491.

Coibion, Olivier, Yuriy Gorodnichenko, and Johannes Wieland. 2012. "The Optimal Inflation Rate in New Keynesian Models: Should Central Banks Raise Their Inflation Targets in Light of the Zero Lower Bound?" *Review of Economic Studies* 79(4) 1371–1406.

Comin, Diego A., Robert C. Johnson, and Callum J. Jones. 2023. "Supply Chain Constraints and Inflation." NBER Working Paper No. 31179.

Corbellini, Stefano Maria. 2024. "Optimal Monetary and Transfer Policy in a Liquidity Trap." *Journal of Money, Credit, and Banking*, forthcoming.

Correia, Isabel, Emmanuel Farhi, Juan Pablo Nicolini, and Pedro Teles. 2013. "Unconventional Fiscal Policy at the Zero Bound." *American Economic Review* 103(4): 1172–1211.

Curdia, Vasco and Michael Woodford. 2010. "Credit Spreads and Monetary Policy." *Journal of Money Credit and Banking* 42: 3–35.

Curdia, Vasco and Michael Woodford. 2011. "The Central-Bank Balance Sheet as an Instrument of Monetary Policy." *Journal of Monetary Economics* 58: 54–79.

Curdia, Vasco and Michael Woodford. 2016. "Credit Frictions and Optimal Monetary Policy." *Journal of Monetary Economics* 84: 30–65.

D'Amico, Stefania and Thomas B. King. 2013. "Flow and Stock Effects of Large Scale Treasury Purchases." *Journal of Financial Economics* 108(2): 425–48.

D'Amico, Stefania, William English, David Lopez-Salido, and Edward Nelson. 2012. "The Federal Reserve's Large-Scale Asset Purchase Programs: Rationale and Effects." *Economic Journal* 122(564): 415–446.

Dávila, Eduardo and Andreas Schaab. 2023. "Optimal Monetary Policy with Heterogeneous Agents: Discretion, Commitment, and Timeless Policy." NBER Working Paper No. 30961.

Debortoli, Davide and Jordi Galí. 2017. "Monetary Policy with Heterogeneous Agents: Insights from TANK models." Unpublished manuscript, Universitat Pompeu Fabra.

Del Negro, Marco and Christopher A. Sims. 2015. "When Does a Central Bank's Balance Sheet Require Fiscal Support?" *Journal of Monetary Economics* 73: 1–19.

Del Negro, Marco, Gauti Eggertsson, Andrea Ferrero, and Nobuhiro Kiyotaki. 2017. "The Great Escape? A Quantitative Evaluation of the Fed's Liquidity Facilities." *American Economic Review* 107(3): 824–57.

De Vroey, Michel. 2016. *A History of Macroeconomics from Keynes to Lucas and Beyond.* Cambridge University Press.

Diamond, Douglas and Philip Dybvig. 1983. "Bank Runs, Deposit Insurance, and Liquidity." *Journal of Political Economy* 91: 401–419.

Diba, Behzad and Olivier Loisel. 2021. "Pegging the Interest Rate on Bank Reserves: A Resolution of New-Keynesian Puzzles and Paradoxes." *Journal of Monetary Economics* 118: 230–244.

Diba, Behzad and Olivier Loisel. 2022. A Model of Post-2008 Monetary Policy. Unpublished manuscript, Georgetown University.

Dickens, William T., Lorenz F. Goette, Erica L. Groshen, Steinar Holden, Julián Messina, Mark E. Schweitzer, Jarkko Turunen, and Melanie E. Ward-Warmedinger. 2007. "How Wages Change: Micro Evidence from the International Wage Flexibility Project." *Journal of Economic Perspectives,* 21(2): 195–214.

Dixit, Avinash K., and Joseph E. Stiglitz. 1977. "Monopolistic Competition and Optimum Product Diversity." *American Economic Review* 67: 297–308.

Doepke, Matthias and Martin Schneider. 2017. "Money as a Unit of Account." *Econometrica* 85(5): 1537–1574.

Dotsey, Michael, Robert G. King, and Alexander L. Wolman. 1999. "State Dependent Pricing and the General Equilibrium Dynamics of Money and Output." *Quarterly Journal of Economics* 114(2): 655–690.

Dupraz, Stéphane, Emi Nakamura, and Jón Steinsson. 2019. "A Plucking Model of Business Cycles." NBER Working Paper No. 26352.

Eggertsson, Gauti. 2010. "Liquidity Trap." *Monetary Economics.* London: Palgrave Macmillan UK: 137–145.

Eggertsson, Gauti. 2011. "What Fiscal Policy Is Effective at Zero Interest Rates?" *NBER Macroeconomics Annual* 25: 59–112.

Eggertsson, Gauti and Paul Krugman. 2012. "Debt, Deleveraging, and The Liquidity Trap: A Fisher-Minsky-Koo Approach." *Quarterly Journal of Economics* 127: 1469–1513.

Eggertsson, Gauti and Cosimo Petracchi. 2021. "Mr. Keynes and the 'Classics'; A Suggested Reinterpretation." NBER Working Paper No. 29158.

Eggertsson, Gauti and Michael Woodford. 2003. "The Zero Bound on Interest Rates and Optimal Monetary Policy." *Brookings Papers on Economic Activity* 1: 139–233.

Eggertsson, Gauti and Michael Woodford. 2004. "Optimal Monetary and Fiscal Policy in a Liquidity Trap." *NBER International Seminar on Macroeconomics* 2004, 75–144.

Eggertsson, Gauti, Neil R. Mehrotra, and Jacob A. Robbins. 2019. "A Model of Secular Stagnation: Theory and Quantitative Evaluation." *American Economic Journal: Macroeconomics,* 11(1): 1–48.

Einaudi, Luigi. 1936. "Teoria della Moneta Immaginaria nel Tempo da Carlomagno alla Rivoluzione Francese." *Rivista di Storia Economica* 1.

Erceg, Christopher J., Dale W. Henderson, and Andrew T. Levin. 2000. "Optimal Monetary Policy with Staggered Wage and Price Contracts." *Journal of Monetary Economics* 46.2: 281–313.

Feinstein, Charles. 1972. *National Income, Expenditure and Output of the United Kingdom, 1855–1965.* Cambridge: Cambridge University Press.

Feldstein, Martin. 1997. "The Costs and Benefits of Going from Low Inflation to Price Stability." In: Christina D. Romer and David H. Romer (eds.) *Reducing Inflation: Motivation and Strategy.* University of Chicago Press: 123–56.

Feldstein, Martin. 1999. "Capital Income Taxes and the Benefit of Price Stability." In: Martin Feldstein (ed.) *The Costs and Benefits of Price Stability*. University of Chicago Press.

Fernandez-Villaverde, Jesus and Daniel Sanches. 2019. "Can Currency Competition Work?" *Journal of Monetary Economics* 106: 1–15.

Fisher, Irving. 1933. "The Debt-Deflation Theory of Great Depressions." *Econometrica* 1(4): 337–57.

Fisher, Stanley, Ratna Sahay, and Carlos Vegh. 2002. "Modern Hyper- and High Inflations." *Journal of Economic Literature* 40: 837–880.

Friedman, Milton. 1956. "The Quantity Theory of Money—A Restatement." In: M. Friedman (ed.) *Studies in the Quantity Theory of Money*. Chicago and London: University of Chicago Press.

Friedman, Milton. 1960. *A Program for Monetary Stability*. New York: Fordham University Press.

Friedman, Milton. 1963. *Inflation: Causes and Consequences.* Bombay: Asia Pub. House.

Friedman, Milton. 1964. "Monetary Studies of the National Bureau." In: *The National Bureau Enters Its 45th Year*, New York, NY: National Bureau of Economic Research, 7–25, 44th Annual Report.

Friedman, Milton. 1968. "The Role of Monetary Policy." Presidential address delivered at the 80th annual meeting of the American Economic Association. *American Economic Review* 58(1): 1–17.

Friedman, Milton. 1969. "Optimum Quantity of Money." In: *The Optimum Quantity of Money and Other Essays*. Chicago: Aldine Publishing Company.

Friedman, Milton. 1970a. "A Theoretical Framework for Monetary Analysis." *Journal of Political Economy* 78.2: 193–238.

Friedman, Milton. 1970b. "The Counter-Revolution in Monetary Theory." IEA Occasional Paper, no. 33.

Friedman, Milton. 1989. "Quantity Theory of Money." In: Eatwell, J., Milgate, M., Newman, P. (eds.) *Money*. The New Palgrave. Palgrave Macmillan, London: 1–40.

Friedman, Milton. 1993. "The 'Plucking Model' of Business Fluctuations Revisited." *Economic Inquiry* 31: 171–177.

Friedman, Milton and Anna J. Schwartz. 1963. *A Monetary History of the United States, 1867–1960.* Princeton University Press.

Friedman, Milton and Anna J. Schwartz. 1976. "From Gibson to Fisher." *Explorations in Economic Research*, volume 3, number 2 (Conference on International Trade, Finance, and Development of Pacific Basin Countries, December 6-7, 1974).

Friedman, Milton and Anna J. Schwartz. 1986. "Has Government Any Role in Money?" *Journal of Monetary Economics* 17.1: 37–62.

Fujiwara, Ippei, Tomoyuki Nakajima, Nao Sudo, and Yuki Teranishi. 2013. "Global Liquidity Trap." *Journal of Monetary Economics* 60(8): 936–949.

Gagliardone, Luca and Mark Gertler. 2023. "Oil Prices, Monetary Policy and Inflation Surges." Unpublished manuscript, New York University.

Galí, Jordi. 2008. *Monetary Policy, Inflation, and the Business Cycle: An Introduction to the New Keynesian Framework*. Princeton University Press: Princeton, NJ.

Galí Jordi. 2009. *Unemployment Fluctuations and Stabilization Policies: A New Keynesian Perspective*. MIT Press, Boston MA.

Galí, Jordi. 2020. "The Effects of a Money-Financed Fiscal Stimulus." *Journal of Monetary Economics* 115: 1–19.

Gerali, Andrea, Stefano Neri, Luca Sessa, and Federico Signoretti. 2010. "Credit and Banking in a DSGE Model of the Euro Area." *Journal of Money, Credit and Banking* 42: 107–141.

Gersbach, Hans. 1999. "How to Avoid the Consequences of Anticipated Monetary Policies." *Economic Theory* 14: 729–740.

Gertler, Mark and Peter Karadi. 2011. "A Model of Unconventional Monetary Policy." *Journal of Monetary Economics* 58: 17–34.

Gertler, Mark and Nobuhiro Kiyotaki. 2010. "Financial Intermediation and Credit Policy in Business Cycle Analysis." In: Benjamin M. Friedman and Michael Woodford (eds.) *Handbook of Monetary Economics* 3: 547–599.

Gertler, Mark and Antonella Trigari. 2009. "Unemployment Fluctuations with Staggered Nash Wage Bargaining." *Journal of Political Economy* 117(1): 38–86.

Giannoni, Marc and Michael Woodford. (2017). "Optimal Target Criteria for Stabilization Policy." *Journal of Economic Theory* 168: 55–106.

Gibson, Albert H. 1923. "The Future Course of High Class Investment Values." *Banker's Magazine* 115: 15–34.

Giovannini, Alberto and Bart Turtelboom. 1992. "Currency Substitution." NBER Working Paper No. 4232.

Golosov, Mikhail and Robert E. Lucas. 2007. "Menu Costs and Phillips Curves." *Journal of Political Economy* 115(2): 171–199.

Goodfriend, Marvin. 2005. "Narrow Money, Broad Money, and the Transmission of Monetary Policy." *Models and Monetary Policy: Research in the Tradition of Dale Henderson, Richard Porter, and Peter Tinsley*. Board of Governors of the Federal Reserve System.

Goodfriend, Marvin and Robert G. King. 2005. "The Incredible Volcker Disinflation." *Journal of Monetary Economics*, 52: 981–1015.

Goodfriend, Marvin and Bennett T. McCallum. 2007. "Banking and Interest Rates in Monetary Policy Analysis: A Quantitative Exploration." *Journal of Monetary Economics* 54(5): 1480–1507.

Goodhart, Charles. 1999. "Myths about the Lender of Last Resort." *International Finance* 2(3): 339–360.

Gordon, Robert J. 1977. "The Theory of Domestic Inflation." *American Economic Review*, 67(1): 128–134.

Gordon, Robert J. 2013. "The Phillips Curve is Alive and Well: Inflation and the NAIRU during the Slow Recovery." NBER Working Paper No. 19390.

Gorton, Gary. 2017. "The History and the Economics of Safe Assets." *Annual Review of Economics* 9: 547–586.

Gorton, Gary and Guillermo Ordonez. 2022. "The Supply and Demand for Safe Assets." *Journal of Monetary Economics* 125: 132–147.

Gorton, Gary and George Pennacchi. 1990. "Financial Intermediaries and Liquidity Creation." *Journal of Finance* 45, 49–71.

Greenwood, Robin, Samuel G. Hanson, and Jeremy C. Stein. 2015. "A Comparative-Advantage Approach to Government Debt Maturity." *Journal of Finance* 70(4): 1683–1722.

Greenwood, Robin, Samuel G. Hanson, and Jeremy C. Stein. 2016. "The Federal Reserve's Balance Sheet as a Financial-Stability Tool." Proceedings of the Jackson Hole Symposium of the Federal Reserve Bank of Kansas City.

Guerrieri, Veronica and Guido Lorenzoni. 2017. "Credit Crises, Precautionary Savings, and the Liquidity Trap." *Quarterly Journal of Economics* 132(3): 1427–1467.

Hall, Robert. 2005. "Controlling the Price Level." *American Journal of Economics and Sociology* 64: 92–112.

Hall, Robert and Ricardo Reis. 2015. "Maintaining Central-Bank Solvency under New Style Central Banking." NBER Working Paper No. 21173.

Hamilton, Earl. 1947. "Origin and Growth of the National Debt in Western Europe." *American Economic Review* 37(2): 118–130.

Harding, Martin, Jesper Lindé, and Mathias Trabandt. 2023. "Understanding Post-Covid Inflation Dynamics." *Journal of Monetary Economics* 140: S101–S118.

Hayek, Friedrich. 1937. *Monetary Nationalism and International Stability.* London: Longmans, Grenn. The Graduate Institute of International Studies, Geneva, Publication Number 18.

Hayek, Friedrich. 1948. *Individualism and Economic Order.* The University of Chicago Press.

Hayek, Friedrich. 1976. *The Denationalization of Money.* Institute of Economic Affairs, London.

Hazell, Jonathon, Juan Herreno, Emi Nakamura, and Jon Steinsson. 2022. "The Slope of the Phillips Curve: Evidence from U.S. States." *Quarterly Journal of Economics* 137(3): 1299–1344.

Hetzel, Robert L. 1987. "Henry Thornton: Seminal Monetary Theorist and Father of the Modern Central Bank." *Economic Review,* Federal Reserve Bank of Richmond, 1–16.

Hicks, John. 1937. "Mr. Keynes and the 'Classics'; A Suggested Interpretation." *Econometrica* 5: 147–159.

Holden Steinar. 2004. "The Cost of Price Stability: Downward Nominal Wage Rigidity in Europe." *Economica,* 71(282): 183–208.

Hume, David. 1752. *Political Discourses: Of Money.* Edinburgh, printed by R. Fleming for A. Kinkaid and A. Donaldson.

International Monetary Fund. 2005. *World Economic Outlook,* September 2005.

Jacobson, Margaret M., Eric M. Leeper, and Bruce Preston. 2023. "Recovery of 1933." NBER Working Paper No. 25629.

Kaplan, Greg, Benjamin Moll, and Giovanni Violante. 2018. "Monetary Policy According to HANK." *American Economic Review* 108(3): 697–743.

Kareken, John and Neil Wallace. 1981. "On the Indeterminacy of Equilibrium Exchange Rates." *Quarterly Journal of Economics* 96: 207–222.

Keynes, John Maynard. 1930. *A Treatise on Money.* Vols. I–II, New York: Harcourt, Brace and Co.

Keynes, John Maynard. 1936. *The General Theory of Employment, Interest, and Money.* New York. Palgrave Macmillan, London.

Keynes, John Maynard. 1940. *How to Pay for the War.* MacMillan and Co., London.

Khan, Aubhik, Robert G. King, and Alexander L. Wolman. 2003. "Optimal Monetary Policy." *Review of Economic Studies* 70(4): 825–860.

Kim, Jinill and Francisco J. Ruge-Murcia. 2009. "How Much Inflation Is Necessary to Grease the Wheels?" *Journal of Monetary Economics* 56.3: 365–377.

Krishnamurthy, Arvind and Annette Vissing-Jorgensen. 2011. "The Effects of Quantitative Easing on Interest Rates: Channels and Implications for Policy." *Brooking Papers on Economic Activity* 2.

Krugman, Paul. 1998. "It's Baaack! Japan's Slump and the Return of the Liquidity Trap." *Brookings Papers on Economic Activity* 2, 137–187.

Kydland, Finn E. and Edward C. Prescott. 1982. "Time to Build and Aggregate Fluctuations." *Econometrica*: 1345–1370.

Law, John. 1705. *Money and Trade Considered, with a Proposal for Supplying the Nation with Money*. Edinburgh. Printed by the Heirs and Successors of Andrew Anderson, Printer to the Queens most Excellent Majesty.

Leeper, Eric. 1991. "Equilibria under 'Active' and 'Passive' Monetary and Fiscal Policies." *Journal of Monetary Economics* 27: 129–147.

Lombardo, Giovanni and David Vestin. 2008. "Welfare Implications of Calvo vs. Rotemberg-Pricing Assumptions." *Economics Letters* 100(2): 275–279.

Loyo, Eduardo. 1999. "Tight Money Paradox on the Loose: A Fiscalist Hyperinflation." Unpublished manuscript, Harvard University.

Lucas, Robert E. 1972. "Expectations and the Neutrality of Money." *Journal of Economic Theory* 4(2): 103–124.

Lucas, Robert E. 1973. "Some International Evidence on Output-Inflation Tradeoffs." *American Economic Review*: 326–334.

Lucas, Robert E. 1982. "Interest Rates and Currency Prices in a Two-Country World." *Journal of Monetary Economics* 10(3): 335–359.

Lucas, Robert E. 1994. "Review of Milton Friedman and Anna J. Schwartz's 'A Monetary History of the United States, 1867–1960.' " *Journal of Monetary Economics* 34.1 (1994): 5–16.

Lucas, Robert E. 2002. "Macroeconomic Priorities." *American Economic Review* 93: 1–14.

Lucas, Robert E. and Nancy Stokey. 1987. "Money and Interest in a Cash-in-Advance Economy." *Econometrica* 55, 491–513.

Magill, Michael, Martine Quinzii, and Jean-Charles Rochet. 2020 "The Safe Asset, Banking Equilibrium, and Optimal Central Bank Monetary, Prudential and Balance-Sheet Policies." *Journal of Monetary Economics* 112: 113–128.

Mankiw, Gregory. 1985. "Small Menu Costs and Large Business Cycles: A Macroeconomic Model of Monopoly." *Quarterly Journal of Economics* 100(2): 529–539.

Mankiw, Gregory and Ricardo Reis. 2002. "Sticky Information vs. Sticky Prices: A Proposal to Replace the New Keynesian Phillips Curve." *Quarterly Journal of Economics* 117(4): 1295–1328.

Masciandaro, Donato, Goodhart, Charles and Stefano Ugolini. 2021. "Pandemic Recession and Helicopter Money: Venice, 1629–1631." *Financial History Review* 28(3): 300–318.

McLeay, Michael and Silvana Tenreyro. 2019. "Optimal Inflation and the Identification of the Phillips Curve." *NBER Macroeconomics Annual* 34: 199–255.

McKay, Alisdair, Emi Nakamura, and Jón Steinsson. 2016. "The Power of Forward Guidance Revisited." *American Economic Review* 106(10): 3133–58.

Meltzer, Allan H. 1963. "The Demand for Money: The Evidence from the Time Series." *Journal of Political Economy* 71.3: 219–246.

Mian, Atif and Amir Sufi. 2011. "House Prices, Home Equity-Based Borrowing, and the U.S. Household Leverage Crisis." *American Economic Review* 101: 2132–2156.

Michaillat, Pascal. 2014. "A Theory of Countercyclical Government Multiplier." *American Economic Journal: Macroeconomics*, 6(1): 190-217.

Mises, Ludwig von. 1912. *The Theory of Money and Credit*. Trans. H. E. Batson. Indianapolis: Liberty Classics.

Mortensen, Dale T. and Christopher A. Pissarides. 1994. "Job Creation and Job Destruction in the Theory of Unemployment." *Review of Economic Studies* 61: 397–415.

Nakamura, Emi and Jón Steinsson. 2008. "Five Facts about Prices: A Reevaluation of Menu Cost Models." *Quarterly Journal of Economics* 123(4): 1415–1464.

Nakamura, Emi and Jón Steinsson. 2010. "Monetary Non-neutrality in a Multisector Menu Cost Model." *Quarterly Journal of Economics* 125(3): 961–1

Nakamura, Emi and Jón Steinsson. 2013. "Price Rigidity: Microeconomic Evidence and Macroeconomic Implications." *Annual Review of Economics* 5(1): 133–163.

Niepelt, Dirk. 2023. "Money and Banking with Reserves and CBDC." *Journal of Finance*, forthcoming.

Nisticò, Salvatore. 2007. "The Welfare Loss from Unstable Inflation." *Economics Letters* 96(1): 51–57.

Nisticò, Salvatore. 2012. "Monetary Policy and Stock-Price Dynamics in a DSGE Framework." *Journal of Macroeconomics* 34(1): 126–146.

Nisticò, Salvatore. 2016. "Optimal Monetary Policy and Financial Stability in a Non-Ricardian Economy." *Journal of the European Economic Association* 14: 1225–1252.

Obstfeld, Maurice and Kenneth Rogoff. 1983. "Speculative Hyperinflations in Maximizing Models: Can We Rule Them Out?" *Journal of Political Economy* 91(4): 675–687.

Park, Seok G. 2012. "Central Banks Quasi-Fiscal Policies and Inflation." IMF Working Papers 2012(014), A001.

Phelps, Edmund S. 1967. "Phillips Curves, Expectations of Inflation and Optimal Unemployment over Time." *Economica* 34(135): 254–81.

Phelps, Edmund S. 1970. "Introduction: The New Microeconomics in Employment and Inflation Theory." In: E. S. Phelps et al., *Microeconomic Foundations of Employment and Inflation Theory*. New York: Norton.

Phillips, Alban W. 1958. "The Relation between Unemployment and the Rate of Change of Money Wage Rates in the United Kingdom, 1861–1957." *Economica* 25(100): 283–299.

Piazzesi, Monika, Ciaran Rogers, and Martin Schneider. 2021. Money and Banking in a New-Keynesian Model. Unpublished manuscript, Stanford University.

Piergallini, Alessandro. 2006. "Real Balance Effects and Monetary Policy." *Economic Inquiry* 44(3): 497–511.

Quinn, Stephen and William Roberds. 2014. "Death of a Reserve Currency." Atlanta Fed Working Paper 2014-17.

Ramsey, Frank. 1928. "A Mathematical Theory of Saving." *Economic Journal* 38(152): 543–59.

Reichlin, Lucrezia, Adair Turner, and Michael Woodford. 2013. "Helicopter Money as a Policy Option." VoxEU.org.

Reis, Ricardo. 2013. "The Mystique Surrounding the Central Bank's Balance Sheet, Applied to the European Crisis." *American Economic Review*, 103(3): 135–140.

Reis, Ricardo and Silvana Tenreyro. 2022. "Helicopter Money: What Is It and What Does It Do?" *Annual Review of Economics* 14: 313–335.

Romer, David. 2000. "Keynesian Macroeconomics without the LM Curve." *Journal of Economic Perspectives* 14(2): 149–169.

Rotemberg, Julio. 1982. "Monopolistic Price Adjustment and Aggregate Output." *Review of Economic Studies* 49: 517–531.

Samuelson, Paul A. and Robert M. Solow. 1960. "Analytical Aspects of Anti-Inflation Policy." *American Economic Review* 50(2): 177–94.

Sargent, Thomas J. 1982. "The Ends of Four Big Inflations." In: R. Hall (ed.) *Inflation: Causes and Effects*. Chicago: University of Chicago Press.

Sargent, Thomas J. 2011. "Where to Draw Lines: Stability versus Efficiency." *Economica* 78: 197–214.

Sargent, Thomas J. and Robert Townsend. 2009. *Questioning Carlo Cipolla*. Unpublished monograph, New York University.

Sargent, Thomas and Neil Wallace. 1975. "Rational Expectations, the Optimal Monetary Instrument, and the Optimal Money Supply Rule." *Journal of Political Economy* 83: 241–254.

Sargent, Thomas and Neil Wallace. 1981. "Some Unpleasant Monetarist Arithmetic." *Federal Reserve Bank of Minneapolis Quarterly Review* 5(3): 1–17.

Schilling, Linda and Harald Uhlig. 2019. "Some Simple Bitcoin Economics." *Journal of Monetary Economics* 106: 16–26.

Schwartz, Anna. 1989. "Banking School, Currency School, Free Banking School." In: Eatwell, J., Milgate, M., Newman, P. (eds.) *Money*. The New Palgrave. Palgrave Macmillan, London: 41–49.

Selgin, George. 1994. "On Ensuring the Acceptability of a New Fiat Money." *Journal of Money, Credit and Banking* 26: 808–826.

Sidrausky, Miguel. 1967. "Rational Choice and Patterns of Growth in a Monetary Economy." *American Economic Review* 57(2): 534–544.

Sims, Christopher. 1994. "A Simple Model for Study of the Determination of the Price Level and the Interaction of Monetary and Fiscal Policy." *Economic Theory* 4: 381–399.

Sims, Christopher. 1999a. "The Precarious Fiscal Foundations of EMU." *De Economist* 147: 415–436.

Sims, Christopher. 1999b. "Domestic Currency Denominated Government Debt as Equity in the Primary Surplus." Unpublished manuscript, Princeton University.

Sims, Christopher. 2000. "Fiscal Aspects of Central Bank Independence." Unpublished manuscript. Princeton University.

Sims, Christopher. 2013. "Paper Money." *American Economic Review* 103(2): 563–584.

Sims, Christopher. 2022. "Optimal Fiscal and Monetary Policy with Distorting Taxes." Unpublished manuscript, Princeton University.

Sims, Christopher and Tao Zha. 2006. "Were There Regime Switches in US Monetary Policy?" *American Economic Review* 96.1: 54–81.

Smets, Frank and Rafael Wouters. 2007. "Shocks and Frictions in US Business Cycles: A Bayesian DSGE Approach." *American Economic Review* 97(3): 586–606.

Smith, Adam. 1776. *An Inquiry into the Nature and Causes of the Wealth of Nations.* Edited by Edwin Cannan. The University of Chicago Press: Chicago.

Stein, Jeremy C. 2012. "Monetary Policy as Financial Stability Regulation." *Quarterly Journal of Economics* 127.1: 57–95.

Stella, Peter. 2005. "Central Bank Financial Strength, Transparency, and Policy Credibility." *IMF Staff Papers*, Vol. 52, No. 2: 335–365.

Stella, Peter. 2008. "Central Bank Financial Strength, Policy Constraints and Inflation." IMF Working Paper No. 08/49.

Svensson, Lars. 1985. "Money and Asset Prices in a Cash-in-Advance Economy." *Journal of Political Economy* 93(5): 919–944.

Svensson, Lars. 2010. "Inflation Targeting." *Handbook of Monetary Economics.* Vol. 3: 1237–1302.

Taylor, John B. 1979. "Staggered Wage Setting in a Macro Model." *American Economic Review* 69(2): 108–13.

Taylor, John B. 1993. "Discretion versus Policy Rules in Practice." *Carnegie-Rochester Conference Series on Public Policy* 39: 195–214.

Teranishi, Yuki. 2015. "Smoothed Interest Rate Setting by Central Banks and Staggered Loan Contracts." *Economic Journal* 125(582): 162–183.

Thornton, Henry. 1802. *An Enquiry into the Nature and Effects of the Paper Credit of Great Britain.* Edited with an Introduction by F. A. v. Hayek. New York: Rinehart & Company, Inc., 1939.

Thornton, M. K. and R. L. Thornton. 1990. "The Financial Crisis of A.D. 33: A Keynesian Depression?" *Journal of Economic History* 50: 655–662.

Tobin, James. 1972. "Inflation and Unemployment." *American Economic Review*, 62(1): 1–18.

Tsinikos, Konstantinos. 2018. "Equivalence between Tighter Borrowing and Lending Constraints." *Theoretical and Applied Essays in Macroeconomics*, Ph.D. Dissertation, Chapter 1, University of Rome "Tor Vergata."

Ueda, Kazuo. 2012. "The Effectiveness of Nontraditional Monetary Policy: The Case of the Bank of Japan." *Japanese Economic Review* 63(1): 1–22.

Vissing-Jorgensen, Annette. 2023. "Balance Sheet Policy above the Effective Lower Bound." Conference Proceedings, ECB Forum on Central Banking (Sintra).

Wallace, Neil. 1981. "A Modigliani-Miller Theorem for Open Market Operations." *American Economic Review* 71: 267–274.

Walsh, Carl, 2002. "Teaching Inflation Targeting: An Analysis for Intermediate Macro." *Journal of Economic Education* 33(4): 333–347.

Walsh, Carl. 2017. *Monetary Theory and Policy.* MIT Press.

Werning, Ivan. 2011. "Managing a Liquidity Trap: Monetary and Fiscal Policy." National Bureau of Economic Research Working Paper 17344.

White, Lawrence H. 2014. "Free Banking in History and Theory." George Mason University Working Paper in Economics No. 14-07.

Wicksell, Knut. 1898. *Interest and Prices.* Richard Kahn (trans.). London: Macmillan, for the Royal Economic Society, 1936.

Williams, John. 2016. "Monetary Policy in a Low R-Star World." *FRBSF Economic Letter* 2016-23.

Williamson Samuel. 2023. "The Annual Consumer Price Index for the United States, 1774-Present." MeasuringWorth, http://www.measuringworth.com/uscpi/.

Wolf, Christian. 2023. "Interest Rate Cuts vs. Stimulus Payments: An Equivalence Result." Unpublished manuscript, MIT.

Woodford, Michael. 1990. The Optimum Quantity of Money. *Handbook of Monetary Economics*, Volume 2, Ch. 20, 1067–1152.

Woodford, Michael. 1995. "Price Level Determinacy without Control of a Monetary Aggregate." *Carnegie-Rochester Conference Series on Public Policy* 43: 1–46.

Woodford, Michael. 1998. "Public Debt and the Price Level." Unpublished manuscript, Princeton University.

Woodford, Michael. 2000. "Monetary Policy in a World without Money." *International Finance*, 2(3): 229–260.

Woodford, Michael. 2001a. "Imperfect Common Knowledge and the Effects of Monetary Policy." NBER Working Paper No. 8673.

Woodford, Michael. 2001b. "Fiscal Requirements for Price Stability." *Journal of Money, Credit and Banking* 33(1): 669–728.

Woodford, Michael. 2001c. "Monetary Policy in the Information Economy." In *Economic Policy for the Information Economy*. Kansas City: Federal Reserve Bank of Kansas City: 297–370.

Woodford Michael, 2002. "Inflation Stabilization and Welfare." *The B. E. Journal of Macroeconomics*, vol. 2(1): 1–53.

Woodford, Michael. 2003. *Interest and Prices*. Princeton, NJ: Princeton University Press.

Woodford, Michael. 2010. "Financial Intermediation and Macroeconomic Analysis." *Journal of Economic Perspectives* 24: 21–44.

Yun, Tack. 1996. "Nominal Price Rigidity, Money Supply Endogeneity, and Business Cycles." *Journal of Monetary Economics* 37: 345–370.

INDEX

Page numbers in italics indicate figures and tables.

coins: Dark Ages and, 355; debasement
of, in medieval period, 294; Florentine Florin, 3; "good" and "bad," 357n1;
Italian republics, 359; seigniorage, 50–52
Commercial Paper Funding Facility, 237
commitment, 172; adoption of "flexible
inflation targeting," 155–56; New Keynesian (NK) model, *168, 169*; optimal
policy under, 152–63; standard, 154–55;
timeless perspective, 153, 154, 155, 172,
262, 265
consolidated budget constraint, 25, 89, 98,
126, 182
consumer(s): borrowing limit, 16; budget
constraint, 45, 96–97; intertemporal
budget constraint, 16, 34, 49, 57, 66, 81,
84, 98, 124; liquidity services of cash,
44–47; monetary economy, 13–17; safe
assets model, 270–72
consumer demand function, 35, 35n27
consumer price index (CPI): core inflation
rate, 295, *296*; inflation expectations,
295; United States, 8, *9*; Zimbabwe
hyperinflation, *331*
consumption demand of good, 121
COVID-19 pandemic, 117; central bank
policies, 357; global economy and, 356;
inflation, *9*; inflation and economic
activity, 320; labor markets and, 326;
macroeconomic stabilization role, 236;
missing disinflation and, 320–21; monetary and fiscal policies, 11; post-inflation,
10, 357; unconventional monetary policy, 215; unemployment rate, *296, 297*;
world economy and, 200
credit crunch: financial crisis (2007–2008),
253–56; frictionless real rate of interest,
243
credit-easing policies, 263
credit spread, 239, 258; forward guidance,
261–62
cryptocurrency: competition, 62–74; government currency, 62; launching a fully
backed, 72–74; medium of exchange,

64, 70–72; optimization problem, 63–
64; private currency, 62; store-of-value
properties of money, 63; threatening
to monetary sovereignty, 76; types
of money used, 68–70; use of government money, 67–68; using only private
money, 70–72; verifying legitimacy of
transactions, 358–59
cryptography guarantee, 358, 361
currency, 4–5; central bank theory of the
price level, 28–32; competition, 77; concept of, 11; controlling value of, 359–61;
cryptocurrency competition, 62–74;
debates about money and, 94n4; definition of, 3, 4; determining the value
of, 22–32; digital, 4, 357; disanchoring,
294; dominance of, 358; fiscal theory
of the price level, 24–27; introducing
competition in, 357–58; legitimacy of
cryptocurrency transactions, 358–59,
361; metallic, 3; moving to system, 356;
paper, 3, 4, 266; properties in model,
45; properties of, 14; roles of, 11–12;
single, within national borders, 357n1;
"stable monetary framework," 360, 362;
transition from metallic coins to paper
money, 40–41; units of, 59. *See also*
cryptocurrency
Currency School, 41

Dark Ages, coins and, 355
debt, government, 101, 103, 126, 177, 182,
215, 272, 284
debt deleveraging, 245–53; aggregate
demand (AD) equation, 248–49, 251;
aggregate supply (AS) equation, 251,
252; borrowers and savers, 246; economy under, 247; flow budget constraint,
245, 247; frictionless real rate of interest,
243; household debt, 242; paradox of
"flexibility," 252–53; paradox of "toil,"
252, *252*; shock, *251*
"demanders" inflation, Keynes' theory of,
308

interest rate rules: New Keynesian (NK) model, *168, 169*; optimal policy under, 164–68

intermediaries: safe securities, 106–7; securities market, 98–99

intermediation: financial, 92; private equity, 361

International Monetary Fund, 171

intertemporal budget constraint: borrowing limit, 46, 81; consumer, 84–85, 100; consumer optimization and derivation, 16–17, 17n10, 365–67; consumer problem representation and derivation, 81–82, 368; consumers, 49, 57, 64, 66; derivation of, 82n5; derivation of borrowing limit and, 46, 367, 368; optimal allocation, 83

intertemporal resource constraint, consumers, 335

Jamaica, high inflation and, 332
Japan, policy rate, 202, *203*

Keynes, J. M., 61, 202, 298, 299, 300, 301, 302, 308, 310, 311, 392

Keynesianism, 302

"Keynesian" label, 114

Keynesian unemployment, 308–11

Keynes-Tanzi effect, 335

Korean War, 325

Krugman, P., 239, 242, 245, 252, 263, 264, 389, 393

Kydland, Finn, real business cycle theories, 114

labor-force participation: concept of, 307; log-linear approximation, 324

Lagarde, Christine, on central bank backing, 357

laissez-faire equilibrium: liquidity crisis, 281–82; welfare, 286

laissez-faire policy, money and banking, 358

Law, John, proponent of "real bills" doctrine, 41n2

Lehman Brothers failure, 356–57

liquidity: facilities, 216n9; supply of, 287–89; supply of public and private, 101–4

liquidity policy: central banks, 78–79; optimal, of central banks, 87–90

liquidity trap, 201, 202–6; channels for unconventional monetary policies, 236–38; credit spreads, 238, *239*; financial crisis, 242; forward guidance, 225–30; helicopter money, 206, 207–15; managing central bank's reserves, 230–36; outline of, 206–7; references, 239–41; unconventional monetary policy, 206, 215–25

lira, 4

Livingstone Survey, 295, *296*

log-linear approximation: benchmark New Keynesian (NK) model, 132–35; derivation of, 132–35, 370–72; NK model with banking sector, 184–90

loss function: derivation of, as second-order approximation, 192, 380–81; derivations of, 151, 373–77; minimization of, 192; target variables, 151

Lucas, R. E., 74, 113, 116, 117, 135, 314, 326, 351, 384, 388, 391, 393

Lucas, Robert E.: review of *A Monetary History*, 113; on macroeconomics, 199; on monetary nonneutrality, 116–17

Main Street Lending Program, 238

markup shock(s), 139; aggregate demand (AD) equation, 158, 159, 162; aggregate supply (AS) equation, 159; frictionless real interest rate, 159, 169–70, 173; inflation targeting, 159–62; inflation targeting (IT) equation, 157–58, *158*; targeting rule, 157; temporary, *158*; temporary increase in, 144–46, *145*. *See also* AS-AD graphical analysis

Smith, Adam: on quantity of notes in circulation, 41; real-bills doctrine, 41, 41n2

sovereign debt, 266

stable monetary framework, 355, 360, 362

Steinsson, J., 115, 265, 311, 320, 327, 389, 393, 394

stochastic difference equation, 159–60; derivation, 378–79

store of value, 11, 12; borrowing limit, 45–46; currency, 14, 15, 45; function of money, 3, 5; government money, 92, 93; real money balances, 47

subjective-paper guarantee, 358

Sweden, inflation target, 150

taper tantrum, episode of, 230–31

tax policy, 26–27; authority of, 26; interest rate and money supply, 53, 53n12; real tax rate and real debt, 26n17

Taylor, J. B., 24, 135, 166, 172, 194, 396

Taylor principle, 166

Taylor rules, 172, 194; interest rate, 24, 24n15

Temporary Liquidity Guarantee Program, 238, 268, 285

Term Asset-Backed Securities Loan Facility (TALF), 237

Thornton, Henry, on origins of monetarism, 41

tight money paradox, 345–48; hyperinflation and, 345–48

Townsend, Robert, on inflation, 293

treasury: budget constraint, 48; budget constraint of, 18–19, 211; central bank and, 27; equilibrium, 20–22; monetary economy, 13, 17–19; solvency constraint, 19

treasury debt, 342n7; backing of, 80, 96, 212, 267, 333; central bank purchasing, 27, 335, 342, 342n7; Chilean, 332n1; government bonds as, 274; households holding, 88, 180; interest rates of, 84,

347; issuance of, 27, 213; purchasing, 27, 201, 208; U.S. Treasury, 18–19, 208

Turner, Adair, on helicopter money, 240

uncertainty, introduction to model, 95

unconventional monetary policies: assets of Federal Reserve System, 217; balance-sheet policies, 206; channels for, 236–38; credit spreads, 238, 239; effectiveness of, 224–25; irrelevance of open market operations, 218–23; relevance of open market operations, 223–25

unemployment: Keynesian, 308–11. See also inflation-unemployment trade-off

unemployment rate: inflation and, 295; United States, 295, 296

United Kingdom (UK): inflation target, 150; monetary aggregates and inflation, 42; Phillips curve, 299, 300; policy rate, 202, 203

United States: abandoning the Gold Standard, 74; adoption of Gold Standard, 59; American Recovery and Reinvestment Act (2009), 208; Consumer Price Index (CPI), 8, 9; core CPI inflation rate vs. unemployment, 322; dollar, 294; federal debt by Federal Reserve, 209, 209; inflation and unemployment, 297; inflation rate and unemployment rate, 296; inflation target, 150; monetary aggregates and inflation, 42; policy rate, 202, 203; quasi zero policy rate after financial crisis (2007–2008), 203; treasury, 18–19, 208

unit of account, 11, 12; currency, 14, 45; function of money, 3–4; government currency, 104; government money, 92; monetary system, 38; "safe assets," 109; safe securities, 95

"unpleasant monetaristic arithmetic": inflation and fiscal/monetary policies, 342–48; scenario of, 332; term,